SOCIAL PSYCHOLOGY
OF MODERN JAPAN

Japanese Studies
General Editor: Yoshio Sugimoto

SOCIAL PSYCHOLOGY OF MODERN JAPAN

Munesuke Mita

Translated by Stephen Suloway

KEGAN PAUL INTERNATIONAL
London and New York

First published in 1992 by
Kegan Paul International
UK: P.O. Box 256, London WC1B 3SW, England
Tel: (0171) 580 5511 Fax: (0171) 436 0899
E-mail: books@keganpau.demon.co.uk
Internet: http://www.demon.co.uk/keganpaul/
USA: 562 West 113th Street, New York, Ny 10025, USA
Tel: (212) 666 1000 Fax: (212) 316 3100
Reprinted 1995

Distributed by
John Wiley & Sons Ltd
Southern Cross Trading Estate
1 Oldlands Way, Bognor Regis
West Sussex, PO22 9SA, England
Tel: (01243) 829 121 Fax: (01243) 820 250

Columbia University Press
562 West 113th Street
New York, Ny10025, USA
Tel: (212) 666 1000 Fax: (212) 316 3100

© Munesuke Mita 1992

The publishers gratefully acknowledge the assistance of the
Japan Foundation in the publication of this volume.

Printed in Great Britain

British Library Cataloguing in Publication Data
Mita, Munesuke
Social Psychology of Modern Japan. –
(Japanese Studies Series)
I. Title   II. Suloway, Stephen
III. Series
305.895

ISBN 0–7103–0451–X

Library of Congress Cataloguing-in-Publication Data
Mita, Munesuke, 1937–
Social psychology of modern Japan / Munesuke Mita: translated
from the Japanese by Stephen Suloway.
550pp.   216 cm. – (Japanese studies series)
"This volume is a re-edition of materials written in Japanese and
originally published in several books – Preface.
Includes bibliographical references and index.
ISBN 0–7103–0451–X
1. Social psychology – Japan.   2. Japan – Social conditions – 1945-
I. Title.   II. Series: Japanese studies series (Kegan Paul International)
HM251.M523   1992   92-3483
302'.0952 – dc20   CIP

Contents

Tables

Figures

Preface

A well-known observation on the mental posture of Japanese in traditional communities is that they are fond of 'looking out from behind a reed screen.' The reed screen or *sudare* keeps out the heat and glare of summer while inviting cool breezes into the house, and incidentally allows you to observe the bright outside world without being observed in your private, inner world. This metaphor, penned by the pioneering folklorist Kunio Yanagita, tells something of the core problem in Japan's relations to other parts of the world throughout the past 120 years: a lopsided information gap.

Since the Meiji Restoration of 1868, Japan has absorbed information from the foreign world with a vigorous curiosity. The history, arts, customs, and social systems of other nations, especially those of the West, have been stressed almost constantly in all media, starting with primary school textbooks. But the reverse flow of information has been sharply limited. It is due in part to the 'reed screen posture,' and perhaps in part to filtering processes in other societies. At any rate, a sort of one-way window or 'magic mirror' has been formed between this archipelago and the world.

Until a few decades ago, only a handful of Western specialists penetrated beyond the 'samurai, harakiri, geisha girls' sort of picture. By the 1980s the image had changed radically to one of 'ultramodern' techno-economy: Sony, Toyota and the like. Traditional or ultramodern, either aspect consists only of *parts* of the reality of contemporary Japan. The society is fundamentally a combination of cultural particularity and 'modern' universality, and the key to grasping it in its totality is *the way of combination*.

A factual investigation of the processes and postures of combination must focus in turn on the four main phases of modernizing and modernized Japan. Those are: the stylized response to Western civilization in the late nineteenth century, at the dawn of the modern period; the erection and operation of the peculiarly Japanistic modernization system (the Meiji regime), which grew out of that response and dominated the society to 1945; the climactic, uprooting phase of modernity, marked by social-psychological flux and drama, during the 'rapid economic growth' era that peaked in the 1960s; and today's 'postmodern' society, colored by the emerging mentality and culture of new generations.

In this volume I have set out to sketch the mentality or social psychology of modern Japan in its entirety, using quantitative and qualitative data that recount the diversity of the dramas of encounter between cultural particularity and modern universality. The diachronic process of modernization through the above phases has brought about a synchronic coexistence of generational variations, with all kinds of tensions and conflicts and also synergies among them. Taken together, these provide the key for understanding the structure and dynamism of contemporary Japan.

Part One is a historical survey of the feelings of the people, based on analyses of popular songs during the century after 1868. The patterns and moods of anger, sadness, joy, love, etc. may offer the general reader a vivid sense of the shifts in the hearts and minds of the common people, which underlie the cultural expressions, political decisions or economic motivations that are more often discussed.

Part Two is a mental history of Japan in the context of the social structure which evolved from 1868 and operated until 1945. Being academic theses, these four chapters might tax the patience of the general reader, but the vignettes and summaries which can be found by scanning may hold some interest and convey the sense of things. The first two chapters identify archetypes of popular response to the pressures and new cultural forms which grew out of the encounter with Western civilization, during and just after the Restoration period. The third and fourth chapters deal with the authoritarian system of modernization which was in place through the mid-twentieth century, focusing respectively on the ideology of primary school textbooks, and on the actualities of the psychology of 'successism' which served as the driving force for industrialization.

Part Three is a series of excursions toward the matrix of postwar social, psychological and cultural ferment. It begins by tracing the transitions in mass thought from 1945 to the early 1960s, through the themes of bestselling books. The remaining chapters focus on various strains and problems as psychological consequences of the 'rapid growth' experience which transformed the social structure between the 1950s and 1970s, and formed the basic structure of contemporary Japan. The topics include: the revolution in the sense of 'home'; patterns of dissatisfaction and anxiety in daily life; the changing nature of white-collar work and status; desires and uncertainties of the marginal elite; and the hellish side of alienation in the city.

Part Four surveys the changing layers of mentality in contemporary Japan. Two chapters discuss the statistical results of attitude surveys in the 1970s and 1980s; the first highlights generational changes in value orientation and in views on sex, gender, the family, etc., and the second focuses on the emerging mentality of the younger generations in the 'postmodern' stage of society. The last chapter provides an overview of social, psychological and cultural change in postwar Japan, giving weight to the situation of the 1970s and 1980s.

This volume is a re-edition of materials written in Japanese and originally published in several books, with titles translatable as *Mental Structure of Modern Japan* (2nd edition, 1984), *Logic and Sentiment in Modern Japan* (1971), *History of Feelings in Modern Japan* (1967), *Social Psychology in Times of Change* (1967), and *Social Psychology of Modern Society* (1979). Only the last chapter was originally intended for translation, having been written for the catalog of a photography exhibition held in Paris and Tokyo in 1990.

Hence each chapter is relatively independent of the others, and may be read or skipped according to the reader's particular interests.

The fact that most of this book was not written from the start with an international audience in mind may be a demerit. At the same time, the reader may profit from sharing at first hand what a Japanese observer recorded about and for the Japanese, without any external considerations.

The translation was carried out in three steps. First, Stephen Suloway, an editor of the quarterly *Kyoto Journal*, made a translation in the ordinary sense, which was finely accurate in itself and based on a deep understanding of the originals. Next, I thoroughly checked his draft, marking insertions, deletions and alterations on most of the pages, restoring certain of my original implications and connotations, and indicating my own preferences of expression. Finally, he refined the checked text. Thus the author can take joint responsibility for this version, although most of the labor and quality belong to the translator. The manifold cooperation with Steve was a memorable and joyful experience, and a stimulating intercultural exchange in itself. I am indebted to my friend in Hawaii, Shin'ichi Yoshifuku, for introducing him to me.

I would like to express my special gratitude to Professor Yoshio Sugimoto of LaTrobe University, Melbourne, who persuaded me to add my work to the Kegan Paul Japanese Studies series, of which he is the general editor. I am also deeply grateful for the support of the Japan Foundation for this work. Further, I express my thanks to Norio Nakamura, of the editorial staff of Kōbundō, for administrative assistance.

There has been much argument as to whether Japanese culture is 'unique.' My answer is, yes and no. Certainly it is unique, but *uniqueness is not unique to Japan*. Every culture on earth is unique, respectively and respectably. I stand against the ethnocentrists who advocate the 'uniqueness' of Japanese, and only Japanese, culture. I also stand against those 'universalists' who are blind to uniquenesses, and hence to the difficulties of understanding different cultures. I was once informed by a professor from Bali, Indonesia, that there are eleven different cultures in Bali, and it is impossible to talk about 'Balinese culture' in general. It was one of the experiences which opened new vistas for me in thinking about the 'manner' of understanding a different society.

It will be a great delight for me if my limited work can help our neighbors to understand some of the reality of the culture and society of our archipelago, which is surely unique and multifaceted, just as *every* culture and society on our planet is unique and multifaceted.

Munesuke Mita
Tokyo, 1991

Translator's Preface

Japanologists informing the West are all too rarely Japanese, and it is a pleasure to take a small step to remedy the imbalance.

The fact that Mita Munesuke is a prestigious professor and well-known writer in Japan does not automatically make him right. His work does show that a deeply revealing study of Japan can be framed broadly enough to provoke reflection on human society in general. It also demonstrates that a frank, universal and critical perspective on Japan should not automatically be disqualified as 'bashing.'

Mita is the engaged sort of scientist. In his many academic and popular writings, he expresses an impassioned questioning of society, and still he is the dispassionate examiner of data and hypotheses. He is also a sweeping, eclectic thinker, and a writer of poetic sensibility. It is his uncompromising practice of all those things at once that makes his work so dense and rich, so challenging and rewarding. (Challenging especially to the translator, who had no choice but to leave some nuances by the wayside.)

It has been my privilege to enter a step further into Professor Mita's mind by working closely with him on the translation. Fulfillment also springs from my belief that this book helps point the way, through its content and its method, to a grammar of human culture, a geography of mind, in alignment with my own aspirations.

My greatest debt is to the Japan Foundation, for the grant that allowed me to spend a year on this work. The Yoshifuku Shin'ichi family, and Douglas Fir generously provided workspace to a peripatetic scribe. Matsuya Toshirō, Toyoshima Mizuho, and Shimura Tameki rescued me from linguistic pitfalls, and Nakamura Norio kindly coordinated.

May the reader enjoy this journey through the harmonies and conflicts of modern Japan as much as I have.

Stephen Suloway
Kyoto, 1991

xix

Note: Japanese names in the text, except in the author's preface are written as they appear in Japanese, with the family name first.

PART ONE

A HISTORY OF FEELINGS IN MODERN JAPAN

1 Popular Songs as Social Psychological Data

When I was sixteen I worked for the summer in a biscuit factory. My job was to catch the grill as it came out of the oven on a belt, pick it up with a thick cloth mitten, place it on the edge of a packing tin at the rear, slide the biscuits in, and put the grill back on the belt, over and over. The early shift ran from five to one and the late shift from one to nine, so the changeover days were rather long. There was a song that the teenage employees would all sing at the start of the morning shift, at lunch in the workers' dining room, and at the end of the late shift. Forever attached to my memory of that song is the bitter-sweet aroma that was a fixture of the place. It went something like this: 'We are in our youth, Love's our only truth, We need no money or position, Hopes for love fill up our vision, 'Tis paradise upon this earth.' No doubt I could look up the correct title and words, but that is not where my interest lies.

Written out, this is clearly nothing more than a common sort of ditty. Yet when the boys sang it softly to themselves as they came one by one across the factory site on a summer evening, the darkness seemed to descend with a weighty solitude, as if calling into question the very existence of their youthfulness. 'Paradise upon this earth.' With that final line, comprehension poured in like yanks of the tail, one after another, in the torrid air. In the stasis between the lightness of the verse written on the page, and the heaviness of the song of the softly singing youths, I was able to glimpse for the first time the secret of the popular song.

The figures and images in popular songs are often fantastic and unconnected with the actual lives of the singers and listeners: a wanderer in the Siberian icefields, a girl on a fruit-laden South Seas island, a fugitive gangster and so on. Yet within the totality of the feelings of the millions of people which are tossed into and conveyed by those dreamy, fantastic figures and images, there lies the essence of the popular song as a *social phenomenon*. In order to interpret the popular song, it is necessary to

3

undertake a deciphering of the truths which are mixed in and lyricized among the fabrications and illusions.

Consider the following letter, written by a village maiden to a soldier at the front. (From *Letters of Farmers Killed in the War*, compiled by the Farm Village Culture Roundtable of Iwate Prefecture.)

Dear beloved Kamata-sama,

When the north wind blows wildly I know it is you, my beloved, whom I must tell, and as I draw near the window an icy storm slips in and passes before my eyes. At those moments, in this breast, the cruel days of an Iwate woman with no tidings are so lonely. Every day passing by one after the other brings a bit of torture to my heart. Getting through each day is the only thing, and still, after all, I am alone. And I don't even have a letter of yours to read. My feelings will never change. Won't you take into your heart the eternal love that I am sending to you?

You must always keep the photo I sent close by. We were two people together in a cold and fleeting world.

When I had a letter from you I did a little dance of joy. Couldn't I have a look at another? In just a brief time I devoted the best of my love to you, Tadao. I want you to remember me in your heart forever. Tadao, even pure love between two people may bring sadness. We exchanged promises and yet our time for parting came more quickly than a stroke of this brush.

Maybe it was all a dream. A figment of my imagination. I want you always to be happy, Tadao. Though I told you I want always to belong to you alone, I have no news at all from you. But you will reply sometime, I know you will. I shall wait.

For now, then, I hope this brings the memory of my lonely heart to your male heart. I am overtaken by sadness, my eyes are so clouded with tears that I can no longer see the words.

Take care of yourself. Know that here in Akita a woman whose time is brief prays that you may have happiness always.

Suzuki

Lance Corporal Kamata Tadao, from the village of Yumoto in Iwate prefecture, carried this letter with him until he was killed in action at age 23 in Nobalichen, the Philippines, on February 17, 1945.

The popular song is one of the many popular arts which furnish what may be called expressive patterns (*kata*) representing the feelings of the masses for a particular era. But they are all substitutes, and the endless variety of nuance in the feelings of the masses is *tripped up* at every step by the hackneyed stereotypes of their formulations. When the intellectuals are summoned, they make short work of criticizing popular art forms, usually by pointing out that the stereotyped mannerisms are interminably boring. Studies of popular art as such tend to lead to that single predictable conclusion. But for those who wish to chart the morphology of the popular mind, a reverse strategy is necessary. Penetration behind the mannerized, stereotyped *surface* is the inevitable point of departure, in order to ascertain just how much acute emotion, how much lofty aspiration or how much utter desperation lies disguised beneath. Identifying mannerism in the expressive patterns of popular art is a presumptive thing to do; the really difficult question is, to what extent is it possible to plumb the depths of the feelings of the age which lie behind the mannerism?

The intellectuals have usually dismissed popular songs with only cursory, and derisory, attention. This results from the delusion that the stereotypical outward form of the presentation makes an open-and-shut case for a poverty of spirit.

My awakening to the popular song coincided with my awakening to history. Most of the youths who were humming "Tis paradise upon this earth' will likely pass their careers at that factory or a similar one. Some could have earned high-school diplomas in night classes, one or two have spoiled their chances with a criminal offense, others might have become hardworking union members; but after pouring all their energies into the plowing of their respective paths, they will all disappear soon enough, one by one, into the depths of the flow of history. Against the giant tide of history, it is possible to view the single human life as a futile exercise. Yet conversely, when history is understood as the rushing torrent of the myriad dreams and realities of those individual lives, each with its inimitable colorations, we can sense the awesome depth and power with which

5

it presses forward. My high school classes left me with an image of history that was nothing more than its shrivelled, cast-off skin.

I was possessed by an ambition to repossess history, to reconsider that countless nameless mass of people cycling just once through life, the thronging conglomeration of discord and fantasy and selfishness and devotion in which I, too, participate.

It is not possible, of course, to see directly into the minds of those people. To observe something invisible, such as a change in temperature, our only handhold is to measure an associated visible sign, like the height of a column of mercury. To allow us to make inferences about the feelings of generations past, what signs have been left behind to serve as our handholds?

There are two types of records of the feelings of an era. One is documents which were actually written by the masses: letters, diaries, certificates, and literary or journalistic contributions. The other is the various popular arts, including not only songs but also theater, literature and cinema.

Surviving documents written by the masses themselves do present the feelings of the age rather directly, and yet the reality is not quite so simple. To begin with, such records must have been penned by people who had both the basic skill of writing and some intellectual training, and thus for most eras written records represent only the thoughtfulness of that fraction of the general populace who were relatively elevated and knowledgeable. The distinction becomes much smaller in the postwar era, but as we move back through the ages, the range of people capable of producing such documents and records becomes progressively more limited.

Tsurumi Shunsuke did groundbreaking research for his book *The Marginal Arts (Genkai geijutsu)*, which covers *hayashi* (meaningless syllables sung to music), nicknames, store names, doodles, and playful gestures. But for our purposes those materials would have to be unearthed and arranged in a comprehensive and systematic manner.

Works of popular art, moreover, are clearly made not by the people but rather *for* the people. This raises the issue of the refraction factor introduced by the artist's mediating role. Of course if a work of popular art is to have some hope of success, it must hold a sounding board to one facet or another of the mentality of the masses of its time. We can look back, then, at successful works of popular art – hit songs, popular broadcast programs, bestselling books and the like – and expect them to reflect some aspects of the particular feeling of the people of that time, or at least those of a particular social class.

The refractory role played by the writers of Japanese popular songs, and by the external pressures operating upon them, was most striking, naturally, during the Pacific War. As will be seen in the text, during this period an untold number of senitmental songs were banned from sale, while many war ballads (*gunkoku kayo*) and other military songs were disseminated as a matter of policy. The suppressed songs were nevertheless passed along orally, and were favorites on both the battle lines and the home front, while the many songs promoted with wholesale propaganda by the military authorities and the Information Board were sung only on official occasions, their parodies being much more popular. The authorities distributed many phonograph records of 'Marching Songs,' but it was always the 'Bivouac Song' on the flip side, typically a plaintive tune in a minor key, that proved more popular.

After phonograph records appeared on the scene in the late 1920s, it was not infrequent that a song which was already popular at the grassroots level would be picked up by a record company, and the recording would amplify its success. The writers of many of these remain anonymous. Meanwhile, even with enthusiastic promotion in the mass media, unpopular songs simply stayed unpopular. Each year, dozens of songs on which record companies had pinned their hopes would end instead in complete obscurity. Sometimes songs that had been promoted in the mass media without response would, at a later time or with slight alteration, garner unexpected success. Those who follow the music industry can cite various cases to prove that if the lyrics of a 'popular song' don't match the feelings of the people at the moment, then the promotional muscle of the record company will not be enough to generate sales.

What decisively distinguishes popular songs from the various other popular arts – theatrical performances, popular novels, films, or broadcast programs – is that the people of the time do not enjoy them in a merely passive manner. For part of what is required to make a popular song popular is that the masses actively *participate* in it, by singing it to themselves (or singing it out loud, or in unison). Thus the popular song, more than other forms of popular art, corresponds to the dominant

7

emotions of the masses as well as to their *moods*, and this relationship can be quite fecund.

In contrast to the documentary sources of social history – literary contributions, diaries, letters, certificates – the popular song, first, requires neither writing ability nor intellectual training. The act of singing is far more basic than that of writing, and is thus open to a much broader spectrum of people, while also being more commonly connected with daily routine. Second, the very term 'popular song' indicates that it is inherently a *mass* phenomenon, and thus it avoids the danger, so common with manuscripts, of being idiosyncratic to the individual involved.

We may conclude, then, that as a repository of the mass feelings of its time, the popular song, properly qualified and delineated, is one of the finest types of material.

Yet while they function as mirrors, popular songs do not provide faithful, planar reflections of popular feelings. They contain many peculiar refractions and chromatic dispositions, for they are as stylized, as glorified, as materialized, and as hyperbolized as actual everyday experience. Stylized, in that the content is reduced to a set of *kata*, or formal types, of basic expression and their variations: 'I'm a bird on a sorrowful journey,' 'Empty-seeming love in my distant hometown,' 'The flow of the water, the soul of the man.' Glorified, in that sundry everyday experiences and impressions are trnsposed into 'beautiful' images: snowy steppes, tropical islands, foggy harbors, or exotic cities; the sloughed skin of a cicada, late autumn rain, morning dew, or erupting volcanoes.

Materialized, into figurations that are not unlike dream symbolism. The psychological solitude of the 'lonely crowd' is transposed to the physical solitude of the 'solitary traveler' or 'stray bird,' memories are a 'spinning wheel,' blocked feeling a 'cage.'

Hyperbolized, into ultimated forms which heighten everyday circumstances or feelings: the spatial maximization of 'Shall I go, shall I return, under the Northern Lights?' or 'Ten thousand miles, far, far from home'; the dramatic circumstances of a wandering orphan, tramp or fugitive; or the direct magnification of feelings, such as 'Staking my life on love.'

To pursue the actual images of the feelings of an era through popular songs, we must proceed by decoding the signs within them, by tracing back through the displacements and colorations of the mirror's refractions.

The material used for this study consists of 451 *ryūkōka* or popular songs, one or more of which were current during each year from 1868, the beginning of the Meiji period, through 1963. They are taken from the 497 songs listed in the 'Annual Table of Japanese Songs' at the end of Shigure Otowa's *Collected Songs and Ballads of Japan (Nihon kayōshū, Shakai Shisōsha, 1963)*. Two of the songs on Shigure's list were immediately eliminated: the title *Dodo-itsu* is the name of a song style rather than a particular song, and two of the 1911 entries – *Murasaki choitone bushi* and *Choitone bushi* – are in fact the same song. (Since some songs of recurring popularlity appear two or three times, there are only 482 different songs, although the recurring titles are included in the tabulations for their respective years, in Table 1.1.)

Table 1.1 *Popular songs selected for analysis*

Seven-year interval	A	B	C	C/A × 100
1868–74	39	6	33	84.6
1875–81	23	3	20	87.0
1882–8	37	3	34	91.9
1889–95	42	6	36	85.7
1896–1902	39	1	38	97.4
1903–9	33	1	32	97.0
1910–16	31	2	29	93.5
1917–23	23	2	21	91.3
1924–30	41	5	36	87.8
1931–7	53	9	44	83.0
1938–44	32	2	30	93.8
1945–51	36	0	36	100.0
1952–8	32	4	28	87.5
1959–63	34	0	34	100.0
Total	495	44	451	91.1

A   Songs listed in Shigure's Annual Table of Japanese Songs.
B   Songs disqualified because of unverifiable lyrics.
C   Songs analyzed for this study.

Among the remaining 495 songs, there were 44 (43 different) for which the lyrics cannot be verified. Thus a total of 451 songs (91.1 per cent of the full list; 439 different works) were qualified as the material to be analyzed. Table 1.1 shows the distribution over time of the numbers of songs analyzed and excluded.

As the table makes clear, there is no extreme polarization in the chronological distribution of the songs which were selected.

Although there is some fluctation over time in the proportion of unverifiable songs, still for each interval at least 83 per cent of the songs listed by Shigure are included in the analysis.

For analysis of motif, the following affect categories were established: anger (*ikari*), resentment (*urami*), despair (*yake*), self-scorn (*jichō*), jest (*odoke*), joy (*yorokobi*), hope (*kibō*), ambition (*haki*), chivalry (*gikyō*), sarcasm (*fūshi*), criticism (*hihan*), longing (*bojō*), coaxing affection (*amae*), wooing (*kudoki*), flattery (*kobi*), jealousy (*shittō*), banter (*hiyakashi*), resignation (*akirame*), lingering attachment (*miren*), loneliness (*kodoku*), nostalgia (*kyōshū*), aspiration (*akogare*), blocked feeling (*heisoku-kan*), wandering (*hyōhaku-kan*), and impermanence (*mujō-kan*). The assignment of the songs to the various categories was carried out by three judges, with the concurrence of two or more required for each categorization. (A table of the songs and the assigned affect categories is included in the original edition of this study, *kindai nihon no shinjō no rekishi*, Kodansha, 1967.).

In addition to motif analysis, various other analyses were carried out with respect to themes, vocabulary, rhythms, musical scales, major and minor keys, and the communication structures of the songs. Only the motif-related aspects of the overall study are included in the present volume.

The quantitative trend analyses at the beginning of each chapter, and the summary table in the Appendix are presented in terms of 7-year periods. The reasoning behind this arrangement is as follows.

Modern Japanese history, in my view, can be broken into the following periods: the *formative period* from the Meiji Restoration of 1868 through 1889, spanning the developments which are generally known as 'civilization and enlightenment' and the people's rights movement; the *solidification period* from 1889, the year the imperial constitution was promulgated (local governing bodies and the national Diet took form around the same time), through 1910, including the wars with China and Russia and the industrial revolution; the *period of ripe maturity* from 1910 – the year of the annexation of Korea and the 'era-ending' assassination plot known as the Great Treason Incident – through 1931, coinciding roughly with the Taisho era; the *period of collapse* (or of coercive revamping) from the Mukden Incident of 1931 – the plunge from the climax of so-called *eroguro* (erotic-grotesque) culture into 15 years of war – through the defeat of 1945; and the immediate postwar period to 1952, when the US military occupation ended and the Japan-US Mutual Security Pact came into effect.

When those watershed periods are lined up, their respective timespans are 21 years, 21 years, 21 years, 14 years and 7 years, all of which happen to be multiples of seven. Taking 7-year intervals as the standard is thus quite convenient, for it guarantees at once the equal spacing required for quantative analysis, while the reliance on historical turning-points promotes a basic homogeneity of characteristics within each interval.

2   The History of Anger

Refractions of anger

Very few of the popular songs of Japan since the Meiji Restoration are direct expressions of anger. Among the 451 representative songs surveyed for this volume, anger is a motif of only 15.

Perhaps the popular song, in all times and places, is by nature something which does not lend itself to themes of anger. The peculiar thing is that songs of anger, however few, were in fact the typical popular songs of a certain time in Japan. For it is not the scarcity or frequency of expressions of anger that we shall observe here, but rather their historical ebb and flow as shown by their chronological distribution.

The popular songs that deal with anger are concentrated between 1883 and 1906, in the middle to late Meiji period. They disappear entirely with the waning of Meiji, and after their exit from the stage of popularity, between 1906 to 1924, the main motif shifts first to *ressentiment* or bitterness, and then to *despair*. Those two motifs remain visible in popular songs without interruption well into the postwar era, although from 1925 onward they are never dominant in quantitative terms. Instead, during the Showa period the major song motif is *resignation*, which here also includes the distinct emotion of *miren*, or lingering attachment.

Column A of Table 2.1 shows the percentages and relative rankings of representative popular songs with these motifs, through the 95 years following the Meiji Restoration. It traces a double and triple refraction of the feelings of anger at the bottom of the hearts of the Japanese people, charting an inward burrowing of their expression from direct anger to *ressentiment*, then to despair, and then to resignation and a regretful sense of lingering attachment.

The intensity of the critical spirit expressed in popular songs exhibits a virtually parallel transition, as shown in column B. It

12

Table 2.1 *Motifs of anger and criticism in Japanese popular songs*

	Anger	Ressenti-ment	A Despair	Resignation and miren	Criticism	B Sarcasm	Self-scorn
1868–74		6.1	6.1		6.1	[12.1]	3.0
1875–81		5.0			10.0	[25.0]	
1882–8	[11.8]	2.9	5.8		[20.6]	11.8	2.9
1889–95	[13.9]	2.8	8.3	2.8	[19.4]	11.1	
1896–1902	2.6			7.9	5.3	2.6	
1903–9	12.5	[28.1]	9.4	21.9	18.8	[28.1]	21.9
1910–16	3.4	6.9	[20.7]	6.9	3.4	[20.7]	13.8
1917–23			[19.0]		9.5	19.0	[23.8]
1924–30		5.6	2.8	[19.4]		2.8	8.3
1931–7		4.5	6.8	[18.2]			[11.4]
1938–1944		6.7	3.3	[20.0]			3.3
1945–1951		2.8	8.3	[22.2]	2.8		2.8
1952–8		10.7	10.7	[50.0]			[10.7]
1959–1963		2.9	5.9	[23.5]		5.9	[14.7]

Figures are percentages of representative popular songs with a given motif in each time period, derived as follows:

$$\frac{\text{Number of songs in time period with given motif}}{\text{Total number of songs in time period}} \times 100$$

Boxes indicate the most common motifs in category A or B for each time period. Figures below 10% are excluded.

is deflected and driven inward from criticism to sarcasm, and then from sarcasm to self-scorn.

(Among European languages, the word which is closest to the retroceded form of anger known in Japanese as *urami* is the French *ressentiment*. The model of the feeling is longstanding *ressentiment* toward the strong on the part of the unjustly oppressed, resulting from their powerlessness to secure or restore their rights.)

Logic and emotion in *minken enka*

It is no surprise that most of the songs of anger which are concentrated in the middle and late Meiji years were *minken enka* (people's-power songs) that were sung in the streets by young men who were active in the people's rights movement.

What sort of rage was it that was expressed in those prototypes of the modern Japanese song of anger? A good place to start is with a model example of the early *minken enka*, the very widely popular 'Dynamite Song' (1883–7):

> People's power activists   Rain down their tears
> To polish the brave spirit of Yamato
>
> (Chorus)
>> Strengthen the nation and public welfare
>> Power to the people
>> If it doesn't happen
>> Dynamite boom
>
> Oh, happy dream
> Of lifting extraterritoriality
>
> (Chorus)
>
> Forty million compatriots   For your sake
> In red prison uniforms   We would suffer
>
> (Chorus)

As the refrain clearly indicates, the value which drives the singers' aspirations is an undifferentiated combination of national interest and people's power. They sought to convey an inseparable connection between the anger of the 'people's power advocates' toward the autocratic government dominated by the Satsuma and Chōshū clans, and the anger of 'the brave spirit of Yamato' toward the imperial powers which were pressuring Japan. Other popular songs of the 1880s offer similar examples, such as the line, 'For your sake and the sake of the nation, the sake of the people' from 'Reform Song' (*Kairyo bushi*, c. 1888). The *minken enka*, then, reveals a tight mutual embrace of the concepts of state power and people's power.

So much for the logical structure of the *minken enka*. If we track their emotional structure, a duality of a different dimension can be seen: an entwining of the spirit of the *bushi* or samurai class and that of the *chōnin* or merchant class. With the lyrics, '. . . polish the brave spirit of Yamato . . . If it doesn't happen, dynamite boom,' the people's-power confederates are 'donning fine woven caps with hairy legs sticking out of their ragged clothes, strutting in high *geta* while carrying stout walking sticks, shaking their fists as they sing' (from Soeda Tomomichi's history, *Enka no meiji-taisho shi*). They had a special taste for send-up lyrics, juxtaposing lofty or silly concepts with the warrior's lot, such as 'martial melancholy,' 'samurai of the universe' or 'samurai dancing a jig.'

Their songs also contained subtle overtones of the humor of *chōnin* culture. It shows in the lyrics of 'Dynamite Song.' Another example: 'The cat will find a way to reach the ladle, Neatly trimmed whiskers underneath the nose, How very fine it is to let a beard grow out, But is it a rat's tail or a cat's whiskers?' (*Ukiyo bushi*, 'Floating World,' 1884) This passage, satirizing the beards which were the symbol of those in power at the time, is based not upon *bushi* anger with its frankness of expression, but upon *chōnin* defiance with its expression refracted through jokes. The emotional foundation of *minken enka* consists of a unique combination of the pluck of the pre-Meiji samurai and the defiance of the merchant class. This suggests something about the character of the social classes who supported *enka* at that time.

Thus the logical structure of the people's-power song of the 1880s – the prototype of the modern *enka* – presents a dual connotation of the concept of people's power and the concept of state power, leaning somewhat to the former; while its emotional structure presents a dual connotation of the bushi ethos and the chōnin ethos, again leaning somewhat to the former.

During the ensuing two decades, as the Meiji regime moved toward solidification by promulgating the constitution, convening the Imperial Diet and waging campaigns against China and Russia, and as the Russo-Japanese War revealed the contradictions within the system; how did the *enka* evolve?

Anger changes direction

The exceptional popularity during 1889 of *Yukai bushi*, 'Happy Song,' marked a turning point in the history of *enka*. The song had several variations with a common refrain,

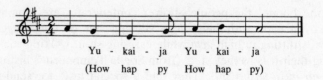

Yu - kai - ja Yu - kai - ja
(How hap - py How hap - py)

The prototype lyrics were:

> Mt Fuji straddles the two lands of Kai and Suruga
> Making an eight-faceted glittering jewel
> There are the white clouds, cold even during summer
> Manifesting a spirit so noble and pure
> Soaring on high between the spaces in the clouds
> Showing independent unyielding spirit
> The temperament of the men of Yamato
> Riding, fencing, practicing archery
> For the sake of the nation they are uplifting
> Take care that the northern gate is always kept locked
> Give your all, your all for the sake of the nation
> Giving all in its name for all nations
> With the reverberation, such great happiness
> How happy   How happy

Here the people's-power concept has disappeared and the *enka* has been squeezed down to the single theme, 'for country.' That was the year that the Meiji constitution was promulgated.

Although *enka* with strong state-power coloration had been sung in the earlier years, and refrains such as 'overthrow clann-ism' were still heard occasionally thereafter, the years 1889 and 1890 are the dividing line where *enka* lyrics suddenly lose the people's-power hue, and the state-power theme becomes domi-nant. The logic behind this shift in content is eloquently pre-sented in the following verse from a 'happy song' entitled 'The Imperial Diet Song' (*Teikokugikai no ka*, 1889)

> Ripening to a civilized nation, the right of freedom
> Is budding firmly, and in our country
> The period of barbaric stubbornness
> Is yielding to calm and flexibility
> Through the trying events of 1873
> Ex-Ministers Itagaki and Goto

Were the first to sow the popular-election
Seed of the flower of Diet politics
And then with the passing of succeeding years
Basking and growing in the favor of
The winds of enlightened civilization
The freedom of man and the wisdom of the people
Receive blessings from heaven in equal measure
The people who are born into this world
Won't be pushed and pressed upon by others
And pressed and pushed indeed they should be
Restrained, the fountain rises
The voice proclaiming the inauguration
Of the Diet resounds in all directions
Until it is heard by the Wise Emperor
Promulgation of the constitution is granted
Government by representation is allowed
At the outset of constitutionalism
All of the citizenry of Meiji
Stand proudly before their unborn descendants
   How happy   How happy

According to the general view of the time, the people's rights movement had triumphed with the granting of the constitution and the inauguration of the Imperial Diet, despite the limit on electoral participation to high-bracket taxpayers making up a mere 1.24 per cent of the citizenry, and further despite the conferring of control upon the nobility in the House of Peers.

As a result, the anger of the *enka* was henceforth not directed at discrimination or oppression within the country, but rather took up urgently and wholeheartedly the cause of discrimination and oppression against minorities abroad. Here is a verse from another of the 'happy songs' entitled 'Treaty Revision' (*Joyaku kaisei*, c. 1893).

Show enthusiasm, sincere men who love the country . . .
Remember the *Normanton*
And the *Chishima* accident
When so many countrymen
Died with their resentment
There is no means for dispelling
The deep delusion of our countrymen

When it comes to extraterritoriality
The thought is mortifying and embittering

Profligate, passionate countrymen
Invigorated, flourishing for country
Sharpening the sword of righteousness
Flying the banner of public opinion
If the current treaty is not abrogated
Decisively cut in two at a stroke
Under the sword of Japan
It shall be our great urgent task
To obtain a resplendent treaty which shall place
The Imperial virtue of the divine free land
Of the Orient high in the eastern sky
   How happy   How happy

When the British freighter *Normanton* sank off the coast near Wakayama, only the British crew were saved while twenty-three Japanese drowned. Due to inequitable treaty provisions, this inhuname conduct went without adequate investigation, leaving the nation smoldering with resentment. A similar incident occurred when the battleship *Chishima* collided with the British ship *Ravenna*.

The anger of a nation subjected to such discrimination and inequity, and the belligerent demands for release from the pressure of the Great Powers, became directly connected with Japan's own dream of becoming one of the Great powers by pressuring other Asian nations.

Doku Shin Ro Futsu Ei Bei   Shikkei kiwamaru genkotsu
  bai
Germany China Russia France Britain America   Extreme
rudeness, blow after blow

That refrain, from the anonymous 'Clenched-fist Song' (*Genkotsu bushi*), puts quite bluntly the dual orientation of the nationalism of the time, as well as the identification between the emotional motifs involved.

> Rupturing Japan-China negotiations . . .
> The Chinese are readily overthrown
> The Great Wall breached
> Only a mile to the walls of Peking
> Praise praise praise . . . Happiness happiness . . .
> – 'Dance of Joy' (*Kimbu bushi*, 1893)

This famous song was popular during the year *before* the Sino-Japanese War. In fact, songs such as this were prophetic and history-making in their character and their content. They articulated an ideology and social psychology which, by using as an intermediary a sense of destiny lopsided with emotion, served as conduits for shifting toward the *outside* the popular hostility and anger that had been pent up inside the country since the beginnings of the Meiji state.

It would be a mistake to say that this sort of social psychology was shaped and fomented in a purely artificial way. Granted, too, that such an orientation of dissatisfaction could not have arisen completely spontaneously. Yet a general sense of, and even a proclivity to, mistrust and fright of foreign countries was present within the traditional community consciousness. Anxiety over external pressures, along with a backlash against the 'hairy barbarians' of the West, had permeated the populace since the time of the Black Ships and the opening of the ports in the 1850s and early 1860s. More directly, thanks to the oratorical campaigns orchestrating the takeover of Korea through military incidents in 1882 and 1884 and the Treaty of Tientsin of 1885, there had been a worsening of sentiment toward China, at least among those Japanese who read the newspapers.

Thus these *enka* became popular by catering to this aspect of the general social psychology of the Japanese at the time, and by becoming popular they amplified it.

This type of *catering-and-amplification relationship* between the social psychology of the masses and popular songs can also be seen in the circumstances which created 'Come On, Russia' (*Roshia koi*), a song which was popular immediately before the Russo-Japanese War of 1904–5.

> The eastern peace has been disturbed
> Specious pretexts have been used
>   Roshia koi   Roshia koi
> The sharp-edged sword of Japan
> Has reached the limit of endurance
>   Roshia koi   Roshia koi

The martial songs of the Russo-Japanese War contain less of the type of bare-knuckled anger that was vented in song at the time of the Chinese war, and are more strongly colored by fun.

> Leasing Port Arthur in '95
> Reneging after only nine years
> Chirippu charappu
> Appuku chikiriki appappaa
> Ryusei ryusei appuku chikiriki cha
>   – 'Prosperity Song' (*Ryusei bushi*, c. 1904)

As the contradictions of the Meiji order came to light after the Russo-Japanese War, *enka* once again sang temporarily of political criticism and popular anger.

> Oh, this world of gold, this world of gold
> Orders from hell come in gold
> Gold if you laugh and gold if you cry
> Once gold, twice gold, three times gold
> Gold divides parent and child
> Gold cuts the love of husband and wife
> We slander infernal greed
> We denounce those blind with self-interest
> Sometimes it hurts or itches
> But if it's for gold it's all right
> Stay away from trials and troubles
> Of others so they don't hex us
> – 'Oh This World of Gold' (*Aa kane no yo ya*, c. 1907)

> It's no good
> Oh the sharecropper's suffering is no good
> Toil unceasingly
> Wait for the harvest, and look

> All the rice goes to the landlord
> While my poor family cries of hunger
> – 'Song of Tribulation' (*Tsumaranai bushi*, c. 1908)

However, these songs scarcely attained general popularity (according to the cultural historian Fujisawa Morihiko). In qualitative terms, they certainly contain some disguised popular anger, but it is a deflected expression, not direct and outspoken as in the *minken enka* of earlier years.

After striking a final chord in 1910 in 'Tex-tex Song,' the motif of anger drops from sight in the world of the Japanese popular song.

We might expect that the rightful heirs of the anger motif in later years would be war songs or workers' songs. Yet in contrast to songs connected with the Chinese and Russian wars, in war songs of the Taisho and Showa periods the anger motif is mysteriously absent. In the government-made war songs and others which conform to them, that is, in songs which came from the top down, the main motifs are the pride and ambition of giving one's all for the nation, and the heroic spirit. Favorite war songs thrown up from below, meanwhile, have motifs of sorrow, homesickness, wandering and impermanence. In virtually none of them is there any expression of anger or hate for enemy peoples. Songs of worker or peasant defiance, meanwhile, never joined the ranks of the really popular or well-loved songs until after the Pacific War.

The history of *ressentiment*

Of course the populace under the Meiji regime did not become so happy that they simply forgot their feelings of anger. Under the pressure and guidance of control mechanisms which had been perfected and strengthened, part of the anger was converted into motive power for foreign aggression and personal advancement, as noted below. The rest of it was deflected inward in the form of *ressentiment* or bitterness or despair, taking temporary residence within the gut of the system.

Songs of bitterness came briefly to popularity after the Russo-

Japanese War. During the last few Meiji years, *ressentiment* and sarcasm were the biggest motifs in the world of popular song. Songs such as 'Oh This World of Gold' and 'Song of Tribulation,' cited above, are more appropriately viewed as expressions of *ressentiment* or despair than of anger. The *ressentiment* motif is also concealed within two songs to be covered below: 'Song of Resignation' and 'Tex-tex Song.' Popular songs outside the *enka* style ranged quite widely in theme, including such titles as 'Involuntary Return,' 'Song of the Golden She-Devil' and 'Clear White Summit of Fuji' from 1909 and 1910, but a great many of them in some way or another have the motif of *ressentiment*.

The outstanding songs of *ressentiment* at this time were the exceedingly popular 'Midnight Reminiscence' (*Yowa no tsuioku*, also called 'Ballad of Osaburō') and 'Rain on My Sleeve' (*Sode shigure*, also called 'Ballad of Soeko'). These songs concern the case of Noguchi Osaburō, who was suspected of killing his lover Soeko's elder brother, and was sentenced to death for an unrelated crime.

> Oh the world is a dream or an illusion
> Alone in prison upon awakening from
> A solitary dream and everywhere around
> The evening is quietly growing older
> The shadow faintly pierces the window
> Oh his shadow, pierced by the moon
> In the abandoned dew-laced cemetery,
> Quietly sleeping elder brother,
> Shining upon that grave
> Recalling again the world recalling the self
> Spending the entire night crying
> And upon the parting from my beloved wife
> The shadow likewise rests . . .
> – 'Midnight Reminiscence' (*Yowa no tsuioku*, 1906–8)

> A paulownia leaf shows that autumn is come
> Could two months have already passed?
> You, enduring prison, your body
> Must be so sad
> Day after day thinking only of that
> Unable even to sleep at night . . .
> Thinking of you and me in this world,

It is not a mysterious
Turn of fate,
Separated by the laws of tradition
And the cold rules of man's world,
Against my will, I must sing of myself
As a childless woman, one who knows not love
While cursing the world and its people,
I could endure it, I could wear it
If just once I could touch
Your warmhearted blood. . . .
All alone in this cruel fleeting world
A mischievous one, a sinner
Is how they slander me and so
If I am a sinner I will join hands and weep
With another sinner, and will cross
The River Styx to the next world
       – 'Rain on My Sleeve' (*Sode shigure*, 1908)

These linked songs, both written to the same slow waltz tune
(the music of 'Beautiful Nature,' reproduced in Chapter 4), are
huge pieces with some hundred lines each. They hold an important place in the history of Japanese popular songs, because their
contents represent in various ways the bridge between the world
of the *enka* and that of the *kayōkyoku* which came into existence
during the Taisho period.

Their overarching motif – subsuming the other motifs of impermanence, pent-up feeling, loneliness, and longing – is the griev-
ance of the powerlessness of an average individual in the face
of society in general and the legal system.

The police, who considered Osaburō guilty from the start,
could not turn up enough evidence. Yet the public had their way
with him, first by presuming him to be the criminal guilty of
murdering the brother, and on top of that, by celebrating as
their hero the very Osaburō whom they took to be the offender.

My beloved darling is floating
Motionlessly, arrested
For a heinous crime, how sad it is,
Ah, yet for that moment when
Surely you killed my flesh, my brother,
I feel hate and resentment too,

23

> Yet because I know that everything
> Springs from your deep love for me
> All my resentment has died away
> No sword can be lifted against love
> The compassion of a parent
> The sympathy of flesh and blood cannot
> Compare to the bond of
> Pure sympathy between two lovers . . .
>
> – 'Rain on My Sleeve'

What cries out for attention here is the public sentiment which required such an immoral hero, to the point of embellishing the facts to create him.

At this time the primary themes of literature, in highbrow naturalist novels as well as popular domestic novels and *shinpa* plays, were Meiji social restriction and individual love, and the home was usually the crucible for their complications. The conflict between the Meiji system and individual love was in a sense the theme of the age, part of the magnetic field created by the poles of the 1908 Boshin Imperial Rescript (an exhortation to moral rearmament, emphasizing family ethics) and *Seitō* (a radical women's-emancipation magazine of the time). Amid a field so *charged with meaning*, sympathy is heartily summoned through the dramatization of Osaburō as the hero who sinned against the Meiji order for the sake of love, and of Soeko as the pure sacrificial heroine.

Resentment toward Osaburō over the murder of the brother is not the motif of the song, being cancelled by his *love* for her. Active resentment colors Soeko's mental attitude only in the following two lines: 'Oh how I resent the gossip of people who don't know my heart' and 'How I resent the cruel law which severs the bonds of feeling.'

These verses transcend the particular circumstances of the heroine who sings them. They are applicable to the universal circumstances of the masses living under the Meiji regime. Those are on one hand a grudge against the 'premodern' which remained in Japanese society, and on the other hand a grudge against the 'modern' which was imposed from above. Within the actual lives of the people within the Meiji social order, the premodern and the modern were not simply in opposition to each other, but rather existed as a double yoke. *Ressentiment*, according to Max Scheler, is made up of three elements: one is the emotional extension of hatred, jealousy and animosity; another is the feeling of powerlessness due to the inability to vent those emotions against opposing persons or social groups; the third is the constant re-experiencing of such powerless hostile feelings.

The secret by which the protagonists of this macabre episode evoked such broad-gauged sympathies must be that they were the spokespersons for an unmentionable *ressentiment* which lurked at the depths of the hearts of the people. Their actions were a figure for the twisted resentment of the surrounding masses who strung them up as heroes for their time.

'Song of Resignation' (*Akirame bushi*, 1908), a song which was popular at the same time as the ballads of Osaburō and Soeko, portrays this *ressentiment* or bitterness against the modern and the premodern in Meiji society in a more realistic way.

> What have you come to this world to do?
> To pay your taxes and your interest
> Born into this fleeting world
> To our unfortunate role we are resigned
>
> Be my mother-in-law* a devil* or a snake
> A young wife* must meekly submit
> Naturally she serves her time
> Without a word, to my fate I am resigned
> – 'Song of Resignation' (*Akirame bushi*, 1908)

The words with asterisks were censored out by the authorities. That this was the only popular *enka* of the time to be censored indicates which topic the rulers of the time reacted to most sensitively (with the extraordinary exception, of course, of the emperor system). By appealing to the actual feelings of the masses, it strikes at the ideology of the family-nation, the pivot of the mechanisms of internal control of the Meiji regime.

Nevertheless, even with its words intact, this song is quite a retreat from the spirit shown in a verse from 'Yoshiya' in the 1870s: 'Be my mother-in-law a devil or a snake, I plant myself down with the right to love.'

'Song of Resignation' continues:

> Arduous overwork and yet more bitter overwork
> Fulfilling duty is something that must be done
> The desire for some sort of rights
> Is not possible, we are resigned

This is of course ironic; no doubt some resisted with all their might. Yet therein lies one endpoint of the history of the *enka*, which runs through so many refracted layers from loud insistence on people's rights through national sovereignty to sarcasm.

> Won't you please give up, oh won't you please give up
> Won't you please give up, it's the safe way
> I am an animal born to be free
> So I give up on giving up

These words might seem to conceal an irrespressible spirit of resistance. Yet in fact it is no more than a self-abusing/self-amusing resistance which is hinted at in the posture of the words.

Two years later, in 1910, came the swansong of the popular motif of anger.

> A child on the back, a swelling belly, No-ya And then
>   the car
>   'Tis-really-quite-'ard Shameful-tyr'nny Needs a push
>   Up-it's-gone-tex-tex
>
> Cold wind leaking through the cracks No-ya Let's have a
>   try
>   'Tis-really-quite-'ard Shameful-tyr'nny Wheel of poverty
>   Up-it's-gone-tex-tex
>
> Had to give up the house and the fields No-ya Now it's
>   every day
>   Yo-heave-ho-no-ya Shameful-try'nny Day laborer
>   Up-it's-gone-tex-tex
>
> Wages go down, prices go up No-ya But all complaints
>   'Tis-really-quite-'ard Shameful-try'nny Are prohibited
>   Up-it's-gone-tex-tex

Birds and insects, they all have nests   No-ya   I'm a human
    being
  'Tis-really-quite-'ard   Shameful-try'nny   I have no house
  Up-it's-gone-tex-tex

Don't trifle with the peasant   No-ya   Staying alive
  'Tis-really-quite-'ard   Shameful-try'nny   Thanks to whom?
  Up-it's-gone-tex-tex
                              – 'Tex-tex Song' (*Ze-ze bushi*, 1910)

The hyphenated refrains appear in the original in *katakana*
script and with slightly distorted pronunication, such that at first
glance or first hearing, one does not grasp any meaning. For
example, the word for tax or taxes, *zei*, is distorted to *ze*. These
artifices were reportedly a means of pulling the wool over the
eyes of the censors. Yet it may well follow that the refrains were
also incomprehensible to the very populace who read, heard and
sang them. And for some of those who did understand, it must
have made the idea of resistance somewhat self-consoling or self-
abusing.

That was the same year that the poet Ishikawa Takuboku
published 'Today's Pent-Up Age' (*Jidai heisoku no genjō*). It
was the time when the Meiji system had reached its point of full
completion, and was about to move from overripe maturity into
a period of stagnation.

The emotion of 'anger' is not simply hate plus repulsion. It
also 'springs from a sense of violated justice' (Hashikawa Bunzō,
'Lost Anger'). Consequently, for it to materialize *as a common
emotion*, there must be a common value system to support the
anger. Anger of a citizenry toward authority requires a widely
shared counter-value, supported by a broad anti-authoritarian
movement. Anger directed toward another country requires that
the nation feel oppressed by some other nation. However, the
solidification of the Meiji regime (via the crushing and absorption
of the people's rights movement), and the transformation of the
Japanese from an oppressed to an oppressing nation (via victories
over China and Russia and the annexation of Korea), had the
effect of eliminating those two premises by which anger may
materialize as a common emotion.

There was one song that seized the spirit of the masses and

stayed widely and continually popular during the transition from the Meiji to the Taisho period.

> Is that Miss Okaru going by palanquin?
> I am being sold and taken away
> Goodbye Father, goodbye Mother
> And goodbye to my love
> Won't you write me sometimes?
>   Don-Don
>
> I don't like to drink by nature
> But I'm drowning the sorrow of parting
> Stop drowning your cares in sake
> Your body is wasting away
> Who will take care of things later?
>   Don-don
>
>   – 'Don-don' (1911–13)

Here, once again, there is no loud demand for rights or freedom or happiness. What is conveyed is the desperation and resignation of the masses at the bottom of the regime who silently endure their reluctant lives.

'Don-don' carries various motifs, including that of despair, a key motif during the Taisho period; and the motifs of resignation and lingering attachment, which are important during Showa.

Let us return to the topic of *enka*, specifically to their original form, the people's-power songs. Figure 2.1 charts the phase changes undergone by their dual logic and emotional structures, along with the progression of the Meiji order from solidification through full maturity.

Figure 2.2 illustrates the basic trends of the anger motif of the people's-power *enka*. On the one hand it turned into state-power *enka* aiming its fury outside the country, and on the other hand, as songs of sarcasm and self-scorn, it was deflected into the sphere of humor and joking.

The motif of anger first spouted up as opposition to the solidifaction of the Meiji regime, materializing mainly as the people's-rights songs. Its logic and feeling then changed forms and followed two paths. On the one hand it reversed itself and became an advance guard and driving force for the program of the regime

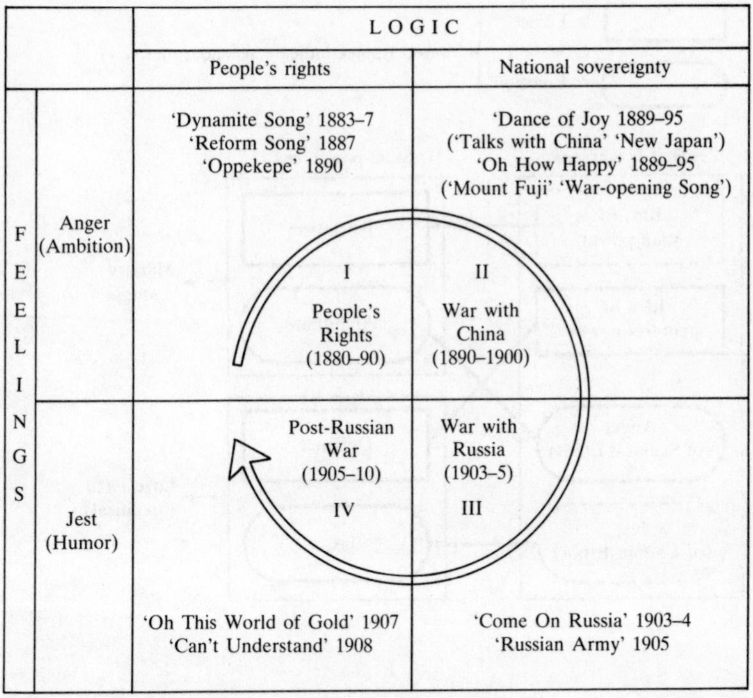

		LOGIC	
		People's rights	National sovereignty
F E E L I N G S	Anger (Ambition)	'Dynamite Song' 1883–7 'Reform Song' 1887 'Oppekepe' 1890 I People's Rights (1880–90)	'Dance of Joy 1889–95 ('Talks with China' 'New Japan') 'Oh How Happy' 1889–95 ('Mount Fuji' 'War-opening Song') II War with China (1890–1900)
	Jest (Humor)	Post-Russian War (1905–10) IV 'Oh This World of Gold' 1907 'Can't Understand' 1908	War with Russia (1903–5) III 'Come On Russia' 1903–4 'Russian Army' 1905

Figure 2.1 *Phase changes in Meiji period* enka

itself, alongside such systemic building blocks as the constitution, the Diet and the wars. On the other hand, it was deflected and apoliticized, and remained adrift at the bottom of the system, in the lower reaches of actual personal feelings, where it took the forms of *ressentiment*, bitterness, despair and lingering attachment (*miren*).

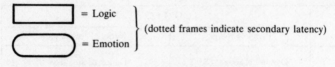

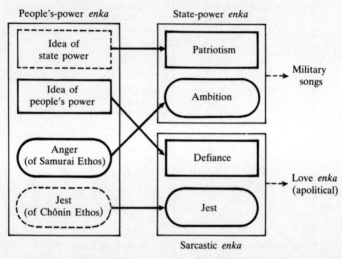

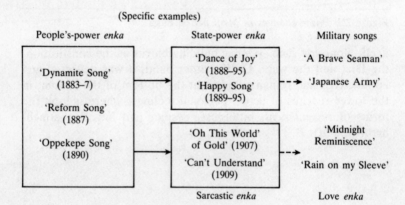

Figure 2.2 *Tracks of the motif of anger in* enka

3 The History of Tears

The vicissitudes of tears

'Tears' is the most frequently used noun in Japanese popular songs after 1868 (the next most frequent is 'dream'). It occurs in 83 of the 451 songs taken up here, or nearly twenty percent. Its distribution increases steadily over time, as follows:

					%
Early Meiji	(1868–89)	1	song(s) of	95	1.0
Later Meiji	(1890–1912)	12		112	10.7
Taisho	(1913–25)	6		46	13.0
Early Showa	(1826–45)	28		99	28.3
Postwar	(1946–63)	36		98	36.7

A closer inspection of the occurrence of the symbol of tears, by 7-year intervals, is presented in Figure 3.1. There is a dramatic proportional increase from 1903, about the time of the Russo-Japanese War. Thus the period when tears was the key symbol of Japanese popular songs is exactly that period which was examined in Chapter 1, when anger twisted inward to resentment or bitterness, and criticism shaded into sarcasm.

In musical terms, it was at precisely this time that songs in the minor-sounding *tan-onkai* scale began to be well liked.

Before the Sino-Japanese war, the word 'tears' appeared in only two songs. One was 'Dynamite Song' (1883): 'People's power activists rain down their tears. To polish the brave spirit of Yamato . . .' (see Chapter 3). The other was 'Song of Nankō' (1900): 'Falling from the luxuriant green leaves of Sakurai . . . Is it tears or fluttering dewdrops?' In both cases the tears are cried by active political personages; they were not the tears of the masses themselves, but those of the elite. Yet of course in the background were the tears of the majority of the 'people' who backed or participated in the people's power movement, and the majority of the 'subjects' who shed their own tears over the legend of loyal Nankō's untimely death, which goes far

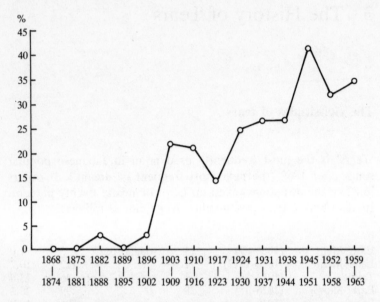

Figure 3.1 *Proportion of popular songs using the word 'tears'*

toward explaining why the people loved to sing these songs. These political personages were a far cry from the mass of the people, and yet they were spokespersons for one or another aspect of the people's feelings during the various phases of Japanese modernity. The people were connected to those in the political sphere, in reality or in fantasy, through the medium of sympathy for their sorrows.

But by the late Meiji period, when tears became a key symbol in the Japanese popular song, the tears of active participants in the political sphere were no longer mentioned. Instead we hear for the first time of the tears of the people, as the direct victims of war or of punishment or some other function of the nation. The song which pioneered this type of expression, and which still reverberates at the deepest level of the feelings of Japanese a half-century later, is 'Comrade in Arms,' a song from the Russo-Japanese War, set in Manchuria. (See Chapter 11.) This was the first Japanese popular song to contain the adjective 'sad' (*kanashii*).

The next songs about tears, just after the Russian War, were 'Midnight Reminiscence' and 'Rain on My Sleeve.'

Oh it's completely, completely a dream
Elder brother, give me leave
Wife and child, give me leave
Tears of repentance are streaming down
Sprinkling on my sleeve like village rains . . .
      – 'Midnight Reminiscence' ('Ballad of Osaburō' 1906)

The pillow here upon my lonely bed
Has been moistened so many times
By hot tears as I recall the memories
Of one who has passed away, and of destiny . . .

I am not supposed to be someone
Who sheds tears of resentment in vain
No, I should not give in to weeping and mourning
I know, but then once again, the unceasing tears –
How could I possibly not have these feelings . . .
      – 'Rain on My Sleeve' ('Ballad of Soeko', 1906)

These songs were the first to exhibit several of the patterns of later Japanese popular songs, including those which constitute the structure of 'tears.' First, the tears that no one sees in a place such as a 'lonely bed; second, the tears of 'resentment' at having lost what little love one could latch onto amid cold society and cruel fate; and third, the tears which overflow uncontrollably despite the norm consciousness of 'not giving in to weeping and mourning.' Popular songs of the 1920s and later are sprinkled with examples of each of these patterns.

'Tears' surrounding the love of men and women

From 1910 onward, there are no more songs containing tears which relate directly to politics, either actively or passively evoked. Instead, beginning with several of the most popular songs of 1909 and 1910, and continuing throughout the Taisho and Showa periods up to the 1960s, the tears which are sung of almost always flow in connection with love between a man and a woman in the private sphere.

In the middle of the Taisho period, tears temporarily took a very low profile. Aside from a few comical uses between 1915 and 1923, the year of the Tokyo earthquake, the word virtually never appears. Generally speaking, the first few years of the Taisho period make up one of the few brief periods marked by cheerful songs infected by the rejoicings of the populace. Another was the time of the Sino-Japanese War in the 1890s.

But by the early Showa years, gloomy tears are found in song after song, including 'I Love You' (*Kimi-koishi*, 1929), 'Black Lily Flower' (*Kuroyuri no hana*, 1929), 'Is Drink Tears or Sighs?' (*Sake wa namida ka tame-iki ka*, 1931) and 'Song of a Bar Hostess' (*Jokyū no uta*, 1931).

> I'm a night-blooming flower at a drinking spot
> With my red lipstick and my brocade sleeves
> Dancing so gaily under the neon lights
> Sadly, sadly fading away   Flower of tears
>
> I'm a sorrowful flower at a drinking spot
> A virgin by night and a mother by day
> My sleeves are filled with hidden tears from long ago
> Growing late and heavy   These are not dewdrops
>
> It rains and it rains   It rains tonight again
> Growing late and sad   On the streets of the Ginza
> And the tears are falling   A long-lost lover
> Memories, memories in the falling rain
> – 'Song of a Bar Hostess' (*Jokyū no uta*, 1931)

These songs, which date from the peak of the escapist '*ero-guro* (erotic-grotesque) nonsense' culture, portrayed the countless sorrows that were crushed underfoot by a gay urban civilization which bloomed unseasonably, smack in the middle of the financial panic and the collapse of the rural economy.

The frequency with which tears were mentioned in popular songs reached a climax just before the Pacific War, between 1937 and 1940.

> The sunset is red   My heart is sad
> Hot tears   Moisten my cheeks . . .

The flowing voyage   Yes, the tears
Fleeting withering memories . . .
      – 'Lakebottom Hometown' (*Kotei no furosato*, 1937)

To the lake with mountains of loneliness
I came all alone   With sorrowful heart
Unable to bear   The pain in my heart
Burning up   The dreams of yesterday
Faint smoke   Of old letters
                – 'Lakeside Inn' (*Kohan no yado*, 1939–40)

The moment when 'Lakeside Inn' achieved widespread popularity was during wartime when, on grounds that sentimentality
could not be tolerated, it was banned by an order from the
Information Board.

After the commencement of hostilities with America in 1941,
all expressions of sadness were suppressed and the word 'tears'
was eliminated from popular songs. 'Lakeside Inn' was one of
the last few songs which offered thoroughgoing articulations of
sadness. Here are excerpts from two others:

When I look there   There where he points
The flow of the river Tone   The flowing moon

The moon I used to view   Smiling long ago
Today   Today   I see with a face of tears
  – 'Moonlit Night on the River Tone' (*Ōtone tsukiyo*, 1939)

Wistful memory of all those tears I cried
Alone there on the banks of the stream
On the night my sister married
That hill, this stream, my childhood friends
Doesn't anyone long for the old hometown?
      – 'Who Doesn't Yearn for Home?' (*Dareka kokyō o
                              omowazaru*, 1940)

The days when it was permissible to express sadness as sadness
turned retrospectively to a kind of happiness, as the wartime
control of sentiments took over.

35

Sorrow in broad daylight

It is said that after the war the Japanese had become 'dry,' yet the proportion of postwar popular songs with 'tears' in them is 36 out of 98, or more than 1 in 3.

At first, they were tears for those who had lost their flesh and blood or their lives in the war ('Who made me such a woman . . .' in 'Amid the Falling Stars,' 1946); or the tears of those who were separated from their native land and dreamed of reunion ('The hot tears when I reach home . . .' 'Repatriation Ship,' 1947); or the tears of those in love who were taken far away or left behind in the wartime and postwar confusion ('Far, so far away you went . . .' 'In the Shade of the Chestnut Tree,' 1947; 'I'll Keep Waiting for You,' 1948–9).

Those were the typical new subjects and situations of sorrow in the postwar period. On the other hand, the new *quality* of postwar sadness is lucidly expressed in 'Blue Mountain Range' (*Aoi sanmyaku*, 1948).

> Wet with rain On the ruins of the fire
> A nameless flower Looks upward
> The glittering peak Of the blue mountain range
> That familiar feeling
> When I see it the tears Run once again
> – 'Blue Mountain Range' (*Aoi sanmyaku*, 1948)

The composer directs that this song be played 'lightheartedly.' With a C-minor melody barely concealing sorrow, it sings not of sadness hidden by dark of night, but rather of a sorrow in broad daylight, with the sun pouring radiantly down. This sort of image of sorrow is repeated in such songs as 'Nagasaki Tolling' (*Nagasaki no kane*, 1949): 'The supremely clear blue sky, Feels like sadness with this pain'); and 'Thistle Song' (*Azami no uta*, 1951: 'A mountain has a mountain's thoughts, The ocean has the ocean's sorrow). It is also connected to the brightness of the tears in 'Let's Walk with Our Eyes on High' (*Ue o muite arukō*, 1961, popular abroad as 'Sukiyaki Song') – 'Let's walk with our eyes on high. So the tears will not drip down . . .'

In contrast to the restricted human sadness exemplified by the ballads of Osaburō and Soeko, these songs embody a new form of emptiness and sadness which possesses humanity once it has been *liberated*, as from the many restrictions of prewar society.

The pearling of sadness

From 1961 to 1963, amid what was known as the 'mood of tranquility' just after the turbulent renewal of the 'Ampo' Japan-US security pact, the symbol of 'tears' appears in some 40 per cent of the popular songs treated here (11 of 27 songs). If we add in others which use the verb *naku* (cry, sob, weep), the total reaches 18, or two-thirds.

Songs such as 'The River Flows' (*Kawa wa nagareru*) and 'Let's Walk with Our Eyes on High' (both 1961) are not simply about lost love, or about poverty or parting, or the sadness of any other specific subject. Instead they scoop up an amorphous sense of sorrow which flows in the depths of the 'tranquility.'

On the other hand, a set of songs from the same years embodies a pattern of sadness that has not changed from the prewar era. They include 'Hundred-Times-Worshipping Lady' (*O-hyakudo koi-san*), which took the Recording Grand Prize; and the 1961 revival of 'I Love You' (*Kimi koishi*). Another is "Ship of Tears" (*Namida-bune*, 1962):

> . . . and the last teardrop
> Soaks into my rubber mackintosh
> No matter what   Just a sailor gull
> I shall not cry, shall not regret   On the northern sea
> Sprouting forth in the ocean   The flower of love

Here is an image of the world which is qualitatively the same as the one presented in 1934 by 'Life of a Meiji Woman' (*Meiji ichidai onna*): 'Hold no resentment for affairs of this world, A life like a single shot of fireworks . . .' (See Chapter 11). Once again we find a loving objectification of the feeling of resignation from life, and a figure of the self desperately shaking off bitterness and sadness. The rampant narcissism of the image of 'a single shot of fireworks' or 'flower of love,' which objectifies the slice of life of the self, acts nectar-like to enfold and heal the wounds of the spirit.

As the pearl oyster envelops an object which pierces its body with mucus and makes it round, so the Japanese wrap an injury to the heart with beauty, and objectify it. 'Pearling' is an apt term which we may use for this function of the spirit by which, rather than removing the cause of sadness, the sadness is given value through beauty as just that sadness.

> Upon the pale violet one day
> The sun of tears will fall in drops
> > – 'Lakeside Inn' (*Kohan no yado*, 1939–40)

> Here and there on teardrops
> Of flower petals glistened
> The dew that evening
> – 'Hill Overlooking the Harbor' (*Minato ga mieru oka*, 1947)

In this line of songs, which extends through 'Red Handkerchief' of 1963 ('Touchingly wet with bitterness/And yet the tears . . .'), tears are in some measure objectified as an aesthetically admirable phenomenon. The crying may even be sung of as something fortunate, as if tears are a symbol of youth:

> Released tears   So full with glistening
> Sorrowful nineteenth   Spring oh spring
> With so much fragrance   In the scattering white dew
> Crying nineteenth   Spring oh spring
> > – 'Nineteenth Spring' (*Jū-kyū no haru*, 1933)

The pearling of sadness reaches its peak in this verse from 1961:

> When the rain stops   In the acacias
> The dove flies   Toward the blue sky
> Purple is the color   Of the wings
> At the edge of the bench
> My cast-off skin is left   Growing cold
> Searching for that person   Far away
> A shadow taking flight
> – 'When the Rain Stops in the Acacias' (*Akashia no ame ga yamu toki*, 1961)

There are the youth of Japan, rapturously enchanted with the beauty of their own sadness.

4 The History of Joy

The baseline for Meiji Romanticism

Joy is a motif in 9.8 per cent of the representative songs of Japan's first modern century (44 of 451 songs between 1868 and 1963). As shown in Figure 4.1, songs of joy reached two clear heights of popularity. The first began in the late 1880s and peaked a few years later at the time of the Sino-Japanese War, coming to an end just before the Russo-Japanese War of 1905. The second spanned a decade at the beginning of the Showa period, in the 1920s and 1930s.

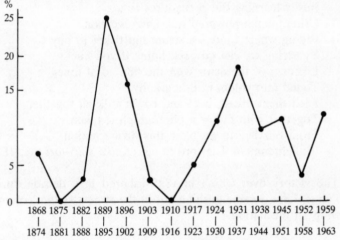

Figure 4.1 *Proportion of popular songs with the motif of joy*

Joyous songs of the early Meiji years were about the dawning period of Restoration, and the attendant liberation from the restrictions of the old era. They tended especially to sing ingenuous praises for the prospects of 'civilization and enlightenment.'

> Gradually everything is opening up
> The result of the reign of enlightenment

> A postcard will do the job
> News by wire and steamships in the mountains . . .
> – 'Enlightened Otsu-e Song' (*Kaika Otsu-e bushi*, 1869–72)

> In the progress of the Empire of Japan
> Japanese classics are all read and discharged
> Discharged duties are thrown away
> Away down the rails goes the horse-drawn car
> Horse-drawn car brings the mail around
> Around I went for a bottled refreshment
> Fresh response sent by electric wire
> Electric-wired lamp then caught my eye
> I deposit my savings for a long time
> Time makes Japan open more and more
> More and more the machines are in movement
> Movements of protest are now inactive
> Active energy goes into business
> Busily learning the procedures to use
> Using human-powered rickshaws we ride
> Riding where there's a steamship ticket to buy
> By spring we can go back home if you like
> Likeness of the actor with the fine vocal tones
> Toned into colors in lithography
> Feed them bread, beef and cow's milk all together
> Together with father a photograph is taken
> From our hearts we bless this divine nation . . .
> – 'Enlightenment Tagword Song' (*Kaika shiri-tori uta*, 1884)

The victory over China in 1895 ushered in a decade during which joyfulness came gushing out in the streets as the 'common feeling' of the nation.

> One fluttering flag is raised
> Flagship *Matsujima* sets out resolutely
> Hip hip hurrah for the Japanese Navy

> Two hawks wondrously nesting
> A sturdy treasure ship named *Takachiho*
> Hip hip hurrah for the Japanese Navy
> – 'Warship Counting Song' (*Gunkan kazoe bushi*, 1894)

The East Asian troubles are happily over
Pachu tenrai yan
Japanese flag erected in Taiwan
Men meto e-estorintan
Tekeshutto Hey let's go and see
    – 'Sound of the Winds' (*Tenrai bushi*, 1895)

This sort of 'joyfulness to pieces' of a nation giddy with victory would wilt into shame with but a moment's regard for the humiliation that must have been felt by the people of China. Yet it cannot be comprehended as merely the arrogance-drenched egoism of a victorious nation. The other ingredient of the mood in Japan was an outpouring of emotion at their own liberation from feelings of humiliation, insecurity and tension. These had arisen, of course, from the historical coercions of the great powers of Europe and America, and had been smoldering since the arrival of the Black Ships and the resulting unequal treaties of the 1850s. Now all that had been wiped away at a single stroke, by transfering the blame onto another people. Their unabashed delight which in some ways resembled the disdain of an upstart, was in large part relief at the reversal of a long national humiliation.

Blessing this reign comes the treasure ship
Laden with gold, silver, lapis, and agates
Wealth and honor and unending happiness
So fine, so fine
So fine, so fine, at last
– 'So Fine So Fine At Last' (*Yoi to yoi to yattose bushi*, 1895)

Such was the prevailing attitude during the last few years of the century, one of the rare intervals in modern Japanese history which brimmed over with cheerfulness.

Spring is so delightful
Couples under the cherry blossoms with sake
Faint moon behind the blooming garden trees
Rustling in the rain and wind
Briefly they bloom and then they scatter
    – 'Four Seasons of Kyoto' (*Kyo no shiki*, 1895)

41

This song, with its succeeding verses on 'delightful' summer, fall and winter, was again popular in 1909–10 and 1911–12, in an *enka* format with the title 'Four Seasons Song.'

Two fresh-feeling songs which remain popular today for school songs, *Minato*, 'The Harbor' and *Natsu wa kinu*, 'Summer Has Come,' date from this particular period.

> The sky, the harbor, and the evening so clear
> Shadows of countless ships 'neath the moon
> Lively sampans going to and fro
> The waves rolling in are turning to gold
> — 'The Harbor' (*Minato*, 1896)

This was the time of the flowering of Meiji romanticism in literature, most notably the poet Shimazaki Tōson's refreshing celebration of the joys and sorrows of youth in *Collection of Young Greens* (Wakanashū, 1897), Bansui's *Universal Sentience* (*Tenchi ujo*, 1899), Kyūkin's *Twilight Flute Collection* (*Botekishū*, 1899) and Yosano Akiko's *Tousled Hair* (*Midaregami*, 1901).

> Welling up and flowing from the many slopes
> Beyond floating mountains the ocean's lute
> The profound melodies of a hundred rivers
> All melting together in the waves
> In the time of mellow clear skies
> From afar can be heard
> The sound of tides in spring
> — Tōson, 'Sound of the Tides' (*Chōon*)

Corresponding to the sentiments of this well-known poem were the undulations of the music of 'Beautiful Nature' which came like a fresh breeze into the world of folk songs at the turn of the century. Previously, Japanese folk songs (including regional *min'yō* ballads, popular *zokkyoku* shamisen songs, and urban political *enka*) were all in simple-duple and simple-quadruple time, with the simple-triple rhythm appearing only as a rare exception. At this point a new wave of songs, characterized by a relaxed and refreshing triple rhythm, was enthusiastically welcomed by a broad section of the public, probably centered on the urban middle and upper classes. The 'era of fresh poetry'

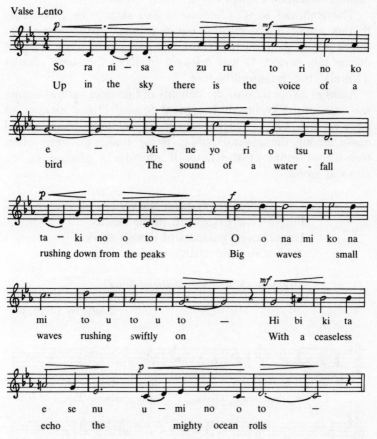

Utsukushiki Tennen ('Beautiful Nature')
Words by Takeshima Hagoromo
Music by Tanaka Hotsumi

which had been proclaimed by Tōson has arrived in the world of popular song as well.

In the lyrics, we find many carefree songs celebrating the joy of living as suggested by the beauty of nature. Among the songs that were best-liked nationally were 'Flowers' (*Hana*), which extolled the splendor of the Sumida River in spring, and 'Eight Miles in Hakone' (*Hakone hachiri*), which sang of inaccessible mountain passes. By 1903, the 24-year-old composer of those two songs, Taki Rentarō, had earned a place as one of the foremost exponents of Meiji Romanticism, alongside the poets

Kitamura Tokoku, Shimazaki Toson, Yosano Tekkan and Yosano Akiko. Indeed, it was these songs which provided the popular baseline of sensitivity for Meiji Romanticism.

'The Railroad Song' (*Tetsudo shōka*) sings with a bouncing rhythm about not a natural but a cultural phenomenon, the bright side of the industrial revolution which took place in Japan during this period. It was released in 1900, the same year as 'Flowers' and 'Beautiful Nature.'

Another celebration of the delights of life amid natural beauty was 'Colorful Flowers of Luxuriant Spring' (*Haru ranman no hana no iro*, 1901) a higher-school festival song which spread easily among the general public. Being similar to some other elite-school songs of the time, it provides a glimpse of the national mood.

> Colorful flowers of luxuriant spring
> Purple glow from a rift in the clouds
> Undarkening paleness of dawn's shadow
> Adding in some tranquil radiant light

Tetsudō Shōka ('The Railroad Song')
Words by Ōwada Tateki
Music by Ta Baiga

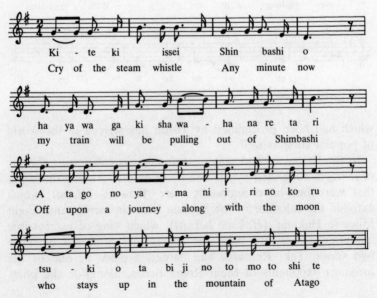

Ki - te ki issei Shin bashi o
Cry of the steam whistle Any minute now

ha ya wa ga ki sha wa - ha na re ta ri
my train will be pulling out of Shimbashi

A ta go no ya - ma ni i ri no ko ru
Off upon a journey along with the moon

tsu - ki o ta bi ji no to mo to shi te
who stays up in the mountain of Atago

Birds are chirping butterflies dancing
And the light of the scattering blossoms
– 'Colorful Flowers of Luxuriant Spring' (*Haru ranman no hana
no iro*, 1901)

'Four Seasons Song' (*Shiki no uta*) which was popular throughout this period is actually a parody of 'Fighting Spirit Song'
(*Shiki no uta*) from the time of the war with China. The transformation is symbolic. Even more symbolically, the tune of
'Beautiful Nature,' which gave voice to the people's exhilarating
joy of life at the turn of the century, reached new heights of
popularity when it was used for the ballads of Osaburō and
Soeko, 'Midnight Reminiscence' and 'Rain on my Sleeve' which
carried the feelings of blockage, grief and resentment of the
ensuing period after the war with Russia (see Chapter 2).

While the musical component of the popular song deserves
proper analytical attention alongside the lyrics, these two
examples seem to show that a given melody does not necessarily
have a fixed emotional orientation. It can be quite changeable,
at least in so far as the general public is concerned. (Of course
the emotional content of the lyrics may also be polyvocal, to one
degree or another.)

After the victory over Russia in 1905, the brightness which
was so continually evident during the turn-of-the-century years
went missing.

The two faces of urban paeans

Upbeat songs were relatively numerous during the first half of
the Taisho period, but in only a few of them does the motif of
joy come through loud and clear. This typical example celebrates
the joys of lower-middle-class life:

A small potted rose flower
Catching the dew of your love
Pale red color of the flower
Smiled for the first time yesterday . . .
– 'Rose Song' (*Bara no uta*, 1917)

The second climax of the joyful popular song came at the beginning of the Showa period. These songs were mainly about the pleasures of the consumption side of urban life. Some of the most famous are 'Tokyo Parade' and 'Dotombori Parade' (1929), 'Willows of Ginza' (1932), and the explosively popular 'Tokyo Ondo' (1933) and 'Tokyo Rhapsody' (1936).

One of their common characteristics is that almost all of them are about the busy streets of Tokyo or Osaka. Another is that, in contrast to the carefree, unclouded brightness of the turn of the century, they sing of joy as the obverse of sadness.

> My darling Ginza willow of long ago
> Who knows of the ruin of age
> Dancing to jazz, staying out and drinking
> At dawn a dancer's rain of tears
> – 'Tokyo Parade' (*Tokyo kōshin kyoku*, 1929)

On the heels of a financial panic in 1927 came the global economic collapse, bringing disaster to the northeast and other rural areas: countless hungry children, deaths from starvation, people collapsing in the streets, wives and children sold into service. It was only on the major thoroughfares of the big cities that happiness and enjoyment were likely to be found. Having been lured away from villages where the lights had gone out, tens of thousands of young women traded with bitter pleasure on the glittering 'red light-green light' streets.

The last gleam in the series of urban paeans was 'Tokyo Rhapsody' of 1936. Its breathless, fly-about rhythm reminds one of nothing so much as being *driven* to a compulsive quest for enjoyment.

Public life came under quasi-martial administration after the abortive coup by young officers in February 1936, and in the following year the Marco Polo Bridge incident served to drag Japan into the quagmire of war with China. The heavy atmospheric pressure enveloping the society led to 'singing night and day' (words from 'Tokyo Rhapsody'), and what better than the phantasmagoria of a rhapsody? For most of the public, this song was clearly not about their own lives, but was an illusion of 'flowering Tokyo' as a dream paradise.

'Tokyo Rhapsody'

Words by Kadota Yutaka
Music by Koga Masao

Paso Doble

Hanasaki hanachiru yo i mo – –
Flowers blooming flowers falling, very fine

Ginza no yanagi no shi ta de – ma – tsu – – wa
Waiting beneath the willows of Ginza

Kimi hi to ri kimi hi to ri Ae ba yu
You all alone you all alone When we meet

ku – – ti – ru – – mu –
we will go to a tea – room

Ta no shi mi ya ko – ko i no
This is happiness this is love

mi ya ko – yu – – me no para dai
only It's a dream para-

su yo – hana no To – – kyo –
dise flowering Tokyo

The switch from liberation to harmony

The joyful songs of Meiji times reflected a sense of carefree *exaltation*. Those of Taisho times went along with lower-middle-class *well-being*. The early Showa songs of joy were lined partly with a decadent *gaiety*. In the immediate postwar period, the joyful popular songs echoed what might be called a bombed-out sense of *liberation*.

'Tokyo Boogie-Woogie,' which the emaciated Kasagi Shizuko not so much sang as screamed from dance stages everywhere, pointedly embodied one element of the contemporary mood. Therefore this song feels almost pathetically distant from the emotional atmosphere in which we find ourselves twenty years later. For a popular song which articulates the feeling of its time, however, a short life span is nothing to be ashamed of. It is this song to which we turn in order to summon a compelling sense of the postwar mood.

> Tokyo boogie-woogie   Floating on the rhythm
>   In your heart you love it   What a thrill
> Echoing way across the ocean   Tokyo boogie-woogie
> The dance they call the boogie   Dancing 'round the world
> It's a dream for lovers   Yes that song   Let's give it a whistle
>   Blow that tune together with your love
> The song of someone's heart that's burning up   In the voice
>   of that sweet sweet lover   I want to dance it with you
> Underneath the   moon that's out tonight
> Tokyo boogie-woogie   Floating on the rhythm
>   In your heart you love it   What a thrill
> Song of the century   Song of the soul   Tokyo boogie-woogie
>   – 'Tokyo Boogie-Woogie' (1948)

Partly because of such provocative lines as 'Come on and boogie-woogie, Keep the beat with taiko drums, Come dance it with a splash now, Sing it out,' this song was frowned upon by the cultured people of the day, conservative and progressive alike, as a degenerate piece of reckless desperation. Perhaps it would be more appropriate to call it a song of abandonment than a song of joy. If it were played on the radio today at full volume, it would bring a blush to our faces. Yet wasn't it just such sweaty enthusiasm that enabled the Japanese to get back on their feet and pull through in the years just after the war? 'Light in the Cottage' and 'Apple Song' from the same period may still strike a chord somewhere in the Japanese heart today, but it was not from there that postwar Japan was born.

Hattori Ryoichi composed both 'Tokyo Boogie' and another hit of the same year, 'Ginza Can-Can Girl.' The latter is in part an echo of the early-Showa lineage of urban hymns, but it portrays the Ginza district as no longer just a domain of male mastery (as in 'At dawn a dancer's rain of tears'), but as a place where the postwar woman can strut, hurling defiance: 'I'm never scared of tigers or wolves.' More than simply a half-bantering document of manners as seen through male eyes, this song expresses the sense of liberation of young women, at least those who lived in the cities. Blustering, 'I might have no house, I might have no money, But I won't be deceived by some man,' it exudes a vitality that is one part desperation (like 'Tokyo Boogie'). At the same time, in contrast to the homemaker ethic of the 1960s, it encompasses alternative designs for the well-being of women.

Yet another hit of 1948 composed by Hattori, 'Blue Mountain Range,' presents joyfulness backed up by this sense of liberation in a more calm and serene style.

In bright young singing voices
The snowslides are melting
Cherries cleave the snow   Of the blue mountain range. . . .

Goodbye to the old clothes
Goodbye to those lonely dreams
Cherries cleave the snow   Of the blue mountain range . . .
– 'Blue Mountain Range' (1948)

There the desperate life force of 'Tokyo Boogie' and 'Can-Can Girl' has disappeared. Instead we find faint praise for what in Chapter 2 was called 'sorrows in broad daylight.' This was the longest-lived of the three songs.

Virtually no popular songs with motifs of joy reached major popularity during the ensuing years up to the early 1960s, a period which is roughly demarcated by the end of the American occupation in 1952 and the turbulent renewal of the Japan–US security pact (Ampo) in 1960.

Outside the sphere of the commercial popular song, however, the 1950s saw the rise throughout the nation of the *utagoe* Singing Movement, which attracted huge numbers of the young. Upbeat songs became the province of local 'singing clubs' where people would gather to sing as amateur performers or en masse. Most prominent was 'Song of Good Fortune' (*Shiawase no uta*), which was so widely loved as to penetrate the strata which normally support the popular song. 'Song of Good Fortune' was not about happiness due to the blessings of the moment, but about working together to build good fortune in the future. It was sung especially on such occasions as the wedding of a member of the group.

> Good fortune is our desire
> We work so very hard
> Dripping sweat in devotion to the future
> Building a bright world
> Let's sing together a song of good fortune
> Let's chase its resounding echoes
>   – 'Song of Good Fortune' (*Shiawase no uta*)

In the realm of popular songs, 'joyous songs' assumed renewed priority during the so-called tranquil mood which followed the ebb tide of the Ampo political uprising. Two examples from 1962 were 'Darling Baby,' *Kawaii beibi* ('How wonderful it is to be in love, Spending these days of youth together with you, Forever, until forever . . .'); and 'We're in Love, You See,' *Koi shiteirun da mon* ('The earth is just a tiny little star, Plenty of happiness, plenty of heaven . . .').

In 1963 two songs were on the lips of virtually the entire country: 'Walking along with Eyes on High' (*Ue o muite arukō*) and 'Hello, Darling Baby' (*Konnichiwa aka-chan*).

> Hello, darling baby   Your smiling face
> Hello, darling baby   Your crying voice
> That tiny little hand Round dark eyes
> So glad to meet you   My name is Mommy
> Hello, darling baby   It's your life

Hello, darling baby   Here's to your future
This good fortune   Is your Daddy's wish
– 'Hello Darling Baby' (*Konnichiwa aka-chan*, 1963)

The 'Song of Good Fortune' which was popular during the Singing Movement of the 1950s had sung of a hopeful resolve for happiness in the future. In the 1960s, many songs-of-good-fortune praise the happiness which is here in the present. The singer seemed to outdo herself with the vocal power of the line, 'This good fortune is your daddy's wish.' In 'Clap Your Hands If You Are Happy' (*Shiawase nara te o tatakou*, 1964), happiness is celebrated by clapping and stamping, snapping fingers and tapping shoulders. 'Forever with You' (*Kimi to itsumademo*), an epitome of perfect happiness and contentment, is similar.

Only a tenth of modern Japanese popular songs are songs of joy, as noted at the opening of this chapter. Although it is a sparse history, we may note that at this writing (in the mid-1960s), the proportion of joyous songs has climbed to its third post-Meiji peak.

At the turn of the century joyous songs were subjectively untroubled. Objectively speaking, though, there was in fact an underside to the industrial revolution, such as the Ashio copper mine poisoning incident (see Yokoyama Gennosuke's 1898 book on Japan's lower-class society). In the joyous songs of the second peak around 1930, danger cast a dark, clear shadow. Dare we state that today we seem to have reached a period of untroubled, joyous songs which are appropriate in both the subjective and the objective sense?

The echoes of the turn-of-the-century songs of joy were interrupted by the gunshots of the Russo-Japanese War, and the gay songs of the 1930s were drowned out by the flames of the Second World War. Is today's giant chorus of 'songs of good fortune' destined for uninterrupted sonorous ascendance?

5 The History of Love

Love from a distance

People may automatically equate popular songs with expressions of romantic love, but of course this is not always true. A little less than half of the 451 songs chosen for this study have romantic love as a theme, including cases where it is a secondary or indirect theme (209 songs or 46.3 per cent). Yet if we trace the chronological distribution (the dotted line in Figure 5.1), the stereotype takes on more accuracy as history progresses. In fact, during the two decades following the Pacific War, the proportion of love songs exceeds 70 per cent (71 of 98 songs).

It is since the Taisho period that romantic love songs have occupied the mainstream of popular songs. Of course before that time there were more than a few *zokkyoku* and *min'yō* folk songs about romantic love. But the great majority of pre-Taisho

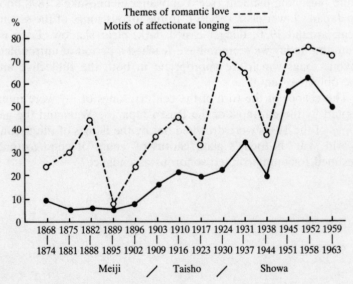

Figure 5.1 *Proportion of popular songs with motifs of love*

popular songs were regional folk songs describing local scenery, songs about the new modern lifestyles, political criticism, social satire, or war songs. (Some of those did have secondary themes of romantic love, and they are counted as such in the calculation above.)

On closer inspection, we find that songs with a theme of romantic love (*ren'ai*) are not limited to songs with a motif of deeply affectionate, yearning love (*bojō*). The latter type was rare during the 1870s and 1880s in particular, when songs about 'love' were usually bawdy songs of coquetry, jealousy, jesting or idle banter, set mostly in red-light districts. Their emotional motif could be considered to be the 'playful' side of romantic love.

Yet in premodern times, local folk ballads often sang of love which was both yearning and easygoing. For the elements of society who sang folk songs, romantic love was not play.

Bojō is a yearning, affectionate love for someone who is esteemed more highly than oneself, accompanied by a sense of distance. A parent does not feel *bojō* toward a child, nor does a situation with the potential for union qualify as yearning love. For the gay blades in the pleasure quarters, romantic love is 'play' because a distance is maintained between the self and the love affair. In the case of *bojō*, yearning love, the distance lies between the loving and the loved, not between the lover and the love, and there is no place for 'play' to intervene.

The tears roll unwiped

The transition in the proportion of popular songs with the motif of yearning love is shown by the solid line in Figure 5.1. There is a steady increase in the late Meiji years just after 1900, and by the 1930s it becomes one of the most important motifs in popular songs, resuming its increase after an enforced decline during the Pacific War.

Songs of romantic love appeared during the modern century in 1910, a decade after the flowering of Meiji Romanticism in literature, with 'Pure White Peak of Mt Fuji' (*Masshiroki Fuji no ne*) and 'Handful of Sand' (*Ichiaku no suna*).

> The tears roll unwiped down my cheek
> Expressing a handful of sand
> She who I cannot forget

The form is quite traditional – the words are a *waka* poem by Takaboku, the melody is a *rōei* chant – but the content incorporates a sense of youthful joy and sorrow which was very fresh at the time.

> Pure white peak of Mt Fuji   Verdant isle of Eno
> Even as we gaze upward, now come tears
> Twelve who shall not return   To these heroic souls
> Our hearts and our spirits consecrate prayers

This song commemorates a boating accident at Shichirigahama in 1910, in which twelve male middle-school students on a school outing lost their lives. After the event, a teacher at the nearby Kamakura Girls School composed it for the students to sing. It is not actually a song of romantic love, yet in it we can see the intercourse of male and female hearts, in an open, group manner. It was several years later that the song reached nationwide popularity.

School songs and popular songs

Upbeat songs of yearning love came into vogue in the early Taisho years, including 'Kachusha's Song' (1914), 'Love is a Delicate Wildflower' (1915), and 'Rose Song' (1917).

> Lovely Kachusha
> The heartache of parting
> Now before the fleeting snows have melted
> Let us sing out a prayer to the gods

Matsui Sumako sang this famous song during the performance of Tolstoy's *Resurrection* at the Teikoku Stage by Shimamura Hogetsu's Dramatic Arts Theatre. Shimamura and Sōma Gyofu jointly wrote the words, and the composer was Shimamura's live-in student, Nakayama Shinpei, then 26. Nakayama belonged to that generation of sentimental youth who lived through the time of the flowering of Meiji Romanticism, which was also the first generation to be educated after the *yo-na-nuki* major scale was designated as the official scale for school sings. (This was influenced by well-known songs which used the scale in whole or in part, such as 'Summer Hasn't Come' and 'Harbor,' both in 1896). Nakayama taught primary school while he was living and studying with Shimamura, and 'Kachusha's Song,' in the same scale as school chorus songs, immediately fascinated children and spread throughout the country, to the point where a ministerial order was issued banning primary students from singing it. This was no accidental success; the story goes that Nakayama had from the start intended to use the school scale as a pattern to create a folk-style song.

For Nakayama, the song was the first in a string of nationwide hit favorites which established him as one of the leading popular composers of modern Japan. More than a dozen of his songs from the Taisho and early Showa periods were successful enough to be included in the representative songs analyzed in this book (see Appendix). Nakayama can also be credited with establishing what is known as the *kayōkyoku* scale, centered on the *yo-na-nuki* minor scale.

The school choral melodies and military melodies based on the minor *yo-na-nuki* scale were in a sense opposites, representing the obverse and reverse sides of modern Japanese emotion.

(A note on the *yo-na-nuki* scale)

The Western scale of do-re-mi-fa-so-la-ti-do was formerly taught in Japan as hi-fu-mi-yo-i-mu-na. In the *yo-na-nuki* scale, the fourth and seventh tones are removed, leaving a pentatonic scale, do-re-mi-so-la. Just after 1900 the national program of choral education in the schools was changed over to this pentatonic pitch. From that time, most of the well-known educational chorus songs were composed on this scale, as were the vast majority of other group-oriented melodies such as military and school songs (and 'The Railroad Song'; see Chapter 3).

Played in a minor mode, this scale sounds quite similar to a scale called *miyako-bushi* or the *in* scale, a traditional mode that was widely used from classical times. Sonobe Saburō explains,

'When the fourth tone (the dominant) of the *yo-na-nuki* penta-tonic minor scale is taken as the tonic, the ascending scale becomes the *miyako-bushi* scale. . . . Thus, in a manner of speaking, the *yo-na-nuki* pentatonic minor scale contains the *miyako-bushi* scale.' (From *Nihon minshu kayō shiki, Regarding the History of Japanese Popular Songs*). See Figure 5.2.

If this scale is played on a piano or harmonica, the peculiarly Japanese feel is immediately apparent. Taki Rentarō's 'Moon on Castle Ruins' (*Kōjo no tsuki*) was the first modern Japanese song in which this scale was intentionally used, and it is one of the secrets behind the distinctive 'Japaneseness' which made the song a favorite. It was left to Nakayama Shinpei to adapt this melodic key to the realm of the commercial popular song.

The *yo-na-nuki* pentatonic scale is not unique to Japan, but is used in many parts of Asia including China, Java, India, Mongolia, Annam and Kampuchea. It is also often used in the folk ballads of Scotland (for example, 'Auld Lang Syne') and Ireland ('The Last Rose of Summer'), which is no doubt one of the reasons that those two foreign tunes have proved to be enduring favorites in Japan. But the traditional attachment to the minor *yo-na-nuki* pentatonic scale is considered, in comparative sociology, to be a notable characteristic of the Japanese. (See Max Weber, *Musiksoziologie*.)

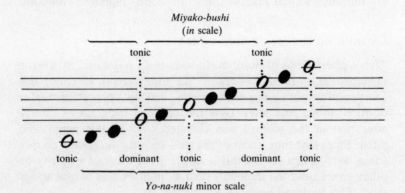

Figure 5.2 *The* yo-na-nuki *and* miyako-bushi *scales*

Love in the light, love in the shadows

In the first years of the Showa period, the brightly cheerful type of yearning love song became rather rare, and a sad sort of love set between twilight and night occupies the mainstream.

The ship sails tonight   Reluctant farewell
Upon the dark waves   Falls the snow . . .
> – 'Setting Sail' (*Defune*, 1927)

The darkness of night   Presses in   Sufferings   Oh, my
Someone is casting shadows   Upon this troubled heart . . .
> – 'Darling Lover' (*Kimi-koishi*, 1929)

A lamp of many colors   Flickers and goes out
The heart of a woman   Has but a short memory
> – 'Naniwa Ballad' (*Naniwa ko-uta*, 1929–30)

At night a falling   Momentary shower
Of your sadness   Melodiously
You are singing   And whistling. . . .
> – 'A Moment's Shower' (*Shigure hitotoki*, 1932)

Amid this stream was Koga Masao's 'Yearning for a Shadow,' which took the nation by storm in 1932. That song, along with 'Is Sake Tears or Sighs?' and 'Beyond the Hills' which he composed at about the same time, confirmed his status as Nakayama's successor on the throne of the popular scene, and inaugurated the era of the 'Koga melody.'

> Yearning
> For a phantom shadow   In the rain in the sun
> Wretched under the moon, wretched   My desire
>   Fire in my breast   Concealed yet burning
>   My heart is pining   Shedding silent tears
>
> So miserable
> I pick up the guitar   And strum
> To console   What only aches
>   Interminable showers   Dying autumn
>   Lonely quavering sound   My heart grieves

> For you
> Long life   Is frostbitten
> Spring forever unseen   This my destiny
>   Is it worth prolonging   This cast-off shell
>   'Tis a fleeting shadow   This love of mine
>   – 'Yearning for a Shadow' (*Kage o shitaite*, 1932)

This tune is regarded as the quintessential Koga melody, while the lyrics are a seamless litany of the tearjerking catchwords of the Japanese popular song: phantoms, shadows, rain, the moon, desire (*omoi*), burning breast, guitar, rainshower, autumn, you (*kimi*), life, spring, fate, cicada shell, love (*koi*) . . . Yearning, burning, pining, aching, consoling, strumming, silently sobbing . . . Lonesome, sad, miserable, fleeting, wretched . . . What a masterful job of composition from nothing but the emotional buzzwords! If a popular song were written by a computer, this is what it would be like. (See the dictionary of symbols in the Appendix.)

'Kachusha's Song,' which proclaimed the era of the Nakayama melody, and 'Yearning for a Shadow' typify the two basic types of the Japanese song of yearning love: love in the light and love in the shadows, love in a major key and love in a minor key.

It is coincidental that 'Darling Lover' and 'Naniwa Ballad' date from the year of the Wall Street crash, and that 'Yearning for a Shadow' was released just at the time of the Shanghai Incident (the onset of full-scale war in China). But it was no accident that through an era leading from economic depression to the desperation of war, the melancholy color of popular songs of yearning love also deepened. As people sang along 'to console what only aches,' they must have loaded onto that sorrowful romance not merely the sufferings of lost love, but also the 'frostbitten' misery brought on by awareness of the setbacks and dead ends that occur in various areas of life.

During the war, songs about yearning love were frequently coiled up in an exoticism which fired people's dreams of going to the Asian mainland. Examples from 1938, the year after war broke out in China, are 'Manchurian Maiden'; 'Shanghai Blues' ('Tears in my eyes, dreaming of Szechuan Road in Shangahi . . .'), and 'Foggy Shiba Road.'

The one I parted with On misty Shiba Road
May he pass safely Across the straits
I shall not forget For he is one
Who has dedicated his life To his country
       – 'Foggy Shiba Road' (*Kiri no shiba-ji*, 1938)

Two senses of distance

Just after the war, 'Apple Song' (see Chapter 9) carried on the line of cheerful love songs which dated from 'Kachusha's Song,' while the gloomy line in the style of 'Yearning for a Shadow' was carried on by another Koga composition, 'Hot Springs Town Elegy' (*Yu no machi ereji*). This is a fine example of a Koga melody, making ample use of *yuri* grace notes.

(*Note*: Yuri, or *kobushi*, is a singing technique by which a note is stretched and quavered. It appears in typical form in 'Hot Springs Elegy' in the opening words, 'Izu no ya-maaaa ya-aaa-ma,' and later at 'yu – no- keeemu-ri,' for example. It is a peculiarly Japanese vocal technique, used in traditional songs with shamisen accompaniments, and differing from Western vibrato or tremolo. Sonobe points out its similarity to melisma, which is used in some folk songs and ancient ballads of southern and eastern Europe. There may well be some connection between *yuri* and the fact that sung Japanese words always end with vowels; for the technique is difficult to use with words ending in consonants, such as the English 'wind' or 'love.')

The feeling of distance is a part of yearning love, as defined earlier in this chapter. In popular songs such a sense of distance is promoted by two main social factors which are in the background. One is the spatial distance which exists between one's birthplace and a 'foreign' place, due mainly to population movements into Tokyo and other large cities. The other is differences in status which exist as a result of class and status distinctions.

Songs of yearning love in which the first factor operates to interpose a sense of distance from the hometown, are typified by 'Lone Cedar of Farewell' (see Chapter 10), 'From the Apple Village,' and 'Train of Sorrow' (all 1956).

'Hot Springs Town Elegy'
Words by Nomura Takao
Music by Koga Masao

I   zu no ya   ma ———— ya   ———— ma
Pale   moon   in   the   mountains

— tsu ki a   wa —— ku   A ka — ri — ni —
of   Izu   Steam   from

— mu — se — — bu   yu — no   — ke — — — mu — ri
the   baths   smothered   by   the   light

A   — a   — —   hatsukoi no   — kimi o tazu — nete —
Oh   searching   for   you   my   first   love

Koyoi mata gi ta   — tsu   ma —   bi — ku
Playing   the   guitar   once   more

— ta bi — no — — — ri
again   tonight

Crying crying as I ran   Drizzle on the platform
Tokyo-bound night train   Hear the blurring whistle . . .
                    – 'From the Apple Village' (*Ringo mura kara*, 1956)

The window separating us   So far away
I can't bear it any longer   Looking back
                    – 'Train of Sorrow' (*Aishu ressha*, 1956)

These are vivid illustrations of the horizontal type of spatial distance, while status differences represent a vertical type of distance.

A love song which throws up this vertical type of distance is 'Ship of Tears' (*Namida-bune*, 1962):

The crying is over and the last teardrop
Soaks into my rubber mackintosh
No matter what   Just a sailor gull
I shall not cry, shall not regret   On the northern sea
Sprouting forth in the ocean   The flower of love

Having fallen in love one cannot hesitate
But having said no   Then never again
I shall never dream   Just a sailor gull
Pillows of herring   In the northern sea
Sorrows of the moon   Ship of tears
                    – 'Ship of Tears' (*Namida-bune*, 1962)

This song illustrates a process which the popular arts in general are wont to perform, an unconscious process of duplication whereby the countless separate, concrete feelings that sigh during a given era are first abstracted and universalized, and then once again poured into the concrete configuration of a certain typical circumstance. The people empathize with the image which is thus formed on the basis of their actual personal feelings which are backed up by millions of individual experiences, and invest it with their own slightly (or very) different emotions. 'No matter what, just a sailor gull. . . . I shall never dream, just a sailor gull . . .' Here is a sense of discrimination, actual to the point of pain. Like a fisherman's lamp which lights up the dark surface of the sea, the song lights up the existence of countless social distances, the scraps of many yearnings that were deflected by those gaps, the untold millions of broken bits of love for which there is no solace other than song.

6   The History of Chivalry

The structure of *gikyō*

The motif traced in this chapter is *gikyō*, a term that has no exact counterpart in English. 'Chivalry' or 'heroism' are the closest equivalents, but it is still something different. *Gikyō* may be defined as 'voluntary abandonment of an intense attachment or inner urge for devotion' to a person or a group.

Some may criticize this definition as emphasizing only the passive side of chivalry. It is true that chivalry signifies the choice of devotion to a person or a group as a way of life and *action*, while the abandonment of an inner attachment is merely its passive premise. But the core of emotional resonance felt by the Japanese toward various forms of *gikyō* is evoked not by the effect of a given deed, but by the act of *abandonment of an attachment*. It is something of an aesthetic of self-denial.

The same pattern is evident in the locus of the climax (*yamaba*) and the tear-wrenching scene (*nakidokoro*) in popular drama, from the *naniwa-bushi* recitations of the latter nineteenth century through the *shinpa* and *shinkokugeki* forms of early modern drama. The deep emotional sympathies of the people are directed more toward the underlying attachment given up by the hero or heroine, especially the inner feeling of tearing oneself away from the attachment, than toward the action which is chosen.

The forms of speech which represent *gikyō* chivalry in Japanese popular culture are not 'to serve' or 'devote,' but 'to give up' or 'tear oneself away.' The core feeling is *active abandonment*.

The conventional theory holds that *naniwa-bushi* and *shinpa* remained popular as a result of identification on the part of a public which had been compelled toward self-sacrifice. While this does touch on a fundamental point of the mentality of the audiences, it does not sufficiently explain the intensity of their active sympathies.

63

The values which orient acts of *gikyo* in popular culture are not rooted in a devotion to concepts that transcend this world, such as belief in a supreme God. The devotion is to individuals and groups who are immanently *present* in this world. Likewise, universal principles such as peace or freedom are not invoked. The values involve a particular devotion, to a person or group with whom the individual is connected in a specific relation. Yet at the same time, insofar as *gikyō* involves abandoning the happiness of fulfilling one's own urges or attachments – and often it means inevitable death, a categorical denial of one's own life – it can be regarded as a martyrdom to values which transcend life. In other words, the sense of values underlying chivalry involves *both transcendence* of life *and presence* within the world.

History offers various examples of peoples who, objectively or subjectively, have enjoyed the fruits of happiness. There have also been many peoples who, objectively or subjectively, have been denied the possibility of pursuing human happiness, so that one by one they live out their once-only lives nursing a pent-up grudge at the depths of their feelings. In some cases there were periods when the idea that the unsatisfactory conditions could objectively be overcome was widely embraced, but these were exceptions, occuring on the cusps of a few historical turning points. People have usually held the view that 'fate' was the underpinning of the conditions of their time and their lives, and that their own efforts were limited to making choices at a few crossroads within the bounds of that fate. Hence the only way they could endure that 'fate' was to attach value in some form to the unhappy fate itself; they had no choice but to *endow misfortune with meaning*. This necessitates the erection of some life-transcending value. If the ultimate value of life is taken to be happiness, what is required is a standard which transcends the value of happiness, and attaches meaning to misfortune itself.

Some peoples have been able to accomplish this through beliefs which internalize world-transcending value standards. But for the Japanese, who have virtually nothing in their traditions of thought concerning thorough transcendence of the present world, it goes against the grain to believe in a transcendent god for the achievement of personal salvation. What they require for personal salvation is a value standard which *transcends life* and also *dwells within the world*. This would have to lie within the norms of a group (*giri* and *okite*, or obligations and rules) which transcend individual happiness; or in some form of beauty. What brings these two together is the *ethical beauty* known as *gikyō* or *ninkyō* (the chivalrous spirit).

Hence *gikyō* was one of the most perfectly fulfilling means of personal salvation open to the oppressed Japanese people. Through it, the absurdity of their self-sacrificing destiny is given value in itself, and life with its scant happiness is imbued with meaning. The people nod in deep assent to such a rite of validation. In that sense, for the Japanese, *gikyo* chivalry was a functional equivalent of salvation by faith.

Chivalry in political songs

Gikyō was relatively strong as a popular song motif during two periods in Japan's modern century. The first was in the middle of the Meiji period, from the time of the people's-rights movement through the 1894–5 war with China. The second was during the '15-year-war' in Manchuria, China and the Pacific. (See Figure 6.1).

At the very beginning of the Meiji period, when popular songs still consisted largely of witty *dodoitsu* shamisen songs, the motif of chivalry was virtually nowhere to be found.

In modern popular songs, the heroic spirit made its first significant appearance in the *minken enka* or people's-power songs.

> People's power activists   Rain down their tears. . . .
> My fidelity is immovable   Forever it shall stand. . . .
> Forty million compatriots   For your sake
> In red prison uniforms   We would suffer. . . .
>   – 'Dynamite Song' (1883–7) (see Chapter 1)

These lines suggest that the chivalrous spirit handed down from former times was one of the key emotional foundations for the people's power movement. Then, unchanged but with its loyalty redirected, it shifts roles to the *kokken enka* or state-power songs.

> Even if our corpses are left in the fields
> For Emperor and for country

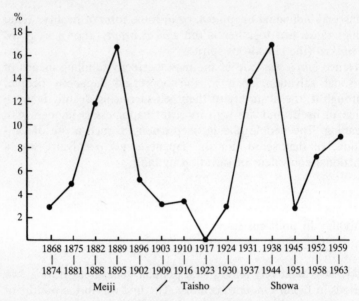

Figure 6.1 *Proportion of popular songs with* gikyo *chivalry motifs*

> Abandoning ourselves is our duty
> Never surrendering an inch, advancing onward . . .
> – 'Finish It Off' (*Yattsukero bushi*, 1884–92)

The numerous songs about chivalrous heroism which were popular during the Sino-Japanese War could just as well be seen as extra verses to this song. Many were even less interesting, stereotyped formulas.

> For the sake of country I'd go anywhere
> We'll win in the end
> Whether we go through fire or water
> – 'We'll Win in the End' (*Yatton makase*, 1894)

> Cutting off my coiffure, sweeping back my hair
> And serving as a nurse, all in service to the nation
> – 'Song of Service' (*Yakkorya bushi*, 1894)

During the last Meiji years and the Taisho period, songs of chivalry were never so popular as the above songs. Yet there was the other side of the same coin: *Naniwa-bushi* and *shinkoku-*

geki, and the associated *yagi-bushi* songs about legendary swords-
men such as Kunisada Chuji, were consistently popular through
the Taisho period.

Striding through flowers and storms

The second flourishing of gikyō in popular songs was during the
Showa period. From around 1930 through the defeat of 1945,
songs of chivalrous heroism were able continually to capture the
hearts of a people living through war.

It began in 1929 with the popularity of 'Ballad of Kutsukake,'
the first in a series of *matatabi ko-uta* or wandering gambler's
ballads.

The people's-power songs had sung of the heroism of those
who would reform the system, while the songs of state power
and the Chinese war extolled the heroism of those who would
play their parts in the system. They all overflowed with clarion
ambition. But the heroism of the gambler's ballad was mainly
one of *desertion*, of flight from the system into a solitary life of
brooding over echoes of abandoned attachments.

> The strength of the spine   The best of nerve
> When entangled in love   Falls to tears
> A lone migratory bird   Living as a voyager
> There goes Kutsukake Tokijirō
>   – *Ballad of Kutsukake* (1929)

Even a sense of frailty, of fragility in the face of 'love,' is openly
expressed and provides part of the song's charm.

> An iron will   Unbent by force or money
> When entangled in love   Turns weak
> The Asama volcano   Beneath three wisps of smoke
> A man   Kutsukake Tokijirō

The following year brought the purge of leftists known as the
March 15th Incident, and the assassination of the radical Diet-
man Yamamoto Senji. As those events slid onward to the time

of *tenko* 'conversion' oaths, 'Ballad of Kutsukake' can be seen to have prophetically set out the composition of the feelings of Japan's rebels. 'Traitors' to the Imperial nation who would unwaveringly maintain their integrity in the face of threats, torture or offers of cash from the authorities, would crumble instantly at a single mention that 'your poor mother must be at home crying her heart out,' and sign the renunciations. Indeed, 'an iron will, unbent by force or money, when tangled in love turns weak.'

Rebellion and martyrdom

If 1929 was the year of 'Ballad of Kutsukake,' the first of a series of 'wandering gambler' songs, it was also the year of 'Tokyo Parade,' the pioneer of a series of paeans to urban life and the pleasures of modernity. Similarly, 1933, the year of 'Akagi Lullaby,' was also the year when 'Tokyo Ondo' took the cities by storm. 'Pure-hearted Man' and 'Wandering' shared 1936 with 'Tokyo Rhapsody.' Urban paeans and wanderer's ballads . . . These parallel phenomena, set against a background of ruin in the rural areas and the impoverishment of the urban lower class, reveal the pleasure culture of the big cities to have been a gaudy but empty flowering, like fireworks.

Compared to the urban paeans depicting the manners of the present time, the wandering-gambler series, which are all set in former times, seem at first glance to be quite 'unreal' or separated from the lives of the people. Yet they do reflect something which lies at a deeper level within the emotions of the *real* life of the people, namely, the *unrealistic* world of chivalrous heroism. However old-fashioned and reactionary they may have sounded in contrast to rampant modernism, they must have resonated with feelings of resentment and mistrust of the system at the bottoms of people's hearts. Those are the feelings which lie disguised within the wretchedness of the fabled gamblers who live in opposition to the world.

A tragic dialectic in the history of modern Japanese emotions was being propelled forward as the road toward war was opening up – the oppressive sense of uncertainty among the rural population and the urban lower classes, set against the culture of modernism. This tragedy is played out in the ambivalence of Kutsukake Tokijirō, who has forsaken his hometown:

> Even standing taller, it can't be seen, I know
> But I can't help trying   Stretching out again
> The hometown where I was born   Is a distant sky
> And the one I love   Is a hundred miles away
> — 'Ballad of Kutsukake'

Put another way, the tragedy resides within the contradictory feelings of the people, who loved the image of the traitor and the gambler for its ambivalence.

At the foundation of the gambler's chivalry is a worldview shot through with a sense of transient impermanence:

> Don't we live only once anyway,
> Falling and floating along to the other world?
> — 'Wandering' (*Ruten*, 1936)

Unable to go beyond reality to establish an implacably critical stance, this world-sense of transient impermanence was ultimately transformed instead into a heroism that functioned as a link in the system:

> Flowers that have bloomed   And are ready to fall
> To fall splendidly   For the sake of the country
> — 'Cherry Blossom Classmates' (*Doki no sakura*, 1944)

Let us trace a little more of the process and the mechanism by which heroism underwent the conversion from rebellion to martyrdom.

> Never mind the world of changing times and seasons
> Nikichi of Kira is simply a man
> — 'Theatre of Life' (*Jinsei gekijo*, 1936–7)

These lyrics posit the world of 'men' (such as the legendary warrior Kira no Nikichi) as the standard for fixed values, taking a viewpoint which goes beyond chasing after the temporal world. At the same time, they renounce any criticism of concrete historical realities ('changing times and seasons'). How things will change is an issue of no concern to these men:

> To live a life   The same as Nikichi
> In this world of honor   And of human feelings

Thus 'Theatre of Life' treats duties and feelings as the set of worldly values. But a year later, in 'Loving Husband's Journey' (*Tsumagoi dōchū*, 1937), the facets of discord between duty and feeling are brought into the light, the feelings are dismissed, and a man's road in life becomes the discharge of duties:

> To my beloved wife   A divorce note is tossed
> The long sword is taken   On a long journey
> – 'Loving Husband's Journey' (*Tsumagoi dōchū*, 1937

The 'manly way' of living is seen as the path of the loyal subject, living apart from his loving wife and beloved home in the crisis of the Empire. Since it was not possible in reality to alter this fate, the masses finally prepared themselves to endure the absurd, as if they were heroes who had chosen the path of suffering by themselves, through a process which *beautifies fate as heroism*, and *transforms suffering into value*.

And still, the core of the people's emotional sympathies lie not with the deeds which were chosen as results, but rather with the abandoned emotional attachment. That is what the title says and the whole song is about.

> For our part   Let us hold no regrets
> We shall meet again   In another floating world
>
> I pledge in my heart   Never to cry
> Yet teardrops betray me   While I pledge
> So much folly   In our hearts
> What reason to cry   On this morning's breeze
> – 'Loving Husband's Journey'

That was the year of the Marco Polo Bridge Incident, after which there was no turning back from the quagmire of full-scale war with China. The following year, the General Mobilization Law brought the war effort into every aspect of the lives of the citizenry. The Resource Mobilization Plan sent 390,000 jobless into the streets (by government figures), and direct and indirect controls on everything from cloth to foodstuffs grew tighter and tighter. As the public was being thus drawn into the wartime regime, 'Journey's Night Wind' (*Tabi no yokaze*), with its words squeezed up from the bottom of the singer's guts as if to shake off and suppress the loves within people's hearts, shot to explosive popularity from September 1938.

> Striding through flowers, conquering storms
> The road a man must take through life. . . .

A balladeers' corps was sent to China that year to console the troops.

The performance of happiness

Very few postwar songs were clearly concerned with chivalry or heroism. 'Train of Sorrows' (1956–7) and 'Kiriko's Tango' (1962–3) sing of embarking alone on a journey, parting voluntarily from the object of affection. These are similar in a way to the theme of Nikichi and the loving husband, but the heroic meaning has grown vague.

> Because I love you   So much so much so much
> Because I love you   I have parted
> Kiriko you had faith   In me
> That's what makes it   So hard for me . . .

While still sympathizing with the emotional pattern of separating from an attachment and embarking on a journey, the postwar Japanese had lost sight of the pattern of an object of common fidelity. By then a hero might move on of his own accord, not for the sake of some external rules, but for the well-being of the partner herself.

Moreover, where once the system had been molded by suppressing the desires and affections of the citizenry, the new postwar order, on the contrary, thrived by stimulating their desires and affections, with respect to consumer goods as well as personal relations. In this day and age, people are constrained to be 'happy.'

In parallel with the mode of life demanded by the former regime, which was to cast away all thoughts of happiness and go off to fight, today the system demands the casting away of any unhappy thought (and don't forget to never stop smiling). With this about-face, the function of chivalry or heroism, as a means of self-deliverance through the glorification of strengthened conformity, is forced to make a formal turn of 180 degrees.

> The one who charmed me yesterday
> Is with someone pretty today
> Even as momentary dreams are broken
> A bus girl cannot be discouraged
> 'All aboard!'
> Cheerfully   Cheerfully   Moving along
>
> A drunken passenger's nastiness
> How to get used to those terrible words
> I let a single teardrop fall
> But all the same, I'm a Tokyo bus girl
> 'All aboard!'
> Cheerfully   Cheerfully   Moving along
>   – 'Tokyo Bus Girl' (1957)

Although it has been transformed and is a far cry from what is known as chivalry or heroism, we find here that same mental device which, on a personal level, glorifies the conditions to which one is subjected, and somehow converts them to affirmative feelings. Here it is taken on by people in contemporary society, where one is always compelled to be jovial and suppress any dark feelings. The performance of happiness must be performed happily. Cheerfully, cheerfully . . .

7 The History of Lingering Attachment

The double structure of miren

Miren is a lingering feeling of attachment which remains even after it has become impossible to form or maintain a relationship with the object of the emotion. The main reason why the actual relationship has become impossible may be an internal norm consciousness, or an external impediment such as death, physical distance or social separation. In general, however, the term *miren* comes most naturally to mind with respect to situations complicated by a powerful *norm consciousness* by which one tries to eliminate or suppress one's own affection.

The proportional peaks and troughs of the *miren* motif in post-Restoration popular songs are shown in Figure 7.1. After a peak immediately following the Russo-Japanese War, the motif

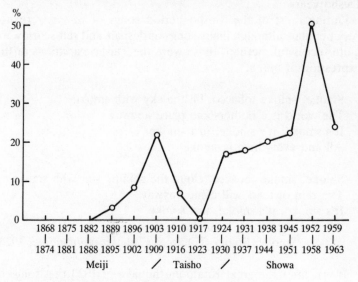

Figure 7.1 *Proportion of popular songs with* miren *motifs*

disappeared completely in the Taisho years, became frequent again around the beginning of the Showa period, and thereafter remained an important theme, appearing in some 20 per cent or more of popular songs.

The *miren* motif can be found in songs from pre-modern times, such as this *dodoitsu*:

> Miren remains in the marks of my clogs
> On the snow this morning of bitter parting
> Though determined never to expect his return
> A similar footstep makes my heart leap in vain

Miren appears as a major theme in about 1906. Leading the way were those twin ballads which germinated several of the motifs of the Taisho and Showa popular song, Yosaburō's 'Midnight Reminiscence' and Soeko's 'Rain on My Sleeve' (see Chapters 1 and 2).

Newspaper personal-advice columns and tragic *shinpa* plays chronicled and soothed the sufferings of the urban masses during the last few Meiji years. The flow of emotions in popular songs was covered in Chapter 1, up to the sense of resignation expressed in 'Don-don,' which was extremely popular into the Taisho years.

During most of the Taisho period songs of *miren* were not very popular, although many songs of despair and self-scorn were quite successful; perhaps those were the Taisho variations of the expression of *miren*.

> Smoke, smoke tobacco, fill the sky with smoke
> The world is a bothersome place anyway
> It's smoke, it's smoke, just smoke
> All and everything is smoke
>
> Smoke, smoke tobacco, cloud the shining sun with smoke
> The rain of tears will come anyway
> It's smoke, it's smoke, just smoke
> All and everything is smoke
>   – 'Smoke, Smoke Tobacco' (*Tabako nome-nome*, 1923)

It was after the great Kanto earthquake of 1923 that songs of *miren* once again took on proportional importance, a position they would keep to the time of this writing. Specifically, among songs of romantic love between 1924 and 1945, 21 of 65 (32.3 per cent) were about lingering attachment, and from 1945 to 1963, 29 of 71 (40.8 per cent). In other words, 1 in 3 hit love songs of the Showa period sang of *miren*, with the proportion even higher after the war.

The pioneer of the series, a song which typifies the *miren* pattern of the closing Taisho and opening Showa years, was 'Left Useless' (*Sutare mono*, 1924)

> I'm the one the world has thrown away
> Because of you I'm obsolete
> It's you who cast me out
> Under the sky of a wandering voyage
>
> A winter's evening in a silken shawl
> Faintly tinged by the blue moon
> Faintly. . . . Sadly
> The hot tears roll down
>
> Like a quiet drizzle falling
> Sobbing alone and lonely
> Faintly. . . . Sadly
> The hot tears roll down
>   – 'Left Useless' (*Sutare mono*, 1924)

The first verse is obviously influenced by a leading popular song of the later Taisho years, 'The Boatman's Ballad' (see Chapter 10), while the mood of the second and third verses corresponds with the sadly lyrical images of the painter Takehisa Yumeji, who dominated the popular culture of the time. With the *double-layered viewpoint* of the heroine, who recounts her own subjective misfortune even as she is intoxicated with the beauty of a lingering sadness objectified within a painted tableau, this song displays the mechanism referred to in Chapter 2 as 'pearling' of heartaches.

The stance which objectifies, for aesthetic enjoyment, the sentimentality of a lingering attachment had not been seen in earlier songs. From this time onward, though, there is a clearly visible, narcissistic formula of equivalence in which beauty compensates for the ache of a lingering attachment.

Departing ships and wandering gamblers

The world of Takehisa Yumeji was reflected in a series of sentimental songs of the twenties, *Yoimachigusa*, which sets his own
poem to music. The atmosphere is exemplified in these lyrics:

> Setting sail this evening?   A breaking heart
> Amid the dark waves   Snow is falling
> Though the ship is out of sight   With a parting ballad
> Even the plover in the offing   Are crying
> > – 'Setting Sail' (*Defune*, 1927–8)

From then on, through the prewar and war years, songs of
miren frequently utilized the image of parting with the man
setting sail from a harbor as a formula for the feeling of lingering
attachment.

> The waves must be rough
> On the Sea of Genkai   Oh
> Can't bring him back any more   Ah, this miren
> On a boat   On a boat
> > – 'Hakata Night Boat' (*Hakata yobune*, 1936)

Overlapping the same time period was a series of ballads about
the wanderling gambler's life which gave shape to the *miren* on
the part of the man who set out on the journey. In these songs,
the conflict between internalized norms and desire or attachment
is portrayed as the conflict between *gikyō* chivalry and *miren*.

> A tearful farewell can be forgotten
> But the unfinished business of crying is fatal
> > – 'Ballad of Kutsukake' (1929)

> No regret for such a woman
> But the tears flow for no reason
> > – 'Theater of Life' (*Jinsei gekijō*, 1936)

> A male willow never cries
> Only shadows sway in the wind
> > – 'Night Wind Voyage' (*Tabi no yokaze*, 1938)

Miren and *gikyō* both tend to find expression especially in situations where conflicts arise from the urge of a strong norm-consciousness to suppress an intense desire or attachment. While *gikyō* (chivalry) stands on the side of the norm consciousness which works to suppress the affection, *miren* (lingering attachment) is on the other side, in the strength of the sentiments which remain even after the desire is suppressed.

As the wartime system grew stronger during the 1930s and early 1940s, the proportion of songs with love themes was declining, yet among those songs that did treat love, *miren* motifs gradually increased. Women's songs such as 'Setting Sail' and men's songs such as 'Ballad of Kutsukake' and 'Night Wind Voyage' seem secretly to hint at the *miren* of those left behind and of those going off to war.

The popular 'Lakeside Inn' was suppressed by the authorities because of its sentimental, lingering attachment, but it was nevertheless transmitted orally. Its soliloquy was widely sung not only by maidens on the home front, but also among soldiers:

> Oh, the shape of the mountains and the water of the lake
> Quietly, quietly the twilight falls
> Embracing this silence, this sadness
> I go on a solo journey . . .
> – 'Lakeside Inn' (*Kohan no yado*, 1938)

> Arms folded restlessly   Eyes turned upward
> Soaring with clouds   In the distant sky
> Far from the homeland   We left behind
> How strongly we feel   Love for our homeland
> – 'Wheat and Soldiers' (*Mugi to heitai*, 1938)

The tears of sacrificial pawns

A decade after the war there was a remarkable surge in the frequency of the *miren* motif (see Figure 8). No less than half of the leading popular songs between 1952 and 1958 included a *miren* motif in some form or another. This sudden intensity coincides exactly with the peak interval of suicide in modern

Japanese history. The highest prewar suicide rate (22.2 per 100,000 population in 1932) was exceeded during each of the six years from 1954 to 1959. That was the time when the streets were overflowing with the unemployed and small businesses were going bankrupt in droves. See Figure 7.2.

The seven years from 1952 opened with a statement by the minister of trade and industry that, 'Suicides due to small-business bankruptcy are inevitable,' and closed with a boom in business administration studies. During this time, for various reasons including the disordered postwar environment, political, economic and labor institutions rushed pell-mell through the repatterning of society, into the era of the gigantic organization. In a sense it was a time of 'primitive accumulation' for the spotty prosperity of the 1960s, or in other words, it was the period when *the weak were weeded out* from various areas of society. The desires of the masses, once liberated by the 'postwar situation,' were again frustrated or twisted, and countless ambitions, aspirations and attachments at the bottom of society were turned back before the impregnable fortress of the gigantic controlling organizations. (Also, during this period the motif of resentment was more common than at any time since the Taisho years.)

During the recession and widespread unemployment of the early 1930s, *men's* songs of disappointed love, which on the whole are not common in Japan, became popular one after

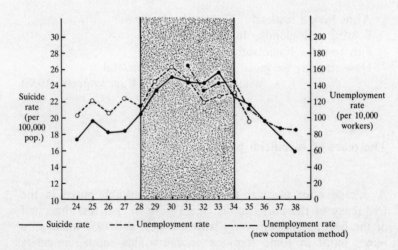

Figure 7.2 *Rates of suicide and unemployment*

78

another, reflecting an 'ill fortune' in various spheres of life other than love (as in 'Is Drink Tears or Sighs?' from 1931). During the social period of the 1950s, love songs with *miren* motifs likewise seemed to express feelings of loss and lingering attachment from a wider variety of life situations.

Through a mechanism of projection, feelings from various life spheres are frequently transferred into spheres which are easily lyricized (e.g. love). Such *selective figuration* of various types of feeling is one reason why the analysis of motifs (or orientations of feelings) in popular songs is more crucial than that of themes or subjects. It is not through their thematic content, but rather through their emotional *motifs* that popular songs 'detonate on contact' deep inside the people of their time.

> Miren, is it?   Is there such a thing?
> Thrown away   Thrown away
> Then somehow picked up   Rubbish of love
> – 'Rubbish of Love' (*Dōse hirotta koidame no*, 1956)

> You see, I told you so
> Come to drink   At the saloon at the harbor
> Anything a man might say   How stupid
> That you would take him seriously, so seriously
> – 'I Told You So' (*Dakara itta janai no*, 1957)

However bashful they may seem as we look back on them today, these plaints were not merely about lost loves. They were vessels for the feelings of the time, into which one could pour the sense of loss from various areas of life, many of which were too prosaic to lend themselves to direct lyricization.

> The journey's fallen leaves   Soaked by the showers
> Flowing without end   The guitar plays
> Hopes and dreams   Fleetingly dying away
> Songs and tears   Are migrating birds

> Worn out by drink   Wasted by regret
> A man wanders   The guitar plays
> Neither that day nor you   Will ever come again
> The call of another country   The night wind

79

In the corner of a saloon   On a dark backstreet
Just a moment's roost   The guitar plays
Even the flickering light is sad   In the flourescent
Shadows, nothing but   Lonely crying
           – 'Shower of Fallen Leaves' (*Ochiba shigure*, 1953)

Only two major hit songs after the war display the motif of *miren* in spheres other than love. One of them was this verse:

Those big dreams   I was carrying
When I left home,   Now I set them afloat
In a sake cup   And let out a sigh
Chanchiki okesa
The moon is blurred   With okesa tears
           – 'Chanchiki Country Song' (*Chanchiki okesa*, 1957)

Here, in the shadows of the 'winners' of the postwar game of social reorganization, are concentrated the regrets, the despair and the self-scorn of the many stragglers who fell short of their goals.

Shouting *miren*

From Taisho through the postwar years, almost all the songs of *miren* tirelessly repeat the same patterns of expression: 'Even when I drink sake, why don't I get drunk?' ('Toast of Tears,' 1948); 'Streamers of miren that I can't cut away' ('Ferryboat Song,' 1952). And more recently:

It was a memory   The tears can't wash away
After all   I'm no good at all
Ah   No good at all
The eyeteeth   Of endless miren
Silently   Bite my lip
                 – 'Regretful Heart' (*Miren-gokoro*, 1963)

But here is an exception, from the years just after the defeat:

Though I call out to you   At the top of my lungs
No one comes back   An echo comes back
It's the toll   Of Francesca's bell
I'm out of my mind   Please just once
Pass along   These words of miren
     – 'Francesca's Bell' (*Furanchesuka no cane*, 1948)

In these lines *miren* is not simply a gutless abjection, to be *washed away* by tears or drink. Nor is the *miren* frame of mind being 'pearled' upon itself in abandonment to quiet *narcissism*. Instead, a new means is unveiled: with no effort to hide the tears, *miren* is shouted out at the top of one's lungs, splendidly sentimental though it may still be.

Compared to the inward gnawing of such lines as 'Faintly, faintly, plaintively' ('Left Useless') or 'The pain every night' ('Is Drink Tears or Sighs?'), the expression of *miren* 'at the top of my lungs' hints at the novel possibilities which were dangled before the Japanese by the postwar situation. And the fact that now, in the 1960s, we have retreated to lines such as 'It was a memory the tears can't wash away, After all I'm no good at all, Ah, no good at all,' hints that something has been lost by the Japanese in the past two decades.

The multiple structure of 'Rain at Kudanzaka'

The second postwar hit that sang of miren in a sphere outside romantic love was *Ame no Kudanzaka* ('The Rain at Kudanzaka') in 1961.

Panting, I tilt my umbrella to look up
The giant torii gate   Hazy in the rain
Mama has come   Finally come
To the shrine   Where my sweet darling lives
How I wish we could meet   Even one single glimpse

I step carefully   Across the wet pebbles
Someone like him   Walks, who knows where
Anyway there is no returning   I'm grumbling, I know

If he were alive   He'd be about that age.
Tears of old age   Well up before I know it

Hands placed together   Bowing in prayer
The falling petals   Sheathed in raindrops
Forgive me, son   You died so well
I can only speak well of you   The oppressive lie
Must stay hidden   With your mother
                    – 'Rain at Kudanzaka' (*Ame no Kudanzaka*, 1961)

(Kudanzaka, in Tokyo, is the site of Yasukuni Shrine, which honors the war dead.) In this dialogue with the dead, particularly the last three lines, there is a multiple construction so complicated as to strain comprehension. First, the mother is compelled to praise her son for having died a 'proper' death. But in light of a mother's true feelings, this praise must be a lie. With the forgiveness of her darling son, the mother must always keep her feelings of lingering attachment hidden.

Her brief soliloquy wanders through three viewpoints. First, at this time 16 years after the war, the traditional norm of 'He died well, I can only speak well of him' still survives among the mothers' generation. This is the standpoint of *gikyō* heroism oriented toward the country. But for a mother, such a chivalrous standpoint has to be negated as an 'oppressive lie.' She shifts from *gikyō* to *miren*.

But to simply dismiss the traditional norm, the values for which her son lived and died, is to personally render hollow and meaningless both his way of life and his way of death. The only thing holding these bereaved mothers back from despair is the sense that their sons died meaningfully, 'splendidly' as martrys to the fatherland. That myth furnishes the value of immortality that is celebrated as the 'god' of Yasukuni Shrine. Unable to endure the 'postwar' ideas which would strip away the phantom glory from their sons, the mothers must refrain from criticizing the old norms. Hence they cannot hold firmly to the *miren* standpoint, they can only cling all the more tightly to the values which drove their sons into death. Thus the *miren* standpoint which negates the *gikyō* standpoint is in turn negated.

Chivalry does not give way to *miren;* miren *gives rise to chivalry.* This is the 'oppressive lie' of the oppressed people. But this mother does not simply return to the same standpoint of the norm that 'You died so well, I can only speak well of him.' For if she were to do so, after having allowed herself to enter into the spirit of *miren*, then she should apologize first of all to Emperor and country. But it is her son whose pardon she begs. The old norms have become the oppressive grounding for those left behind, not because they are substantively correct, but because they are the sole basis by which meaning can be imparted to the life and death of the mothers' loved ones. In other words, due to *the failure of postwar ideas to generate any other values* that could furnish the dead with a sense of meaning.

Here too is a clue to the above-stated historical riddle – how miren in the postwar period fell back from the explicit shout of 'Francesca's Bell,' retreating once again to private tears and sighs in the shadows.

8 The History of Jest

Three phases of jest

We have seen how, at the end of the Meiji period after the Russo-Japanese War of 1905, resignation and lingering attachment (*miren*), despair and self-scorn, transience and loneliness became the dominant motifs of the popular song. Earlier, during the period spanning the people's-rights movement and the war with China and Russia, it had been criticism and irony, ambition and anger, hope and joy which had held sway. Going further back to the years just after the Meiji Restoration, we find that jest stands out as the leading motif. In the present study, it appears in 19 out of the 33 songs from 1868 to 1874 (57.6 per cent), and in 14 of the 20 from 1875 to 1881 (70 per cent). Although it was no longer the main motif after the mid–1880s, jest by no means disappeared. At least one or two amusing songs are among the most popular in every 7-year interval thereafter. (See Figure 8.1.)

Several of the songs that were current around 1870 were humorous ditties of the sort which had been supported for many years by the petit-bourgeois *chōnin*, embodying their *iki* spirit of understated pride and elegant, stylish entertainment. (Unfortunately, the elaborate wordplays of those songs cannot be rendered into another language.)

Alongside that older type of song, other popular songs of the 1870s make light of the many currents of events set loose by the Restoration, or of the new fashions of the 'civilization and enlightenment' movement.

Quite a few humorous songs were enjoyed simply for fun, usually making use of such devices as puns, counting games or nonsense syllables. But the greater number were designed to express various other feelings under the guise of humor.

> If a beard marks the high official
> Cats and mice are all high officials

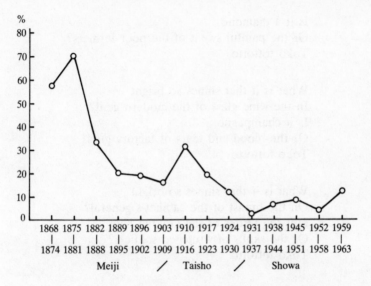

Figure 8.1 *Proportion of popular songs with humorous motifs*

> If a high official never bows
> How does he get into a mosquito net?
> – 'High Officials Song'(*Kan-in bushi*, 1875)

This was one of a series of sarcastic songs about the sense of privilege displayed by the new officials. They were sung mainly in Tokyo, where they served as a means of dispelling the resentment of the city's inhabitants toward the newly ascendant ruling clans from Chōshū and Satsuma, and their bureaucrats and police. In this way the traditional streak of jest in the popular song gradually acquired a sting.

By the middle of the Meiji period, as popular songs began to express a feeling of national prosperity and a sense of unity among the citizenry, the sharpness was directed toward the international pressures which were enveloping Japan.

Several saracastic *enka* about Meiji Japan's wartime enemies, China and Russia, were mentioned in Chapters 2 and 4. After the Russo-Japanese War, the humor of sharp-tongued enka was once again turned toward the contradictions of domestic society.

> What is it that shines so bright
> On the hairpin of the nobleman's mistress?

85

Is it a diamond
Or the painful sweat of the poor farmers?
Toko tottotto

What is it that shines so bright
In the wine glass of the modern gent?
Is it champagne
Or the blood and tears of factory girls?
Toko tottotto

What is it that shines so bright
On the breast of the cabinet's general?
Is it the Order of the Golden Kite
Or the skulls of wretched soldiers?
Toko tottotto

If this world worked just as we want it
Rickshaw pullers, stablemen and farmers
Would ride in carriages pulled by
Modern gents in Western clothes
Toko tottotto

> – 'Trumpet Song' (*Rappa bushi*, 1905)

When Japan entered the First World War, the degree of frenzy that was seen during the wars with China and Russia was certainly not apparent. 'Tsingtao Song' (1914) aimed its sarcasm not so much at the enemy country, as at the government which drove the masses into the war. ('Who said Tsingtao was so fine? . . .') At the same time it is a smile of self-scorn by the masses themselves who were willingly driven to serve. This subtle duality in 'Tsingtao Song' was part of a transition at the time, a conversion of popular-song jest from an arrow of sharp sarcasm aimed at the strong, to a pathos-laden, self-exploiting smile directed toward oneself.

Here is a song from a few years later in which the humor has shifted almost completely to the bitter smile of self-scorn:

I was so happy to find a wife
But the same entree always turns up
Croquettes   Croquettes

Today it's croquettes   Tomorrow it's croquettes
All year round it'll be croquettes
           – 'Croquette Song' (*Korokke no uta*, 1918)

Such songs of the Taisho period are suffused with smiles of sorrow at the realization of the common dreams of the Meiji masses (a secure position for Japan on the world stage and continuing modernization at home), and with smiles of bitterness at the disillusionment from the Meiji-era vision of utopia. The theme of 'Tsingtao Song' is the internal grief of the Imperial Japan who was now one of the Great Powers, while 'Croquette Song' treats the internal sadness of modern life itself. 'Who said Tsingtao was so fine?' 'I was so happy to find a wife.' The comical opening lines are humor brought forth by the emotional fall of the masses, after the utopia they had wholeheartedly desired had slipped through their hands.

Thus the expression in humorous popular songs shifted over time from joy to jests of anger, and then from anger to jests of sadness.

The tramp and the dandy

Other songs with a simpler, unshadowed sort of humor were also favored in the Taisho years. 'Tokyo Song' (1919) is also known as 'Pai no pai' from these lines:

Rame chantara gitchon chon de pai no pai no pai
Pari koto panana de furai furai furai

– a jumble of fun about ramen noodles, pie and 'fried bananas from Paris.' It goes on to portray the easygoing, prosperous mood of Tokyo before the great earthquake:

Tokyo's center is Marunouchi
The Diet buildings and Hibiya Park
The smartly designed Imperial Theatre
The imposing castle is Police Headquarters
Rows of ministries at Babasakimon

> Marine Building, Tokyo Station
> Where are the trains puffing off to?
> Rame chantara . . .

and indulges in a bit of sarcasm about 'pilfering pickpockets and beggars . . . in Tokyo's bustling Asakusa.'

But from the earthquake of 1923 into the Depression years, humor once again mixed a stern self-scorn with its ironic smiles.

> I'm the stylish man they call
> The village's number-one modern boy
> Conceited, swollen-headed, with a triumphant air
> I arrived on the Ginza in Tokyo
> Well, now, the style of the moment
> Is a blue shirt with a bright red tie
> A derby hat with horn-rimmed spectacles
> And baggy sailor pants
>
> The girl I fell in love with
> Has black eyes and bobbed hair
> She's short with a beautiful body
> And she's insolent down to her toes . . .
>
> Do you know that my
> Father's the landlord and mayor
> The mayor is rich and I, his son,
> Am still a bachelor
> Oh, how grand it is
> When there's status and money
> Even if a man is homely
> The ladies fall right in love . . .
>   – 'The Dandy' (*Share otoko*, c. 1925–30)
>
> From the blue sky wads of money are falling
> Softly against my noontime snoozing cheeks
> Five thousand, ten thousand, a hundred thousand, a million
> But I woke up before I could spend it
> Wah hah hah ha   Wah hah ha
> Flat broke, a wallet full of air
> A tramp has it easy these days

I'm drunk, I'm drunk on a half cup of sake
Drunk, and every girl is a beauty
Sharing a cigarette with a friend
Gives smoking a different flavor
Wah hah hah ha   Wah hah ha
Flat broke, a wallet full of air
A tramp has it easy these days

A prolie's heaven, a cheap hotel
Curled asleep hugging my knees, so cute
Hearing the rain on my blanket pillow
The departed missus came to my dreams
Wah hah hah ha   Wah hah ha
Flat broke, a wallet full of air
A tramp has it easy these days

If there's no money it's no cause to fret
Even with money your hair grows gray
Even the rich have only one grave
Crying or smiling, the same fifty years
Wah hah hah ha   Wah hah ha
Flat broke, a wallet full of air
A tramp has it easy these days
                    – 'Song of the Tramp' (*Rumpen bushi*, 1931)

However bad the times may be, tramps didn't make up much of the population, and the dandy of the song was not so common in real life. But it was not only the tramp who sang his song, and the people laughing at the dandy did not necessarily lack any resemblance to him. These caricatures gave concrete expression to situations which were to some degree personally familiar to many of the urban masses.

During the war, when tight-lipped expression was the only thing permitted by the authorities, the humorous song was forced to travel in the disguise of informal parodies. *Miyo tokai no yo wa akete* ('Look up to the shining sun on the eastern sea') became *Miyo Tojo no hage atama* ('Look up to the bald head of [Prime Minister] Tojo'). *Katte-kuru-zo to isamashiku* ('I'm going to win at the front, courageously') became *Yatte-kuru-zo to isamashiku* ('I'm going to win at her front, courageously').

> The octopus who was called up yesterday
> Is the glorious fallen   In battle today
> When will the skeletal remains return
> They won't return   Cause it has no bones
> > – Parody of 'Lakeside Inn' (*Kohan no yado*)

Three strains of postwar jest

There are three lineages of humorous popular songs in postwar Japan. One of them follows the rhythm shown in the illustration, with content typical of the long-established *ko-uta* ballad form.

Included in this line are 'Tonko Song' and 'Yatton Song' which rode a wave of old-style revivals to popularity between 1949 and 1951. During this period the Dodge deflation policy brought on the insolvency of some ten thousand businesses, and hundreds of thousands of laid-off workers flowed into the streets. Japan was approaching the big postwar economic turnaround, amid the uproar of the emergency procurement boom for the staging of the Korean War. These songs carried both the sunny smiles of procurement contractors who were celebrating springtime in their world, and the desperate, tearful smiles of small-business owners and workers who were suffocating in a recession. They were heard in the second-floor sitting rooms of high-class restaurants as well as in rope-curtained street stalls.

> 'Don't drink, don't drink'
> Is what you always tell me
> But how can I go without drinking?
> Drinkers can only drink
> Put yourself in my shoes
> It's impossible to stop drinking
> Just because you say so
> > Hey, waitress   Bring me one more
> > > – 'Yatton Song' (*Yatton bushi*, 1951)

Here jesting thrives in the full variety of its functions, sometimes a vessel of joy, sometimes a vessel of sadness, possibly a vessel of anger.

The second lineage of humor sings in a light, witty style of the workaday joys and sorrows of people in particular professions. It includes such titles as 'I'm the Engineer of the Super Express' (1950) and 'The Young Patrolman' (1956). The most popular was 'City Sandwichman' of 1952.

> I'm the clown   Of the town
> I'm out again today   With my foolish smile

Although humor stands alongside the motifs of transience and *miren* as one of the most common elements of the Japanese popular song, this is virtually the only song that uses words which refer directly to jesting. Here, humor is self-objectified as a performance. It recounts just how much pathos can be lodged within its smiling countenance. In this respect, it is the leading edge of the role of humor in Japanese song.

> Horn-rimmed glasses   And swallow-tailed coat
> Swallowing my tears   Guess I'll smile
> But if I must cry   I'll look at the sky
> Sandwichman   Sandwichman . . .

If it were only the sandwichman whose situation is presented in this song, surely it would not have reached such a degree of popularity. It seems to have concretized and condensed into an exaggerated form the situation of the shop clerk, sales representative or average salaryman, who at first glance have nothing whatsoever in common with the sandwichman. The lyricist, by the way, was a schoolteacher.

When people are who are filled with sadness find it necessary to put on a smiling face, they *make jokes*. In today's society, where we are compelled constantly to be cheerful, joking plays a mediating role in resolving the contradictions between the private feelings of the individual and the expectations of society. Or it plays the role of a shunt which switches the *feelings* of sorrow and nothingness to *expressions* of laughter.

The third line of humor, epitomized by *Suudara bushi*, centers around the songs of Ueki Hitoshi, including 'With a Bang' (*Don-*

to bushi), and 'Okay, Until Then' (*Hai, sore made yo*). The first of them was 'Gratefully' (*Arigataya bushi*, 1960).

> Gratefully   Gratefully
> Gratefully   Gratefully
> Out of money   Worry and fret
> Jilted by a woman   Cry and cry
> Stomach's empty   Eat some rice
> Life is finished   Go to heaven
> Gratefully   Gratefully
> Gratefully   Gratefully
>   – 'Gratefully' (*Arigataya bushi*, 1960)

These songs, like many previous humorous songs, can be sung in two ways: as lighthearted praise for a world at peace, and as a full dose of bitter self-scorn. Both moods are current in today's society, and one of the major attractions of these songs is that they can be freely arranged and sung according to one's mood or situation.

> Planning to drink just a little drop
> And before I know it   Barhopping
> Waking up   From a snooze on a station bench
> Now this   Is no good at all for the body
> Yeah I know I know   But I can't seem to stop
> Ah   Looky   Floating   Su-wimming-wimming-ly
> Swimmingly   Float-float-floating . . .
>
> Suurararatta sui-sui
>   – 'Suudara Song' (*Suudara bushi*, 1961)

Among Ueki's other songs, 'With a Bang' is more inclined toward the lighthearted side ('A salaryman's someone with a comfortable trade . . .'), while 'Okay, Until Then' leans to the morose ('You're all I live for . . .'). Ueki's lighter aspect, the celebration of a world at peace, can be traced all the way back through the 'pai no pai' 'Tokyo Song,' and the songs just after the Sino-Japanese War, to the early-Meiji songs of praise for 'civilization and enlightenment.' The other aspect of his songs, the bittersweet self-scorn and irony, can be traced back through 'The Dandy' in the Taisho period to the Meiji *enka*.

Yet when his songs first appeared, the lines that were immediately on people's lips everywhere were the uniquely onomatopoetic 'Sui sui suurararatta sura-sura sui sui' and the instantly famous 'Yeah I know, I know, but I can't seem to stop' (*Wakatchyairu kedo yamerarene-e*). His vocalizations will long be remembered for this 'feel-good' onomatopoeia.

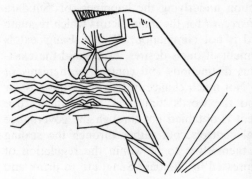

Look of a ninawa-bushi *performer*   *Look of Ueki Hitoshi*
(caricature by Matsugawa Yasuo, from
Nihon Dokusho Shimbun, November 27,
1961)

This is precisely the opposite of the traditional *naniwa-bushi* recitation technique which deeply influenced the singing styles of Japanese popular songs. The *naniwa-bushi* technique calls for maximum constriction of the throat and nose during exhalation, so that the voice is repeatedly distorted and squeezed. In contrast, Ueki's singing style, which was described by Terayama Shūji as 'the voice of someone who has just inhaled a nasal decongestant,' shoots cleanly out without the slightest restriction. It is precisely the *lack of a sense of restriction* in Ueki's singing that is highlighted by the sounds of 'Sui-sui,' 'suu-suu,' and 'sura-sura,' and they work well together with the famous 'I can't seem to stop.' They liberate the life impulse by sidestepping any concern for ethical norms or future results.

The way of life implied in this attitude gives new emphasis to the desires of the here and now, and slips lightly around all the rules of behavior which govern them. Through the lenses of the guiding pattern for prewar expressive patterns, this is improper behavior, a deviation from the norm, and accordingly it takes on significance as a latent critique of the system. But the dominant styles of the existing system have come more and more to rely not so much on the suppression of desires as on the *systemic internalization of desires*. The affirmation of given types of desire functions as a factor of conformity and reinforcement of the status quo, rather than as a critique.

The lack of restriction underlying the happiness of 'Suudara Song' depends on a *disregard* for the main factors which regulate desires. But disregard is not elimination. 'With a Bang' extols the substantive enjoyment of one's desires, even amid the existing barriers and status distinctions and control mechanisms of work (as in the line, 'Not much chance of becoming the boss or the manager . . .' and the words 'timeclock and punchcard'). This state of fulfillment is obtained not through the governance of desires by external controls, but rather through the scaling down of the desires themselves to fit within the regulation of work. The desires expressed in 'Suudara Song' are to drink and snooze, to blow the annual bonus at the racetrack, to reach out to a charming woman at first sight. A major prop of that carefree attitude is the fragmentation and diminution of the desires themselves. Therein lies the latent nihilism of today's Japanese, who lack a conscious awareness of nihilism.

If happiness is perceived as only that happiness which can be gotten amid the present realities, then it is easy to become happy. Here is happiness as a sort of *tautology of value judgment*, turning any feeling of disappointment on its head.

9 The History of Loneliness

Traveler on the ice

It is a truism among the Japanese that songs about sadness or lingering attachment or homesickness or impermanence are not sung in order to divert the mind or to forget. Their larger function is to *deepen* the feelings all the more by purifying, intensifying and objectifying them, and thus plumb the depths of the abyss and stay the tremblings of the soul. The real-life effect of these sorts of songs is recounted in one of Oshima Michiko's letters in the runaway bestseller *Gazing at Love and Death*. When she sings 'Going Back North,' popular in 1961, 'I grow excessively sad, but it puts my heart at peace.' This is no extinguishing of sadness.

At the same time, through the technique of 'pearling' misfortunes, liabilities on the level of happiness are converted into pluses on the level of aesthetic value. For the Japanese this is a means of transcending the self.

The initial appearance of loneliness as the main motif of a modern popular song was in 1917:

> Shall I go, shall I return, under the Northern Lights
> Russia spreads endlessly to the north
> In the west the sunset, in the east the dawn
> The bell tolls in midair
> Ardent love laid bare in the wilderness
> Horses treading the ice
> People are so cold, have pity on me
> The bars of the town are still far away
>   – 'Song of Wandering' (*Sasurai no uta*, 1917)

Next is 'Exile's Journey' (*Ruro no tabi*), in 1922, followed by 'Left Useless' (*Sutaremono*) in 1924. This series is discussed in Chapter 10, but let us note here that they are all songs about wandering. In Japan in the modern era, the feeling of loneliness

95

is above all expressed in connection with homesickness and transience. For the *loneliness of having left home* is the archetypal feeling of loneliness for modern Japan.

'Wandering Song' ruminates upon the scene of a lone traveler standing under the aurora borealis in Siberia. What is the meaning of, 'People are so cold, have pity on me'? The phrase hints at a hidden meaning of the symbolic image of the solo traveller. In the vocabulary of Japanese allegory, a journey is traditionally a symbol of life, and a solo journey is the symbol of a lonely life. The loneliness in the wanderer's ballads of the 1920s and 1930s gives concrete form to the loneliness of the soul amid the multitude, by projecting it into the loneliness of the body amid the 'journey's sky.' In the background is the early-Showa buildup of the big cities and the large-scale influx of people from the countryside. Wouldn't their natural first, deep impression be 'People are so cold, have pity on me'? In the history of Europe, it was said that the air of the city was the air of freedom. For most of the people of modernizing Japan, and perhaps many other 'developing' societies, it was more the air of loneliness.

As if in a dream, where various elements of real life are dissolved into fragments and then displayed as a jumble of strange shapes, in the song the images of cold urban 'air' and personal loneliness, of unease about the purpose of life and helplessness, and the sense of distance from home, are made into a gorgeous montage: wandering in the endless icy wilderness beneath the glow of the northern lights.

The lyricists of songs which caught on widely, such as Kitahara Hakushū ('Song of Wandering'), had the ability to produce portrayals which crystallize and concretize, which juxtapose in enchanting images the fragmentary unease and loneliness, or the aspirations and joys and nostalgia at the depths of the popular consciousness of their time.

Kitahara also wrote the lyrics of 'Orange Blossoms,' a song which achieved well-loved popularity comparable to 'Roamer's Journey' and 'Left Useless.' Here he created a vessel for an even more universal nostalgia and loneliness, which takes as its theme not the homesickness of spatial distance, but that of temporal distance – nostalgia for the elapsed days of the past.

> How I cried there   There beside the orange blossoms
> All of them, all of them   So delicately soft

The orange blossoms   Still bloomed
So whitely, so whitely   Ever they bloomed
                    – 'Orange Blossoms' (*Karatachi no hana*, 1924)

Songs aching with rupture

The first Showa songs of loneliness, immediately after those
wanderers' songs, fairly ache with ruptured communication:

> Pulling on the thread   Sheltering my pain
> You'll never know   How I pine
> Such is life   Such is life
> Oh, Dotombori Canal
>
> Love's siren call   Reaches so far
> Reaches everywhere   If I wait
> Such is life   Such is life
> Oh, Dotombori Canal
>
> Blinking flickering   Multicolored lights
> You'll never know   This woman's heart
> Such is life   Such is life
> Oh, Dotombori Canal
>   – 'Naniwa Ballad' (*Naniwa ko-uta*, 1929–30)

This is a song of intense desire, and she does not concede that
it cannot be realized. On the other hand, singing from the man's
side of the communication breakdown:

> Even if I waste away to nearly nothing
> Don't ask this heart about it
> After all it's a man's road
> What can a woman know of it?
>   – 'Pure-hearted Man' (*Otoko no junjō*, 1936)
>
> For this woman   I have no lingering attachment
> Why then must   The tears flow

97

A man's heart,   One must be a man,
Thought I understood   Disappointed
                  – 'Theatre of Life' (*Jinsei gekijō*, 1937)

The pathos of this acute despair at the lack of communication between two people's hearts does not arise from a mass-society context which assumes from the start a fundamental discontinuity between one individual and another. Rather, it comes from the pain of betrayal within actual personal relationships, when there is a deep-seated belief that mutual understanding is definitely possible.

Like a flower left in bloom
Oh, my heart is sad
Like a black lily flower
Oh, my shadow is sad
    Believing the words of the heartless
    Dreaming of happiness so many times
    Hollow heart, lonely dreams
    Quickening hopes in the nighttime sadness
Like the color of the black lily flower
Oh, my heart is sad
Like the scattered dew
Oh, my shadow is sad
    Believing the words of the heartless
    Dreaming of happiness so many times
    Wind on my cheek when the tears dry up
    Quickening hopes in the nighttime sadness
          – 'Black Lily Flower' (*Kuroyuri no hana*, 1929)

Here once again we find a typical pattern of objectifying feelings of loneliness in an attempt to enjoy them aesthetically.

Solidarity through loneliness

In 1931, the year when prewar 'modern life' reached its ultimate form in the big cities and mass culture was at its peak, 'Song of a Bar Hostess' was one of the most popular songs (along with

'Is Drink Tears or Sighs'). Its straightforward loneliness is not a purely private thing, but a loneliness set in the context of a multitude of strangers.

> Dancing so gaily under the neon lights
> Sadly, sadly fading away   Flower of tears
>
> I'm a sorrowful flower at a drinking spot
> A virgin by night and a mother by day
> – 'Song of a Bar Hostess' (*Jokyū no uta*, 1931)

The loneliness of chatting familiarly in a group situation, unable to speak of the real feelings of one's own separate life, is the quintessence of loneliness amid the crowd of contemporary society.

When this sort of loneliness resonates with that of others, people link up sympathetically. This is the paradox of loneliness as a unique moment of *solidarity*.

> I'm a withered eulalia on the riverbank
> You too are a withered eulalia . . .
> – 'Boatman's Ballad' (*Sendō ko-uta*, 1921)
>
> How pathetic   Fellow orphan
> Mooring ships   Again today with you
> – 'Boatwoman's Song' (*Onna-sendō uta*, 1955)

During the rapid spurts of rural migration to the swelling cities, in the 1920s and again in the late 1950s, under the 'foreign sky' one heart could 'touch' another in its maximum depth only through the respective senses of loneliness.

Clarion sentimantalism

'Apple Song,' which was popular immediately after the war, is meant to be played in 'marching style,' and although it was played that way in such settings as black-market stalls, that was not necessarily the tone when individuals sang it to themselves.

99

Namiki Michiko sang it in a way which draws out all the latent sorrow of the C-minor melody.

> My lips come close   To a red apple
> The blue sky   Is silently watching
> An apple says   Nothing at all but
> I understand so well   How an apple feels
> — 'Apple Song' (*Ringo no uta*, 1946)

As they hummed this song to themselves, people would ruminate upon loneliness under the brightness of a sky gone cloudlessly blue over the rubble and ashes. This touches on the domain of clarion sentimentalism, connecting with the sun-drenched sadness of 'Blue Mountain Ridge' (1948) and 'Nagasaki Tolling' (1949; cf. Chapter 3), and the sunny loneliness of 'Walking Along with Eyes on High' (1961). 'Apple Song' and the other immediate-postwar-era songs of loneliness recalled and grieved for the severed human ties during the war, the draft calls, deaths in action, air raids, deployments, internments and evacuations.

> You have gone so very far away
> The eyes remaining in my breast
> My memories   When lingering alone
> In the shade of the marronier   Hot tears
> Still overflowing today   Eternal memories
> — 'In The Shade of the Marronier' (*Maronie no kokage*, 1947)

> Still darkening today   On a hill in a foreign land
> It must be painful, friend   It must be hard
> Wait patiently   The storm will pass
> The day of return will come   Spring will come
> — 'A Hill in a Foreign Land' (*Ikoku no oka*, 1947)

> People spread and scattered   All alone
> For how long   For how long
> And I, nestling against a pillar
> Goodbye goodbye   When will you come back?
> — 'Night Station Platform' (1947)

> Waiting for you   Waiting for you
> Not-yet-come evening   Lonely evening

Flower at the window   A single flower
Pale-colored rose
                    – 'Waiting for You' (*Kimi mate domo*, 1949)

Other examples include 'Nagasaki Tolling' ('My wife has been summoned to heaven, Separated, on the journey alone,' 1949); and 'Can't-forget-you-Blues' ('Clasping memories of your face, Driven nearly crazy every night, Still I know you won't return').

Reversal of loneliness

The prototypical Japanese lyric of loneliness, that of people in the cities who are separated from their hometowns, has thus come to be expressed in subtle alternation with the spirit of grief for wartime separations.

Alone in the twilight of the city
Plaintively playing a flute
Though it's a slender fleeting bamboo flute
You know my heartfelt wishes

Taking a stroll just for fun and
Returning, it was a space in the memories
Smiles of the flowers float gently
A melody that makes me cry

City of flowers at twilight
In the window a lonesome journey's star
Feelings approach blowing blowing a tune
The wind, would you send it to him
         – 'Plaintive Bamboo Flute' (*Kanashiki takebue*, 1946)

Telling my fortune   By the flow of the stars
Where shall I roost   What shelter tonight
In a heart that is hardened   There is no romance
The tears are all cried   They're dried up
   Who made me   Such a woman

101

Having a cigarette   Whistling a tune
On an aimless evening's   Wanderings
Worn to a shadow   People turn and look
Under the city lamplight   Lonesome misery
  Who made me   Such a woman

Where is she now   Little sister who starved
Could I see my mother   Just once
As I bite my lip   The sadly bright red lip
Even the dark night wind   Cries and blows
  Who made me   Such a woman
– 'By the Flow of the Stars' (*Hoshi no nagare ni*, 1946–7)

A few years later, the stage of loneliness shifted from the city to the village, as song themes began to shift from the loneliness of being *separated from* the home village, to the loneliness of being *left behind* in the home village.

Do you remember   Our hometown village?
How many years have passed   With no news from you?
Sending off to Tokyo   Bright red apples
So bitter to see
Oh my   In my heart

Do you remember   The evening we parted?
Crying, crying I ran   Through the light rain
The inbound night train's   Blowing whistle
Unending rocking
Oh my   Of my heart

Do you remember   When we were children?
Those hills and streams   Where we played together
Haven't changed a bit   Since the old days
It's time to come back
Oh my   To my heart
        – 'From the Apple Village' (*Ringo mura kara*, 1956)

Brilliant red sunset-glowing sky
A hawk wheeling round
He-ey, he-ey,
Can you see Tokyo from up there?
            – 'Evening Hawk' (*Yuyake tonbi*, 1957)

In this lonesome country village
My young heart   Was on fire
For that lovely girl   Who left me behind
And went off to Tokyo
   Oh moon of the apple orchard   Good evening
   If you hear some news
      Be sure to tell me, now
      – 'Good Evening, Moon' (*O-tsuki-san komban wa*, 1958)

Village life became so depressing in the late 1950s that even those in the city would sympathize with the loneliness of those left behind before indulging their own loneliness.

   Far   Far
   Even with memories   Far sky
   When you reach Tokyo   Be sure
   To send word   She said
   Those tears   On a red cheek
   Like an apple

   Calling   Calling
   Secretly on a moonlit night   I called out
   She hasn't become a bride   Still
   She fervently waits   For me
   How old is that girl
   Yes, well past twenty   Long ago
   – 'Farewell's Lone Cedar' (*Wakare no ipponsugi*, 1956–62)

Urban loneliness, rural loneliness

As the urban component of the population climbed past 50 per cent, the disparity between farm and factory income increased, so much that the traditional position of the first son was reversed. The era of second and third sons as lifetime dependents was giving way, and the beneficiaries of primogeniture grew envious of their younger brothers who had gone off to the cities. Now the heirs who were obligated to stay at home were the lonely ones.

The decade which brought that turnabout, from the late 1950s, was also the time when the vivid images of urban culture were thrust into the middle of the daily life of the village, thanks to the rapid diffusion of television. Before long, the rural youth were finding their role models not among the wrinkled generation of their fathers, but among the contemporary generation of smart urbanities. And so the loneliness of those left behind in the hometowns grew even keener in comparison to the loneliness of those who had left.

Of course loneliness did not disappear from urban life. As we shall see below, it began to change from the loneliness of separation from the hometown, to the even deeper loneliness of *people without a hometown*, of living truly alone.

10 The History of Nostalgia and Yearning

The paradox of folk songs in vogue

Regional folk songs enjoyed widespread popularity during two periods in modern Japanese history: the last decade of the nineteenth century, and the late 1920s and early 1930s. Only a few isolated examples achieved much currency at other times.

Before examining the characteristics of the two periods of popularity, we should take a moment to consider exactly what is meant by a folk song *coming into vogue*. Is a folk song something that can be 'popular' one year? Is a song that is popular a folk song?

The life of a folk song consists in the deep interrelationship of the customs and history of a particular *region*. Conversely, the life of a popular song lies within its tendency to spread without limit beyond the particularity of a given region. Another essential element of a folk song is that it is passed on and sung *continuously* over a long period of time, transcending particular eras. And conversely, the essence of a popular song lies in its sensitive reflection of the social psyche at a particular historical moment.

The paradox of the folk song that comes into vogue is that it must lose something of its inherent nature. Popularity does not necessarily signify a strengthening of the folk song or of the communal lifestyles and feelings which sustain it. It may be a phenomenon which occurs in the process of their deterioration.

In most cases, the popularity of regional folk songs nationwide, or at the least in the major cities, derived from the flow of population out of the regions to the cities, as well as the incorporation of the villages into the national communications network.

The first folk-song boom had two crests, in 1889 and 1896. In 1889 the national system of city, town and village administrations was promulgated, establishing the political and social piping that links Tokyo with the regions. In 1890, magnificent celebrations in honor of the proclamation of the imperial constitution were

105

held in every city, large and small. Citizens who did not even know the provisions of the constitution plunged into the intoxication of this strange 'festival' honoring the aggregation of central and regional authority. It was for that day that the still-current *banzai* ('viva') shout was invented. In line with the purpose of molding a sense of civic unity, the larger celebrations included performances of folk songs from the various regions of the country. Everyone present could hear a national selection, made up exclusively of cheerful numbers, of such folk traditions as Ise Ondo, Nagoya Jinku, Oiwake Bushi, Tosa Bushi, Sansa Shigure, Soma Bushi and Echigo Jinku.

The Tokaidō railway linking Tokyo and Kobe was opened during the same year, followed by the Tohoku line to northern Honshu in 1891 and the Shin'etsu line to Niigata in 1893, greatly facilitating the flow of people as well as images.

Following these conditions, the vogue for folk songs in 1896 expressed the heightened sense of civic unity spurred by victory in the Sino-Japanese War. It was then that regional folk songs put down roots in the cities for the first time. After the turn of the century, only the odd occasional folk song reached popularity, such as 'Kawachi Ondo' after the Russo-Japanese War and 'Yagi Bushi' in 1916.

The second folk-song boom, at the beginning of the Showa period, was initially stimulated by the 'first hometown dance and folk song festival' which was organized in 1925 by JOAK, the Tokyo station of the national radio organization. This was billed as a 'regional revival,' but in fact the folk songs of this period did not come from the villages to the cities, for they had been freshly composed in the cities and diffused to the whole country, including the villages. Nearly all of these 'new folk songs' were written by Nakayama Shinpei between 1924 and 1935. The lyrics were mainly touristic and 'patriotic' toward the provinces, obviously conscious of visitors from the cities.

The standpoint of the outsider is apparent in the new folk songs. Lines such as 'Shima Springs lies beyond this world' or 'Away from the world, Tenryūkyō' were clearly not the ideas of the local residents. The epitome of this situation was the very popular new-folk-song line, 'Habu Harbor sunset, gentle sunset'; the real Habu Harbor, on the island of Oshima, faces east! (The lyricist candidly confessed that he wrote the line while imagining Hirakata, on another coast in an entirely different part of Japan.)

Local areas thus came to be viewed as objects. As the new folk songs curried favor with the urbanities, they touristified the local areas and hometowns themselves, treating regional culture as a commodity for sale. The 'new folk song,' as distinct from the folk song, had been born.

From folk songs to songs of hometowns

Three themes arose together in popular songs during the late 1920s and 1930s. Songs about hometowns, songs about the cities, and songs about wandering gamblers all appeared one after the other (see Figure 10.1).

Tellingly, songs about hometowns became popular for the first time just as folk songs rode out their last great wave of popu-

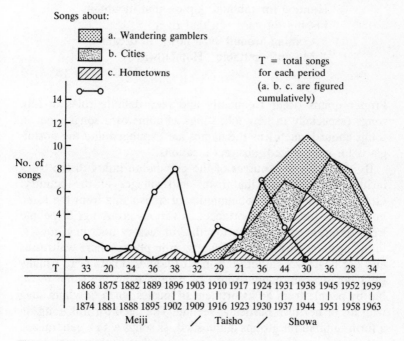

Figure 10.1 *Folk songs and songs about hometowns, cities and wandering gamblers*

107

larity. The folk songs, which by then were originating in the cities, are already none other than hometown songs. What is the difference between folk songs (or new folk songs as hometown songs) and hometown songs? Let us compare verses from the best-known examples of each form.

> In Kochi in Tosa   On the Satsumaya Bridge
> I saw a monk   Buy a fancy hairpin
>   Yo-sa-koi   Yo-sa-koi
>
> I'll show you the Mimase rapids   Opening up Urato
> Katsura Beach   Is famous for its moon
>   Yo-sa-koi   Yo-sa-koi
> > — *Yosakoi bushi* (Tosa folk song)

(Local place names are used for wordplay in the Japanese. *Mimase* also means 'I'll show you,' *Urato* can mean 'back door.')

> Hunting for rabbits   Up on that mountain
> Fishing for carp   In that river
>   Coming around even now   In dreams
>   My unforgettable   Hometown
> > — 'Hometown' (*Kokyō*)

Proper nouns occur frequently and play definite roles in folk songs (especially in new folk songs as hometown songs), but in songs about hometowns the names are expunged and the nostalgia is for generalized, abstract locations.

By the 1920s the sources of the population influx to the cities included virtually all the towns and villages of the country. Gradually the various communities of transplants from the same hometowns faded in importance, as various groupings of people from different places came together in factory boarding houses, in the upstairs back rooms of shops, or in places where waitresses and bar hostesses gathered. Songs of homesickness were usually sung not by comradely groups of people from the same town, but by people from an assortment of locales, each of whom sang with his or her own particular feeling. The need for folk songs in a form suitable for groups diminished, as songs with a generalized content of nostalgic homesickness, such that each person could substitute a personal image of his or her own home, began to spread: 'Leaving home, coming all those thousand miles'; 'Do you remember our hometown?' 'Hometown days, far away in my dreams.'

Rural paeans, urban paeans, continental paeans

If traditional folk songs sung in the cities aroused the nostalgia of people who had left the countryside, then the new folk songs sung in the cities aroused feelings of aspiration among urbanites. Nostalgia, including homesickness, is an attachment to one's previous life and experience, a state of mind which faces toward the past. Aspiration, on the other hand, faces toward the future. Incidentally, songs of nostalgia and songs of aspiration display very similar frequency curves over the history of modern Japanese popular songs, as shown in Figure 10.2.

Before the 1920s only two songs about homesickness were significantly popular, aside from some military songs which included yearnings for the distant homeland during service on

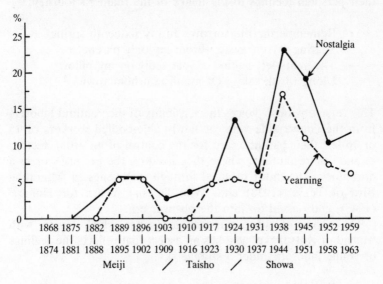

Figure 10.2 *Proportion of popular songs with motifs of nostalgia and aspiration*

the Asian continent. Then during the final Taisho and opening Showa years of the 1920s, song after popular song took up the theme. The first was 'Roamer's Journey' (*Ruro no tabi*, 1922):

> Drifter adrift   Destination of flight
> Siberia in the north   And Java in the south
> On which land   Shall my grave be set
> On which land   Will I turn to earth
>
> Yesterday to the east   And today to the west
> A roamer's journey   How much longer
> Even an island will do   Amid the offing
> Of the endless sea   I long for a genuine home
>   – 'Roamer's Journey' (*Ruro no tabi*, 1922)

In comparison with the song which is considered its forerunner, 'Wandering Song' ('Shall I go or shall I return, under the Northern Lights . . .'), 'Roamer's Journey' had much more to do with the real range of action of the nation at the time (the military expedition in Siberia, from 1918 to 1922). But the third verse suggests that a much broader base of people entrusted their personal feelings to the image of the roamer's journey:

> Remembering the sorrow   In my sixteenth spring
> Tearing myself away   From my only parents
> The years left behind   Float sadly on my pillow
> I long for the sky   Of my distant hometown

This verse obviously voices the sensibility of the youthful laborers from the countryside who, as newly able-bodied workers of 15 or 16 left their parents' care for the control of an urban factory or shop or restaurant, where they lived on the premises or in a dormitory. The motif survived through such songs as 'Migrating Bird of Tears' (1932) and 'Who Doesn't Yearn for Home?' (1940), and passed on into the postwar era.

The series of wandering-gambler songs which began with 'Ballad of Kutsukake' also has an aspect that reflects the feelings of young laborers under a strange sky.

> Even if I stretch it can't be seen, I know
> But I can't help trying   Looking back once again

Hometown where I was born   It's a distant sky
And the one I love   Is a hundred miles away
                – 'Ballad of Kutsukake' (1929)

The gathering in the cities of groups of laborers who have left their native villages behind is by no means unique to Japan. It is a universal feature of the formative periods of capitalist societies. Nevertheless, the question arises as to why the motif of home-sickness carries such heavy weight, qualitatively and quantitat-ively, in Japanese popular songs. The answer seems to lie in the particular pattern of *dekasegi* (seasonal migrant labor) followed by young Japanese. They were not proletarians in the literal sense of having been chased away from their native homes by enclosure and the like, nor were they rootless *Heimatlos* who had turned their backs on their hometowns. As the daughters and junior sons of farm families who sought work in the cities to supplement household finances and reduce the number of mouths to be fed, they were *warmly seen off* at the hometown station, and never forfeited their native homes. In this respect, there was a sweetness to their loneliness and sadness. That is, there was a beauty and an ease in their nostalgia, and thus also in Japanese songs of homesickness.

Parallelling these songs of nostalgia was another series of popu-lar songs with a motif which, on its face, was the opposite: longing for the bright lights and tree-lined avenues of the city. Some of the titles were 'Tokyo Parade' and 'Dotombori Parade' (1929), 'Willows of Ginza' (1932), and 'Tokyo Ondo' (1933).

As the military involvement in China intensified after the Mukden and Shanghai Incidents of the 1930s, the theme of nos-talgic songs shifted away from being in the city and missing one's native town, to being on the Asian continent far from the native country.

Meanwhile, the themes of songs of aspiration, which until the time of 'Tokyo Rhapsody' of 1936 had aroused yearnings for the cities, shifted toward the continent. Examples include 'Manchur-ian Maiden' (1937–8), 'Flowerselling Maiden of Shanghai' (1939), 'Canton Dancer' (1939) and 'Soochow Nocturne' (1940).

Night in China   A night in China
Harbor lights   In the purple night
Junks sailing in   Boats of dreams

Ah, unforgettable   Fiddler's strains
A night in China   Dreamy night

Night in China   A night in China
In the willow window   A lantern swings
A red birdcage   A Chinese maiden
Ah, inconsolable   Song of love
A night in China   Dreamy night

Night in China   A night in China
A night waiting for you   At the rainy railing
Flowers fall and scatter   Rouge scatters too
Ah, after I go   Could I forget?
A night in China   Dreamy night
                    – 'China Nights' (*Shina no yoru*, 1938)

These songs can be said to have played a role in the general mobilization of the dissatisfied national spirit toward service on the continent. In fact, the military authorities bought and distributed some of them by the hundreds of thousands.

On the other hand, sentimental and nostalgic songs, such as 'Lakeside Inn' and 'Who Doesn't Yearn for Home?' were generally suppressed (except in versions which had been altered so as to instill fighting spirit).

In other songs, even the feelings of homesickness of the soldiers themselves were exploited and channeled toward an active fighting spirit.

As we departed   From our country
Courageously we vowed   To return victorious
Doing the glorious deeds   Or dying as we try
When the bugle sounds   The call to advance
The waves of flags   Sending us off
Come back to life   In memories
                    – 'Bivouac Song' (*Roei no uta*, 1937)

Dear mother   Pardon the delay
I remain   Very healthy
Though it may sound proud   I'd like to show
My iron helmet   With all the bullet marks
From here on the continent   Up until today
                    – 'News from Shanghai' (*Shanhai tayori*, 1938)

With such faces   And such voices
My wife and children   Sent me to great deeds
Though tattered   The fluttering flags
Still float   Among the distant clouds
                    – 'Praying at Dawn' (*Akatsuki ni inoru*, 1940)

The collapse of the hometown

We saw in Chapter 1 how the sense of emotional blockage during
the final Meiji years changed during the Taisho and early Showa
eras to vague yearnings for the ocean or exotic moods, which
gradually coalesced into the concrete image of the Chinese continent. With the loss of the Pacific War the citizenry's dreams of
the continent were shattered, and the yearnings shifted once
again toward America or Hawaii or exotic moods within Japan.
    Oka Haruo's carefree rendition of 'Long-Awaited Cruise to
Hawaii' (1948) provided one outlet for popular feelings of dissatisfaction during and after the war. Another was 'Seaman in Love'
(1949) – 'Time to leave port, happy sound of the departure
gong . . .' The yearnings for wandering exoticism of the postwar
masses also found voice in 'San Francisco Chinatown' (1949–51),
'Nagasaki Elegy' (1947), and 'Pomelo Seller of Nagasaki' (1948).
(Nagasaki has historically had an exotic appeal in Japan.)
    Other songs, such as 'Foreign Hills' (1947) and 'The Night
Grew Late in Muntinglupa' (1951), suggest thoughts of the
defeated homeland by Japanese who were overseas, and at the
same time were songs of grief sung during the years of mourning
for youths lost to war.

        The wind rocks dreams of memories
        Again today, singing a song of no return . . .
    – 'The Shade of the Marronier' (*Maronie no kokage*, 1947)

        The hill we reached together you and I
        The hill overlooking the harbor . . .
    – 'The Hill Overlooking the Harbor' (*Minato ga mieru oka*,
                                                            1947)

113

> White flowers were blooming
> Days of hometown dreams, long ago
> – 'When White Flowers Bloom' (*Shiroi hana no saku koro*,
> 1947–50)

> Smoke in the mountains   At twilight
> The retreating figure   Of he who departed
> Turning around   A wave of the hand
>   Growing faint   Ah   The pale sunset
>   Crimson-stained   Longing
> – 'Smoke in the Mountains' (*Yama no kemuri*, 1952)

During the second phase of the postwar period, from 1952 to 1958, the main themes of nostalgia and aspiration reverted once again to the prewar combination of rural-urban shuttling.

The 1951 song 'Let's Go to Tokyo' ('Let's go, If we go, Everything will work out fine'), which by itself seemed to have the power to pull teenagers like Terayama Shūji away from home, was banned from sale. But in 1956 and 1957, the shop counters in every town in the country were lined with records arousing ambitions for the glittering metropolis: 'Tokyo, 3 AM' ('You look fine in your bright red dress . . .'), 'Tokyoites' ('Tremolo of rain on rows of trees . . .'), 'Tokyo Bus Girl' ('With your young dreams and love . . .'), and 'We'll Meet in Yūrakuchō.'

It is noteworthy that these songs were clustered between 1956 and 1958, the time when it was said that 'the postwar era has ended,' when *danchizoku* (apartment dwellers) and *katei denka* (household electrification) were fashionable words, when the rapid diffusion of television and weekly magazines marked a structural change toward a communications-intensive life. They fell precisely amid the most conspicuous period of emergence of Japanese mass society.

In perfect parallel came a spate of popular songs about rural youth gone to the cities and yearning for their native towns, clustered in 1956 and 1957. 'Lone Cedar of Farewell,' 'Train of Sorrows,' 'To the One I Long to See,' 'The Sights of Tokyo,' 'This is Tokyo, Mother,' 'Come Back Soon.'

The contrasting scheme of 'urban loneliness' and 'rural warmth,' which infused songs of the prewar era, was in the process of breaking down in those songs of the 1950s. Hence the entreaties by those left in the village to 'come back soon' or 'be sure to send word when you get to Tokyo,' as well as inviting mother up to the city and saying to her, 'This is Tokyo, mother, you've seen the pictures?' There is now even a sense of superiority on the part of those who have left for the cities, and the homesickness comes like a sympathetic heartache for the families and lovers who have been left behind in the deserted villages. This is a complete turnabout from the prewar songs of homesickness. Songs about the miserable solitude of the city even came to include the title 'Me with No More Hometown to Return To' (*Kaeru kokyo mo nai ore sa*). The image of being able to return at any time to the warmth of the village was collapsing.

The deterioration involved here corresponds with the inversion of feelings of loneliness which was discussed in Chapter 8.

The final flourish of city folk and rural folk in the late 1950s came in 'Leaving My Home in Tosa in the South' (1959). This song made no waves when it was recorded with *enka*-style vocalization, but it became a hit when Peggy Hayama sang it in the liberated western style. This suggests that during the second phase of the postwar period, urbanization and modernization had finally become more than an external living environment for the young rural natives, penetrating to the core of their personalities. After 1959, the song of sentimental homesickness went into steep decline.

In the third phase of the postwar period, after the Ampo uprising of 1960, 'Kitakami River Nocturne' (1961) can be cited as the representative hit song with the motif of homesickness. Here we no longer see a nostalgia for the communitarian interpersonal relations of home and village, for it is nothing more than scenes of nature along the river which are made into a beautiful memory, as the setting of first love. Homesickness seems to have been transformed into the urbanite's yearnings for nature.

> Those eyes   As if moistened
> With gentle fragrance   Of white lilies
> Bring back the memories   The memories
> Night of the moon   On the Kitakami River banks

> When the evening torches   Were burning
> Faintly in my heart   First love

Bring back the memories   The memories
Murmurings   On the Kitakami River banks
– 'Kitakami River Nocturne' (1961)

Formerly, when the young natives of farming villages took their summer servants' days-off, they would leave the city and scatter to their villages in pursuit of the warmth of the home communities. Now when the young urbanites take their summer holidays, they leave the city and scatter to the seashore and the mountains in search of 'nature' as the stage-trappings of their youth. Although they trace the same paths of behavior, there is a significant difference between those for whom the village is the ultimate base of life, and those for whom it is the city. Between the prewar songs of homesickness and 'Kitakami River Nocturne' there is a perfectly identical distance. The city-reared youth of today also often feel a 'nostalgia' for nature, but instead of an actual sensation which is footed in their direct life experience, it is typically nothing more than the generally accepted, glamorized concept of nature. It is a yearning under the name of nostalgia.

11 The History of Feelings of Transience

Impermanence and wandering

The feeling of impermanence (*mujōkan*) is made up of two elements. One is keen *perception of change* occurring over time in the actual world, including the self. The other is *cathexis*, or investment with significance, of *things which go away or die away* (as opposed to things which are growing or being created). When the element of awareness is stronger, the feeling of impermanence becomes a transcendent affective neutrality; this farsighted type of feeling is typified in the extreme by a Buddhist priest who has attained 'enlightenment.' When the element of cathexis is stronger, the feeling of impermanence is colored by a boundless attachment to that which has passed on; this is the exclamatory (or grieving) type.

In contrast to that awareness of change over time, the feeling of wandering (*hyōhakukan*) is inherently an awareness of *change in space*. As with the feeling of impermanence, cathexis of the feeling of wandering has entirely to do with the *path* which runs past (not the goal toward which one is to proceed). Hence the feeling of wandering can be defined as *awareness of the self as one who goes away*.

Another common feature of the feeling of impermanence and that of wandering is an awareness of *the uncertain nature of the future*, for change is seen not to occur in accord with any schedule previously determined by the ego or a trascendent entity. Consequently, even when attention is directed toward a future destination, one would use such expressions as 'unknown places' or 'which town tomorrow?' The sensations of evanescence, of futility, of helplessness that are entailed in the recognition of this non-volitional sort of change can be expressed in a word as transience (*utsuroi*), either temporal transience (impermanence) or spatial transience (wandering).

Adjectives which express impermanence are fleeting, futile,

117

ephemeral; verbs of impermanence are to scatter, to pass, to go away, to flow; symbols of impermanence are a flower falling away, the water's flow, a migratory bird, a journey.

Adjectives expressing wandering are desolate, lonely, ephemeral; verbs of wandering are to roam, to flow, to cross, to pass, to drift; symbols of wandering are flowing water, floating grass, water plants, a journey, a migratory bird, birds (gulls, wild geese, swallows), the wind, waves, clouds.

The frequency over time of motifs of transience in popular songs is charted in Figure 11.1. It appears little by little from the end of the nineteenth century, begins to play a major role after the war with Russia, levels off in the Taisho period, and appears in some 40 per cent of popular songs during the 15 years of war up to 1945. After the war it by no means disappears, occurring continually in about 25 per cent of all the songs in this study.

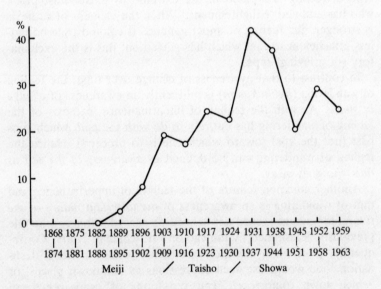

Figure 11.1 *Proportion of popular songs with transience motifs*

Transience on the battlefield

The motif of transience first appears in fairly distinct form in the military songs of the Sino-Japanese War.

> The gun barrel's echo   Dies away
> After it even insects   Do not chirp
> – 'Women Following the Army' (*Fujin jugun uta*, 1894)

The sense of transience on the battlefield reached its apex in 'Comrade in Arms' (*Senyū*). Written just after the Russo-Japanese War of 1905 and current well into the post-Pacific War era, it is Japan's longest-running and most broadly popular war song. This points up the meaning of war as a social basis which actualized and molded the sense of transience among the Japanese.

> 1   Here hundreds of miles away from
>   Our country, in the red light
>   Of a Manchurian sunset lies my friend
>   Under the stones at the field's edge
>
> 2   I remember sadly how up to yesterday
>   He was marching straight ahead
>   Heavily punishing the enemy
>   Here the hero sleeps
>
> 3   Ah, at the height of battle
>   I marched on never thinking
>   That the friend who was next to me
>   Could so suddenly be felled
>
> 4   Though under stern army discipline
>   Could I turn my back on this?
>   I picked him up, 'Stay with it!'
>   Laid a dressing as the bullets flew
>
> 11 Arms around shoulders, we would say
>   We are going to lose our lives
>   When I die I trust my bones to you,
>   We pledged between the two of us

12   Though I never expected it, I continue
Alone in this mysterious life
Beneath the red sunset of Manchuria
Digging the grave of my friend

13   On this perfectly clear moonlit night
With heavy heart I take the brush
And send these final particulars
To the parents of my friend

Within the individual lives of the people who went to the front, 'Comrade in Arms' signifies a confrontation with the death of one's intimates and oneself ('We are going to lose our lives'), in the context of having been driven far from home by the authorities ('Here hundreds of miles away from our country'). The soldiers were compulsorily placed amid intense temporal and spatial change, and the future uncertainty of both themselves and the surrounding world ('Though I never expected it, I continue alone in this mysterious life'). It is the very definition of transience.

While the war songs from the Chinese and Russian wars sang of the impermanence of the lives of individual soldiers *amid* the war, the following two songs, which were popular in the years between those wars, sing of the sense of impermanence in the grand sweep of historical time which enfolds the wars themselves.

In the twilight at the crossing
Of the verdant village of Sakurai
Reining in his horse under the shade of a tree
Knowing full well his worldly fate
Scattered upon the hidden sleeve of armor
Is it tears or gathered drops of dew?
         – 'Song of Nankō' (*Nankō no uta*, 1899–1900)

In spring   A flowery feast on the castle tower
As the sake cup goes round   The thousand-year-old pine
Spreads out its branches   Providing shade
The shining days   Where are they now?

In autumn   Camp colored by the frost
Of honking passing geese   Their numbers reflected
Upon a planted sword   Glinting flowing
The shining days   Where are they now?

Now the ruined castle's   Feeble moon
Its unchanging light   Shining for whom?
Only the katsura tree   Remains at the fence
Only the storm   Sings in the pines

Heaven's light   Never changes
The worldly figures   Moving up and down
Throwing the light   High and low
Oh ruined castle's   Feeble moon
                    – 'Koujou Castle Moon' (*Kōjō no tsuki*, 1901)

This sense of impermanence is in fact the *world-sense* in which
the historical consciousness of the Japanese people is rooted. It
stands in conspicuous contrast to the sense of *progress* upon
which the ideological historical consciousness of modern Europe
is founded. While they have a common premise of a keenly
sensed recognition of change, in Japan the cathexis is poured
into *that which passes or dies away*, and not into phenomena
which are growing or being created. The process of change is
not taken as a link in a purposeful conscious process according
to the will of god or of human beings; instead the indeterminacy
of the direction of change is emphasized. In other words, it is
the difference between an awareness of the self as a participant
in the flow of history, and an awareness of the self as a castaway
upon the flow of history, or as an admiring spectator standing
on the bank.

The water's flow and the human self

Just after the Russo-Japanese War, the feelings of transience
within the lives of the people (which were swayed by the norms
of the time and other external conditions, and could not be
freely designed), oozed forth in such popular songs as 'Midnight
Reminiscence,' 'Rain On My Sleeve,' and 'Don-don Song' (all
discussed in Chapter 1).

    Is that Miss Okaru going by palanquin?
    I am being sold and taken away . . .
                    – 'Don-don Song' (1911)

It may happen that you may fall
Into the fate of passing away
With the dew on the execution ground
'Tis such sad news to hear . . .
                    – 'Rain on My Sleeve' (1908)

From this time onward, the awareness of transience, in the form of feelings of impermanence or of wandering, became a central motif of Japanese popular songs. As early as 1912, the motif was archetypically presented in a simple form:

Sasa ya sasa-sasa sasa ya sasa
Kikaku to gengo wa hashi no ue
Mizu no nagare to hito no mi wa
Ashita mataruru takarabune

Grass and grass-grass grass and grass
Poets and warriors on the bridge
The water's flow and the human self
Tomorrow waits the treasure ship
                    – *Nara maru kuzushi* (1911)

In the image of the water's flow, feelings of impermanence and of wandering are fused together. This framework was carried on through such songs as 'Gondola Song' (1916) and 'Boatman's Ballad' (1921–2).

Life is short   A girl must love
Before the reddened lips have faded
Before the ardent blood is cooled
Tomorrow's months and days   Do not exist

Life is short A girl must love
Before her black hair has faded
Before the heart's flames die away
Today will not   Come again
                    – 'Gondola Song' (1916)

The gondola that floats on the water is never once mentioned in the words of the song, but as the title, it serves as guiding image of the entire song.

122

I am the riverbank's   Withered eulalia
And you too are just a   Withered eulalia
Somehow the two of us   Are in this world
Flowerless unblooming   Withered eulalia

If we live or if we die   You know, my dear
In the flow of the water   What shall we change
As for you and as for me   As boathands
On the Tone River   We shall earn our passage
                    – 'Boatman's Ballad' (*Sendo ko-uta*, 1921–3)

When the self is compared to something in a Taisho or early-Showa popular song, it is almost always something fleeting, something helpless, something transient: water grasses, withered eulalia, a flower left in bloom, scattered dew drops, a cast-off cicada skin, a deserted boat, a migratory bird.

I'm a blade of watergrass   Blowing in the wind
Flowing and flowing and flowing endlessly. . . .
– 'Song of Wandering' (*Sasurai no uta*, 1917) (cf. Chapter 9)

Like a flower left in bloom
My heart is so lonely . . .

Like scattered drops of dew
My shadow is so fleeting
   – 'Black Lily' (*Kuroyuri no hana*, 1929) (cf. Chapter 9)

Spring forever unseen   This my destiny
Is it worth prolonging   This cast-off shell
'Tis a fleeting shadow   This love of mine
         – 'Yearning for a Shadow' (*Kage o shitaite*, 1932)

Those plovers   Are not crying
I am a forlorn   Boat adrift . . .
                – 'Island Maiden' (*Shima musume*, 1932)

Rainy day or windy day   I spent it crying
I'm in the floating world   A migratory bird . . .

This dream or that dream   All is scattered
I'm a tearful   Voyaging bird . . .

123

My dear old   Hometown sky is distant
With nowhere to go   Voyaging bird . . .
– 'Tearful Migratory Bird' (*Namida no wataridori*, 1932)

This sort of temperament of sadness and helplessness is not universal among premodern societies, where the self is safely anchored in the world of the community. Nor does it tend to be seen in modern societies, where a suitably strengthened self has been established within a civic world. The emotional motif of these songs is the desolation, helplessness and misery felt by those whose sense of self has been formed within a community world, and who are then cast willingly or unwillingly into the circumstances of modernity. The structural contradictions between society and personality which appear during the transition from premodernity to modernity give rise to *a self which lacks both external and internal underpinnings*. This is clearly the 'floating grass,' the 'withered eulalia' the 'boat adrift,' the 'bird migrating through a floating world.' These are the key emotional symbols of modernizing Japan, made up of Japanese premodern substance and Western European modern form.

The emotional landscape of the large numbers of Japanese who had abandoned their hometowns for the cities after about 1919 was specified in the previous chapter as 'Drifter adrift, destination of flight . . . On which land will I turn to earth?' – the theme lines of 'Wanderer's Journey.'

'Border Town' (*Kokkyō no machi*, 1934) expands upon the same theme. Like 'Wanderer's Journey' its structure consists of a poetic image presented clearly in the first verse, followed by a gradual articulation of its down-to-earth meaning as it descends through the atmosphere of the raw sighs of the people.

Even the sleigh bells   Echo with desolation
The snowy wilderness   The city lights
Crossing beyond a mountain   Stars of a foreign land
The border   Covered with frost

Away from home   A thousand distant miles
I have the feeling   That it's out of reach
That distant sky   Stares firmly down
There are nights   To make a man cry

Hopes for tomorrow   Are not completely gone
No one to turn to   All alone
And the red sunset   Moves me to tears
But it's no use   For a bird of passage
— 'Border Town' (*Kokkyō no machi*, 1934)

The opposite intellectual poles of tradition versus modernity (of Japan versus the West), and the poles in people's daily feelings of *home versus city* (or countryside versus Tokyo), cast their shadows across each other and drum up resonances of their associated experience.

Emblems and emotions of wandering gamblers

The string of ballads about wandering gamblers in the early Showa years is also based upon the feelings and life structure of the working class who still bore the smell of the farm in modernizing Japan.

Sonobe Saburō offers the acute perception that in the world of popular songs, some expressions of homesickness and of longing for the city 'had hidden within them some of the true nature of the song of the wandering gambler.' Yet it seems more accurate to stand that observation on its head, and conclude that the song of the wandering gambler is basically the *shadow* of the feelings of homesickness and yearning which inherently arise in that stratum of society.

The popularity in 1929–30 of the pioneer of the wandering gamblers' songs, 'Ballad of Kutsukake,' was not followed immediately by a succession of similar hits. It was in 1934–5 that the genre reached its full stride in a dozen widely popular songs, including 'Akagi Lullaby.' These songs caught the spirit of the people at the moment when the ebbing tide of the early-Showa erotic-grotesque cultural movement was mixed with the rising tide of militarism. They freshened the touch of the winds of the time, which were blowing the culture of pleasure and degeneracy and nihilism intact onto the battlefield.

I floated and floated on the beach town riverbank
Floating with the merry shyness of the willows

125

A gaze recalled as I launch a little boat
And the sulky night wind steps in uninvited

I won't cry about the ways of the world
Life is like a single shot of fireworks
While it burns and scatters the stage set is switched
And for a woman all the more

Neither pride nor kindness stands against this floating world
It is all just bubbles on the water
I won't cry, I say through my tears
As the moon looks down on a crumbling silhouette
     – 'Life of a Meiji Woman' (*Meiji ichi-dai onna*, 1935)

The procession of similar songs over the next several years captured the spirit of the people as they turned toward battle:

Anyway we'll be going yonder just one time
Falling and flowing and then we pass on, you know . . .
     – 'Flux' (*Ruten*, 1936)

Tossing a beloved liaison upon the rocks
The professional gambler's watery journey . . .
     – 'Loving Husband's Journey' (*Tsumagoi dōchū*, 1937)

Migrating geese   Crying in disarray
Where is tomorrow's   Roosting place . . .
     – 'Mt Akagi Full Moon' (*Meigetsu Akagi-yama*, 1939)

These songs were particular favorites among soldiers because the army at that time was made up primarily of rural natives, and because the traditional values of social obligation and human sympathy (*giri* and *ninjō*), which underpinned the nineteenth-century genre of *naniwa-bushi* songs, held strong sway in the military world. As they camped at some foreign hill or valley without knowing if they would be alive or dead on the morrow, the soldiers no doubt picked out the images of the wandering gamblers' songs as expressive catharsis for the sense of transience of their army life.

In the army songs of the Meiji era, in the wanderer's songs of the Taisho era, and in the gambler's ballads of the Showa era,

feelings of impermanence and feelings of wandering are insepar-
ably fused. Between the visualized, concrete expressions of the
sense of wandering, and the conceptualized, abstract expressions
of the sense of impermanence; between that which expresses and
that which is expressed, there are simultaneous and alternating
exchanges of roles. Within the cycle of feelings becoming symbols
and symbols turning back into feelings, the sense of transience
of the Japanese is endlessly amplified.

Impermanence permeates the starting point

The chapters on sadness and loneliness touched on feelings of
transience just after the war, which grew out of the loss of kin
during the war or separations and solo ramblings during the
general confusion, as well as the sense of wandering and impermanence among those who returned from the front, defeated
and futile, and those who saw loved ones snatched away from
them.

Rocked and rocking   On the back of the back of the waves
Returning boat   On a course with the moon . . .
              – 'Repatriation Boat' (*Kaeri-bune*, 1946)

A flower of the field   Living fleetingly
In the world of people   On the undulating waves . . .
              – 'Nagasaki Tolling' (*Nagasaki no kane*, 1949)

The wind rocks the dreams of the memories
Singing again today a song of no return . . .
– 'In The Shade of the Maronnier' (*Maronie no kokage*, 1947)

Afterwards, up through the early 1960s, the forms of
expression for feelings of transience in popular songs showed
almost no change, simply repeating the patterns which had been
molded before the war. This suggests that there was some continuity in the various social conditions that reproduced those
modes of feeling.

> Makes me feel happy   And makes me cry
> Hateful, that evening's   Wind of voyage
> – 'Woman Boathand' (*Onna sendōuta*, 1955)

> Pillows of herring   In the northern sea
> Sorrows of the moon   Ship of tears
> – 'Ship of Tears' (*Namida-bune*, 1962–3)

Amid that stylistic context, out of the singing houses emerged 'Going Back North,' a song which can be called the germ of a new sense of transience with a feel unknown before the war. In this, the song of someone who is leaving Tokyo on a journey 'back north,' we may see whether the classic plan of the modern Japanese popular song, with its two poles of the city and the hometown, is transmitted intact.

> The window   Wet with evening dew
> The capital   Already far away
> A lone traveler   Going back north
> The tears   Flowing endlessly

> The dreams   Have died in vain
> Wandering in darkness   Again today
> Distantly desiring   Emptily hoping
> Affections   Have left me

> Now I go   Silently
> What more   Should I say
> Farewell, homeland   Dear ones
> Tomorrow   Who knows which town
> – 'Going Back North' (*Hokkikō*, 1961)

The lyrics are somewhat inconsistent. Why should leaving the capital and going back north mean 'farewell, homeland'? Surely this is not a journey into Siberian exile. And what can it mean to quit the homeland and 'go back' to the north? . . . Regardless of the apparent contradictions, what is unequivocal in this song is the singular unity of its emotional atmosphere, which appealed to something deep inside a certain generation, a certain layer of society.

There had previously been songs about throwing up the city

and going back home, but this one has no sense of returning to the 'beloved' home, to the 'warm' bosom of one's parents, for it sings only of the despair of one who is quitting the capital.

Aside from soldiers at the front, the typical source for feelings of wandering in Japanese popular songs up to this point was the groups of people who had left their hometowns during the decades of modernization, who still identified with their native villages as home even when they took in the 'journey's sky' of city life, whose reference groups were back in the country homes of their forebears and their childhood. For people of those generations, quitting the capital and 'returning' to the north would have felt quite literally like a reversion to the starting point, with no room at all for the feeling of 'farewell, homeland.' For the generations of hometown departees, the logical contradiction in 'Going Back North,' would align as a note of *emotional* discord.

The emotional equivalence between leaving the city and leaving the homeland can work only insofar as one's reference group has been entirely transferred to the city, and the home village has lost significance as life's base. For this singer, there is no 'hometown' in the sense of a peaceful place to live, where he is warmly welcome at any time. Like it or not, the city has become the ground upon which he makes his stand. This is why it is possible for the feeling of leaving the capital to be presented in polarized form as 'farewell, homeland.' It defines the generation, the layer of society for whom the atmosphere of the song is not only emotionally consistent but deeply appealing. What seems an obvious logical contradiction is in fact an articulation of the feeling among contemporary Japanese of having *lost the starting point*.

Popular just after 'Going Back North' was 'The River Flows,' in which the singer speaks for those who live in the city and have no home to which to 'return.'

> Blighted leaves   Floating again today
> In a city valley   The river flows
> Insignificant   Hopes are dashed
> Into eyes   Stained with sorrows
> The twilight   Water glares
>
> At the foot   Of a bridge of memories
> So many dreams   Covered with rust

Somebody   With a cold heart
Somebody   Parting for love
Now crying   In the wind which blows through

Through the valley   With the pale lamps
The river flows   So straight
Covered with dust   Of the world, of people
And yet I live   Gazing at the water
Do not sigh   Tomorrow will be bright
    – 'The River Flows' (*Kawa wa nagareru*, 1961–2)

The heroine of this song is not personally 'flowing' like the protagonists of the Taisho roamers' songs, the Showa wandering gamblers' ballads, and the city-to-home return-trip songs. She is gazing at what flows by while she stands at a single spot. Her memories lie not someplace far away, but before her eyes at the foot of the bridge on which she stands, 'covered with rust.' Rather than feeling a transience traceable to the helplessness of being separated from life's starting point, she finds an impermanence which permeates that very starting point in the here and now. The sudden turnaround to a happy ending comes without any tangible clue, as nothing more than the singer's earnest instruction to herself.

The situation can no longer be resolved through a 'return' to the mother's bosom or the native village or the soil of the homeland, for it has become the pervasive sense of impermanence which arises from the uncertainty of individual life in this thoroughly modernized society.

Appendix to Part One
A dictionary of modern Japanese
emotional symbols

In Osamu Dazai's novel *No Longer Human*, there is a conversation about tragic nouns and comic nouns. Just as some European languages have masculine, feminine and neuter nouns, for persons with poetic sensitivity, there are also nouns which are tragic or comic. Trains are tragic, for example, while buses and trams are comic. The playwright who inserts even a single tragic noun into a comedy is said to have failed a fundamental test.

Various nouns have their own characteristic emotional atmospheres. When effectively deployed in a poem or play or story, they communicate more splendidly than direct expressions of emotions. Conversely, if used inappropriately, they can spoil the atmosphere of the work. In Japanese *haiku* there are seasonal theme words, such as waterfall or tree frog, which besides identifying the indicated things, play the secondary role of indicating the season (in this case, summer). In other genres of Japanese writing, nouns such as dice or folded-paper cranes or seashore, besides identifying objects, also indicate emotional atmospheres (transience, longing and nostalgia, respectively). It is impossible to attain a full understanding of songs, poems or even prose without knowing the commonly sensed *emotional values* of the nouns within a given culture. In addition to dictionaries of the things which are indicated by symbols, we may need a dictionary of the emotions which are narrated by symbols.

There are several types of reasons why a certain noun may embody a particular emotion in condensed form. It may be that a key attribute of the thing which the noun indicates is stereotyped as a certain feeling; thus a cicada's shell calls to mind the brevity of its lifespan and becomes a symbol of transience and impermanence, and wild geese symbolize wandering. Or there may be a tendency for the existence or the awareness of the thing itself to be associated with a specific emotion; hence folded-paper cranes denote longing, and raindrops loneliness. Or it may be that the biological or psychological disposition of the thing calls an emotional atmosphere to mind, as rain denotes gloominess or sadness, and blue sky hope or joy. Or it may be that the form or the function of the thing works as an embodiment of some mental or emotional phenomenon; hence a spinning wheel signifies memories, and a cage means emotional blockage.

When a culture selects certain nouns as symbols of certain emotions, there may be other factors at work as well, including ethnic patterns of empathy, cultural phonetic preferences, and traditional mannerisms of expression.

Systems of emotional symbols work like the rings of a tree to disclose moments in the history of the lives of a people. Through comparisons of these symbols, which will differ at least a little with various peoples and eras, we can gain a handhold for comprehending the emotional temperament at the depths of the mental structures of each people and era.

As a first step in this job, here is a dictionary of emotional symbols which appear in the songs of the people of modern Japan. We might next compare the overall pattern of symbols and the emotional implications of individual symbols to those in the songs of other cultures, to pre-modern Japanese song forms and folk songs, and to various other artistic genres of the modern era, in order to more thoroughly map the emotional disposition of the people of modern Japan.

Autumn wind (*Aki kaze*)   Impermanence
Black lily (*Kuroyuri*)   Sadness
Blighted leaves (*Wakuraba*)   Disappointment
Breeze (*Soyo-kaze*)   Blessings, good fortune ('Sweet gentle breeze of the hills in spring')
Bubbles (*Awa*)   Impermanence ('Everything is fleeting bubbles of water')
Caged bird (*Kago no tori*)   Blocked feeling ('I'm a caged bird unable to go out')
Cherry blossoms (*Sakura*)   1 Gallantry. 2 Tranquility
Cicada shell (*Utsusemi*)   Impermanence ('Short-lived shadow of a cicada shell')
Clouds (*Kumo*)   1 Aspiration, hope ('Yearning toward the rose-colored clouds') ('Huge clouds of hope are forming'). 2 Impermanence, wandering

Dew (*Tsuyu*)   Impermanence ('The self of fleeting disappearing dew')

Dice (*Saikoro*)   Impermanence

Evening (*Yoi*)   1 Sadness. 2 Loneliness

Fallen leaves (*Ochiba*)   Impermanence

Falling star (*Nagare-boshi*)   Impermanence

Festival (*Matsuri*)   Nostalgia

Fields (*Nobe*)   Nostalgia

Finger (*Yubi*)   Tender love

Fire (*Hi*)   1 Ardent love ('Lit a fire . . . in my heart'). 2 Anger. 3 Heroism, sincerity

Fireworks (*Hanabi*)   Impermanence ('Life is like a set piece of fireworks')

Flowers (*Hana*)   1 Love, longing. 2 Joy

Flute, Bamboo Flute (*Fue, Takebue*)   Sadness, loneliness

Fog (*Kiri*)   Sorrow, sadness ('The fog rolls on saying goodbye')

Foghorn (*Muteki*)   Sorrow, sadness ('I wish I could cry like a foghorn')

Folded paper cranes (Thousand cranes) (*Orizuru, Senbazuru*)   Longing

Guitar (*Gitaa*)   1 Loneliness. 2 Longing

Harbor (*Minato*)   1 Nostalgia. 2 Aspiration. 3 Exoticism

Hills (*Oka*)   Nostalgia ('The hills where you and I came together')

Insects' chirping (*Mushi no koe*)   1 Impermanence. 2 Loneliness

Journey (*Tabi, Tabiji*)   Transience, impermanence.

Lake (*Mizuumi)*   Sorrow ('The lake quietly recounts the sadness')

Lamp (*Akari*)   Nostalgia ('A red lamp on a street of elegies')

Lane (*Komichi*)   Nostalgia

Letter (*Tayori*)   Nostalgia

Lullaby (*Komori uta*)   Nostalgia

Man (*Otoko*)   Heroism, pride

Migrating bird (*Watari-dori*)   Wandering

Moon (*Tsuki*)   1 Loneliness ('The moon in the window sadly alone'). 2 Impermanence ('The moon we watched smiling long ago'). 3 Feelings from afar

Mountain, Mountain range (*Yama, Sanmyaku*)   1 Nostalgia. 2 Hope, aspiration

Night fog (*Yogiri*)   Sorrow, lingering regret

One-sided waves (*Katase nami*)   Unrequited love ('One-sided waves make me cry again tonight')

Pillar (*Hashira*)   Loneliness ('Nestling against a pillar')

Playing cards (*Karuta*)   1 Impermanence ('Floating and sinking of a transience world of cards'). 2 Despair ('For this heart weary with cards and liquor')

Plateau (*Kōgen*)   Brightness containing sadness

Rain (*Ame, kosame*)   1 Sadness ("Tis the rain of a night of sobbing'). 2 Lingering attachment. 3 Indifference ('The night rain indifferent to the flowers'). 4 Quiet longing ('Song of the rain soaking into my heart'). 5 Gentleness ('More gentle than the rain')

Raindrops (*Amadare*)   Loneliness ('Drops of rain engraving with no sound of one I love')

Red string (*Beni himo*)   Love

Roses (*Bara*)   Good fortune, joy, hope

Sake   Despair

Sea gull (*Kamome*)   Transience ('In what place at dawn? In company with the gulls')

Setting sail (*Debune*)   Lingering attachment

Setting sun (*Yūhi*)   1 Wandering. 2 Sadness

Shade of a tree (*Kokage*)   Loneliness

Ship, Boat (*Fune, Kobune*)   Wandering, impermanence ('Faithless ship of a single ruinous night')

Sky (*Sora*)   1 Hope (Dreams fluttering in the distant sky'). 2 Nostalgia, sorrow, loneliness ('Silently watching the blue sky')

Small island (*Kojima*)   Loneliness

Spinning wheel (*Itoguruma*)   Memories, nostalgia ('The spinning wheel's passing months and days')

Stardust (*Hoshi-kuzu*)   Sorrow

Stars (*Hoshi*)   1 Hope. 2 Impermanence

Station (*Eki*)   Nostalgia, lingering attachment

Steam whistle (*Kiteki*)   Nostalgia, sorrow

Stray bird (*Hagure-dori*)   Loneliness, wandering

Stretching (*Senobi*)   1 Lingering attachment ('Even if I stretch I couldn't see it, I know'). 2 Feelings from afar ('Standing on tiptoe to see the distant sky')

Sugoroku (Japanese *parcheesi*)   Impermanence

Swallow (*Tsubame*)   Transience ('Wet swallow with an uncharted tomorrow')

Tape (*Tēpu*)   Lingering attachment
Tolling (*Kane*)   Impermanence
Traces (*Omokage*)   1 Longing. 2 Lingering attachment
Train (*Kisha, Ressha*)   Sorrow, grief, nostalgia
Twilight (*Tasogare*)   Sadness, loneliness ('Alone in the twilight of the capital')
Water, Water's flow (*Mizu, Mizu no nagare*)   Impermanence
Water grass (*Mizukusa*)   Wandering
Waves (*Nami*)   Impermanence
Whistling (*Kuchibue*)   1 Loneliness, sorrow ('Parting alone and whistling'). 2 Happiness, hope
Wild geese (*Karigane*)   Impermanence, wandering
Wilderness (*Areno*)   Wandering, solitude
Wind (*Kaze*)   Impermanence ('As the wind changes so too will I change')
Window (*Mado*)   1 Aspiration, hope. 2 Loneliness
Wings (*Tsubasa*)   Hope

Table A1.1 *Proportional occurrence of emotional motifs in Japanese popular songs*

$$\frac{\text{Number of songs in time period with given motif}}{\text{Total number of songs in time period}} \times 100$$

a	Criticism
b	Sarcasm
c	Anger
d	*Ressentiment*
e	Despair
f	Self-scorn
g	Jest
h	Joy
i	Hope
j	Ambition
k	Chivalry
l	Longing
m	Amae
n	Coquetry
p	Bantering
q	Resignation and Lingering attachment (*miren*)
r	Loneliness
s	Emotional blockage
t	Nostalgia
u	Yearning
w	Transience

Time period	No. of songs	a	b	c	d	e	f	g	h	i	j	k	l	m	n	p	q	r	s	t	u	w
1868–74	33	6.1	12.1		6.1	6.1	3.0	57.6	6.1	6.1	6.1	3.0	9.1	6.1	6.1	12.1						
1875–81	20	10.0	25.0			5.0		70.0	5.0	5.0	10.0	5.0	5.0		5.0	15.0						
1882–8	34	20.6	11.8	11.8	2.9	5.9	2.9	32.4	3.9	11.8	23.5	11.8	5.9		2.9	2.9				2.9		
1889–95	36	19.4	11.1	13.9	2.8	8.3		19.4	25.0		25.0	16.7	5.6	2.8	2.8	2.8	2.8		2.8	5.6	5.6	5.6
1896–1902	38	5.3	2.6	2.6			23.8	18.4	15.8		7.9	5.3	7.9			13.2	7.9		5.3	5.3	5.3	7.9
1903–9	32	18.8	28.1	12.5	28.1	9.4	21.9	15.6	3.3		6.3	3.1	15.6	3.1	3.1	21.9	21.9		15.6	3.1		18.8
1910–16	29	3.4	20.7	3.4	6.9	20.7	13.8	31.0				3.4	20.7			24.1	6.9			3.4		17.2
1917–23	21	9.5	19.0			19.0	23.8	19.0	4.8		4.8		19.0		9.5	9.5		9.5	9.5	4.8	4.8	23.8
1924–30	36		2.8	5.6	5.6	2.8	8.3	11.1	11.1	11.1	5.6	2.8	22.2	5.6	2.8	8.3	16.7	22.2		13.9	5.6	22.2

	N																					
1931–7	44	4.5	6.8	11.4	2.3	18.2	9.1	4.5	13.7	34.1	4.5	4.5		18.2	29.5	6.8	6.8	4.5	40.9		
1938–44	30	6.7	3.3	3.3	6.7	10.0	16.7	13.3	16.7	20.0	3.3			20.0	13.3	3.3	23.3	16.7	36.7		
1945–51	36	2.8	2.8	8.3	8.3	11.1	8.3	2.8	2.8	55.6	2.8	2.8		22.2	19.4	2.8	19.4	11.1	19.4		
1952–8	28	10.7	10.7	3.6	3.6	7.1	3.6	7.1	7.1	60.7	7.1	7.1		50.0	14.3	3.6	10.7	7.1	28.6		
1959–63	34	5.9	2.9	14.7	11.8	11.8	11.8	2.9	8.8	50.0	11.8	5.9	2.9	23.5	23.5	2.9	11.8	5.9	23.5		
Number Total	451	30	40	15	26	34	40	91	44	25	38	34	109	18	15	37	62	47	15	37	22	81
Percentage		6.7	8.9	3.3	5.8	7.5	8.9	20.2	9.8	5.5	8.1	7.5	24.2	4.0	3.3	8.2	13.7	10.4	3.3	8.2	4.9	18.0

Note: See Chapter 1.

PART TWO

THE SOCIAL PSYCHOLOGY OF MODERNIZING JAPAN

12 Archetypes of Social Response during the Meiji Restoration

I Topic, data and methodology

1 A search for enduring patterns

As a watershed of transformation in modern Japan, the Meiji Restoration is comparable with no other event except perhaps the defeat of 1945, for it prescribed the fundamental characteristics of Japanese society thereafter. The topic of this and the following chapter is limited to the ways in which the people[1] of Japan parried the upheavals in their lives at the time. The focus is on the molding during the Restoration period of deep patterns which have continued up to the present to orient the ways in which people live in modernized Japan.

Two fascinating themes are omitted from the discussion. The first is an examination of the *causes* of the Meiji Restoration through factors of social psychology. As long as due care is taken to pursue the inquiry properly, so as not to fall into a psychologistic and thus inaccurate interpretation of history, it would no doubt be very fruitful. One could use social psychology to examine the parameters linking, say, socioeconomic factors with the modes of behavior of the groups which promoted the Restoration, or alternatively, to discuss the 'determining functions' which mediate the processes of response to sets of exogenous and indogenous conditions, and so influence the course of history. But that sort of inquiry lies beyond the present purview, even though these two chapters may offer some secondary, piecemeal contributions along those lines.

The second theme would be an investigation through social psychology of the *processes* of the Restoration movement. For example, the dynamics of human relations within and between the various groups which energized it. Again, this interesting line of inquiry is beside the point. We shall cleave to an analysis of *patterns in the people's modes of coping* with the Restoration, as a

141

means for pursuing archetypal patterns in the lives of modernized Japanese.

The reason for these limitations is that my ultimate goal is not to elucidate the Meiji Restoration as an historical phenomenon. I aim instead to grasp in its totality the framework of the social psychology of modern Japan as it has endured into the present. As the first step in that project, let us analyze the modes through which the common people responded to the momentous events of the Restoration period.

2 Sources for symbols (of, for and by the people)

Many excellent studies of the mentality of the Restoration elites have been carried out in the areas of political, economic and intellectual history. But the mentality and attitudes of the common people during the Restoration period have not yet been investigated in a systematic, comprehensive manner.

Of course no opinion polls or attitude surveys were carried out in the early Meiji years. Nor was anyone compiling the sorts of direct behavioral data that might allow us to grasp the situation in quantitative sociological terms, such as statistics on crime, antisocial conduct, suicide, or marriage and divorce. Aside from some fragmentary demographics, the only quantitative data available to us are basic statistics on schools, newspapers, and shrines and temples, as well as some incomplete figures on peasant uprisings and acts of destruction. It is thus virtually impossible to revive quantitatively the social psychology of the period.

The richest source of original data which can serve our purpose, and which exists in systematic form, is the newspaper columns of the day. Newspaper articles can be regarded, first, as records which pertain to the contemporary actualities of social psychology, or to put it another way, as 'symbols *of* the people.' Second, through the arrangement, emphasis and appraisal of the events they cover, news articles offer a handhold on the psychology of the readers whose inclinations they served; in this sense they are 'symbols *for* the people.' Third, in contributions from readers (including letters, parodies, poems, jokes, etc.), we find direct articulation of popular psychology, and thus newspapers also comprise 'symbols *by* the people.'[2]

The first Japanese-language newspaper, in 1862, was the *Kanban Batabia Shimbun*, published by Yorozuya Heishiro, who also established the *Kaigai Shimbun* around the same time. These contained only foreign news and reprints from Chinese magazines, and are therefore of very little interest for data on Japanese social psychology. Then the civil war of 1868 created a broad demand for news, and from that year newspapers covering domestic events began publication one after another, beginning with *Chūgai Shimbun*.[3]

From our standpoint a hundred years on, if we seek to establish hard factual data to probe the social psychology of the period, there is virtually nothing to choose from but these newspapers. Most directly valuable are the articles and comments on phases of life at the time. The authenticity of the news reports is conspicuously weak, with frequent attributions to 'hearsay' or 'crewmen's accounts.' It would be a waste of time to check questionable articles against other newspapers, since their sources may well have been the same rumor mill. While we therefore cannot accept the reported 'facts' themselves as data, we can still accept the social-psychological fact that these rumors actually existed. That a reporter would invent a rumor is not inconceivable, but it was in all probability rather rare. At the most basic level, the authenticity of newspaper articles as artifacts is indisputable, for who would take the trouble to produce a backdated counterfeit edition at a later date?

Do typical patterns of living and coping fall within the newspapers' coverage? We may tentatively assume that they do, and that the coverage reflects to some extent the different generations and social classes, albeit with varying degrees of clarity. Of course it is in the nature of a reporter to emphasize factors which at the time are regarded as more or less atypical, a tendency which must be carefully considered in evaluating the material.

Then again, even though our purpose is to find out what was normal at the time, bias toward the unusual is not such a fatal difficulty as it might seem at first glance. In the first place, marked regional contrasts in societal energy and character were a particular feature of the Restoration period. Something that was in fact normal in one locality was often a natural object of curiosity in others, and hence the stuff of articles. This was most pervasively the case for country folk with respect to the new urban norms of 'civilization and enlightenment' (the rapid adoption of Western customs and inventions); as well as for urban sophisticates with respect to the normalcy of 'quaint' customs in 'remote' villages.

143

In the second place, the Restoration was a period of stormy and historic transformation, and the suddenness with which things constantly *became* normal provoked deeply felt accounts. Third, the peculiar facts appearing in the newspapers often had what might be called a quintessential grain, in that they threw general trends into relief in an extreme or pure fashion. Fourth, when newspaper material is regarded not as a source of fact, but as an indication of where the readers' interests lie (symbols *for* the people), the issue of unusualness evaporates. For, as a rule, newspapers, being commercial enterprises, make every effort to appeal to the habitual interests of the populace.

Coverage of underlying causes and background factors leading up to the reported events is undeniably shallow in Restoration-era newspapers. This reflects both the technical problem of limited space for news accounts, and the immaturity of the journalism profession at the time. On the other hand, during this anomic period of fluctuation in the social and political order, there was less interference from official censors, and less suppression of certain types of news in the name of 'good sense' than in later times.

For data weighted toward the social psychology of the peasants, who made up 80 per cent of the population at the time, we can make use of various documents related to peasant uprisings.[4] These include drawings and descriptions of the disturbances (symbols of the people), lists of demands (by the people), and propaganda posters and proclamations (for the people).

Scores of uprisings occurred during the Restoration period, the largest of them involving tens and even hundreds of thousands of participants. Their modality of demands and action was the tip of the iceberg. Below the surface were the hopes, the stakes, the sympathies and the righteousness of many other peasants who either lacked the resolve to risk their lives by joining in the disturbances, or did not have the opportunity. Unfortunately, we have no reliable way to estimate the size of the popular base supporting the revolts.

At any rate, the majority of the rural population weathered the Restoration upheavals in relative tranquility. In order to shed light on their aspirations, morality, aesthetics and worldview, aside from fragmentary journalistic evidence, we can turn only to anthropological data (mainly, symbols of the people). Such data tends to be weakened by the frequent impossibility of precise dating, as well as by the potential for distortion through oral transmission. Modern historical research has alleviated these handicaps to some extent, but it is still advisable to shore up and confirm anthropological material through other documentary sources whenever possible.

Data on the mentality of the urban *chōnin* or merchant class around the time of the Restoration survives today in the form of popular songs, including many parodies and satires; as well as in graffiti and other scribblings, satirical poems, and posters and handbills from the urban centers of Kyoto and Edo/Tokyo.[5] These can be classed as symbols both by and for the people.[6]

Concerning the *bunmei-kaika* or 'civilization and enlightenment' movement, excellent mines of original data exist in two genres of booklets: the 'accounts of flourishing prosperity' (symbols of the people), and the 'enlightenment manuals' for Western-style living (for the people).[7] These served two functions: to guide those who wanted to adapt to modern customs, and to furnish topics of conversation for others who were merely curious. (Apparently they were typical souvenirs of Tokyo in the countryside, and 'must' reading for local opinion leaders and informational gatekeepers.) As guides they were required to be more-or-less accurate records, while as centerpieces of conversation they were prone to embellishment, exaggeration and rumor. Hence we must be on guard for distortions. Meanwhile, the very fact that the people delighted in such hyperbole, that such rumors circulated, constitutes social-psychological data in its own right.

3   Historical Social Psychology: An Analytical
    Framework of Mentality

Before presenting the data, I will outline an organizational framework for arranging the descriptive and analytical results that will emerge. This schematic discussion will also touch on the nature of the social-psychological approach to history. In particular, what I wish to develop here is a method for the schematization of data and constructs which represent the consciousness of a people.[8]

To begin with, I divide the set of internal elements that regulate people's patterns of behavior into *motivational* factors which impel people to act, and *normative* factors which control the orientation of their actions. Behavior proceeds from motivations (that is, *desires*), but it is shunted by normative factors into actions which are roundabout or retardative, regressive or reactive, substitutive or symbolic. The three basic patterns of this self-regulation arise from sensitivity toward normal, appreciative or cognitive norms. I refer to these three sets of internal factors as *morality, aesthetics* and *worldview*.

The principles or standards which govern the spheres of worldview, morality, aesthetics and desires are of course 'truth,' 'goodness,' 'beauty' and 'happiness.' In sum, people's behavior is motivated by desires which aim toward happiness, and it is modulated and oriented by their worldview, morality and aesthetic, which aim toward truth, goodness and beauty.

These factors usually overlap and operate in tandem. Morals are based on worldview (e.g. the worldview of the 'unbroken imperial line' and the moral of patriotic loyalty). Worldview is skewed by desires and aesthetics (into wishful thinking and other illusions). Morality is internalized so thoroughly that the norm itself ends up as the desire (goodness equals happiness: 'I follow my heart's desire to hew to the golden rule'), and so forth.

This organic constellation of interactive desires, aesthetics, worldview and morality is the totality which I designate as the mental structure or the *frame of consciousness* of an individual, a group or a historical society.

Desires, aesthetics and morality are each a differential mix of countless value judgments, both actual and latent. Only the worldview, even as it influences value judgments, consists of perceptions of reality (actual and latent). This distinction allows us to sum up desires, aesthetics and morality as *value consciousness*, as opposed to *worldview* or the sense of 'reality.'

To recapitulate the elements which govern behavior:

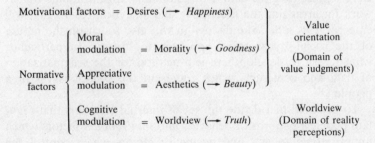

Accordingly, historical social psychology, or the *historical study of the mental framework of the people*, includes these four analytical subject areas.

1 *History of desires*: The history of views of happiness and the 'fruits of life,' and their social and cultural foundations. Patterns and defining factors of desires for wealth, power, fame, etc. Shifts in the content of images of 'success,' and their social foundations. Patterns of dissatisfaction and unhappiness, and the background of prescriptive social factors . . .

2 *History of morality*: Shifts in principles regulating daily interpersonal relations, and their foundations. The history of aberrant behavior and social sanctions. Shifts in objects of loyalty and qualitative changes in the composition of loyalty . . .

3 *History of aesthetics*: Historical changes in aesthetic expression in the popular and 'marginal' arts. Shifts in taste. History of fashion . . .

4 *History of worldviews:* Historical changes in views of the cosmos, humanity and society. Superstitions, myths and illusions. Literacy and diffusion of knowledge. Consciousness of self and position in society, and its shifts in distribution. History of Zeitgeist, of the sense of history, and image of the future, and their foundations . . .

Much more could be said about the nature of historical social psychology, but the preceding descriptive and analytical considerations will suffice to outline the methodology by which historical phenomena are approached in this and the following chapter.

II Eejanaika: liberation of desire and desire for liberation

It is well known that peasant uprisings occurred on an unprecedented scale during the years surrounding the Meiji Restoration.[9] Yet as can be seen in Figure 12.1, there was a trough in the number of incidents during the decisive year of 1867. In

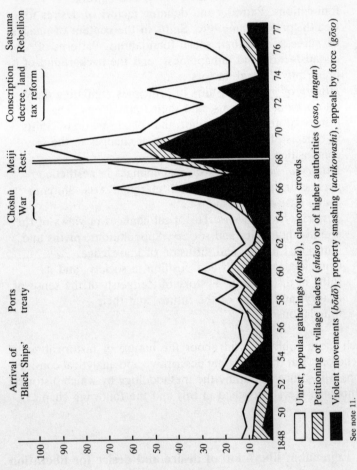

Figure 12.1 *Number of peasant disturbances by year*

□ Unrest, popular gatherings (*tonshū*), clamorous crowds

▨ Petitioning of village leaders (*shūso*) or of higher authorities (*osso, tangan*)

■ Violent movements (*bōdō*), property smashing (*uchikowashi*), appeals by force (*gōso*)

See note 11.

the sharply shrunken area of the graph for that year, as if buried respectably away, lie incidents of 'ecstatic mass violence' in the areas of Nagoya, Tōkaidō, Kyoto, Osaka, Nishinomiya, Edo, Yokohama, Shinshū, Ise, Awaji, Awa, Sanuki and Aizu. Their rallying call was *'Eejanaika'* – 'Why not? It's all right.'[10]

Mass pilgrimages to the supremely sacred Grand Shrines of Ise occurred at intervals of roughly sixty years from 1650 to 1830, and another took place over several weeks in 1867, two decades early. In the worldview of the people of the time, this promoted a perception that extraordinary times were upon them, an amorphous premonition that the time was nigh for a shift in the flow of historical cycles. This sense of extraordinary moment gave rise to an *across-the-board affirmation of desires* (in contrast to the later ethos of the so-called Great East Asian War, when the same historical sense was linked to the total *negation* of desire, as in the slogan, 'Desirelessly, on to victory!')

One of the ordering principles of traditional village society was the alternating cycle of *hare* (festive or ceremonial periods) and *ke* (ordinary everyday life).[12] Entry into the special time of *hare* was seen as an historical turning, the arrival of the 'world of the gods,' and linked with this was a sense of the liberation of desires, to the point of virtually unregulated amplification. The disappearance of mechanisms which regulate desires was a premise of that worldview. Yet paradoxically, hidden within that premise was a sense of powerlessness, of not possessing in oneself the power to mold and constitute the awaited world.

We may surmise the whereabouts of the people's desires on the eve of the Restoration through the many parodies which they sang, and the modes of behavior of the unruly mobs. *As directly expressed*, they were often desires for unlimited amounts of food and drink, and sex.[13] But interestingly, many contemporary materials include testimony of the following character: in Awa, 'As they danced through the house, they would bring out clothing and implements and cash and, with a chorus of *eijanaika*, throw them away or give them to others.' In Kyoto, 'Singing praises of sake, as if they were at a cherry blossom-viewing party in Edo, they would lift the barrel and repeatedly encourage all present to "Have a drink, *eijanaika, eijanaika*." ' In Yamada: 'The Ise pilgrims scattered money around in such great quantities, it was said that a beggar could pick up two thousand coins in a day. Then the beggars scattered the money they had gathered and heedlessly left it where it lay.'

It seems that rather than desires for plenty of food, drink or sex, the true motives behind the wreaking of 'ecstatic mass violence' had more to do with the demand for an escape from the routine framework of contemporary society, in which concern for social sanctions and social advantage placed manifold restrictions on their lives.[14] For the stifled people at the end of the feudal age, the *liberation of natural desires* signified by gluttony and sexual revelry was nothing more than an actualistic form of expression of their *desires for social liberation*. Accordingly, in the songs of the time, rather than *a*moral sexual enjoyment in itself, we find lyrics about adultery and orgies which deliberately reject the existing morals, which are *anti*moral.

This order-smashing energy was naturally directed most vehemently at those oppressors nearest to hand who were *real-life embodiments* of the Tokugawa social order – the village headman and the prominent merchants:

With frenzied cries of 'Eijanaika, eijanaika' they danced through the houses with their shoes on, oblivious of sitting rooms or private rooms, unrestrained by the official dignity of the elders.
They went after the ones who had always been hateful fellows and dictators, and purposefully danced into their houses crying 'eijanaika,' destroyed the floor mats and fixtures and seized what valuable items they could, dancing all the while.[15]

There are various theories concerning machinations from above in all this, although reliable evidence has not yet been discovered. Was it the strategy of the anti-shogunate royalist leaders to make it look as if their own movement was initiated among the people? Or did they instead avail themselves of hidden opportunities to exploit and amplify events which happened to occur? Either way, it is all but impossible to discount the intervention of the political aims of the royalists. With one hand they maximized the release of the order-destroying *energy* enfolded within the people's desires for release from oppression, and with the other they rendered its *orientation* completely innocuous by means of reform-from-above. Through their dual manipulations, the instigators of the Restoration reforms achieved brilliant success, probably exceeding their own expectations.

The people, having stored up their dissatisfactions with the feudal order, did not look within themselves for the power to bring forth a new world. They required the power of a higher realm, be it divine or elite. The top-down-reform pattern of the Meiji Restoration precisely mirrors this structure of the people's consciousness.

Happiness and unhappiness were conceived by the peasant society entirely in terms of good and bad harvests, governed by the meteorological whims of 'nature' which was beyond the reach of human activity. Hence, for example, Shinto talismans are seen as 'lucky omens for a fruitful year.' In line with this concept, a 'merry season' of popular rowdiness simply occurred in the course of things, and the Restoration itself, for the majority of the people, was a shift in the affairs of 'nature', beyond the sphere of their own actions.

Eejanaika was clearly an emotional symbol which 'expressed thoroughgoing affirmation and thoroughgoing renunciation in a single phase' (Nakano Taku). Viewed more elaborately, the affirmation and renunciation contained in this symbol operated in two significant ways. It represented a sweeping affirmation of desires via total renunciation of existing value standards, and at the same time, an affirmation of the 'natural' trend of the times via renunciation of the independent ego. The capacity for critical thought – for the individual mind to actively critique, design and reconstruct the world – was thoroughly relinquished, but by way of compensation, the fulfillment of desires was for the first time sweepingly affirmed. Inherent within this mental posture were the conditions whereby the liberated basic energies of the people would naturally be deflected and channeled into the new social order. And the Resoration reforms, after they were consummated, exhibited a substance which reflected the dual connotations of *eejanaika*.

Yoijanaikae, Along the Sumida River, Viewing the flowers,
    the moon and the snow
Yoijanaikae, No one gets angry, Speaking together and
    understanding each other's heart

In this parodic version of the 'Eejanaika' song, current in Edo in

151

1868 (Meiji 1), the wild, anarchic energy of the previous year's song has completely disappeared. Likewise in *Miyako shin-torioi* ('The Capital's New Wandering Minstrel'), popular at the same time:

'Tis a world of contentment, Progressing peaceably,
Cooling down, Yoijanaika, Yoijanaika,
Gods of happiness have come from on high,
Samurai gentlemen incline toward the temples,
And the people are rejoicing,
And in the hallowed halls of state,
Everyone handling the affairs
The Ministry of the Right, Ministry of the Left,
And the governors and the plenums,
Are supervised by the Councillors. And in the capital,
In Toshū, in Satsuma, in Hagi, Hiroshima, Nagoya and
  Fukui,
All pray first for the eternal Imperial dynasty,
May the reign be blessed with prosperity.

Then, in 1869, the order-destroying eejanaika energy presents itself during the Hida-Takayama peasant revolt:

in the city center a total of 36 samurai residences and houses of prostitution were smashed apart. Pawnshop articles were scattered all about the town. A riotous crowd broke into a newly constructed storehouse packed full of paper, sake and oil, scattering supplies of unavailable paper up to everyone's knees. Sake and oil were spread through the city and the river as people raised hearty toasts and continued to riot.
(*Meiji Shimbun*, 4 May 1869)

On the causes of that riot, an official history of the Nagano region states: 'At the time of the Restoration, [the new] governor of the district wanted to swiftly eradicate previous abuses, but everyone found his orders to be strange. In addition, the people still yearned for the familiar Bakufu administration, and there had been an uproar of complaint in the villages and towns from August or September 1868 onward.' This explanation must be taken with a grain of salt, for it is the account prepared by the Restoration government. We will delve into the real causes of the riot in the next section.

The energy of popular dissatisfaction at the close of the feudal era – the energy expressed in *eejanaika* – took two paths after the Restoration. Some of it was absorbed by the oligarchy who were the beneficiaries of the Meiji state, while some of it followed the opposite political vector, and continued for many years to shake up the lower strata of the Meiji state.

III Early-Meiji zeal: social upheaval and the molding of the anti-establishment mentality

There was a new upsurge of peasant uprisings immediately after the Restoration of 1868 (as shown in Figure 12.1). In terms of social psychology, the popular mood of excitement and exaltation during the early Meiji years was rooted in four aspects of the peasant mentality:

1 *Rebelliousness*, accumulated through the heightening of economic contradictions in the closing years of the feudal era.
2 *Political realism*, born from first-hand experience of oscillations in the system of political control during the late-Tokugawa and early-Meiji upheavals.
3 *Political fervor*, ignited by anti-shogunate and post-Restoration ideology and then, as a result of disillusionment with actual policies, converted to anti-establishment feeling.
4 *Outrage*, at fresh usurpations and authoritarian actions by the Meiji government during its initital consolidation of power.

This section outlines the clusters of factors which made up these salient aspects of the farmers' mood, with emphasis upon the third point, which is the central topic of this study.

1 Economically motivated rebelliousness

The expansion of commerce during the last decades of the Tokugawa regime prompted a multifaceted transformation of peasant

153

consciousness, through a variety of cause-and-effect linkages. Due to the permeation of commodity economics, the poverty of the samurai was shifted onto the shoulders of those who were the economic foundation of the samurai class, the peasants, in the form of taxes. Already near subsistence level (the policy toward them was termed, 'Don't let them live but don't let them die'), now that every drop of surplus value was being squeezed from them, the peasants had a heightened sense of peril. At the same time, the commercialization of crops furnished the upper tier of farmers with the opportunity to accumulate surplus value, leading to segmentation of the farming population, which in turn produced class antagonisms.

The structural parasitism of the upper tier of farmers, who had long exercised feudalistic power as village headmen, patrons and overseers, was doubled and trebled as their windfalls led to usury and other economic machinations, at the expense of the lower-class peasants who were gasping for survival. From the late-seventeenth through the mid-eighteenth century, the farmers-united character of peasant revolts shifted to include aspects of class struggle, notably attacks on landlords and movements to recall village officials. The outbreak and suppression of uprisings had escalated feelings of mistrust for the ruling class among the participants and the other peasants in many districts. These experiences also generated an amorphous body of organizational savoir-faire and 'agitation skills,' which to one degree or another was passed on from generation to generation.

The impoverishment of the samurai class also led to the decline of its social and moral prestige, and in particular placed the warrior families at the financial mercy of wealthy operators. The inability of the daimyo or the local shogunate officials to restrain racketeering – cornering of rice markets or padding of crop taxes, at the expense of peasants and the urban lower class – led to a further loss of respect for feudal authority, and provoked further mistrust and opposition among peasants.[16]

All of these factors, along with the general broadening of the farmer's sphere of life and range of concerns, brought on by the spread of the commodity economy, gradually gave shape to a new morality and a changed worldview among the peasantry. See Figure 12.2.

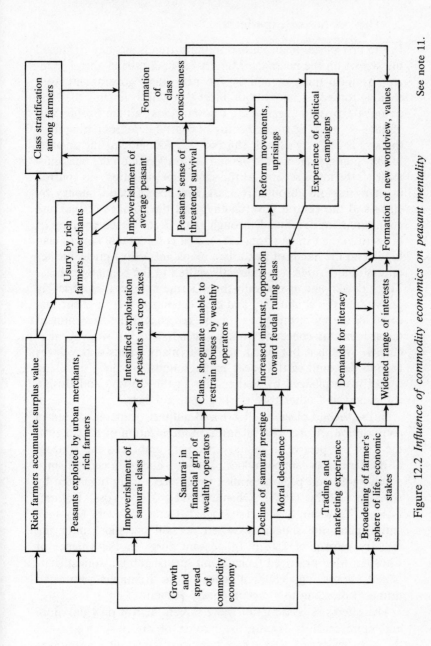

Figure 12.2 *Influence of commodity economics on peasant mentality*   See note 11.

155

2 The politics of experience

In the first place, financial and military trends steadily tightened the screws on the peasants. Military expenditures by the shogunate, by local daimyo, and by the new Meiji government were steadily forced higher by both internal conflicts (notably the 1864 punitive expedition against the Chōshū clans and the Boshin War of 1868–9), and the strengthening of coastal defenses dating from the arrival of Perry's Black Ships in 1853 (demanding the opening of the country). Hence the burden of taxation upon the peasantry grew all the more severe. At the same time, inflation was spurred in many regions through reckless issuance of paper money by clans and the central government[17] and the coinage of bad and counterfeit money,[18] and through the effects of the opening of ports to foreign trade (from 1858). The considerable flow of clan funds into the hands of rich urban merchants drove prices further up, and the burden was indirectly shifted to the common people. These developments naturally made farmers, by now inextricably drawn into the commodity and cash economy, feel their survival to be all the more threatened; and exacerbated their resentment toward the tax-collecting village officials and the wealthy merchants. And last but often not least, many towns and villages around defeated castles, near battlegrounds, or along marching routes were pillaged by soldiers during the Chōshū and Boshin campaigns and other royalist-shogunate conflicts.[19]

In the second place, the increased military preparations led to conscription. Along with technical modernization of armaments, the new perspective in military planning embraced the concept of the farmer as cannon fodder. The idea had been current since about 1840, and peasant armies were successively organized by clans in Chōshū (1849), Obama (1851), Mito, Tosa, Kokura, Geishū, Tsuwano, Kishū, Tsu, Ogaki, Ueda, Echizen, Kawagoe and Sendai; the shogunate raised peasant battalions after the military reform of 1862.[20] In peasant corps in the villages of Chōshū, 'Men practiced fencing and spear-fighting, women sharpened swords, and children practiced as drummers with *taiko* drums,' according to a contemporary account.

The effects of conscription were threefold: Not only did more and more farmers assume the burden of direct service. Also, the very existence of the new practice of peasant conscription implanted anxiety in the hearts of all farmers. And finally, through such formalities as official 'permission to bear a surname and wear a sword', a sense of political constituency and participation was germinated among the peasants.[21]

Third, a slackening of the administrative and judicial apparatus at the fringes of the shogun-daimyo power structures created conditions which were more favorable than ever for the birth and diffusion of anti-feudal thinking. The massive Nagaoka revolt of 1868 (in Echigo) and the ensuing wave of uprisings in the Tōhoku and Hokuriku regions were occasioned by the civil war-induced shakiness of the regime in general.

Fourth, the value hierarchy that was deeply implanted in the minds of the farmers was jolted by such things as the sight of daimyo being routed, and the adoption of the term Imperial Army. 'Absolute' authority was suddenly relative. There was a palpable sense that 'the world is changing,' and accordingly, the traditional fatalistic worldview was crumbling. See Figure 12.3.

3 Disillusioned ideological fervor

In 1863, some *rōnin* of the 'revere the emperor, expel the barbarians' persuasion infiltrated the Ikuno domain in hopes of raising an army, and participated in a peasant uprising. A propaganda handbill they distributed among the farmers read:

> Recently the relations between the Emperor and the shogun have not been good. The exact day is unknown, but the banners will be raised in Kyoto, and then all Japan will be divided in two, east and west. In that year the farmers west of Kyoto will be exempt from taxes, and thereafter they will submit only seventy percent, with a thirty-percent exemption. . . . Those who immediately join our side depending on the degree of their service, will be allowed to carry swords and will be given names, and some will receive salaries or other rewards.

The agitation of these imperial patriots included both the romanticism of revolutionary zealots who staked their personal ideals upon Restoration reform, and the pragmatism of manipulative campaigners who appealed irresponsibly to people's desires.

The 'grand edict' announcing the return to imperial rule, issued on February 9, 1867, included the following paragraph:

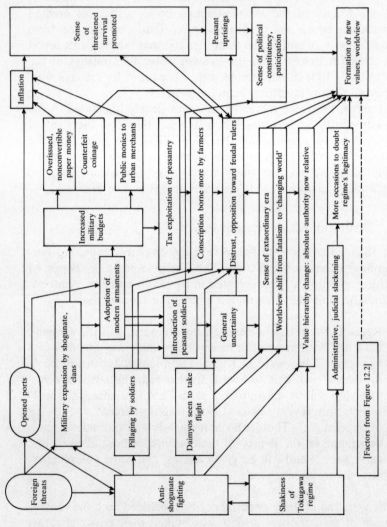

Figure 12.3 *Influence of political realities on peasant mentality*

The recent tendency is for prices to rise remarkably and out of all proportion, to the profit of the rich who grow richer, while the poor tend to grow rapidly poorer, all as the result of unfair administrative orders. The people are the great treasure of the monarch, and on this occasion of the restoration and renewal of all things, his heart is moved by their sufferings. We call upon those who have resourceful and farsighted policies for rescuing us from evil to let themselves be known.

Thus the proclamation of the Restoration made reference to the concrete everday problems of the common people, with a public undertaking to control prices.

At the time, the Restoration was known as *go-isshin*, written with characters meaning 'honorable whole renewal' – signifying reform that was at once sent from above (hence honorable), and thoroughgoing. It later came to be known by the current term *ishin*, literally 'tying anew'.[22]

In March 1867 on the Oki Islands in the Japan Sea, a group of three hundred rural residents (one source says three thousand), including farmers, soldiers and scholars, rose up to demand their rights. In a mass meeting it was decided to exile the district representative of the shogunate: 'Indeed upon this august occasion of the Restoration, he should quickly quit this district which lies in the domain of the Imperial Court.' The leader of the group, who held that, 'Corrupt officials and petty officials should be driven out one and all,' based his value judgment on the authority of the Emperor as transcending the feudal status hierarchy. 'Though until now we have considered ourselves the lowliest, and acted with vacillation and neglect, from today we must be citizens of the Empire.'

Given that the emperor was a quasi-transcendent entity, the concept of 'all people under one ruler' served, in its limited way, as a functional substitute for 'equality under god.'

Following the typical pattern, the autonomous government in Okinoshima, which had risen up to overthrow and expel the shogunate's representative, was officially recognized by the regional administration of the new Restoration government. During the period of civil conflict when organs of shogunate and clan rule still survived, the Restoration government went so far as to directly and indirectly assist peasant revolts, as means of overthrowing them from below.[23] But even during this transition period, the new government felt it necessary to remind the people that they were still under systemic restraint:

> There may be some among the common people who believe that the Restoration has stripped away everything that has obtained up to the present, and that today or tomorrow they will be able to get money without any effort. Let it be known that this is a misunderstanding.
>
> (Proclamation by the Nagasaki law court, March 1867)

On the very day of the announcement of the emperor's five-point Charter Oath in 1868, the five notices which were posted for the public restrained the exercise of actual power by the people. They strictly forbade 'the heretical Christian religion,' and expressly banned the 'establishment of factions for direct petitioning or groups extending beyond home areas.'

A vanguard unit of the imperial army which was deployed in the Kanto region pledged to halve the crop taxes, and were greeted as saviors by the peasants. However, the central command soon judged them to have been carried away by the severe popular disaffection with the old regime, branded them a 'false imperial army,' and executed them.

The head officer of a similar vanguard unit in Hida-Takayama earned the adoration of the populace by ordering a halving of that year's crop levy and cancelling other peasant obligations. A few weeks later the Restoration government discharged and punished him, for having overstepped in directly implementing the ideas that the government itself had floated. His successor rescinded the tax reduction and followed the central-government policy of reliance on the landlords and rich merchants of the area. The result was the Hida-Takayama uprising of 1869 (described in the previous section). It was not motivated by loyalty to the 'familiar' old regime of the clan and shogun, but rather was directly incited by the new government's reversion to old patterns. It was engendered by the contradiction between the stated and hidden agendas of the government, between the people's expectations and the developing realities.

As for the autonomous government of Okinoshima, after the civil conflicts were over and the Meiji government had deposed the Tottori clan and solidified its position, the leaders of the uprising were tried and punished in February 1871, four years after the fact.

In a millenarian *yonaoshi* (world renewal) movement in the Tome district of Rikuzen (now Miyagi) in January 1871, impoverished farmers who had lost their land during a famine in the early 1830s filed suit in the prefectural court, claiming: 'The lands which were conveyed in the past should now, under the purity of the Restoration of Imperial Rule, be returned without any payment, and if by some chance the prefectural government should refuse to make the award, we have no doubt that the noble central government will sustain our petition.' Instead, they were cross-examined by the court, forced to submit a written apology, and dismissed with an admonition to 'be cautious in future.' Whereupon the farmers decided to 'ask some questions through soldiers,' and proceeded to organize an army, only to be quickly subjugated by forces of the Restoration government.[24]

The Restoration of imperial purity had become the restoration of the old power structure. The burdens upon the peasant class were never mitigated. Instead they were forced to assume as well the new burdens of conscription and of supplying revenue for schools and other aspects of modernization-from-above. (See Figure 12.4.)

The Restoration government's *idea* of 'the people' as the supposed 'great treasure of the emperor' stands out from the back-

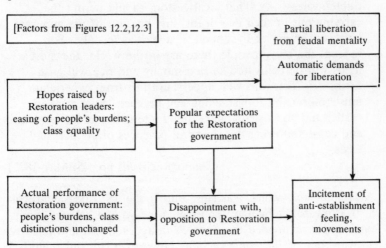

Figure 12.4 *Disillusioned ideological fervor and peasant mentality*

ground of the *reality* of the people's lives. Here is an excerpt from an 1872 memorial 'On Methods of Childrearing' by a prefectural legislative councillor.

> Since assuming my post some time ago it has been my duty to observe local practices. For a long time they have been practicing the bad customs of abortion and infanticide. These corrupt habits are not limited only to the poor, but are also practiced among the middle class. At the extreme, there are cases where babies are murdered after birth with the parents close by.

As a corrective policy, the memorial recommends that 'some monies be granted by the government as capital for raising children.' At the same time, on the bulletin boards in the towns and villages, the terms used were these:

> The essence of humanity is the correct observance of the five cardinal principles of [Confucian] morality. The first principle is filial piety between father and child. Today in this administrative district, poor persons are aborting pregnancies and even resorting to the strangling of newborn babies. Brutal wild eagles are known to cast away their young, but what of humans who are surely meant to rise to righteousness! . . . That local custom should permit the carrying out of such evil deeds, just because of the apparent impoverishment of livelihood, is a serious mistake. For indeed, the more people there are in the world, the more fields will be cultivated so that money and rice will gush forth. . . . You who well understand this from experience must reform this longstanding evil practice, must awaken earlier and go to sleep later. Breed a long line of descendants, and cease following the shameful practices of animals and birds.
>
> (*Shimbun Zasshi*, no. 45, May 1872)

A famous song which was sung during the 1870 peasant revolt in Kashiwazaki, Echigo, entitled *Ahodara-kyō* ('Mock Scripture'), aptly expressed the people's disappointment and mistrust growing out of the contradictions between myth and reality in the imperial state:

Hallelujah, everyone   Won't you listen to us?
The august views of the Imperial Court   Are a pack of lies . . .
In the abode of the gods   All the throats are dry
'Tis all so very splendid   But in truth affairs are wretched[25]

4   Fresh abuse, fresh outrage

Under the crop tax reform which was initiated in 1873, the aggregate quotas for each village went up. Moreover, in many cases the setting of assessments for individual fields within the villages was entrusted to major landlords, who had been designated as representatives of the landholding class. As a result the burdens tended to be shifted more heavily onto minor landowners and tenant farmers, thus intensifying the dissatisfaction of peasants at the middle level and below. Moreover, the local costs of assessing land values and otherwise administering the reform itself were borne by the farmers in each area.[26]

Moreover, while the conversion from in-kind to cash payment may have been an essentially progressive step, the actual result at the time was that smallholders and tenant farmers were left open to the larcenous terms of the merchants who bought up rice with an eye to the tax deadline.[27] Moreover, payment in kind was continued as a provisional measure until the tax rates were determined, but due to a drastic decline in the market price for rice from 1875, conversion at the current price greatly deflated the value of the in-kind payments. This was the direct cause of large-scale peasant revolts during 1876 in Ibaraki, Mie, Gifu, Aichi and Sakai.[28]

Morever, through the Restoration government's reclassification of land into public and private holdings, much of the land which peasants had been utilizing was placed in government ownership or in a few private holdings. The government then acted vigorously to suppress customary usage on lands that had become public holdings. A major result was that poor farmers and tree cultivators, who made up the bulk of the population in mountain villages, were deprived of the traditional bases of their livelihoods.

Moreover, the abolition of the samurai class of feudal retainers led on one hand to the conscription decree of 1873, increasing the burdens and anxieties of the common people; and on the other to the use of public monies for the temporary continuation of the hereditary samurai stipends. Those monies, under the policy of promoting industrialization, tended to be channeled by the government into development capital, leaving the peasant class to foot the bill for public debt as well as taxes.

The first three clusters of factors within the peasant mentality (here classified as rebelliousness, realism, and fervor) constitute the social-psychological grain of zealous exaltation within the early-Meiji peasant movement. The fourth cluster, the fresh sense of victimization, furnished the sparks which ignited the movement, and which were most directly reflected in the demands that were thrown up. (See Figure 12.5.)

IV   Patterns of social demands and their refractions

In this section we shall turn to the demands which were expressed in the scores of documented early-Meiji peasant revolts. More interesting than the demands themselves, of course, are the social patterns with which they were inextricably related. An examination of these patterns, and the ways in which they were frequently refracted in the demands expressed on the surface, will delineate various aspects of the psychology of the peasants at the dawn of modern Japan.

1   Types of demands[29]

The demands voiced in peasant rebellions during the first decade of the Meiji period fall into three categories of substantive opposition to socioeconomic policies and conditions:

I   Demands for abolition or in defiance of *feudalistic restrictions dating from pre-Restoration times*
II   Resistance to the *Restoration government's primal stage of consolidation* through authoritarian measures
III   *Reactionary resistance* to progressive government policies

A final category of demands which were essentially of a simple economic nature is here numerated as 'zero.'

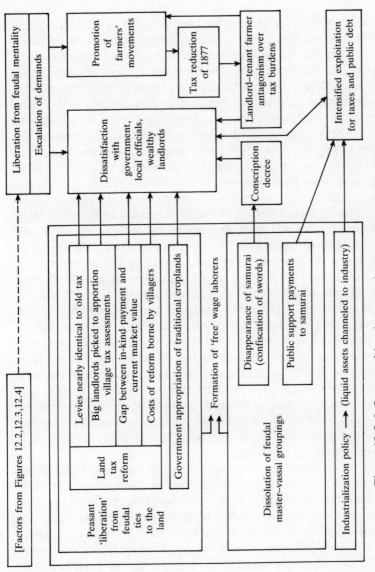

Figure 12.5 *Influence of harsh new policies on peasant mentality*

0   Demands for *protection of livelihood*, mainly economic compensation

The latter range from calls for disaster relief or indemnification of losses, to opposition to army plundering or price inflation; depending on the particular circumstances, some of these are related to category I or II. The most immediately obvious theme of early-Meiji rebellions in general – calls for tax reduction or exemption – tends upon case-by-case investigation to fall into one of the first two categories, of resistance to feudal restrictions or to consoldiation of the new government. Meanwhile, the 'down with the new government' slogan which turned up from about 1871, sometimes in the form of pressure to get rid of local officials, arose from circumstances traceable either to government consolidation (II) or enlightened policies (III) or both.

Table 12.1 classifies the demands expressed in the early-Meiji peasant revolts into these four categories, with an annual breakdown of their appearance. As was just explained with respect to demands for financial relief and for ousting the government, a particular type of demand might fall under category I, II, and/ or III, according to local circumstances at the time. Hence the categorization is somewhat tentative and general, but it will nevertheless be useful as a means of inferring overall trends.

Feudalistic vestiges of the old regime persisted in the first place because the process of forming the modern state was far from complete in the early Meiji years, and also because the new government often relied on them as a framework of control. The first class of demands, those in defiance of the feudal vestiges, consists of efforts from below to supplement the 'total renewal' (*go-isshin*, as the Restoration was then known), as well as to overcome those conditions.

(I–1) *Demands for the removal or indictment of village officials and local administrators*. During the last three months of 1868, a flood tide of uprisings to punish village headmen crested across the northern region which nursed embers from the Aizu war earlier that year. They always included proposals for popular election of headmen. Campaigns involving attacks upon, expulsions or calls for investigation of low-level ruling officials who were holdovers from the Bakufu-daimyo regime (the village and district-level *kimoiri*, *shōya*, *nanushi*, *warimoto* or *kumigashira*), also broke out during 1868 in the provinces of Mimasaka and

Echigo; during 1869 in Rikuzen, Rikuchū and Osaka; and during 1870 in Iyo, Bichū, Mikawa, Bungo and Musashi. In two major region-wide revolts which began in August 1871, in Iyo and in Aki and Bingo, crowds destroyed many homes of headmen who were aligned with efforts to restore daimyo sovereignty.

At that point the Restoration government restructured and renamed the local administrative bodies, yet most of those appointed as mayors (*kuchō* and *kochō*) of the new subdivisions were former headmen from the daimyo days,[30] and the peasants persisted in their movements to drive them out. Uprisings of this nature broke out in succession throughout the country, in the prefectures of Mimitsu in 1872; Iwate, Akita, Ishitetsu, Kokura, Nagasaki, Hiroshima and Ehime in 1873; Shikama and Kumamoto in 1874; Mitsuma in 1875; and Okayama and Miyazaki in 1876. A series of uprisings in Kumamoto during January 1877, on the eve of the Satsuma Rebellion, involved demands for popular election of mayors.

(I–2) *Demands for the disbursement of feudal estates.* The mistrust and rejection of former leaders was directed not only at the village administrations but also at the clans which had ruled the various fiefdoms. As in the 1867 Okinoshima rebellion, the people's bright hopes for the Restoration as a liberation from the yoke of feudal rule could be seen in several uprisings during the first two Meiji years (1868 and 1869). The most notable occurred in six villages of the Otashichi domain in Shinano, in the Gujō domain in Minō, and in 58 villages in the Tayasu domain in Kai.

(I–3) *Demands for equality of social classes.* The smashing of some two hundred and fifty houses by classless peasants demanding equality, during a January 1868 uprising on the Shiakujima islands in Sanuki, seems to have been exceptional. But demands for social equality were not unusual in the so-called intravillage disputes (*murakata* uprisings) by the *komae* farmers, who were traditionally excluded from official membership in the farmer class. In many cases they had managed to accumulate enough wealth to wield some economic power, and came to feel entitled to higher status. The collision of these demands with the old order played an important role in the day-to-day struggles for democratization within the villages.

(I–4) *Refusal of post-route assistance.* Defiance of the shogunate's *sukegō* (assisting village) assignments for transport services

Table 12.1 *Types and frequency of demands in early-Meiji peasant revolts*

Types of demands	1868	69	70	71	72	73	74	75	76	77	Total
I Abolition of feudal systems dating from the Tokugawa period											
1 Expulsion or indictment of local officials	19	23	9	7	2	9	5	1	4	10	89
2 Disbursement of feudal estates	3	2									5
3 Equality of social classes	1	1									2
4 Refusal to provide post-route assistance	2	1									3
5 Change of crop tax to cash levy	2	1	1				4				8
6 Freedom to sell crops		1		1	1						3
II Resistance to consolidation of the Restoration government											
1 Rectification of tax reform (land assessment, devalued kind payments, survey costs, etc.)						6	1	5	15	5	32
2 Opposition to government appropriation (occasional privatization) of village-common mountain and forest lands				1							1
3 Opposition to conscription				1		14	2				17
III Reactions against progressive policies											
1 Opposition to cholera vaccination, telegraphs, railroads, Westernization, etc.			2	3	1	2			1	2	11
2 Retention of discrimination against hereditary outcasts				3	2	5					10
3 Restoration of local clan rule		3		8							11
4 Preservation of Buddhism			1	2	1	3					7

No.	Category	1	2	3	4	5	6	7	8	9	10	Total
0	Protection of livelihood and unclassified demands											
1	Relief or indemnification for bad harvests, natural disasters	2	21	11	1	1	5	3	1	1		46
2	Prevention of or relief for civil-war plunder and impoverishment	4	1									5
3	Prevention of or indemnification for price increases	2	10	3	2	1	1	3		1		23
4	Relief for losses due to bad, counterfeit or outdated currency		5	2			3					10
5	Other demands for rice or money	4	3	1			2		2	3		15
6	Debt deferment of cancellation, lower interest rates, etc.	5	2									7
7	Return of pawned lands, goods	4	3	1						2		10
8	Crop tax reduction, exemption, deferment	8	17	19	11	7	8	3	3	2	1	79
9	Tenant-farmer demands for fee reduction, etc.	10	1	1	1	1		2			4	20
10	'Down with the new government'	1		6				1				8

Multiple demands from the same revolt are entered in various categories, hence annual totals may exceed the numbers of revolts.

The provisional nature of the categorizations is explained in the text. Also, any quantitative analysis of peasant rebellions is subject to various handicaps (see Note 9, below).

The many different demands for rectification of the land tax reform are placed in a single category, as they were intertwined in many revolts. The text provides more detail.

The cutoff date of this table excludes most opposition to cholera vaccination, which peaked in 1879, and to appropriation of mountain and forest lands, which arose during 1879 and later.

Most of the data is from Aoki Kōji, 'Meiji shoki nōmin ikki nenbyō,' *Rekishigaku kenkyū* No. 318, November 1966, pp. 13–27, with additional information from other sources.

between post stations was directly articulated during uprisings in early 1868 in Bichū and in 13 villages in Iwashiro.

(I–5) *Demands to change the crop tax to a cash levy.* This demand appeared early on in two series of rebellions in Iwashiro (Fukushima) in 1868 and 1870. After the 1873 reform which began the change to a cash land tax, opposition to the provisional collection of rice as payment in kind led to rebellions the following January in two areas of Okayama and in Mimizu (Miyazaki). The high price of rice at the time was a major factor.[31] The Wappa Riots in August 1874 in Sakata (Yamagata), which involved ten thousand people, were prompted by the prefectural authorities' concealment of the cash basis of the new land tax, which they attempted to collect in rice as before; the rioters were almost entirely victorious.

(I–6) Demands for freedom to sell crops. From July to December 1869 some thirty thousand peasants in Bungo (Ōita) rebelled with this cause as one of their major demands, and destroyed the designated exclusive dealerships. This demand also appeared in a major uprising in 1871 in Ōsu and in a 24-village uprising in 1872 in Mimizu.

Next is the set of demands raised in opposition to the authoritarian manner in which the Restoration government carried out its primal consolidation of power. Agrarian rebellions reached their historical peak in 1873 (see Figure 1), and most of the large-scale uprisings of that year involved resistance to the land tax and conscription laws which were decreed during the year.

(II–1) *Demands for rectification of the tax reform.* Dissatisfaction with land assessment methods, or with the tax levies for the land survey and for title searches and deed certifications, fueled uprisings in 1873 in Iwate, in Myōtō, and on the islands off Izu; in 1874 in Shikama; and in 1875 in Kagoshima and Gifu.

During 1876 farmers losses were compounded by the depressed rice market, and demands for revised assessments and revaluation of in-kind payments swept the entire country. It began early in the year with scattered small-scale incidents in Tottori and Chikuma. In May in Wakayama, first one group of 17 villages and then another of 8 villages mounted strong but unsuccessful petitions. Movements then arose in June in Toyama, Yamanashi and Yamaguchi, in August in Shizuoka, and in November in Ibaraki and Nagano. Finally, as the result of the Ise Riot which spread in December through several prefectures (see note 28), the government reduced the land tax from three to 2.5 per cent and reduced the supplemental levies by one-fifth to one-third, for an overall tax cut of about 25 per cent.

(II–2) *Resistance to land appropriation*. In the process of assignment of deeds, mountain and forest lands which had been village commons (*iriai*) passed in principle into government ownership, and occasionally into the hands of private landlords. As a harbinger of this conflict, it is known that in 1871 farmers in Nagano planned a rebellion around the claim that it was illegal to award clan lands to the government; beyond that there is no reliable data, although it is commonly believed that the clan's mountain and forest lands had been customarily farmed. The largest incident, in 1880, was the Ueno fodder-land riots which encompassed some eighty villages in Gumma. Similarly motivated uprisings occurred in 1879 in Niigata and in 1883 in Kanagawa and in Minami-tama, Tokyo.

(II–3) *Opposition to conscription*. The earliest uprising of this type was in 1871 in Kōchi, sparked by the announcement that able-bodied men were to register for the prefecture's own draft. In 1873, when the national conscription law took effect, large-scale uprisings occurred in the spring in Watarai, Fukuoka and Ōita. These were dwarfed by incidents that summer, including the three hundred thousand-strong Takeyari Uprising in Fukuoka (one source says one hundred thousand), and revolts involving about twenty thousand people each in Okayama, Tottori and Myōtō. At the same time there were also anti-draft uprisings in Shimane, Hiroshima, Nagasaki, Shirakawa, Ehime and Kyoto. While the 1873 rebellions were concentrated in western and southern Japan, during 1874 other conscription protests occurred in such places as Akita in the north.

Those peasant demands which are significant for their direct connection to the main historical trends of the time (categories I and II) have been described above. Although the documented list of agrarian rebellions is large enough to serve as a springboard for a topology of the 'category 0' economic demands, these are of little importance to the present study. I shall focus instead on the 'reactionary' demands of category III. Belying more complex trends, this is the only set of demands that are strategically significant as data for historical social psychology.

2   Configurations of refraction

Reactionary demands, such as those opposing vaccination or outcast liberation, or supporting clan rule or Buddhism, are by no means a particular, isolated strain of the agrarian rebellions which I have singled out for my own interest. All of the historical data indicates that they were a *common and frequent* element of the early-Meiji uprisings in general.

Since many of those causes did not, objectively speaking, reflect the best interests of the farmers, they may seem to be of 'false' significance. Yet the fact that many farmers risked their lives by standing up to fight for them shows that they were something more than whimsical notions. Clearly, the reactionary slogans were *refracted* articulations of the true interests of the farming population. The modes of refraction are functions of the actual mentality which governed the peasant class.

a   *Defense of Buddhism*
An article in the April (intercalary) 1868 issue of the *Chūgai Shimbun* (no. 26), stated:

> The issuance of the order for unification with Shintō is causing the outbreak of disturbances on a large scale. If it were to lead to the galvanization of the Buddhists it would no doubt immediately shock the whole country like a violent thunderclap, for it would certainly involve forces far greater than those of the daimyo in all quarters. . . . It is to be hoped that His Imperial Highness will bestow his attention on this affair to stave off such a calamity and restore tranquility throughout the land.

This article was translated into Japanese from the English-language *Herald* newspaper (published in Japan). It is the solicitous advice of Western observers, who were estimating the local social psychology in the light of their own dark history of centuries of violent religious wars.

In fact there was surprisingly weak resistance by Buddhists to the new government's order for the merging of religions, and the accompanying 'abolish and destroy Buddha' movement. This confirms that during the Bakuhan days, the Buddhist religious structure had become a hollow shell, a parasite of the political rulers, with no grip on the people's souls.

Nevertheless, spirited resistance was put up on several occasions: the 1870 Echigo uprisings which is famous for the 'Mock-Scripture' song quoted above; the Mikawa Monks Revolt of 1871; an uprising in Shimane the same year; the Irrigation Riots in Echigo involving twenty to thirty thousand people in 1872; and a rebellion by fifteen thousand in three areas of Tsuruga (Kyoto) in 1873. Each of these incidents was the work of followers of Jōdo Shinshū (the True Sect of Pure Land Buddhism). In a time when the people often joined enthusiastically in anti-Buddhist campaigns, when temples generally were targets, not fomenters of destructive attacks, the peculiar belligerence of Jōdo Shinshū is a noteworthy phenomenon.

A major factor behind it was no doubt the notorious intransigence of this sect and its followers. They had displayed especially forceful rejection of Shintō since the rise of Rennyo in the thirteenth century, staying away from customary community practices in their localities to such an extent that people generally said 'We don't know the *monto* [Shinshū believers].' A second likely factor was the close adhesion between the Higashi Honganji school of Jōdo Shinshū and the Bakufu. In the areas where these uprisings occurred, most of the Shinshū clergy and lay supporters were associated with that school.[32] Third, Shinshū religious orders were unusually tight-knit organizations, and hence served as natural core groups and communication networks for insurrectionary activities.

There is another, overriding factor, which is that Shinshū had always had a different social base than the other major Buddhist sects (Jōdo, Zen, Nichiren). From the beginning, Shinshū cultivated followers mainly among the samurai, in power centers as well as rural districts. Hence their base consisted of self-sufficient feudal farmers, which meant that the sect was well represented in those farmers' associations and could rely on their donations to operate and maintain temples. This secure linkage with the local people tended to make the priests, as resident local leaders, responsive to the demands of the farmers who comprised their parish. As a result, the Restoration government's policy of merging Buddhism into Shintō had especially severe repercussions in areas where Jōdo Shinshū was well established. 'Other temples, which typically had income from benefices, were not directly pressed for survival. But Shinshū temples, which depended on donations from followers, were the most vulnerable to the consolidation policy. For them it was a life-or-death matter.'[33]

That difference in social bases is reflected in the differing ways in which Shinshū and the other sects coped with the perilous post-Restoration atmosphere of hostility to special privileges and Buddhism. Since Buddhism at the time basically lacked deep roots in the lives or minds of the people, the prospect of forfeiting the protection afforded by special privileges made the other sects feel helpless, creating a coercive motivation for protective alignment with the new authorities. With religious tracts tending toward such topics as 'Resurgent Zen and Defense of the Fatherland,' 'Pacification and Preservation of the Nation,' or 'Buddhism and National Prosperity,' not only were priests and monks toadying to the government policy, but through their instant conversions they were even seen to be cats'-paws of the anti-Buddhism movement.

As may be guessed from the close connections between the Higashi Honganji school and the Bakufu, the attitudes of those at the upper levels of the Shinshū religious hierarchy, who had long been accustomed to privilege and official protection, were no different than those in other sects. Shinshū orders assisted in the suppression of more than a few peasant revolts,[34] and conversions in line with the government policy were not unknown among the Shinshū clergy.

But in the outlying temples at the lower reaches of the Shinshū hierarchy, due to the close contact with the lives and minds of the common people, there was *never* any kowtowing to authority, but on the contrary a drive to preserve the purity of the faith. In some regions there was resistance to compulsory Shintō worship and to the severing of connections with parishioners, for it was possible for Shinshū to confront the authorities by relying on deep-rooted popular support. While some Buddhist priests went so far as to abandon their own faith to purchase secular privilege, some among the Shinshū clergy gave up their secular privileges in order to *maintain their inner faith*. In some cases they nominally left their orders so as to become economically self-supporting. For example, the parishioners of Iwatoshirosha, a branch shrine in Shirayama, Echizen, were devotees of Jōdo Shinshū who renounced their special privileges to become shrine members when the Buddhism-Shintō merger was decreed. Some one hundred and twenty of them jointly signed a petition which read:

> The noble aims of removing the separations between Shintō and Buddhism are to differentiate the way of the gods [*kami*] and the way of the Buddha, and to further the institution of both ways, and we wish to state that we have no objection. . . . We are returning to the soil and pursuing occupations, devoting ourselves fully to loyal reverence of the Emperor. As shrine parishioners of Shirayama who are carefully observing Shinto rites, we also beg leave to fulfill the dying wish of our ancestral founder and great teacher by serving the way of the Buddha.

The stronghold of the people's rebellious psychology was converted by Jōdo Shinshū into an opportunity to transcend secular values, by way of the logic expressed in the famous Northern Followers Manifesto of 1868:

> Those who follow [the imperial army of the Restoration] are all foes of Buddhism, and though they may find temporary glory in this world, they are sinners who will burn in hell. . . . The time has come to risk our lives so as to reap the grace of Buddha, and therefore, holding fast to our beliefs, when we catch sight of the foes of Buddhism we must kill them without hesitation. Should it happen that we lose our lives at the hands of the foes of Buddhism, we shall surely be transported directly to the Pure Land.

Of course such teachings on transcendence of secular values reflect longstanding Buddhist doctrine, which was subject to different interpretations by the various sects and schools. Shinshū's differing base of social support enabled it to recast that traditional precept into a *functional* entity in the political sphere. In other words, independence from authority, through a combination of the lives and interests of the people, was made into a substantive vehicle for transcendence of secular values.

To put it the other way around, beliefs which could totally transcend the value system of the powers that be, and impart a spiritual base to the defiant people, took form only in an extremely localized fashion. This, then, was one among the key factors which operated on deep levels to prescribe the modes of the people's response to the Restoration, and hence to prescribe the character of the Restoration itself.[35]

b *Opposition to cholera prevention and other modernizations*

The many protests against such reforms as vaccination, telegraph poles, the solar calendar, prohibition of nudity, or the killing of bears, are a well-known aspect of the early-Meiji peasant revolts. Among these, opposition to cholera vaccination was most frequently the direct cause of uprisings (in Okayama in 1877, and in Aichi, Saitama and seven locations at once in Niigata during 1879). The main underlying factor is commonly said to have been a general mistrust of the unfamiliar (and especially the foreign) in traditional 'natural village' society. But a crucial aspect of these reforms is that they ignored the experiental, substantive rationality within peasant customs. In some cases the decrees coercively applied an alien, theoretical, formalistic rationality. In other cases they disregarded the special characteristics and peculiarities of local regions. In the farming villages of southwestern Japan, for example, it was deeply distressing for the people to be forced to wear clothes for summer farm work. Nevertheless, the officials who were sent from Tokyo, eager to make fine records in local administration, brandished concepts of hygiene or slogans about 'good customs' as they imposed what was felt to be a severe restriction.

More significantly, behind these 'misunderstandings' lay a *deep-seated mistrust* among the peasant class of whatever the ruling class did. The way in which a given social class defines its situation at a given moment is naturally colored by the fundamental desires and feelings of that class at the time. In the villages of the 1870s, the key feature of cholera prevention, or of any vaccination, was that it is not medical 'treatment.' The actual effect of a *preventive* measure cannot be ascertained. It is something like a Rohrschach image, an enigmatic phenomenon with various possible interpretations. When something so vague is coupled with a general feeling of mistrust for the people who are performing it, it is bound to be viewed as sinister. Hence, inoculation 'extracts body fat for use as someone else's nourishment'; the iron beds in Western hospitals are roasting grills for obtaining fat; the imported red wool blankets which were popular

at the time were died with 'blood taxes'; the telegraph is Christian witchcraft, and telegraph poles are painted with the blood
of living maidens.

In the magnetic field between the crumbling of the people's
customary world and their fearful anxieties, a few scraps of
non-demonstrative fact (say, electric poles sometimes resembling
crosses) are invested with wild 'meanings' (Christian magic) and
taken as proof to back up the anxieties and fears. Then the
fragmentary facts of 'evil import' are hung together on the axis
of anxiety and fear, crystallized into a coherent whole, and
presto, an entire world of grotesque mythology takes shape. For
example, if you go a Western-style hospital, 'they'll put you on
a grill and take out your insides without your knowing it and
you'll die smiling.'

Rumor is the self-confirmation of anxiety and fear, and it is
also a self-propagating medium. Amid anxiety about a new situation and mistrust toward the action of the ruling class, anyone's
version of a rumor could spread in all directions with no limit
whatsoever.[36]

c Opposition to outcast liberation

Maintenance of discrimination against the hereditary *eta* class of
outcasts (known today as *burakumin*) was demanded in uprisings
in the Himeji-Ikuno region and in Kōchi during 1871; in two
areas of Okayama during 1872; in the 300,000-strong Fukuoka
revolt and in riots in Hiroshima in 1873; and in other incidents.
As an example, here is an item from a petition during the
prefecture-wide 1871 rebellion in Kochi:

> Now that *eta* have new status and are mixed with the farmers,
> we no longer have any will to work. With *eta* farmers there
> can be no smooth progress. The Government Decree has
> wounded us deeply, and we don't know what to do to
> maintain our status.

The situation referred to is this: the restoration government's
'equality of the four classes' left the status of the nobility and
the samurai families unchanged. As far as the farmers were
concerned, social distinctions were left in place for those classes
who ranked above them, but were removed for those who ranked
below them, the merchants and the *eta*.[37] Without the dismantling

of the *system* of discriminatory principles and assigned subjugation, the 'liberation' of the new commoners meant that the peasant class became the bottom level of society.

To make up for the actual troubles which they had to endure, the farmers had been able to turn to the conceptual comfort of their superiority to the *eta*. Then when the object of transference for their sense of oppression was removed, while their real economic political and social oppressions were left standing, the inevitable result was pent-up dissatisfaction.

The issue of the 'new commoners' was at once a sore spot of peasant-class dissatisfaction with the new government's reforms, and the weakest pressure valve for its expression. Its symbolic significance among farmers is suggested by the fact that *shin* (from *shin-heimin*, 'new commoners') was one of the code words they used to refer to government agents sent to expose home sake breweries, along with *saru* (from *salle*, a Western-style hard-floor room) and *megane* (eyeglasses).

The pathetically perverse agrarian reaction to the liberation of the outcasts was inevitable. The farm population was caught in an internal contradiction of the Restoration reforms – between the requirement for a 'unified national citizenry' as a condition for the formation of a modern state, and the necessity for essential continuity of the feudal status hierarchy as the actual mode of control.[38] The resulting peasant dissatisfaction was deflected downward in a retrograde movement, through the weakest spot in the social context, the unshackling of the *eta*.

d *Demands for restoration of local clan rule*

During a peasant revolt in 1866 in Higashi-mimasaka, the homes of rice and sake merchants and village officials were smashed in typical fashion, but no one laid a hand on 'the storehouses of the [clan] Lord wherein the rice tithes are kept, which alone were carefully preserved.' The contrast is underscored by the apparent wonderment of that remark, made by a monk who recorded the events of the rebellion.

When the daimyo domains were abolished and replaced with prefectural administrations in 1871, the deposed daimyo were called to Tokyo. On that occasion:

The farmers of the Asano domain in Hiroshima amassed on the roads and in the castle to prevent the departure of the former daimyo. . . . Farmers set out slowly along the roads to Hiroshima, hoisting banners or carrying bags of first-harvest rice [traditionally regarded as the welling forth of the farmers' personal devotion to the local lord], shouting 'We beg you to stay, we beg you to stay.'

Likewise, one of the formal demands of the united farmers in the widespread rebellion in Tosa the same year was: 'If our Governor [the former daimyo] visits the capital, there can be no happiness among the farmers here.'

Demands for retention or reinstatement of *tonosama* or local daimyo were also expressed in an uprising in 1869 in Morioka, and in many others during 1871 in the prefectures of Hori (Izumo), Matsuyama and Ōsu (both in Iyo, the latter involving 40,000 people), Takamatsu, Fukushima, Okayama and elsewhere. All of these uprisings, as Hirano Yoshitarō has pointed out, 'were movements essentially actuated as vitriolic attacks on the homes of the parasites of the feudal administration (the village heads), and in the destruction of prosperous shops.'

During the pro-daimyo demonstrations in Hiroshima, the most widely circulated rumor was that, 'Three thousand *ryo* were paid out as compensation for the departure of the daimyo, but the headmen who received it are keeping it for their own use and not passing it along to the farmers.' No doubt such a payment was never made. Yet such a rumor would not arise without reason. The point is that the farmers' actions and rumors indicate the disposition of their affections and disaffections under the Bakuhan regime.

In any stratified society, the people have a pervasive ambivalence toward the power system which rules them. On one hand there is a certain momentum of hatred for the system, rooted in the actual experiences and realizations of everyday life; but there is also a certain momentum of loyalty, affection and faith toward the system, due to internalization of the ruling ideology. If the people are socially mature enough to erect a theoretical framework on the basis of their actual experience, then their own principles may check their support for the ruling ideology.

However, in a stratified society where *the people have no mature, theoretically framed social capacity*, the defiant backlash arising from independent realizations hovers within the closed circuit of their routine lives. In their consciousness, truncated by the lack of a theoretical grounding, the conventional mythology (or worldview) and morality are furnished by existing *dogma*. In that case, the people's ambivalence toward the system polarizes into two psychic entities: one is *hatred for petty officials* (or at most, high officials), who are the direct source of the sufferings felt in actual life (the system as palpable enemy). The other is *loyal attachment to the apex of the ruling structure*, which is a distant object of faith (the system as symbol). In 1870 a group of rebelling farmers put it this way: 'We harbor no resentment toward our Lord. We give no quarter to the officials who serve him.'[39]

The tradition of direct petitioning of rulers was born of precisely this psychological structure: mistrust of local and middle-level representatives of the ruling class, versus unwavering trust in the ruler at the top.[40] In the popular storytelling arts of modern Japan, from the *kōdan* and *naniwa-bushi* recitations of the Edo period through the popular novels of the twentieth century, an unbroken current of tales about heroes and allies of the people reflects this image of the system in the mind of the common people.

Such 'apex romanticism' helped to establish the legitimacy of the imperial state. With the convergence of daimyo loyalty into imperial loyalty, this romanticism was transformed into a social-psychological foundation that was at once stable and richly elastic. The well-known result of the elasticity is that malice arising from actual sufferings imposed by the imperial state, and suspicions arising from blunders, have always been absorbed by 'wicked imperial advisors' or lower levels of leadership, while the emperor himself is the perpetual object of innocent, romantic affection.

Of course this shunting process is not so simple or straightforward. When the peasant rebellions shifted into opposition to the tax reform and conscription, the peasant class did begin to look behind the village officials and rich farmers and perceive the central government as the enemy, although only at the regional level. As a result there were cases where, 'The rich farmers and common peasants, who had been mutual enemies at the stage of the "world reformation" movements, became close allies (in Fukui and Okayama), and united in a cooperative struggle under the leadership of the rich farmers' to win mitigation of land tax burdens. (We may assume that this sort of conversion was one aspect of the peasant mentality. Witness the case of Uta Seiichi, who as a village headman had his estate smashed by an 1868 uprising in Aizu, but fifteen years later was a stalwart on the side of the people in the People's Rights Movement in Fukushima.)

The farmers who conducted one typical uprising at this stage, in Aichi at the end of 1876, after concluding that they could not achieve their aims without mounting an appeal to the central government, planned to directly petition the emperor during one of his occasional visits to the prefecture. One of their leaders, a wealthy farmer named Hayashi Kinbei, lost his nerve, finding himself 'somehow extremely terrified at the thought of directly petitioning His Imperial Highness.' Though the people felt walled off from it, a symbol of a newly just system did in fact exist, in the person of the crown of the Restoration government. Scratch the surface of early-Meiji peasant perception, and it is seen to once again hold the ruling structure to be an (all the more) enormous and exquisite institution.

In these processes, we can detect the powerful undercurrents of the peasant mind which would later well up in the People's Rights Movement. We can also glimpse the base of the inner control mechanism which constantly deflected, and channeled into the system, the amorphous dissatisfaction and resentment of the majority of farmers and farmers' children under the Meiji social system.

V   Historical patterns of coping

The orientation of this chapter so far has been toward the people's *rebellion* against the Restoration. This section will outline various other patterns through which the people coped with their situation.

In the typology of people's responses to the ruling value standards of their society, the leading name is Robert Merton. Besides rebellion, Merton identifies four types of behavior: conformity, innovation, ritualism and retreatism. These types are prescribed through theoretical, deductive definitions, and it is these which I borrow here; he also links them to historical, experiential images, but they are drawn mainly with contemporary American society in mind.[41]

The application of Merton's typology to an historical society in a different area and time will throw into relief the *historical differences between theoretically similar types of response*. What were the specific forms in which those types existed in Japanese society amid the historical circumstances of the Meiji Restoration? These will be outlined in accordance with the data.

Likewise, Merton's 'value objectives' and 'systemic norms' are not cast in concrete in a form which applies to all societies and transitional periods. As we apply these terms to Meiji Japan, we must remember that, as in many societies, the value objectives pursued by the *state* and the dominant value objectives of *society* were not necessarily congruent. The specific topic here is the typology of the people's response patterns to the Restoration (not to Meiji society in general), and the present definitions of the value objectives and systemic norms are limited accordingly, as follows: The value objectives are those which were publicly pursued by the Restoration government, the basic pattern being the Charter Oath of 1868.[42] The main systemic norms are the educational, bureaucratic, conscription and taxation systems which were instituted by the Restoration government.

On the assumption that this methodological simplification is appropriate and justified for the topic, I proceed to consider the value objectives and systemic norms of Restoration society, which at the time occurred on various levels and with various meanings.

a   *Conformity*
Conformity involved abandoning 'evil practices of the past' (e.g. the Bakuhan era); sending children to the newly opened schools; seeking knowledge 'all over the world'; and especially, 'strengthening the foundations of imperial rule' by happily complying with the draft. Through these means, 'civil and military officials together, and the common people as well, shall all attain their aspirations.' (Quotations from the Charter Oath.)

Yet it was not until 1891 that the primary school entrance rate exceeded 50 per cent[43] and substantial numbers went into military service. It may be presumed that in the years up to 1877, the majority did not display a thorough degree of conformity. The prestige of the imperial state took root in the minds of most

of the citizenry between 1889 and 1905, from the promulgation
of the Meiji Constitution through the wars with China and
Russia.

Within this context of limited conformity, the newspapers frequently printed 'commendations' of 'exemplary' towns, villages
and individuals.

In the village of Kami-katsura in Kyoto Prefecture, the entire
village is cooperating to raise money for the construction of
an elementary school, and much of the required funds have
been raised by ceasing the distribution of sakē, cakes and
the like during the Bon festival and on other festive occasions
in the vicinity, and donating all of the moneys to the village
fund. . . . In addition they have eliminated unnecessary
expenses, including even trifling matters, in order to assist
in the school construction project, in a truly commendable
village-wide effort. Also, in the village of Furuwatari in
Aichi Prefecture, the elder Ōki Gentaro has received a
commendation from the prefectural government for having
opened an elementary school.

(*Hakubun Shinshi*, September 1872)

The Shiga Prefecture European School was recently opened
without any use of public revenues, entirely through the
efforts of the people, with especial assistance from . . . [list
of names]. . . . Governor Matsuda's office has approved the
admission of female students, and it is to be expected that
in future the prefecture's intellectual talent will flourish.

(*Shiga Shimbun*, no. 1, October 1872)

In the new commoners' [former outcasts'] hamlet of . . . in
this prefecture, the entire population aims to study writing
and ciphering, and having decided on the establishment of
a primary school, every household is weaving straw sandals
during non-working hours . . . the proceeds will be applied
to the school fund, adding up little by little to a great amount.
The exertions of their spirit are beyond praise.

(*Shiga Shimbun*, no. 3, October 1872)

In the new commoners' village of . . . in Nara Prefecture,
since the opening of the school some 33 students have

enrolled, and in addition more than 30 adults are enrolled as evening students. Their diligence is unrivaled, and deserving particular notice among them are Kiyokawa Seihichi, age 69, who poses anagram riddles every evening, and also . . . [list of names]. . . . With untiring diligence, Sumugawa Kiyokazu remained one day in the lecture hall and composed the following poem: 'Blessed by an era in which all is renewed, we cherish the deep blessings of our ruler.' With ever more diligence hereafter, in a few years the new commoners will be above scorn and instead it may well be the commoners who are deserving of contempt.

(*Nisshin Kibun*, November 29, 1872)

With their laudatory style, these articles seem like the materials of a species of generational campaign. Anecdotes of other sorts of model donations were also printed on occasion:

Shiho, a widowed farmer in the village of Kumeda in Musashino, who is ninety-one years old, has been making cotton during her free time and donating it to the government. In return she recently received a gift of money. This laudatory action involved a total of some thirty thousand *zeni*.

(*Taiseikan Nisshi*, November 28, 1870)

Another type of behavior which naturally surfaced was the aspiration to subjective or objective 'success in the world' by participating in the system. This was evidenced by the tendency for young men who had been conscripted for basic training to brag to their neighboring farmers that they were 'army camp veterans,' and for village heads or elders who became mayors or neighborhood chiefs to suddenly adopt imperious manners.

There was one case, around 1880, of a poor farmer's child who for four years walked to and from a middle school nine miles away, sometimes collapsing from hunger on the mountain pass. After graduation he kept commuting, to an academy of Chinese classics. He wove straw into rope late into the night, and when his parents complained about the mounting bill for lamp oil, he bought his own oil and made the rope in a corner of the barn. Having finally saved 10 yen, he left his village, on an island in the Inland Sea, to enroll in a secondary school on Honshū. The villagers told each other, 'He'll soon be the mayor.'

Such was the implication of 'building a school for the village.'

The shift from a society of ascription to a society of achievement, brought about through the nominal 'equality of the four classes,' imparted a fresh sense of purpose to the lives and exertions of industrious peasant youths and their families.

b *Innovation*

In the village that said, 'He'll soon be the mayor,' another young man, a carpenter's son, returned for the New Year's holiday and shocked everyone by covering the parlor of the family house with red carpets and proclaiming, 'I am the mayor.' 'Has he gone crazy?' was the general reaction. After the New Year season, he simply disappeared.

The Charter Oath precept that 'the common people as well shall all attain their aspirations' ignited flames of desire in the minds of village youth, but the systematic means for fulfilling those desires were not freely attainable (see Chapter 15). This gap between goals and means produced various tensions and aberrant behavior. Such legendary criminals as Kumasaka Chōan, Takahashi Oden and Yoarashi 'Nightmare' Okinu were children of this period.

Unfortunately there are no extant crime statistics for the earliest Meiji years, but for example, in 1879 some 118,173 persons were convicted of crimes (excluding disorderly conduct and other very light offenses), or 324 per 100,000 population. This is a far higher proportion than, say, at the peak of the 'erotic-grotesque' culture in 1931, when the corresponding statistic was 230 (151,296 convicted).

Table 12.2 provides additional comparative data. To come a little closer to the actual incidence of deviant behavior, the types of offenses are limited to those for which the figures are relatively unaffected by changes in legal provisions, police capabilities, or enforcement policies. (For example, gambling, intimidation and obscenity are excluded.)

Crimes against property were unusually frequent in the late 1870s. In particular, during the 1880s, robbery – the most drastic criminal expression of frustration created by the gap between people's desires and òptions under the system – reached a level which is unsurpassed in modern Japanese history. The per-

Table 12.2 *Number of convictions by type of crime*

Year	Population (thousands)	Murder	Arson	Robbery	Theft
1876	35,555	376	135	889	22,149
1877	35,870	247	145	1,131	22,458
1878	36,166	535	172	1,506	28,322
1879	36,464	424	219	1,401	31,360
1912	50,577	879	552	556	24,793
1925	60,210	930	470	490	11,686
1963	96,156	1,431	401	1,492	29,121

Sources: Population: *Nihon tokei nenkan.*
Meiji-era crimes: *Nihon teikoku dai-ichi tokei nenkan.*
1912, 1925 crimes: *Keiji oyobi gyōkei tokei yoshi.*
1963 crimes: *Shihō tokei nenpō.*

petrators of these types of sheer criminal behavior clearly make up a very tiny proportion of the general population (the proportion convicted for all crimes reached a peak of 0.584 per cent in 1885). Yet beneath the surface of the conviction statistics, surely there were a good many *daydreams* of gambles, legitimate immorality, and crimes.

Rabbit-selling schemes[44] were extraordinarily popular in the Osaka, Tokyo and Tohoku regions, and billiards flourished in Osaka[45] during the early Meiji years. It seems that as the means provided by the regime were insufficient for realizing the desires ignited by the ideals of 'class equality' and 'success,' there was a rush of speculation and gambling. In one country village of that time, some 80 per cent of those who became wealthy did so through gambling. Widespread speculation mania was the base on which a series of wealthy investors, such as Kōshuya Chūemon and Amamiya Keijirō, built their fortunes.

The numerous attempts to directly petition the emperor during these years were one of the 'transformed patterns' ordained by the exceptional historical circumstances of the time. A village youth who was punished for throwing a petition for 'school expenses' into the emperor's carriage[46] may seem eccentric at first glance, and yet it pierces to the core of the contradictions between goals and means, ideals and reality in the Meiji state. The existence of other, similar cases, and the general frequency of direct petitions may be inferred from this article:

At the Kyōmachi entrance to Nagoya, a man in the crowd wearing a black mask and blue socks attempted unsuccessfully to throw a message case wrapped in white cloth into the Imperial carriage, and immediately fled. At the Uonodana crossing, a man veiled in white cloth approached to petition the Emperor, but he was apprehended and fell unconscious. He is one Jūkichi from the village of Hatchō in the Ōno district of Echizen, and the gist of his message was that having been born under the Empire, his life would have no meaning if he were not a direct retainer of the Court, and he begged to be employed. At Teppōmachi, a man veiled in black cloth proffering a document jumped out and was blocked, and ran away. At Higashiyama, some three hundred members of former samurai families had amassed to request reinstatement of their stipends, but there was no unruly behavior.

(*Chōya Shimbun*, July 2, 1880)

c *Ritualism*

The nature of formal patterns of behavior went virtually unrecorded in the newspapers and other documents of the time. But regarding new laws, proclamations and holidays, there are frequent mentions of 'misunderstanding' or 'failure to grasp the purpose.' It is likely that the numerically dominant type of behavior was conformity with systemic norms only, without thorough conformity to the actual value objectives pursued by the Meiji state.

The systemic norms tended to be observed as formal ceremonies, as against different behavior in the non-formal or private world. A typical example was the New Year by the new calendar, which was celebrated in a perfunctory manner as 'the government-office New Year,' while the real ceremonies were held later at home on the old date. This phenomenon can probably be found in any culture, but among the people of Japan at this time it was certainly a key pattern of formalistic 'conformity.'

d *Retreatism*

There were many cases of suicide by hanging among people who were cornered by difficult circumstances amid the post-Restoration changes, as well as those who had lost their resources through gambling, or who dreaded conscription. The private religions that spread with great rapidity in the post-Restoration years, such as Tenrikyō, Sumiyoshikyō and Konkōkyō, cannot quite be interpreted as a pattern of rebellion, but they may well have been means of escaape for most of the believers.

The cotton region of Osaka and Nara was dealt fatal blows by the importation of raw cotton and the introduction of spinning machines, and the lights went out in the villages as people fled in the night to escape mounting debts. People disappeared from other regions as well. Most of them flowed into the cities and became the lowest of the rabble, with virtual slave status as farmhands, laborers or prostitutes. It is no wonder that so many thousands banded together to set off for Hawaii, America, Guatemala, Shanghai, Hong Kong, Singapore, Queensland or New Caledonia.

Of course the great majority of the people were not driven by economic ruin to suicide or flight, nor reduced by hopelessness to rotting in urban tenements or abandoning their country. Many did forsake their hometowns, and many were driven out by the rural disintegration, to erect new lives in 'second' hometowns. There they displayed resourcefulness and persistence in the face of the recurring struggles brought about by historic changes, and served as the undercarriage and engine for the development of 'modern Japan.'

In the broad sense, the Meiji Restoration was an historical watershed not just of economics and politics, but of social psychology. In each of those dimensions, it represents the *primal consolidation* of the social energies which erected modern Japan.

The complex process of the forfeiture and disintegration of the rural hometowns was delineated by particular structural characteristics: laborers working 'away from home,' entrepreneurs as absentee landlords, intellectuals as 'runaway slaves,' and so forth. Those lifestyles, in turn, contributed particular characteristics to the complex psychology and reality of modern Japanese society.

(1967)

Notes

1   The term 'the people' (*minshū*) is used here to mean those who are not in 'the elite.' The elite being the set of groups within a society or social system who exclusively hold what is socially valued as wealth, authority and prestige. 'Mass' (or 'the masses') is sometimes used as the counterpart of 'elite,' but 'mass' also refers to an historical phase of humanity, as in 'mass society.' To avoid ambiguity, 'mass' and its derivatives are used here only in that historical sense.

2   I categorize historical data on social psychology as follows:

Symbols *by* the people: letters, diaries, essays, readers' contributions to periodicals, etc.
Symbols *for* the people: reports, textbooks, the popular arts, etc.
Symbols *of* the people: documents and publications on folklore and customs, reportage, etc.

3   Major newspapers covering domestic events founded up to 1877, followed by city of issue, frequency (if known) and starting date:

Chugai Shimbun, Edo, about ten times monthly, February 1868
Kōko Shimbun, Edo, April (intercalary) 1868
Yokohama Shinhō Moshi Hosō, Yokohama, semi-weekly, April (intercalary) 1868
Yokohama Mainichi Shimbun, Yokohama, December 1870
Shimbun Zasshi, Tokyo, irregular, May 1871
Osaka Nippō, Osaka, irregular, October 1871
Kaika Shimbun, Kanazawa, thrice monthly, November 1871
Tokyo Nichi-nichi Shimbun, Tokyo, February 1872
Nisshin Shinji-shi, Tokyo, daily, March 1872
Yubin Hōchi Shimbun, Tokyo, five times monthly the first year, then daily, June 1872
Tokyo Shimbun, Tokyo, weekly, February 1873
Asano Shimbun, Tokyo, daily, September 1874
Yomiuri Shimbun, Tokyo, September 1874
Tokyo Akebono Shimbun, Tokyo, daily, June 1875
Bankoku Shimbun, Tokyo, daily (evenings), January 1876
Tokyo E-iri Shimbun, Tokyo, daily, March 1876
Kinji Hyōron, Tokyo, weekly, June 1876
Tōyō Shinpō, Tokyo, once or twice monthly, July 1876
Dan-dan Chimbun, Tokyo, weekly, March 1877

Osaka Shinpō, Osaka, daily, December 1877

Each of these newspapers was issued by a different publisher, with the exception of the Nisshin Shinji-shi and Bankoku Shimbun. (*Source*: Kyoto University National History Research Center, *Nippon kindaishi jiten*, pp. 780–2)

4   The most comprehensive collections of historical material on Restoration-period peasant uprisings are Aoki Kōji, *Meiji nōmin sōjō nenjiteki kenkyū*, Shinseisha, 1967 and *Hyakushō ikki no nenjiteki kenkyū*, Shinseisha, 1966; and Tsuchiya Takao and Ono Michio, ed., *Meiji shonen nōmin ikki roku*, Nanboku shoin, 1931, reprinted by Keisō Shoin, 1953. For excellent detailed accounts of the largest few uprisings, see Ono Takeo, ed. *Ishin nōmin hōki dan*, rev. edn, Tōkō Shoin, 1965.

5   The best collections of Restoration-era urban scribblings, poems, handbills and the like are Umehara Hokumei, ed., *Kindai sesō zenshi*, Hakuhōsha, 1931; and Fujisawa Morihiko, *Meiji ryūkōka shi*, Shunyōdo, rev. edn, 1955. For the late Tokugawa years, see Sakuragi Shō, *Sokumenkan bakumi shi*, Keiseisha, 1905.

6   Popular songs are symbols *for* the people, but since they can be regarded as vicarious expressions of people's feelings, they are quite close in nature to symbols *by* the people. As social-psychological data, symbols *for* the people hold significance in three ways: (1) as *substitute expressions* of the popular mind (almost *by* the people); (2) as the *practical knowledge* of those interested in manipulating the popular mind (almost *of* the people); and (3) as *formative elements* of the popular mind (purely *for* the people).

7   Many of the leading booklets are collected in three volumes of *Meiji bunka zenshū*, Nippon Hyōronsha: *Bunmei kaika hen* (1929), *Zasshi hen*, rev. edn, 1955, and *Fūzoku hen*, rev. edn, 1955.

8   In earlier works I have outlined some basic schematic arrangements of such factors as social psychology and social structure, value orientations and value systems, value systems and belief systems, and the experience of an era and that of the generations within it. See Mita, *Theory of Value Orientation (Kachi ishiki no riron*, Kōbundo, 1966); and *Mental Structure of Modern Japan (Gendai nihon no seishin kōzo*, Kōbundo, rev. edn, 1984).

9   It is impossible to tally or graph by year the total numbers of participants in the peasant uprisings. There are conflicting counts for virtually every incident, and the reports are certainly clouded by varying definitions of what constituted 'participation' (which, furthermore, was not infrequently covert). The figures range from 'upwards of ten' for some incidents, to as many as 300,000 (or 100,000 by another estimate) for the Fukuoka revolt of 1873. Also,

there were uprisings which spread serially across a given region or occurred intermittently over a period of time which in the absence of a clear reporting standard, may or may not have been recorded as single events.

10 'Ecstatic mass violence' is the term used by Hani Gorō ('Bakumi ni okeru shiso dōkō', *Meiji ishin shi*, p. 37). E. H. Norman called it 'mass hysteria' ('Eejanaika ko' in *Kurio no kao*, Iwanami Shoten, 1956).

Other studies in Japanese of the *eejanaika* phenomenon, in addition to those mentioned elsewhere in these notes, include Tsuchiya Takao, 'Ishinshi ue no nansensu,' *Chūō Kōron*, December 1931, and 'Ishin no o-fuda-ori,' *Nihon shakai-keizaishi no shomondai*, 1947; Tōyama Shigeki, 'Kinsei minshu shinri no ichimen – okagemairi yori eejanaika e,' *Shakaiken*, Vol. 2, No. 8, 1947, and *Meiji ishin*, Iwanami shoten, 1951 (pp. 187–98); and Wakamori Tarō, 'Kinsei shōroku shinkō no ichimen,' *Shichō*, No. 49, 1953.

11 Data from Aoki Koji, *Hyakushō ikki no nenjiteki kenkyū*, Shinseisha, 1967, and 'Meiji shonen nōmin ikki nengyo' in *Rekishigaku kenkyū*, 318, Nov. 1966. The figures do not include what are known as intravillage disputes (*murakata sōdō*). This is not because they are of negligible significance, but because a large proportion of them apparently remain undiscovered as of this writing, and it would be premature to graph their annual occurrence.

12 On the *hare* and *ke* cycle, see Kamishima Jirō, *Kindai nihon no seishin kōzō*, Iwanami Shoten, 1961.

13 'At the New Year they changed the straw mats and danced upon them in their shoes, and pounded the New Year rice cakes by setting them out and stamping them with their shoes, and picked them up and ate them with a volley of "eijanaika". . . . As they danced they would flirt with one and grab the arms of two others, saying "Dōdemo eijanaika" ["Anything goes, why not?"].' (Yamaguchi Yoshikazu, *Awa eijanaika*, 1931, pp. 46–7, cited in Hani, op. cit.)

Some lines from various versions of the 1867 popular song *Eejanaika*:

Eejanaika eejanaika, Lay paper on her privates and when
  it's torn lay it again, Eejanaika eejanaika

Eejanaika eejanaika, An earthen cup bumps up with its
  mate, Both get cracked, Eejanaika
Eejanaika eejanaika, You're an octopus and I am too,
  We're stuck together, Eejanaika

Make her ring and ring her again, The big drum-bell at dawn,
A rousing ring, Eejanaika

(From various sources including Shiseki Kyōkai, *Teibō zōshūroku*,
Vol. 1, p. 312; Tamura Eitarō, *Yonaoshi*, Yūzankaku, 1960; and
Mori Hideto, *Taishū bunkashi*, Sanpō, 1964.)

14 ' "Eijanaika' clothing fashions and folk songs are breaking down
the hierarchical order of the Edo-era household, and making it
equitable. Wanton women are wearing men's clothes, blindingly
striped short coats and trousers. Dignified papas wear their daughters' padded silk garments with wigs on their bald pates. It's becoming normal for maidservants to be shop boys and young men to be
maidens.' (Tamura, op. cit., p. 124) The newspaper *Teibō Zōshūroku* reported: 'Schoolgirls look like false samurai, old women are
made young, wives look like husbands in short coats . . .' Conscious
or unconscious, these are fascinating hints of the orientations of
their wishes.

15 Yamaguchi Yoshikazu, *Awa eijanaika*, 1931.

16 One example is the 1868 *yonaoshi* (world renewal) uprising in
Echigo, engendered by collusion between the Nagaoka clan and a
wealthy merchant.

17 Total revenues of the Meiji government from December 1867
through December 1868 were about 33 million yen, of which nearly
90 per cent (29.4 million yen) was exceptional income, mainly from
issuance of paper money, which accounted for 73 per cent of all
revenues (24 million yen). Ibinishi Mitsuhaya, Katō Toshihiko,
Ōshima Kiyoshi and Ōuchi Chikara, *Nihon shihonshugi no seiritsu*,
Tokyo Daigaku Shuppankai, 1965, Vol. II, p. 274.

18 In 1868 Matsudaira Katamori, the daimyo of Aizu, set up a counterfeiting mint inside Wakamatsu Castle, and stamped large volumes
of coins made half of plating. He also permitted wealthy individuals
to engage in private coinage, in exchange for a 10 per cent rake-
off. As a result, prices in the Aizu realm rose suddenly to at least
three and in some cases ten times the levels in the four neighboring
domains. Counterfeiting of plate coins was also undertaken by the
Satsuma and Chikuzen clans, and even by the Meiji government
itself during its earliest years.

19 The sacking of Aizu by imperial troops when Wakamatsu Castle
fell in 1870 was described by Okatani Shigeo, a member of a
traveling government inspection team who happened to be on the
scene: 'After taking Honari two days earlier, the imperial troops
broke through to the city on the morning of 23 August. Orders
had been issued throughout the city that no one was to leave home,
and that everyone should remain calm. Despite such repeated

instructions, as the people of the castle town sat calmly at home on the morning of the 23rd, they were surprised by the attack and quickly fled, abandoning all their possessions. The soldiers moved in and plundered furniture and other things, broke into the antique shops and sold the goods, and even posted signs in the radish fields reserving plots for themselves. After the fall of the castle, the people wanted to return to their labors, but were barred from their family homes until they raised money to buy them back. Such a plunderous attack is without precedent. Wherefore they complained and requested aid, but although there are large relief funds, they have not benefited from them. Their plight is pitiable.'

20 Inoue Kiyoshi, *Nihon no gunkokushugi*, University of Tokyo Press, 1953. A world-renewal uprising in Ueno province in 1868 was directly motivated by the high quota for peasant conscription set by local shogunate officials.

21 Kiemon, a freeholder and tenant farmer on the island of Ōshima in the Inland Sea, had gone up to Edo to serve in the defense of Edo Bay, and come back with news that 'the world is changing.' 'Upon hearing the story of Kiemon's journey, all of the island's farmers concluded that "This is a critical moment." He always ended his tale with the admonition that, "There will certainly be a big war with America and Russia. In that case, Edo will not prevail. Only the farmers can save the Japanese nation."' Miyamoto Tsune-ichi, *Nihon zankoku monogatari*, 4th edn, Heibonsha, 1960, pp. 309–10. (This sort of up-to-the-minute report was probably quite rare.)

22 In fact the name of the Restoration era, Meiji, derives from a line to which an ancient Chinese book of divination fell open: 'The sage faces south and perceives the whole world. First discern [*mei* in Japanese], then rule [*ji*].'

23 For example, an uprising instigated by retainers of the Okayama clan in the Misakutatsuno district in April 1868. (See Aoki Kōji, 'Meiji ishinki no nōmin,' *Shisō*, January 1967, p. 103.)

24 *Tome gunshi*, Vol. 1, p. 193. A similar but much larger-scale movement for retrospective compensation, popularly known as the Goman-koku [50,000 bushels of rice] Rebellion, occurred in the Takasaki domain in 1869; see Hagiwara Susumu, *Gumma kenshi, meiji jidai*, Takagi Shoten, 1959, pp. 104–10.

25 Niigata-ken Naimubu, ed., *Echigo Sado nōmin sōdō*, pp. 475–6. The 'Mock Scripture' song later spread to other localities where it was often heard. It is said that as a result the government occasionally banned Bon Festival dancing (Sonobe Saburō, *Nihon minshu kayō shikō*, Asahi Shimbunsha, 1962, p. 33).

26 The land tax reform raised a total of about 45 million yen, of which some 35 million was supplied by local landowners.

27 'This change to cash payment is a very troublesome thing for the farmers. . . . Very few of the farmers have set aside the whole amount of cash for the annual payment. Most of them take all of their surplus rice for the year and immediately sell it to the merchants in order to raise the cash. Since everyone in the community follows the same pattern, when the payment date draws near the merchants are always ready to pounce on the prey at their feet and squeeze all the profit from them, and the farmers have no way to avoid them. . . . If they neglect the annual payment they will fall into bankruptcy, which they dread as much as strangling themselves with a silken cord, and so with full awareness that they are caught in the merchant's trap, they proceed anyway to sell their rice.' Spoken by a character in an 1874 book, *Discussions on Enlightenment* (*Kaika mondō* by Ogawa Tameji)

28 Kido Tashirō, 'Meiji kyūnen no nōmin ikki' in Horie Ei'ichi and Tōyama Shigeki, ed., *Minken undō no hatten: jiyū minkenki no kenkyū*, Yūikaku, 1959. For example, the uprising in November and December which began in Mie as the Ise Riot and spread to Aichi, Gifu, Osaka and Wakayama. At that time the market price of rice in Mie Prefecture was 3.5 yen per bushel, while the rice value standard for cash tax payment was 5.49 yen. Since one-third of the field tax was acceptable in kind, in terms of cash payment the actual loss was on the order of 50 per cent.

29 New evidence and the new theoretical approaches of recent scholarship mandate a revision of the previous standard classification of early-Meiji peasant demands, in Hirano Yoshitarō, *Nihon shihonshugi hattatsu shi koza*, 1936, reprinted by Iwanami Shoten, 1974.

30 Fujita Shōzō cites historical materials on the 'reappointment' of fedual officials as mayors in the Tokyo-Saitama and Nagano areas, in *Tennosei kokka no shihai genri*, Miraisha, 1955, p. 93.

31 Tokyo market prices for one *koku* of rice, in yen:

1872	January:	4.10	December:	3.60	Average:	3.88
1873		3.60		5.40		4.72
1874		5.60		8.00		7.28
1875		7.60		5.70		7.28
1876		5.60		4.70		5.01

32 Yoshida Hisaichi, *Nihon kindai bukkyōshi kenkyū*, Yoshikawa Kobunkan, 1959, p. 7. On the other hand, the Nishi Honganji school was closely connected with the imperial court.

33 Yoshida, op. cit., p. 50. In this connection, a compelling case has been made that the chief cause of the classic religious rebellion of

the time, the Mikawa Monks Revolt, was an attempt by the Kikuma clan to absorb the temple's mutual financing association (Kojima Kōji, 'Meiji shonen Mikawa no ikkō shūsōjō,' *Nishi-mikawa chiri rekishi ronshū*, 1951).

34 For examples from 1873 onward, see Yoshida Shoichi, 'Meiji ishin ni okeru bukkyō no shakaiteki katsudō,' *Taisho daigaku kenkyū kiyō*, No. 47, 1962, pp. 104–7.

35 A Western scholar has called Jōdo Shinshū 'the closest Japanese analogue to Western Protestantism.' R. N. Bellah, *Tokugawa Religion*, Glencoe, Illinois: The Free Press, 1957, p. 122.

36 The examples in the text illustrate how rumor works as a self-confirming, self-amplifying mechanism of fear, anxiety and mistrust. Valuational sentiments of desire, attachment and malice may also serve as the core of rumor. Rumors in themselves are clearly visible data concerning social actualities, and the investigation of the valuational sentiments behind them is an effective technique for tracing the history of social psychology.

37 Some episodes presenting the typical outlook and situation of the 'liberated' 'new commoners:.

'When the proclamation of commoner status was handed down, the men of a certain village of Seishū spent the day praying for the first time at the main shrine to purify themselves and expiate their former sins (!) [sic], bowing reverently to the deities in thanks for this great blessing from heaven. They lit purifying fires in front of the shrine and took some of the flames home, where they put out the fires they had had burning until then, so as to cleanse their daily meals. Having never before used the divine fire, all of them on this occasion were putting their former tainted and soiled lives behind them and celebrating the circumstances of their rebirth.

'Incidentally, in Toide in Etchū province, a new commoner reported that he went to a certain public bathhouse and asked to bathe, but the owner said: You definitely cannot enter, for surely if the likes of you were to enter then from the following day my regular customers would stop coming and I would lose my livelihood, and it is the same for everyone who is in whatever line of business. Even though equality has been granted, it is not yet actually practical. I know that you have been granted equality, and that you are now said to have become gentlemen and to have lost the *eta* color, but still there is this difficulty, for which no reason can be given.' (*Kaika Shimbun*, No. 1, December 1871)

Also: 'In Sakazuki, Tochigi . . . when they happen to go to a bathhouse or a barber shop, they are often told that it is taboo, that the regular customers would never come to the establishment again and it would ultimately have to go out of business.' (*Tokyo Nichi Nichi Shimbun*, May 4, 1872)

38 A critique of the national census of 1872 by Kyoto prefecture authorities, which complained of the contradiction between the central government's theory and practice. To wit, while the stated goal of the census was 'to break down the lineages of clan membership and thoroughly institute the rights of equality among the four classes,' it demanded individual data concerning class distinctions (such as samurai status or 'penal' status beneath the commoners) and clan dominion. (Fujita, op. cit., p. 85)

39 During the major *nainai-zukushi* uprising in the Matsushiro domain (in Shinano, later Nagano). (Tamura Eitarō, *Kindai nihon nōmin undō shiron*, Getsuyō Shobō, 1948, p. 92.)

40 Many peasant uprisings resorted to direct petitioning of local rulers (*jikoso*) or of supra-local rulers (*osso*), bypassing minor officials. This was a centuries-old, but exceptional procedure of complaint, which entailed risk of death during the feudal era.

41 Merton, Robert K., *Social Theory and Social Structure*, rev. edn, 1957.

42 The text of the Charter Oath of 1868, which was publicly proclaimed as a pledge by the Meiji emperor to his ancestors:

1 An assembly shall be widely convoked and all measures shall be decided by open discussion.

2 High and low shall be of one mind, and the national economy and finances shall be greatly strengthened.

3 Civil and military officials together, and the common people as well, shall all attain their aspirations, and thus the people's minds shall not be made weary.

4 Evil practices of the past shall be abandoned, and actions shall be based on international usage.

5 Knowledge shall be sought all over the world, and the foundations of imperial rule shall be strengthened.

43 *Nihon teikoku tōki nenkan*. School attendance grew rapidly thereafter, exceeding 90 per cent by 1902.

44 'Rabbit selling, popular for the first time since the Bakufu days, has recently reached a level beyond all reason, and industry is being lost. Dishonest merchants ask outrageous prices and ensnare the ignorant in their schemes. The common technique is to use Western paints to disguise the color of a rabbit's fur, pass it off as a unique species, and sell it to someone from a remote area. It is really quite astonishing and lamentable that so much cunning and gullibility exist that these abuses may so often occur.' (*Tokyo Nichi Nichi Shimbun*, September 5, 1872) In the whirligig of this time of rapid

change, the restlessness and humbly raised hopes of the common people were easily exploited through blarney about the enormous value of a red rabbit.

45 'Billiard playing was stopped some time ago, but it is reported that it has been started again in Osaka by swindlers who pose as foreigners. The game is strictly prohibited by the government, for like gambling, it is a recreation so evil that those who indulge in it are likely to finish by losing their homes and all their possessions. As it may presently appear in the Tokyo and Yokohama areas, all are advised never to pick up these balls and never to look into the places where it is played, for it may cause no end of troubles, it is such a terrible, terrible thing.' (*Kanayomi Shimbun*, November 9, 1875.)

46 *Tokyo Nichi Nichi Shimbun*, August 8, 1876. Direct petitioning was illegal and all of the petitioners were punished. From 1870, one hundred cane strokes was the punishment prescribed by law for cutting through the soldiers protecting the imperial carriage. The cabinet reaffirmed this policy in a statement on February 8, 1876: 'Of late, during Imperial journeys there have been some instances of people suddenly breaking through the guards and presenting petitions and memorials. The national laws expressly prescribe that such action is grave misconduct, and any citizen who under any circumstance is led astray by a sense of urgency shall be punished afterward. The people must understand this, in order that this pitiable situation shall not occur.'

13 Archetypes of Social Response during Meiji Westernization

I Civilization and enlightenment

In the narrow sense, and as the area of focus here, the period of civilization and enlightenment (*bunmei-kaika*) spans the years from the return of the Iwakura diplomatic mission in 1872 through 1878. In the broad sense, the rapid Westernization of Japanese culture began with the opening of ports to foreign ships in 1854 and continued through 1890.[1]

Extension: diffusion to the regions and the depths

In December 1871 the Shimbun Zasshi reported that there were already more than forty thousand ricksaws in Tokyo. The article goes on to state that there were only a few dozen of the new-fangled vehicles in Kyoto, and just one each in Shizuoka and Kusatsu. Evidently there was quite a gap between the progress of the capital and that of the regions.

The following year, some government bureaucrats on a trip outside the capital, 'wearing their Western clothes, went for a walk near the government offices in the city of Kawagoe and were surrounded by vociferous crowds of young and old, men and women, exactly as it had been when foreigners were sighted in Tokyo ten years ago' (*Nichiyō Shimbun*, October 1872). This is an apt portrayal of the structure of *bunmei-kaika*. At the time, the pundits quipped that it was not the civilization and enlightenment of Nihon, but of Nihonbashi. In every newspaper there was no dearth of diverting anecdotes at the expense of 'the illiterate and ignorant of the remote backward quarters.'[2]

A popular jingle of the time went, 'Tap a cropped head and it plays the tune of civilization and enlightenment,' for the cutting of the traditional topknot was the conventional sign of a head that contained enlightenment. One scholar has estimated that nationwide, the proportion of men without topknots was 10 per cent in 1872, 20 per cent in 1875, 40 per cent in 1877, 70 per cent in 1880, 80 per cent in 1882, 90 per cent in 1883 and 98 per cent by 1887.

The event which served as the wedge for the full-scale spread of enlightenment to the provinces was the replacement of the feudal domains with prefectural administrations, in 1871. The postal service which began that year between Tokyo, Kyoto and Osaka had been extended to Nagasaki by the year-end. This was also the year of the first census and the nominal abolition of outcast status. During 1872 the plan of the compulsory primary school system was announced, the solar calendar was adopted, and military conscription was begun, all of which directly affected the lives of the common people everywhere. They were caught in the nets of the Meiji government leaders whether they liked it or not.

There are many records of the reactions of the rural peasantry to *bunmei-kaika* as it began to impact their daily lives, from about 1873. A few examples: most official announcements were written entirely in Chinese-style characters, leaving country folk baffled. At the New Year of the old calendar, people would take time off to recite the traditional prayers, but it was altogether unsatisfying because they had to keep their voices down to avoid being scolded by the policeman (who was enforcing the solar calendar). The children were sad because the lotteries were stopped. People were delighted to attend readings of the news-paper, where they heard of events all over Japan and conditions in other countries.

Local newspapers and magazines (published outside the Tokyo-Yokohama and Osaka-Kyoto-Kobe urban centers) also made their debut at this time, appearing first in Kanazawa, Nii-gata and Nagoya during 1871, and in Yamanashi, Nagano and Ibaraki during 1872.[3]

The first wave of *bunmei-kaika* spread with apparent rapidity in local areas for several years after 1871. It was borne chiefly by a particular class of people – the mayors, the wealthy farmers and the newly appointed ward and neighborhood heads. Among these minor leaders there were some who held their own against the central authorities, as representatives of the people. Most of them, however, were opportunists who were eager to rise by showing 'achievements,' and who therefore impatiently pressed superficial enlightenment upon the people they administered.[4]

Such forcible 'enlightenment' naturally spawned various sorts of resistance among the farmers (as seen in the last chapter), weathering a series of aftershocks[5] as it gradually penetrated the rural areas. Not until the 1890s did substantive civilization and enlightenment, beyond the level of the slogan, take root in the lives of the local people.

Bunmei-kaika in the literal sense means 'civilization and enlightenment' in general. But its essence as an historical concept lies elsewhere, in the strange encounter between the basic emotional structure of the Japanese and various elements of Western and modern civilization.

The footfalls of civilization and enlightenment made vivid impressions on the villagers of the grassy countryside, but were absorbed without shaking the bedrock of their traditional mentality. The eminent anthropologist Yanagita Kunio described the process:

> In the peaceful villages nestled against the mountains, with their ancient beliefs in the collective illusions of contented mountain gods and menacing long-nosed goblins, it was said all over the country that in the dead of night badgers ran along the railroad tracks mimicking the sound of the steam engine. This talk was limited exclusively to the time just after the opening of the rail lines. Later, when the primary schools had been newly established, the story of the nighttime sounds was changed to the mimicking of schoolchildren's clamor. When the telegraph reached the villages, the sly badger was said to be in between the houses bawling telegrams. . . .
>
> This sort of talk was by no means limited to particular regions, and every house in the neighborhood always claimed to have heard the same sounds. That the curious new noises led to such reinvigoration of phantoms suggests that they made a very deep impression.

While there was much novelty that was visually and aurally perceptible, the real changes transpired soundlessly at a more profound level. Yanagita continues:

> The convenience of *shōji* [translucent paper doors] had been recognized for quite some time, but so long as the sale of

paper was forbidden under the non-commodity economy, it was not possible to install them in the farmhouses. Then by an odd turn of events, paper gradually flowed into the poorer homes in the form of children's school exercises. In books of pictures from the time, the *shoji* doors of those homes are always covered with copy sheets full of ABC's. Such was the scene in many villages as late as the middle of the Meiji period. Indeed, as the children started attending school, they began to become indispensable appurtenances.

In the common houses the use of *shōji* was seen at first as a simple home improvement, but it was actually a cause of momentous changes. . . . The brightening of every corner of the large structures led to the installation of internal partitions within the home. . . . Plate glass was not manufactured domestically until much later, but highly-prized imported glass came into use and began to be fitted into *shōji* frames, and from that time many people in the countryside began silently gazing out from their homes. . . . During their spare time, young people would retreat to the same window nooks to read books. They gradually came to know and think about things unknown to their elders, and the cramped rooms of their minds began to open outward.

Andon [paper-enclosed oil lamps] that were designed to be set anywhere were in fact unknown before this time. As they became more portable and brighter, and later when electric lamps could be turned on or off in any room, the idea of the home gradually changed. It became difficult to share a house of any size with anyone other than those with whom one was genuinely eager to live. This was the dispersion of fire, as I have called it in a previous work, or in other words, the waning of the influence of the hearth.[6]

Thus the generations were generated in the villages of Japan, and history proceeded quietly at the depths of society to foster the propulsive energy for the modern era.

Intension: transformation of the mental framework

We have seen that 'enlightened civilization' did not shake up the people's basic mentality, at least for the time being. The initial flow washed into their existing frame of desires, aesthetics, morality and worldview, in the form of fragmentary enlightened customs.

The people's version of the combination of 'Japanese spirit and Western learning' is nicely displayed in some lines from various songs which were popular during the 1870s:

> If I want to send a message when others are around
> I will use the electricity of my heart

> How pleasant is a letter after such a long time
> Connections are renewed by telegraph

> What started as a casual temporary treaty
> Grows stronger through ties to the new generation

> Set a meal for his photograph when father is away
> Such a fine way to fortify the family

> Squatting down with the hands for support
> And the hips twisted up – treadle sewing machine

> Now there are three hundred and sixty-five days
> More days for us to meet in the new calendar[7]

There was a clearly identifiable Zeitgeist that was widely operative in the minds of the people at the time. In the contemporary vernacular it was expressed as *hirakeru*, 'to be enlightened' (from a root meaning 'open').

> People say to each other, 'Of all the things on the road of life, what a blessing it is to encounter the world of enlightened ways. Upon reflection it is such a great progress, truly enlightened, so truly enlightened.' The words 'being enlightened' [*hirakeru*] are on everybody's lips nowadays, high and low, genteel and simple.
>
> (*Tokyo Enlightenment and Prosperity*, 1874)

> > Gradually everything is opening up
> > Results of the reign of enlightenment
> > A postcard will do the job
> > News by wire and steamships in the mountains

Wearing shoes while awaiting
Horse-drawn carriages and rickshaws
Low-priced inns are all the rage
And Western barbers and billiards . . .
Kaika Otsu-e bushi ('Enlightened *Otsu-e* Song,' c. 1872)

The image of becoming enlightened (*hirakeru*) is one of release or liberation, of moving from a closed-off situation into brightness. In substantive terms, this meant liberation from several forms of social closure: (1) cultural exclusionism, under the strict Tokugawa policy of national isolation; (2) the sealed-off character of each local area under the feudal daimyo system; (3) social conventions based on ignorance and irrationality; and (4) fixed life destinies, enforced by the feudal system of the four classes.

The new directions opened up by these liberations were: (1) a fresh and ingenuous curiosity about Western culture; (2) a yearning to go the capital, especially among ambitious rural youth; (3) impatience for scraps of civilization, and an urge to compulsively imitate them; and (4) visions of limitless ascent in the world, among all social classes.

The feeling of release was one of the pivotal elements of the sense of becoming enlightened. The other was the assumption of an affirmatively passive posture, a posture that can be called the 'consciousness of the beneficiary.'[8]

Since the arrival of steam trains I always go to see my grandchildren in Yokoyama. It has become normal to pay calls in all directions on a single journey. This country does so much for us that we must fight back tears. It is so convenient, so very convenient.
(*Tokyo Enlightenment and Prosperity*)

In the end, the mentality of enlightenment, that composite of liberation and passivity, did have perceptible impacts upon the desires, the aesthetics, the worldview and the morality of the people. The remainder of this section describes the process in each of those four areas.

a *Desires*
There was a yawning gap between the ideology and the social psychology of civilization and enlightenment.

Bunmei-kaika means quitting the base practices of former times, cultivating intelligence and virtue, diligently pursuing one's occupation, and living as a single nation in a land of tranquility, while recognizing and thoroughly deploring the veritable profligacy of the foolish and ignorant people.

(*Perspectives on Civilization and Enlightenment*, 1875)

The passive sense of liberation provided above all an *excitation*[9] of suppressed materialistic desires. The activities and phenomena which were described in common parlance as 'enlightenment' usually boiled down to either a taste for fine clothes and food, or unfettered behavior on the part of women. It was in the nature of *bunmei-kaika* to lend authority to the pursuit of material pleasure by labeling it as Western: 'as in the "English way" of luxury or the "French way" of ostentation' (*What Is Enlightenment?*, 1880).

Aside from the pursuit of material pleasures, there was wholesale excitation and actuation of other desires linked to worldly values of wealth, influence and prestige. A popular song chanted:

> To marry in the next world is the idiocy of old
> If not it in this world, what's the use?
> I am not attracted by appearance or status
> A fine man is one who is rich[10]

A contemporary booklet on *bunmei-kaika* imputes similar desires to a pair who happen to see the Emperor passing with his entourage.

A: They say today the Emperor is accompanying the Empress Dowager and the Empress in the carriage to visit the old manor, where the plum blossoms are in full bloom. How gorgeous!

B: You shan't be envious, for I aim to succeed, and one day I shall ride with you and some geishas to view the plum blossoms at the new manor.

A (laughing): Stop joking, 'tis the idle boast of a houseboy. You could never do it.

B (holding back laughter): How rude, how very rude of you.

(*Tokyo Enlightenment and Prosperity*)

This tendency was encouraged by bestselling books endorsing the same appetites, such as Fukuzawa Yukichi's *The Encouragement of Learning* (1872) and the translation of Samuel Smiles' *Self-Help* (1871).

Since the number who could aim at actual success was limited, there was a gap between goals and means, between ideals and reality. A part of its expression took the twisted form of speculative gambles, which swept the metropolitan districts. (See Section V of the previous chapter. After rabbit-selling was banned in 1872, the vogue continued with sales of dancing mice, gamecocks, canaries and other get-rich-quick rarities.) Another aspect of *bunmei-kaika* was a mania for inventions and improvements, on the pattern of the rickshaw, and the untold number who plunged into such schemes probably had motivations closely akin to those of speculators and gamblers.

b *Aesthetics*

The sense of modern liberation also extended to color. Gaudiness and beauty were a distinctive characteristic of the *bunmei-kaika* movement.[11] In one contemporary discussion, the concepts of enlightenment are submerged in a discussion of gaudy clothes and love of beauty, as a purported hidden trend of history.

Such a reform that forces enlightened people to revert to barbarous customs of old . . . could never profit the nation . . . and will not last long throughout the country, for people will revert once again to enlightened manners, and the taste for gay colors will prevail among the public. Since the opening of the ports, everyone has been very keen for enlightenment and progress . . . and the public has become quite accustomed to beauty.

(Comparisons of Past and Present, 1874)

At least among urbanites, the blossoming influx of Western civilization resulted in a wider, more diverse range of tastes. For the majority of common people, one look at glass or bricks or ironware was enough to stimulate incipient demand. Booklets about enlightened Tokyo made much of the grand new Western-style buildings.

More importantly, there was a shift in the pure aesthetics of the Japanese, through which the choice of Western manners became a symbol of the status which one assumed in the new society. This led to such promotions as, 'without the graceful adornment of a watch with a gold or silver chain, you cannot be a real, golden man.' The new status symbols ranged from Western clothes, food and buildings to walking along with a Western dog.

> The mansions of imperial appointees were formerly estates like those of the daimyo or the shogun. Now some of them are ornate, three stories high, in the English style, or designed for French-style living. . . . Inside they are fitted out with Western-style chairs, fine dining tables and carpets, with flowers in vases the year round, and colored light from crystal chandeliers. . . . With an assortment of strange utensils, dressed up in vivid colors, they eat beef and mutton, speak English and French (standard Japanese will not do), grow long beards and mustaches, and strive for white-skinned natures.

> (*Tokyo Enlightenment and Prosperity*)

c *Worldview*

The speed with which literacy spread through Japan in the early Meiji years is virtually without parallel in the modern history of any nation.

The first indication of the Restoration government's mass-education policy was an instruction to 'establish primary schools' in the Prefectural Administration Order of February 1869. Public schools were opened in earnest after the Education System decree of August 1872, with its famous exhortation that 'on no account shall a village have a household without learning, nor any household a member without learning.' The decree divided the nation into eight university districts, each to contain 32 middle-school districts, which were each to comprise 210 primary school districts, and directed that schools be established accordingly. This was a grandiose plan, for it envisioned a total of 53,760 primary schools, whereas in 1965 there were only 22,676. As early as 1875, the Education Ministry listed 20,692 public primary schools, although only 3,806 of them were newly constructed; about two-fifths were in temples or shrines and about one-third in homes.[12]

More significant are the proportions of children actually enrolled in primary school. In 1876 Nagano Prefecture led with

63.2 per cent, followed by Yamanashi with 59 per cent, and Tokyo and Osaka with 58.8 per cent each. The national average in 1879 was 41.2 per cent (58.2 per cent of boys, 22.6 per cent of girls).[13]

At the beginning, most of the primary school texts, especially at the first-grade level, were direct translations of American Wilson readers. These were full of phrases that were rather odd in Japanese and in Japan. They also contained explanations and illustrations of the 'five types of people in the world' (Asian, European, African, Malay, American), and model essays on the idea of mutual understanding of their differences. Thus school attendance meant that radically different worldviews were glimpsed by children who had been dozing in the 'Asiatic indolence' of Japanese villages. During the 1880s errand boys in sake shops and fish markets would prattle about 'the different types of people in the world.' At least one critic of the school system admitted (in a newspaper essay bemoaning the lack of morals education) that the schoolchildren of Iwate Prefecture were well versed in the names and historical outlines of countries on all continents.

For the authorities, the fast spread of literacy served several important objectives. One was making the people receptive to official communications (i.e. government instructions).[14] Another was the promotion of trade and industry, so as to build national prosperity and military strength.[15] Third was the cultivation of capable individuals for administrative positions. Fourth were the reformist ideals which, along with the slight pressure of the nominal commitment to 'equality of the four classes,' were an early motif of Meiji government policies.[16] And fifth was the diplomatic necessity, which later took on greater importance, for Japan to be seen from abroad to have become a 'civilized' nation.

Among the people, there was some resistance to the enforced burden of school expenses, as well as some apprehension that the ability to read and write would lead to dissolute living or a slackening in household duties. Yet the groundwork of demand for literacy was very much in place. First, the commodity economy was spreading, and rudimentary reading, writing and ciphering were indispensable for the selling and stocking of goods. Schools operated by Buddhist temples for the children of common people had been proliferating across Japan for a century, well before the quickening of educational interest brought on by the opening of foreign trade in the 1850s and the Restoration reforms.[17]

Second, the sphere of life and the range of interests of the people were fast expanding, as government authority was centralized and new modes of transport and communication came into use in the new commercial economy. The framework of everyday life was expanding beyond the scope of direct experience, and the center of gravity was shifting toward the pseudo-environment of society at large. With this structural change, the ability to decode and manipulate symbols became more functional and attractive.

Third, the slogan of 'equality of the four classes' held out before the people, at least on the ideal level, the dream of unlimited elevation of social status. Scholastic education was perceived as just such a ladder of ascent. (See Chapter 15 on Successism.)

So much for the worldview impacts of mass education. What was the worldview of the *bunmei-kaika* movement itself, as expressed in the contemporary popular books and pamphlets on enlightenment? Let us survey a representative tract from 1873, entitled *Civilization and Enlightenment*, by Katō Yoshikazu:[18]

First and foremost is the theme of escape from the magical worldview: 'Under reason, the world never contains mysterious things.' 'In truth, apparitions are not apparitions.' 'Goblins disguised as foxes and badgers are disproved by reason.' 'In truth, long-nosed goblins do not exist.' The tract goes a step further to espouse a new perception of subjective identity:

> Those who are surprised that mysterious things can be explained are being manipulated by their halters. But civilized, enlightened people who are free of such personal convictions can well infer the true nature of any sort of thing and understand the reason of its occurrence. It is well to use one's own discrimination to decide which things should and should not be believed.

Yet the author takes a different tack in a section explicating 'Reasons for Veneration of the Gods': 'it is none other than a matter of faith, and to say that such a belief is mistaken would be to turn one's back on the essential meaning of this section, which may be summed up as filial piety and patriotism.' He goes on to argue adroitly for the legendary emperor system. 'Of course there are mysterious things written in the books about the Age of Gods . . . but as these concern matters from the time of the first separation of heaven and earth, in truth they must certainly include mysterious things. In China and in the West as well, every explanation of original creation includes mysterious things, but aside from the establishment of the order of heaven and earth, there is no place for mysterious interpretation.' This sort of tolerance for the miraculous existed side by side with the fundamentally empirical, rationalistic outlook of *bunmei-kaika*, allowing the development of the following creative theology: 'Just as it is impossible for a mosquito to understand how it could formerly have survived underwater as a larva, so it is impossible for us today to understand what occurred in ancient times.'

In its basic character, this material is quite typical of the 'enlightenment books' of the time. They begin by criticizing the magical worldview and presenting the rationalistic outlook. Then they stop short at the boundary of the government-certified ideology. Finally, they play to the galleries by glossing over the implicit contradiction, with a leap of reason through some arbitrary metaphor. Such wisely sophomoric glosses were served up to the people precisely in order to deal with the paradoxical duality of *bunmei-kaika* teachings, and of the Restoration itself.

d *Morality*

During the time when direct translations of Wilson readers were used as primary textbooks, the ethical content of public education was a transplant of the American protestant ethic.

> God gives nothing to those who do not work hard. Those
> who work hard are rewarded. Studying should be thought
> of as the mother of happiness. Those who strive shall succeed,
> and those who are lazy shall reap no reward. Do not think
> that if you do not work today it can be done tomorrow, nor
> that if you do not work this year it can be done next year.
> Time flies like an arrow, it goes and it never returns.
>
> (Third-year primary school textbook)

These textbooks were in wide use from 1873 up to about 1887. The nature and extent of their moral impact on the Japanese mind during the formative period of capitalism offers fascinating ground for future research.

Intellectual historians tell us that such enlightened thinkers as Fukuzawa Yukichi, Taguchi Ukichi and Mori Ōgai energetically introduced the morality of the modern citizens' society, centered on concepts of equality of class and gender. But at the time, the actual function which was often served by ideas like 'all people are created equal' was not so much the formation of a citizens' society as the encouragement of success through 'learning.' The drive to succeed was a new social value that was at once desirable and moralistic. It was ethically grounded in the authority and dignity of a pre-established harmony between individual and society, and was thus similar in atmosphere to the values espoused by Bernard de Mandeville or Adam Smith in the eighteenth century. For example, a popular song from the early Meiji years equated success with moral conduct.

> The student who must dress in rags
> Will be wearing brocades in the end
> If you want to know the essence of enlightenment
> Let us call it compassion for others

For a description of how ideas of freedom and equality were grasped at the level of popular consciousness, we may turn to the dialogue of a second-rate novel of the time, *What Is Enlightenment?*:

> Since the imperial government was restored . . . they have taken great pains to give more and more freedom to the people. Isn't it a wonderful thing?
>
> (Part 1, 1872)

> Don't you know that nowadays they have imported what are called rights of independence and freedom from the West? The government has bought them all up and is selling them by the piece throughout the country, even to the lowest classes, and the *eta* are getting a lot of them and entering the ranks of the common people. If you ask me, freedom means behaving just as you please so long as someone else doesn't object.
>
> (Part 2, 1880)

That image of freedom displays in concentrated form the moral sensibility of *bunmei-kaika* as modernization-from-above.

The latent popular foundation for criticism and reform of the deeply rooted old morality would await the People's Rights Movement. In the meantime, the maincurrent of *bunmei-kaika* moral consciousness was authoritarian, catering to the powers that be and the trend of the times. Nevertheless, the value references of the Japanese were rearranged through the substitution of one authority for another.

What were the impacts of the newly predominant value references of 'Western civilization' on the ways of thinking of the people during the formative period of modern Japan? And what potentials did these impacts provide for the modern Japan that was in gestation?

II Reorganization of value reference

Multiple levels of authority

A typical advertisement from the early Meiji era, for a medication called Hōtan (Treasure Pill), reads in part:

> From the ninth-generation successor of Yamamoto Haruyuki
> of Abeno, Izumi, who began furnishing various medicines
> in 1680, which descendant has studied from 1862 with the
> great Dutch Doctor Baldwin, and in 1871 was granted
> License Number One for the Sale of Medicines by the Tokyo
> Imperial University.

The references which are used to promote commodities to the public are fine reflectors of the value orientation of the people at a given time. It should be fruitful to trace the logic of public exhortation, as an aspect of the history of popular awareness of authority. At the outset of the Meiji era, three tiers of authority are clearly visible in advertisements: tradition (as in the uninterrupted family line), government (License Number One), and the West (the great Dutch Doctor). With regard to civilization and enlightenment in particular, the authority of the government and the authority of the West function in series.

> Haircutting is the custom of the civilized Western nations,
> and consequently the Emperor himself does it, to say
> nothing of the common people in general.
>
> (*Tokyo Enlightenment and Prosperity*, 1874)

The flow of authority for 'civilization' is set out here in a straightforward manner: from the West to the emperor to the nation as a whole. (And off went the topknots, as mentioned earlier.) This thinking extended even to the liberation of the *eta* outcasts, the reason for which, the story went, was that the existence of such discrimination 'brings great shame to the Emperor in facing Westerners.' Outdoor nudity was prohibited by a proclamation which stated that it was offensive to visiting Westerners and reflected poorly upon the country. The same justification appeared in a proclamation banning mixed bathing, pornography and tattoos – 'barbarous customs which Westerners look down upon.'

The disposition of the government was often shored up by the authority of the West, for the government of the time was actually unable to hold its own against the criticism of Westerners. Viewed the other way, through the consciousness of the people, the West and 'civilization' itself were imbued with authority for the first time via the disposition of the ruling elite. The solar calendar was accepted not for its intrinsic rationality, but because of a government order; the people referred to it as 'Cabinet dates.' Beef butchers added 'Government Licensed' to their signboards, and even the Westernization of homes was occasionally justified as a 'strict order of the Imperial Court.'[19]

> Of course nowadays the Court is rejecting the old ways and
> embracing the Western style, and there is nothing that can
> be said against it. It has been strongly decreed. . . . One of
> the provisions of the Charter Oath is to seek knowledge
> throughout the world and strengthen the foundations of
> Imperial rule. This is the will of the gods, and not something
> to be discussed lightly.
>
> (*Tokyo Souvenir*, c. 1869)

As we have seen, the value references which oriented government power at the time were in turn often legitimized by appealing a step further to 'civilization' (the West). Thus *bunmei-kaika* had two tiers of value standards: on the actual level, the authority of civilization depended upon the power existing in the government; while on the theoretical level, the powers-that-be relied upon and drew their legitimacy from the authority of civilization.

At the transitional moment when Japan embarked toward modernity, the operative social-psychological dynamic lay in the delicate, interdependent balance between two value references, the particularistic and the universalistic. Two roads toward two different modernities were in gestation: the modernity that served only to select, interpret and manufacture universal doctrines, which those in power often used to legitimize their own policies; and the modernity that served as an independent set of value standards to supervise, criticize and reform the powers-that-be.

Conformity and deviation

In the popular books and pamphlets which furnished the conventional teachings of *bunmei-kaika*, the paradoxical symbiosis of those two modernities in the womb of 'enlightenment' is often revealed ironically. The following discussion is from a booklet entitled *A Dialogue on Enlightenment*, published in 1874. It is purportedly between Kyūhei (a realistic yet unreal moniker meaning 'Old Ordinary') and Kaijirō (a similar name which reads like 'Enlightened John').

Kyūhei: I see. I understand very clearly that the present
political system is very fine, but I have one more question
about what you are saying. You say the government officials
are to be regarded as the servants of the people. And yet
it is they who oversee everything that goes on. Everyone
bows deeply to the salaried government officials. People
respect them as their masters, as Buddhas who feed them by
allowing them to pick crumbs from their beards. But the
officials treat the people as if they were domestic animals
who have come inside the house. Whenever they meet
people they flaunt their authority. Where is the logic in this?
No servant would be so impolite as our government officials.
Shall we prostrate ourselves before our own servants? . . .
[The citizens] should not have to become soldiers and carry
heavy guns. If a bureaucrat complains about that, then the

first thing you should tell him is to remember the
relationship between servant and master, and if he still
complains, then you dismiss him. . . . I cannot quite
understand the actual conditions in the world today. If the
political system had some proper logic, then the people
would not have to put up with public notices and ordinances,
they would not have to worry about paying taxes on the
money they earn through their hard work, and they would
not have to become soldiers and be shot at. That is the way
it ought to be, and if the people were to hear that it was
so . . . they would dance with joy.

'Old Ordinary' is keenly aware of the contradiction of ideals and
reality in *bunmei-kaika*, in terms of the life experience of the
populace. His complaint elicits this response:

Kaijirō: But Kyūhei, I think your logic is quite absurd. . . .
If a body says this is *my* field and this is *my* mountain, and
they are one or two miles away from his home, the reason
that nobody will rob the field or the mountain is because
the government rules the world with law. If a body has ten
warehouses and a hundred plots of land and a hundred
thousand pieces of silver, then he can hold sumptuous feasts
for all manner of beautiful women, for he has enough, and
he need not worry about the poverty of his descendants,
because the government rules this world with law. . . . The
people in general have the right to receive benefit from the
government, and they also have the obligation to give some
benefit in return, for otherwise it would not work.

Kaijirō has let drop a telling reference to the hierarchical social
and beneficiary structures of 'the present political situation.'

Kyūhei: Let's talk about how the police treat offenders. . . .
If it is someone who looks like a bureaucrat, they treat him
very politely, but if it is someone in worn-out clothes such
as I wear . . . if we merely say a polite hello, they
immediately turn tough and treat it as a major incident, and
if they think we have misbehaved they glare at us and purse
their lips . . . and sometimes they beat us with their sticks
until we cannot walk. This is something I have sometimes

seen, and every time I do I am filled with hatred toward the police, and I wish I could slap their faces.

Kaijirō responds to this with similes such as, 'the people are like trees in a garden, and the government is like the gardener who prunes the trees in order to preserve them.'

Predictably, the whole book is set up for a happy ending in which Kyūhei surrenders to Kaijirō's enlightened persuasion. And yet the actual misgivings of the people which form the backdrop for hapless Kyūhei's supporting role are evoked in a moving and memorable manner.

In this pattern, the one which *bunmei-kaika* teachings most often followed, not only does the personal sense of resistance come up short, but the amorphous rebelliousness of the samurai, peasants and merchants from former times is brought to its knees.

On the other hand, the precipitous and reckless introduction of new culture, typified by the early primary school readers, also gave birth to a mental world which spread beyond the goalposts of the oligarchy's intentions. Ienaga Saburō has pointed out that:

Amid the tide of *bunmei-kaika*, Ōi Kentarō studied democracy by way of French jurisprudence, and another theorist of the same camp, Ueki Emori, developed his own ideas while eagerly attending lectures of the Meirokusha and the Mita Oratorical Meeting. The People's Rights Movement could not have developed without the historical premise of 'enlightenment' thought.

Education by means of direct translations, without any commentary or filtering by the authorities, exposed children to the raw wind emanating from genuine documents of Western culture. The core group which was educated under a translated Western primary curriculum (between 1872 and 1879) were those born from 1868 to 1870. This mini-generation happened to produce a series of modern Japan's deepest thinkers: Kitamura Tōkoku, Tokutomi Roka, Kinoshita Naoe, Taoka Ryō'un, Nishida Kitarō and Suzuki Daisetsu. (Of course *bunmei-kaika* was only the first of the forces which shaped their ideas, during the tremendous upheavals from the Restoration through the Popular Rights Movement.)

The shifting posture of authority itself allowed some breathing space for a sense of liberation and autonomy. Here is a vivid portrayal of the circumstances confronting young people in the early Meiji years, part of a purported consultation on personal matters between students at a girls' high school:

Ume: You cannot imagine how upset I am. I never stop worrying. Kiku, you must tell me what I should do. . . . You see, I come from a samurai family, but unfortunately my father died when I was young, so we had very little money to live on and we had a rather hard road. Now my mother, who devoted herself to bringing me up, my dear mother has arranged for me to marry the second son of one of our relatives. He's my cousin. My mother is constantly telling me to get married quickly. She's always talking with the matchmaker. This person I am supposed to marry has lots of pimples and he's very strange. . . . It's not because he's so ugly that I can't stand him. I can put up with that. What I can't stand is that he has no head for learning, no common sense. What should I do? He's very skilled in swordsmanship. But he's never read any Japanese history, much less the Chinese classics. And of course he has read no Western books. I hear that recently he is spending a lot of time with a certain official who is good for nothing. They debate about invading Korea, but they know nothing about it. How stupid . . . I wouldn't want to talk about anything with him! But it's my mother's order. If I disobey her, it will make her very unhappy, and that would be a sin. I am utterly depressed. I'm embarrassed because I can't concentrate. If I try to read a book, all I can do is think about this. I can't even sleep when I lay down. When I'm awake my head is drooping. I have no idea what to do. That's why I've come to you.

Kiku (Laughing): What are you so worried about? There's nothing to be afraid of. You've been going to school for a long time now. Haven't you gotten rid of the old-fashioned ideas yet? In the old days, fathers had absolute authority. If you didn't obey them, you were lucky to stay alive. But your body is made by god, and your parents only raise it. Your obligation to god is the first thing, and your obligation to your parents comes second. Those are the universal rules of human society. Nowadays, authority figures don't have power any more. They can't make their students and children do what they want them to. When your mother orders you to do something, if you have a *reason* to refuse, then it's all right to refuse. Marriage is a moral thing, and people can't be simply ordered into it by their parents. If you say nothing then you'll be married off to that terrible person. You have the *right* to make up your own mind, and it's up to you to assert it.

Ume: But how can I assert my rights?

Kiku: I have high hopes. Very few women have been able to study up to now, so there are not many woman teachers. I am still young, and I am studying, and if I succeed, I will not marry. I'll become a woman teacher and get some money and I'll rely on my own means to support myself. That's freedom. Maybe I'll go to the Shimabara today and to the Kinsugi tomorrow [theaters], or go out and enjoy the flowers and the mountains. Who's to say we can't? Maybe I'll go drinking with some man, and maybe I'll sleep with some wonderful man. Nobody can say I don't have the right. Wouldn't that be nice? If you have money, you can do whatever you want, with actors, with artists, or whoever. Much more so in choosing your husband! Of course you can't get all those things unless you have learning. You must study hard and never give up your freedom.

Ume: That's very good advice. I'm not terribly smart, but from now on I want to start following your advice.

Kiku: If that's so, then you'd best refuse your mother's order straightaway.

Then they entered the lecture hall.

(*An Account of the New Prosperity in Tokyo*, 1876)

What is vaguely described here is the sprouting of the modern ego, within the aperture between the tottering Confucian morality and the newly introduced value systems. It was a trial-and-error process of groping around and testing out various new notions. While we cannot know how much is real and how much is fiction in this particular conversation, it no doubt reflects the state of mind of at least a part of the generation who grew up amid the Restoration conflicts.

The metamorphosis of the capital-yearning sensibility

We have seen above how the various phenomenologies of *bunmei-kaika* were shaped by paradoxical compounds, of the ambient tides of self-determination and external determination, of liberation and opportunism. The socioeconomic factor behind these tides was the rapid promotion by the state of *top-down modernization*, in order to equip a nation where conditions were unripe for spontaneous capitalist development to withstand the external threats posed by Western capitalist powers. In the social-psychological dimension, the medium for the cultivation of top-down modernization was a traditional sensibility that the Yanagita school of anthropology calls 'capital yearning.' This posture of longing for 'refinement' consisted essentially in the immense expectations which rural Japanese placed on the capital (*miyako*), and their 'keen sensitivity to cultural currents' (Kamishima Jirō). That predisposition on the part of the people provided the psychological drive toward civilization and enlightenment, which allowed them to undergo repeated change and social metamorphosis as they responded to top-down modernization.

There were two elements in the capital-yearning mindset. On one side it *encouraged a dynamism toward change*, a spirit of emergence from the obscurity of present conditions, based on longing for the 'yet-unseen world.' On the other side, it *discouraged personal creativity*, leaving no ground for the spirit of digging in and remaking the existing life setting: one could either eagerly await the arrival of the light of metropolitan culture, or set out alone from the village and head for the city. As a result it was fertile ground for submissiveness to authority, and for aspiration to authority (the cult of success).

During the *bunmei-kaika* period this sense of capital-yearning expanded to an international scale. In its aspect of transformational dynamism, it was amplified by the sense of liberation from the Tokugawa socio-cultural yoke of national isolation and class restriction. The other, non-creative aspect was reinforced by two factors: the perception of the overwhelming cultural superiority of the West, and the new centralization of politics, society and culture. The sensibilities which are lumped under the name 'civilization and enlightenment' thus acquired a widened sweep and a diversified range.

The amplitude of the cultural movement was jacked still further by the globalization of the metropolitan horizon. The *miyako* of the original capital-yearning was spatially condensed to a single location (Kyoto) which served as a concrete model. Whether or not a given practice was really the mode in the capital was an issue that could be verified by actual inspection. But in the new pattern of capital-yearning, the *miyako* model was the West – the vast and vague expanse of Europe and America, with its diverse array of nineteenth-century systems and philosophies, from Prussian autocracy to American democracy, from imperialism to communism. Like the blind men and the elephant, the superficial Westernization of the Japanese consisted of continual reassertions of 'real culture' and 'true enlightenment.' Hence the character of *bunmei-kaika* civilization was marked not only by the paradoxical balance between universal concepts and the self-serving interpretations of the authorities, but also by the fundamental multipolarity of civilization itself.

Lacking a single coherent model, Western culture appeared as a *set* of mutually conflicting values, and this was a blessing for modern Japan. The broad scope for interpretation ushered in a season of flourishing debate. In public bathhouses, restaurants and village assemblies, the people criticized each other's 'false' culture, 'uncivilized' behavior or 'crackpot' civilization, and argued about 'real culture' and 'true enlightenment.' Countless sophists became expert at devising temporarily watertight proofs. Above all, the multiplicity of 'civilization' and its interpretations made it all the easier for those in power to pick and choose whatever suited their own purposes. But on the other hand, the disunity of authoritative standards sent shock waves through the absolutism of authority in general, paving the way for the people to think about their own autonomy. Further, it forced intelligent, motivated young people to set their minds to the search for the real basis, the original wellspring of the many faces of 'civilization.'

By redrawing the capital-yearning sensibility of the Japanese along international lines, *bunmei-kaika* toppled the certainty and the substance of their notion of 'metropolitan refinement.' From that time on, modern Japan was constrained or released into its still-unending quest for the ultimately refined version of 'true' enlightenment, amid the many competing strains of civilization.

Notes

1   The English words 'civilization' and 'enlightenment' are used in this chapter as direct translations of *bunmei* and *kaika*. The idiom *bunmei-kaika*, with its implication that Western modernization equals civilization, came into use around 1870 and is used mainly to refer to the cultural movement of that time.

2   An example: 'In the Kami-shitayaji district of Yamagata, the district supervisor had an urgent announcement for the villages, and one day in late March he sent out a circular at twelve o'clock noon. It reached the administrator in the next village at one o'clock in the afternoon and he, being not fully cognizant of the new time system, sent it on to the next village with the notation that it was dispatched at thirteen o'clock. The administrator there, similarly confused about the new time system, noted that he had received it and passed it on at fourteen o'clock. It was successively relayed through fifteen villages, where none of the administrators grasped the time system, finally reaching the village of Chōzenji where the notation was twenty-seven o'clock. It needs be said that by now, government instructions should be thoroughly circulated among the illiterate and ignorant of the remote backward quarters, and administrators should be conscientious in their duties. It is to be hoped that in all quarters the officials will cease this inconsistent practice.' *Shimbun Zasshi*, No. 93, April 1873.

3   The geographical distribution of the early local newspapers forms a belt across central Honshu. It seems to have been no accident that the new culture was most agilely adopted in the region *between* western Japan, with its deeply rooted, high-culture traditions, and northeastern Japan, where the socioeconomic base was still immature. Rickshaws came into use faster on the Chūsandō mountain highway than on the Tōkaidō, the main route between Tokyo and Kyoto. Also, as stated later in the text, the primary school entrance rates were highest at first (surpassing the major cities) in Nagano and Yamanashi prefectures, which also had some of the earliest non-metropolitan newspapers.

4   The following passage from a fictional work of 1880, *What is*

Enlightenment?, portrays the actual situation at the time. A teacher is scolding a village administrator. 'All your efforts are in vain. You have no sense of loyalty. You look only to your own reputation. The newspapers all say that in every prefecture the mayors are educating the conservative villagers and preaching to them every day. They open schools and hire teachers and educate the conservative village people and their own children. For this they are all commended by their prefectural governments. The newspapers say that some of them receive rewards from the Ministry of Finance. You are jealous of all this fine talk, so you go around the village and harass the poor farmers and exploit their energies, taking risks with other people's money, as it were, in order to make yourself famous in the newspapers. You should be ashamed of yourself for even thinking about such a thing. It's like the old Chinese saying that for the success of a single mandarin all the subjects are bled dry. The government does not intend for you to make a few hundred farmers suffer and pay taxes just for the sake of your personal reputation.' Tsuji Kōsō, *Kaika no wa nashi*, Part 2, 1880, reprinted in *Meiji bunka zenshū*, 1st edn, Vol. 20, p. 82.

A non-fiction example: 'Twenty-nine farmers with cropped heads, from the village of Kengendō in Saitama, hurried to the prefectural office, led by one Marubōzu, and reported that on the previous night after midnight they had been suddenly hailed by three men who ordered them all to have their heads cropped, and then roughly cut off their topknots with scissors.' *Shimbun Zasshi*, No. 40, April 1872.

5 In 1880 a village in Nagano conducted a boycott of imported goods including lamps, hats and umbrellas, and even sold the chairs which had been purchased for the village hall the previous year to another village. Around 1882 various localities in Ishikawa, Shimane and Shiga formed alliances to boycott imported goods, and according to a contemporary record, 'The sale of Western goods was suddenly stopped, and Western-style clothes became rare sights on festive occasions,' and various repercussions occurred when imports were later circulated in the areas. (Yanagita Kunio, ed., *Meiji bunkashi, Fūzoku hen*, Yōyosha, 1954, p. 136.)

6 Yanagita Kunio, *History of Culture and Everyday Life in the Meiji and Taisho Periods (Meiji Taishō shi, Sesō hen*, Chikuma Shobō, 1963), pp. 158, 194–6.

7 Lyrics from *Dodo-itsu senshū*, Vol. 8 of *Meiji bunka zenshū*, rev. edn, Nippon Hyōron Shinsha, 1955; except the first pair of lines, from *Kaika dodo-itsu*, Vol. 3, cited in Fujisawa Morihiko, *Ryūkōka hyakunenshi*, Dai-ichi Shuppansha, 1951, p. 194.

8 Types and patterns of response to a social system (see Figure 13.1).

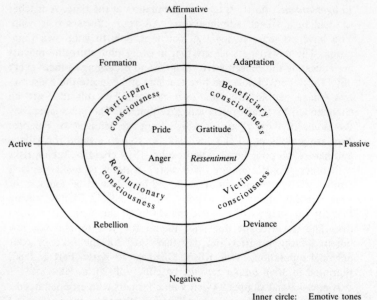

Figure 13.1 *Types and patterns of response to a social system*

9 The term 'excitation' (*reiki*) is used by Kamishima Jirō to denote the accentuation and amplification, by means of acculturation, of elements already existing within a culture. *Kindai nihon no seishin kōzō*, Iwanami Shoten, 1961, p. 183.

10 Lyrics from *Dodo-itsu senshū*, op. cit. 'Insistence on the perennial precept of the Zen masters . . . 'to tend the fields rather than write poetry, to be the one who becomes the moneylender' is actually a preeminent teaching of enlightenment.' Oka Sankei, *Comparisons of Past and Present (Konjaku kurabe*, 1874; reprinted in *Meiji bunka zenshū*, rev. edn, Vol. 8, p. 173.

11 'Women delight in wearing clothing in shades of grape, lavender and plum,' according to the Shimbun Zasshi, No. 81, 1873. Many other reports attest to the popularity of purple in the early Meiji years. And the popular mind today associates the Meiji years with purple; see Chapter 16.

12 Figures from the third annual report of the Education Ministry, cited in Miyahara Seiichi, *Kyōiku-shi*, Tōyō Keizai Shinpōsha, 1963, p. 31.

13 Prefectural figures from Miyahara, op. cit., p. 33. National figures

from the government statistical yearbook, *Nihon teikoku tōkei nenkan*. Primary school enrollment consistently exceeded 50 per cent after 1890, and exceeded 90 per cent from 1902.

14 The *Tohi Shimbun*, No. 2, May 1868, excerpted a letter from Osaka interpreting the remarks of a Frenchman: 'He said that since nowadays most of the proclamations of the renewed government of the Japanese Empire use Chinese characters, eight or nine of every ten people cannot understand their meaning. He said that it is necessary to establish schools in every village to teach the necessary reading skills.'

15 The Education System decree of 1872 emphasized instruction in daily-use characters for 'property management, commercial prosperity, and advancement.' On the other hand, Miyahara Seiichi points out that this also 'served as the logical premise to justify the payment of education fees by the people.' Miyahara asserts that, at least at the time when the Education Decree was issued, 'education in the schools was not meant to instill absolutist ideology, but was intended solely to impart Western technical knowledge.'

16 Because of its permeation by egalitarian ideals, the Education Decree provoked resentment toward the central authorities among conservatives and reactionaries, and even certain 'enlightened' leaders of the Restoration government. Nevertheless, it remained as the framework of education policy until the Revised Education Decree of 1880. Hence it was not simply by chance that such ideals played a role in the molding of Meiji-period attitudes.

17 The spread of temple schools began gradually in the Kyōhō era (1716–35), increased during the Temmei and Kansei eras (1781–1800) and the Bunka-Bunsei period (1804–29), and reached its peak in the Tempō era (1830–44).

18 Quotations from Katō Yoshikazu's *Bunmei-kaika* are taken from *Meiji bunka zenshū*, 1st edn, Vol. 20, pp. 15–23. This is the *bunmei-kaika* tract most often cited by scholars of the movement, although many turn to others as well, in part because Katō was evidently a Shintōist.

19 'Westerners find it very amusing that Japanese go barefoot on floor mats. Wherefore it has now been decreed by strict order of the Imperial Court that it would be well to build houses in the Western manner, and for people to behave according to natural laws, by sitting upon chairs to conduct business during the day and sleeping upon beds above the floor at night.' Yokogawa Akinami, 'Portal to Enlightenment' (*Kaika no ireguchi*, 1873, pamphlet).

14 Value and Belief Systems in Prewar Textbooks

In terms of its dominant value, premodern, communital Japan was an ocean of Harmony – a milieu in which ascribed status and particularized identifications informed the bulk of the people's behavior. In the sea change that was brought on by *bunmeikaika* and the People's Rights Movement, vast amounts of Achievement – an opposite, universalist, non-ascriptive value – precipitated into the society. (See Figure 14.1.) From the multitudes who were buried away in the microcosms of daily life in their hometowns, the early-Meiji sociocultural movements brought forth numerous groups of aspirants who sought to rise in the wider, outer world.

Those two separate, polarized values briefly went their respective ways, but were soon reunited within the finely engineered system of the Meiji state. In the process, Harmony was freed from the traditional fatalism of birth circumstances (via 'equality

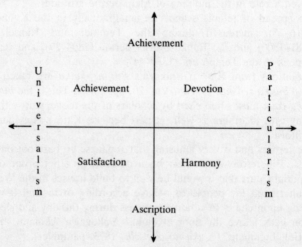

Source: Sakuta Kei'ichi, 'Kachi to kōdō,' *Bunka to kōdō* 1963, p. 37.

Figure 14.1 *General typology of social values*

of the four classes'), and set on new moorings through the institutionalization of the scholastic ladder as the route to success. Meanwhile, the Achievement value which attracted so many aspirants was interwoven into *loyalty* to the nation headed by the emperor, diet and army (as in the transfiguration of the people's-rights movement into assertions of national sovereignty, discussed in Chapter 2). As the energy of ascent was particularized and closed off, the value of Devotion (to the emperor state) swelled up to absorb much of the orientations toward Harmony and Achievement. Devotion became the unifying, supreme principle in late-Meiji society.

The Meiji oligarchy were able to elicit the active energies of the people who had been dozing in localized Harmony, by continually releasing them from the ascriptive value aspect; and at the same time to ensure the loyalty of those who were awakened to universalist Achievement, by continually channeling them into nationalist particularism. The secret of the extraordinary success of the Meiji regime was precisely this enticement of the people's aspirations, out of the contradictions of Harmony and Achievement, and into Devotion in the form of *active loyalty*.

This chapter will look into the reciprocal dynamics of the two early-Meiji impulses – to remain submerged in the Harmonious actualities of daily life, and to Achieve a rational reordering of daily life along value standards which transcended its routines. For it was these dynamics which spawned the value structure of the later-Meiji system, thereby locking in the value orientation of modernizing Japan as a whole, and furnishing the motive force for the modernization process. What, then, were the structural and functional aspects of that fatefully effective Meiji value system?

1 Family state: the value system in morals textbooks

The data which best serve to identify the official ideology that was implanted in the minds of the people during the latter half of the Meiji era are to be found in the contemporary textbooks.

Historically, the key routes by which ruling elites have sought to acculturate their peoples have been religious institutions, schools, and the mass media. In modern Japan, Shintō and Buddhism cannot compare in depth or breadth with religion in the West, either as internal regulating forces in society or as instruments for inculcating the popular mind. The mass media did not attain broad-ranging influence comparable to that of the school system until, at the earliest, the end of the Taisho era in the 1920s. In the later Meiji period, then, it was education in the schools which was overwhelmingly the most important means of instilling values among the people. Moreover, due to the generation gaps opened up by the rapidity of Japanese modernization, home training became relatively ineffectual for the acquisition of modes of social adaptation. By and large, Japanese mothers and fathers have been 'behind the times' ever since Meiji. Finally, the strong role of academic attainments in the determination of career tracks, and hence chances for success in life, makes schooling still more significant in the molding of the Japanese person.

As for the content of school education, during the beginning Meiji years before the consolidation of the government, the texts themselves were not fixed, and education was in fact rather free and unrestrained.[1] During the Taisho era, on the other hand, there was rather widespread advocacy of a free and easy, child-centered style of education, not necessarily adhering to textbooks.[2] In the latter half of the Meiji era, however, education was thoroughly given over to explication, amplification and reiteration of the textbooks.[3] Consequently, at least during this period, textbooks played the decisive role in the education that was conducted in the Japanese schools.

Before proceeding to analyze the contents of textbooks during and after the solidification of the Meiji establishment, it will be useful to trace the basic patterns and changes of textbooks through the forty-odd years of the Meiji era. Karasawa Tomitarō divides them into five time periods:

Period I	(1872–9):	Translated Western textbooks
Period II	(1880–5):	Revival of Confucian ethics
Period III	(1886–1903):	State-approved textbooks
Period IV	(1904–9):	State-compiled textbooks, first series
Period V	(1910–17):	State-compiled textbooks, second series

For the first few years after the Education Decree of 1872,

during the time of 'civilization and enlightenment,' the school-books were direct or abridged translations from the West, mainly America and France. But their contents, some of which actually encouraged the People's Rights Movement, were undesirable to the clan-based oligarchy, especially after the Satsuma Rebellion of 1877, when the government came to view the radicals rather than the conservatives as the main enemies. In 1880, the Ministry of Education banned the use of parts or all of the leading texts of this period, because they 'contain articles which are inappropriate for primary school textbooks.' The ban included even a 'moral training' manual issued by the ministry itself (*Shūshinron, A Treatise on Moral Training*, Abe Taizō, tr.), and one issued by the Imperial Household Ministry (*Meiji-kō sessō, Readings on Meiji Thought*). It also removed such widely used texts as *Taisei kanzen kunmo* (*Western Instruction of Moral Goodness*, translated and explicated by Mitsukuri Rinshō) and *Shūshin kunmō*, (*Moral Instruction*, abridged translation by Nawa Kenji).

The sudden shift in the central government's education policy had begun with a manifesto on 'The Main Points of Education' (*Kyogaku taishi*), drafted by Motoda Eifu on the basis of the Meiji emperor's impressions during his 1878 tour of central Honshu. This document observed that 'searching the world for knowledge' (as mandated in the Charter Oath of 1868) had gone too far; lamented that education at the time was in an 'evil' state of 'placing the moral code of loyalty and filial piety behind the vain emulation of Western manners'; and proposed that 'hereafter the study of morals elucidate the moral code of loyalty and filial piety, and be based mainly upon Confucius.' Such policy reforms were implemented in the Revised Education Decree of 1880. One result was the Plan of Rules for Primary School Teaching, promulgated in May 1881, which elevated moral training from the bottom to the top of the list of educational goals.

Moral training played a central role in Japanese education from then on. The paragon of education doctrine of that time, and the template for morals texts by independent writers, was *Essentials for Children's Study (Yōgaku kōyō)*, a text compiled by Motoda and issued in 1881 by the Imperial Household Ministry. The widely used texts of Period II included *Shōgaku shūshin-*

kun by Nishimura Shigeki, *Shūshin jikun* by Kameya Kō, and *Shōgaku shūshinsho* by Kido Rin.

The decrees issued in 1886 by Education Minister Mori Arinori (on primary schools, middle schools and the imperial universities) greatly strengthened the training of teachers, and inaugurated the system of government textbook approval. While these measures comprised the groundwork for modernizing the educational system, they also strengthened the state's control over the content of education. Then in 1890, the Imperial Rescript on Education[4] substantively and positively prescribed the fundamental value and belief systems which were to be instilled in the minds of the people under the Meiji regime.[5] Representative textbooks from Period III include *Shūshin nyūmon, Shōgaku shūshinkun, Kōtō-shōgaku shūshinkun* (all 1892) and *Shūshin jōkun* (1893), all by Suematsu Kenshō; *Shōgaku shūshinkyō* (1893) by Amano Tameyuki; and *Jinjō shōgakushū* (1890) and *Kōtō-shōgaku shūshinsho* (1891) by Higashikuze Michitomi.

The first clear note of state intent to wholly stipulate textbooks was sounded in 1887 during the ninth session of the House of Peers, in a bill which provided that texts would be free of charge: 'Be it enacted that textbooks for primary school moral training shall be compiled using state funds.' By the late 1890s, notwithstanding the strong objections of Fukuzawa Yukichi and his allies,[6] the pressure for state compilation of textbooks, especially for moral training, was coming to a head. The springboard for its enactment was the revelation in 1902 of a far-reaching bribery scandal concerning state textbook approvals.[7]

The first series of state texts were hastily compiled amid the storm of political pressure. Put into use from 1904, they were of a provisional, tentative nature. For the full development of the value and belief systems of the Meiji regime, we must turn to the second series of state texts, which appeared in 1910–11. Appearing around the time of the annexation of Korea, the launching of the *Shirakaba* (White Birch) humanistic artists movement, and the Great Treason Incident, the second set of state-compiled texts were vehicles of opposition to the modern sense of self and the socialist thought which had begun to sprout in the 'period of blockage' following the war with Russia. As such, they represent the anchoring and the self-confirmation of the dominant value and belief systems of the Meiji order.

Having set the stage, let us now proceed to an analysis of the content of morals courses during each of the five periods of Meiji textbook policy. Tables 14.1 through 14.5 list the value areas covered in representative texts from the respective periods, and the numbers of lessons devoted to each topic. (See Note 8 for explanations of certain value categories.) Table 14.6 shows the relative value emphases for all of the books analyzed in those five tables. (See Note 9 for the methods of calculation.)

Without dwelling further on the details of Meiji education policy, I shall present the basic hypotheses which emerge from the data in the tables. To throw into relief the cardinal characteristics of the five time periods, the data from Table 14.6 are rearranged in Table 14.7 and Figure 14.2.

Table 14.7 *Average numbers of morals lessons emphasizing various types of values*

(Period)	I 1871–4	II 1880–1	III 1892	IV 1904	V 1910
A Civic society	23.7	7.5	8.4	12.8	7.3
B Success	0	29.0	14.4	12.8	11.2
C Family	15.7	12.6	22.8	7.9	11.1
D Nation	12.5	0	4.8	4.3	1.2
D Loyalty to emperor	0	2.5	11.8	10.3	16.8

In the translated Western texts of Period I, there is a relatively very strong emphasis on the values which comprise the morality of civic society – fidelity, contractual obligation, responsbility, ownership, transactions and so forth. In line with this trend, considerable weight is also given to the basic norm consciousness of the modern state, through teachings on citizens' rights and obligations. It is only natural that the contrasting precepts concerning the emperor and the imperial line and the fundamental national character would be absent. Indeed, not one lesson treats the morality of loyalty, between subject and ruler or servant and master. In the area of family, concrete relations with parents and siblings are duly treated, while the abstract concepts of *ie* (household) ideology – ancestors, family name, family precepts – are nowhere to be seen. The fairly numerous lessons on parent-child and sibling relations are centred not on the Confucian ethic of filial piety, but on feelings of love and affection. Again, these patterns are to be expected, as the texts are translations or abridgments of European and American books. In a sense the

Table 14.1 Number of morals lessons emphasizing various values, 1871–4

(Text)	Primary school — Mitsukuri Rinshō, tr. Taisei kanzen kunmō (1871–3)				Higher school — Abe Taizō, tr. Shūshinron (1874)
(Volume)	**I**	**II**	**III**	**IV**	
Syntheses and general essays	1~6		18	1~4	8
Personal values					
Health, hygiene	9				
Independence, self-reliance					
Ambition					
Learning, pursuit of knowledge		4	7		
Effort, diligence		3	5		
Perseverance, patience, moderation		15	16		
Thriftiness, complacency		17			
Other	10			1	
Relations with others					
Honesty, sincerity					
Fidelity, contracts					
Benevolence, kindness		8 9 10 11			10
Tolerance, magnanimity					14 15
Etiquette					15
Friendship, companionship			9		
Gratitude, repaying kindness		12 13			
Employer and employee, master and servant			10		
Other		1 6 14	8		5 9
Family					
Home, family					
Ancestors					
Parent-child, filial piety		2	3	4	11 12
Brothers and sisters		5	6	5	
Husband-wife, man-woman		1		2	
Other		7			

Category	Subcategory	Entries
	School, teacher and student	4
	Neighborhood, town/village	
Nation	Japan, national character	
	Emperor, imperial line	
	Loyalty	
	Flag, national anthem, national holidays	
	Constitution, laws	11
	Citizens' duties	12, 13, 14, 6, 7, 13
	Citizens' rights	15, 6, 7, 6
	Other	9
	International relations	16, 2, 3, 4, 7
Civil society	Vocation	
	Ownership, selling and buying, borrowing and lending	
	Philanthropy, charity	
	Public welfare, civic virtue	
	Industries	17
	Other	6
	Religion, faith	7, 8
	Other	18, 19, 16

Table 14.2 *Number of morals lessons emphasizing various values, 1880–1*

	(Text)	Primary school — Kameya Kō, *Shūshin jikun* (1880)					Higher school — Motoda Eifu, *Yōgaku kōyō* (1881)
	(Volume)	I	II	III	IV	V	
	Syntheses and general essays	6	1 8	8 10 11	2 8 12	8 13	
Personal values	Health, hygiene	2					
	Independence, self-reliance						
	Ambition						7
	Learning, pursuit of knowledge	4	4	1 3	3 5	2 1	6
	Effort, diligence		6	3 2	6		20
	Perseverance, patience, moderation			6	4		12
	Thriftiness, complacency		5		10 11	11	11
	Other		7	7			15 16 19
Relations with others	Honesty, sincerity					4	8
	Fidelity, contracts						5 14
	Benevolence, kindness						9
	Tolerance, magnanimity					7	18
	Etiquette						10
	Friendship, companionship	3					4
	Gratitude, repaying kindess						
	Employer and employee, master and servant					11	
	Other	5	2 3	4 5 9	9 10	5 9 10	17
Family	Home, family						
	Ancestors						
	Parent-child, filial piety	1	–		7	3	1
	Brothers and sisters	1				3	
	Husband-wife, man-woman						3 13
	Other						

School, teacher and student — 3
Neighborhood, town/village — 2

Nation
  Japan, national character
  Emperor, imperial line
  Loyalty
  Flag, national anthem, national holidays
  Constitution, laws
  Citizens' duties
  Citizens' rights — 12
  Other

International relations

Civil society
  Vocation
  Ownership, selling and buying, borrowing and lending — 1
  Philanthropy, charity — 6
  Public welfare, civic virtue
  Industries
  Other
  Religion, faith
  Other

Table 14.3 Number of morals lessons emphasizing various values, 1892

(Text)	Higher primary school Higashikuze Michitomi *Kōtō-shōgaku shūshinsho* (1891)		Primary school Higashikuze Michitomi *Jinjō shōgaku shūshinshū* (1890)			
(Volume)	I	II	I	II	III	IV
Syntheses and general essays						
Health, hygiene		9	30	5		
Independence, self-reliance						
Ambition						
Personal values						
Learning, pursuit of knowledge	12	10	8 9 37	6		11
Effort, diligence	14	11	27			
Perseverance, patience, moderation	10		28		9	
Thriftiness, complacency	8	8	29	8	11	
Other	9 13 16	12	13			6
Honesty, sincerity	15	7	26		8	
Fidelity, contracts	6	6			10	
Benevolence, kindness				10		
Relations with others						
Tolerance, magnanimity						10
Etiquette	7		10 11 12 7 38			
Friendship, companionship			20 36	9	6	5
Gratitude, repaying kindness			25			
Employer and employee, master and servant						
Other			6 17 33		5 7	3 9
Family						
Home, family			21			
Ancestors			2			
Parent-child, filial piety	3 4	3	3 16 32	2	2	2
Brothers and sisters	5	5	4 5 18 19 34	3	3	4
Husband-wife, man-woman			21		4	8
Other						

Neighborhood, town/village							
Nation							
Japan, national character	1	15	24	1	1	1	1
Emperor, imperial line	15	23				2	2
Loyalty	31	1					
Flag, national anthem, national holidays	1						
Constitution, laws					13		23
Citizens' duties				13			15
Citizens' rights				14			
Other	14				14		
International relations				11			
Civil society							
Vocation	7						
Ownership, selling and buying, borrowing and lending				12			
Philanthropy, charity	40	13			7	11	14
Public welfare, civic virtue					12		
Industries	39						
Other							
Religion, faith	22			2			4
Other							

Table 14.4 *Number of morals lessons emphasizing various values, 1904*

	(Text)	*Dai-ichi-ki kokutei shūshin kyōkasho* (State Moral Training Textbooks, 1st Series)							
		Primary course				Higher primary course			
	(Volume)	I	II	III	IV	I	II	III	IV
	Syntheses and general essays	26	27		25 27		28		
Personal values	Health, hygiene	3 15 16	8 9	16	13		21	26 28	5
	Independence, self-reliance		4	7		18	9		16
	Ambition					3			
	Learning, pursuit of knowledge	6		6	14	28	11 12		11 17
	Effort, diligence			27 5	10 9	4 22	26		10
	Perseverance, patience, moderation		24 25	8 11		23 12	10		3
	Thriftiness, complacency		17	17					14
	Other	4 5	11 15	9 10	15 12 11	6 16 19 8 11 17	6 7 8	25	15 4 2 6 7 18 19
Relations with others	Honesty, sincerity	19 20	10 18 19	12 13		7 10	13	15	
	Fidelity, contracts		13	24				16	
	Benevolence, kindness					8 25 9	14 18	20	13
	Tolerance, magnanimity	18	14	15			5	17	
	Etiquette	17	12	23 21 20	16	15	4		8 9 20
	Friendship, companionship						14	3	
	Gratitude, repaying kindness	13	16	16				8	
	Employer and employee, master and servant							6 13	
	Other		6	22 14	17		3		
Family	Home, family	12	1 2 3	3			1	1	
	Ancestors						4	1	
	Parent-child, filial piety	9 10	7	3 4	6	14	3	2	
	Brothers and sisters	11			7				
	Husband-wife, man-woman				26				
	Other			5				5	

	Col 1	Col 2	Col 3	Col 4	Col 5	Col 6	Col 7	Col 8	Col 9
School, teacher and student					1 / 24				
Neighborhood, town/village				25				9	
Nation — Japan, national character	14	23	1 / 2	1 / 3	1 2 / 3 4	1 2 / 5	17 18 19		22
Emperor, imperial line		21				27			23
Loyalty					5				
Flag, national anthem, national holidays						27			
Constitution, laws				24 / 22					
Citizens' duties			20 / 22	20 21 / 23			20 27	21	24 25 27
Citizens' rights			23	23					27 26
Other									
International relations				24			25	24	11
Civil society — Vocation	22	19	24 / 18 / 26				25	11 / 19	
Ownership, selling and buying, borrowing and lending		26		18 / 19		26 / 20	15 16	10 / 12	
Philanthropy, charity	21 25						22	13	
Public welfare, civic virtue		22		8			21 / 13	23 22 7	12
Industries									
Other									
Religion, faith	23	20				24		21	
Other									

237

Table 14.5 *Number of morals lessons emphasizing various values, 1910*

| | (Text) | *Dai-ni-ki kokutei shūshin kyōkasho* (State Moral Training Textbooks, 2nd Series) | | | | | | Higher primary course | |
| | | *Primary course* | | | | | | | |
(Volume)		I	II	III	IV	V	VI	I	II
	Syntheses and general essays	25	26	27	26 27	28	26 27 28	26	26
Personal values	Health, hygiene	6 7	10	22	11		23	13	
	Independence, self-reliance				12 13		12	16	
	Ambition				5				
	Learning, pursuit of knowledge	1 3	6	5	15	18	18 19	12	11 12 13
	Effort, diligence		4		6				
	Perseverance, patience, moderation		23	13	17	15	15	15	
	Thriftiness, complacency	10	7	17			18	18	9
	Other	2 9	11 24 12 16	6 10 12 14 20	16 14	5 8 9 14 17	9 10 11 20 13	11 17 24 9	14 25
Relations with others	Honesty, sincerity	18 19	17	7		7	15	9	
	Fidelity, contracts		21			6	22		
	Benevolence, kindness	22				5	21		
	Tolerance, magnanimity		15	21		22	19		
	Etiquette	8	13	11	18	16			
	Friendship, companionship	4 5	13	8		19			6
	Gratitude, repaying kindness		22	19		23			8
	Employer and employee, master and servant		9		10	20			
	Other		25		25	21		8 20	
Family	Home, family	15	8				8	4	
	Ancestors						8		
	Parent-child, filial piety	11 12 13	1 2	3	8	12	7	5 6	5 22
	Brothers and sisters	14	3	4	9	13			
	Husband-wife, man-woman					27	24		7
	Other		5					7	

Category	Topic	1	2	3	4	5	6	7	8
	School, teacher and student	21					21	1 2	
	Neighborhood, town/village			9 25				3	
Nation	Japan, national character			1 16	1 2 7	1	1		1 3 24
	Emperor, imperial line	16 17	18 19 20	2	3 4 21	2	5 6		2 23 19 20
	Loyalty				22	3	7		22 4
	Flag, national anthem, national holidays			15		4			17 18
	Constitution, laws				23		23		21
	Citizens' duties								
	Citizens' rights						25		
	Other								
	International relations							14	
	Vocation	20		23					
Civil society	Ownership, selling and buying, borrowing and lending			18 26	20 24	25	17		
	Philanthropy, charity						14		10
	Public welfare, civic virtue	24				11	16		15 16
	Industries			24					
	Other				26				
	Religion, faith	23		19				23	
	Other								

Table 14.6 *Percentage of morals lessons emphasizing various values*

	(Period)	I 1871–4	II 1880–1	III 1892	IV 1904	V 1910
	Syntheses and general essays	16.7	11.0		3.1	5.6
	Health, hygiene	1.4	1.0	2.9	4.9	3.7
	Independence, self-reliance				2.4	1.9
	Ambition				0.6	0.6
Personal values	Learning, pursuit of knowledge		6.5	6.2	4.3	3.7
	Effort, diligence		8.5	2.9	3.7	2.5
	Perseverance, patience, moderation		6.5	2.9	2.4	2.5
	Thriftiness, complacency		2.5	5.3	1.8	2.5
	Other	2.8	7.5	6.5	12.2	14.2
	Honesty, sincerity	2.8	8.5	5.3	6.1	4.3
	Fidelity, contracts	11.1	3.5	2.4	1.2	1.2
	Benevolence, kindness	5.6	5.0	1.2	3.1	1.2
Relations with others	Tolerance, magnanimity	2.8	2.5	1.2	2.4	1.9
	Etiquette		3.5	4.8	3.1	3.1
	Friendship, companionship	1.4	2.5	3.4	2.4	3.1
	Gratitude, repaying kindness	2.8	3.5	0.5	1.2	1.9
	Employer and employee, master and servant	1.4	2.0			1.9
	Other	9.7	12.5	6.2	3.1	1.9
	Home, family	8.3			1.2	1.2
	Ancestors			2.9	0.6	1.2
Family	Parent-child, filial piety	4.2	5.5	9.1	4.9	5.6
	Brothers and sisters		2.0	8.4	1.8	3.1
	Husband-wife, man-woman	2.8	5.0	2.4	0.6	1.2
	Other	1.4		0.5		0.6

School, teacher and student	1.4	1.0	2.6	3.1	1.2
Neighborhood, town/village				1.2	1.2
Nation					
Japan, national character			1.0	1.2	0.6
Emperor, imperial line			3.8	5.5	8.7
Loyalty		2.5	6.5	2.4	5.6
Flag, national anthem, national holidays			0.5	1.2	1.9
Constitution, laws	1.4		2.4	0.6	0.6
Citizens' duties	7.0		2.4	3.7	0.6
Citizens' rights	4.2			0.6	
Other		1.0	4.1	0.6	0.6
International relations	1.4				
Vocation	1.4		1.2	0.6	1.2
Ownership, selling and buying, borrowing and lending	5.6		1.2	1.8	1.2
Civil society					
Philanthropy, charity		2.0	3.4	3.1	2.5
Public welfare, civic virtue			2.4	4.9	2.5
Industries				1.2	1.2
Others	2.8		0.5	1.2	0.6
Religion, faith	2.8		2.9	1.8	1.9
Other	4.2				

241

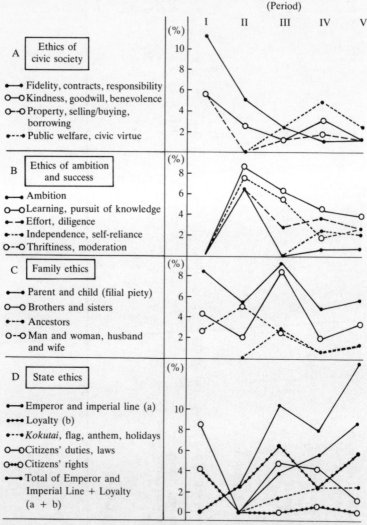

Figure 14.2 *Percentage of morals lessons emphasizing various values*

data provide a lateral comparison of Western and Japanese modernity. But from 1880, as already noted, most of these texts were partially or wholly removed from the nation's classrooms.

In the textbooks of Period II, the topics of property, sale and borrowing, and of citizen's rights and obligations disappear entirely, while the morals of civic society (fidelity, obligation, responsbility) drop to about half the earlier frequency. Meanwhile, the pious ethics of vertical relationships within the family and between ruler and subject are not yet given very high priority. More numerous are topics of individual morality, including success, determination, effort, diligence and thrift. In fact, the last group is noticeably more common than in the prior or later periods (Figure 14.2, Ethics of ambition and success).

By 1879, the government seemed strongly determined to illuminate the people on Confucian ethics. In that year the policy statement on Key Concepts of Education called for young schoolchildren to be initially exposed to illustrations, photographs and explanations of 'loyal retainers, dutiful children and virtuous wives from past and present,' for the purpose of 'drumming into their brains before all else a sense of the moral obligation of filial piety.' Irregardless. and interestingly, the texts of the early 1880s were not thoroughgoing treatises on piety, but instead devoted considerable space to the morals of wordly success, which are governed by the ascent-based value standard of Accomplishment. Object lessons on ambition, learning, endeavor and diligence reached their peak during these formative years of the Meiji regime. They served the function of scooping up the people's hidden anxieties and desires to rise in the world, and pouring them into the channels of the official system.

It was during Period III, under the schema of the 1886 textbook approval law and the 1890 Imperial Rescript on Education, that moral training became substantially dominated by the ethic of the family state, centered on loyalty and filial piety. In one of the leading textbook sets of the time, Higashikuze's *Jinjō shōgaku shūshinsho*, the national flag is depicted in the opening section at each grade level, thus repeatedly 'drumming into their brains' the morals of loyalty and devotion. This was the sort of education received by the children on the home front during the Sino-Japanese War. The figures show that within the emphasis on loyalty and filial piety, it is the latter of the two values which was given higher priority.

During Period IV, the first era of state-compiled texts, the only numerical indications are a slight retreat of the Confucian ethics of filial piety and ancestor reverence, and a slight advance (or resuscitation) of the universalistic morals of public welfare, civic virtue, goodwill and benevolence.

In the second series of state textbooks, the intentions of the

Meiji regime finally reach their full realization, in the erection and thoroughgoing development of a value system based on the principles of loyalty and filial piety. These books bring the inculcation of the grace and dignity of the emperor and the imperial line to an unprecedented level, and are also shot through with teachings about *kokutai* (the emperor system as the national polity or the fundamental character of the nation), and the national flag, anthem and holidays.[10]

That completes the outline of changes in textbook moral values between 1872 and 1911. Returning to our original schema of value typology (Figure 14.1), two major changes were effected. First, the aspirants who were inclined toward the universalistic value pole of Achievement were confined within the limits of loyalty to the established order. This was done by changing the role models for ambitious aspirants, specifically by replacing the likes of Lincoln and Washington with Sontoku and Hideyoshi.[11] Second, those people who were inclined to remain in the somnolence of Harmony were driven over to active Devotion, through the setting out of Ninomiya Sontoku and Kusunoki Masatsura[12] as role models for Confucian fidelity, and the recasting of that Confucian value as *the unity of loyalty and filial piety*.[13][14]

Thus the Meiji regime erected a value system with a dual function, at once *liberating* the vast, latent energy within the premodern community order, and *channeling* it into the sphere of loyalty, to provide motive energy for 'a prosperous country and a strong army.'

The two functions are metaphorically expressed in these closing lines from two volumes of a morals textbook set written soon after the Imperial Rescript on Education.

> The peaks of Tsukuba
> Cast shadows near and far
> But no shadow measures up
> To the shadow of the Emperor
>
> Brilliant as the sun and moon
> Shining in clear skies
> We look up to the Emperor
> As to a lofty mountain

(Suematsu Kenshō, *Kōtō-shōgaku shūshinkun*, 1892 (Vol. 1, Lesson 28, and Vol. 2, Lesson 17)

The first poem offers the people a secure sense of *belonging*, guaranteed by the value standard of 'eternal (imperial) immutability.' The second teaches those who could not remain in their simple hometowns the universal value of making one's name in the wider world. Within this framework of loyalty and patriotism, anyone, no matter how poor or humble, could make an impression on sixty million fellow citizens, and become a model for respect.

The state-compiled morals textbooks include stories of many persons to illustrate obedient devotion. For almost all of them, the path to glory was either to sacrifice their lives for the emperor, or else to place their children in that fatal position.[15]

It is the same with loyalty and patriotism. In the six volumes (for the six primary grades) of the second series of morals textbooks, there are eight lessons with loyalty as the central theme, and no fewer than seven of them are stories of citizens giving their lives in real or simulated battle.[16] This is the clearest indication of the aggressive, realistic import of 'loyalty.'

But the quintessential embodiment of loyalty as the supreme behavioral value – a veritable short course on morals which was taught to successive generations in the second set of state texts up through 1945 – is the lesson on 'Yasukuni Shrine.'

Yasukuni Shrine is on Kudanzaka hill in Tokyo. At this shrine, the people who have died for the nation are worshipped. On the festival days in the spring and autumn, Their Imperial Highnesses the Emperor and Empress Themselves dispatch a messenger to offer Their respects. It is due to the express intent of His Imperial Highness that such a warmhearted celebration is held in honor of the loyal retainers. We who are deeply aware of the august blessings of His Imperial Highness must learn from those who are worshipped here, and do our utmost for the sake of the nation and the Emperor.

With that, every citizen, no matter how poor or humble, has the chance through a single deed to be forever enshrined as a spirit who defended the fatherland, as a god. Furthermore, the value is supported by that 'most authentic and solid' ground, the 'eternal and immutable' Empire. In other words, this is a device for satisfying both the ageless desire for solid *ground* and the ageless desire for *heaven*, a focal point for coverging both the anxiety of alienation and the anxiety of obscurity, or a means for their prevention.

> The finest flowers are cherry blossoms,
>   the finest men are warriors.
> The august Shrine of Yasukuni provides
> A world surrounded by cherry trees.
> The souls of the people who have scattered as flowers
> Gallantly for the sake of the Nation
> Here find quietude.
> Life is light and duty is weighty.
> As we fulfill that duty, it is surely safe
> To sacrifice our lives for the Emperor.
> Deep within the bronze torii, behind the shrine fence
> Grandly we shall be celebrated.
> Our glory will survive the generations.

('Yasukuni Shrine', song from the state morals textbook, second series, grade four)

What was the justification for that value which held the high ground, the value of the Empire itself? Searching through all the textbooks from that era, the only 'evidence' we can discover is the 'boundless benefit' which we ourselves and our ancestors before us have received from the emperor and the imperial line. With that device, the sense of 'original grace' which lies at the depths of the racial religious consciousness of the Japanese was adroitly ladled up and served into loyalty to the emperor-system state.

Appearing hand in hand with the precept of boundless imperial blessing, and apparently just as effective (or more so) in fastening loyalty within the conscience of the people, is the accomplished 'fact' of the imperial succession, which is of course based on myth.

For more than two thousand five hundred and seventy years from the enthronement of Emperor Jimmu until today, in succession over the generations, there have been imperial descendants who rose to the position of Emperor. Among the many nations in the world, there is no other which has been blessed as we in the Japanese Empire have been blessed with an unbroken line of emperors . . . All of our ancestors have honored the Emperor and devoted themselves to the path of loyalty and patriotism.

> (State morals text, 2nd series, grade give, first lesson)

The mainstay for the groundwork of the *value system* (the moral consciousness) of loyalty and patriotism, was the *belief system* (the worldview) of the unbroken imperial line and its eternal immutability.[17] In other words, in the schoolbooks which laid the foundations for 'morals,' a unique and significant role was reserved for 'history.'

2 'The unbroken imperial line': the belief system in history textbooks

Among the several methods used to inculcate the value system of the ruling ideology of the Meiji regime, the task entrusted to history education was made clear as early as 1881. The General Plan for Primary School Teaching that was promulgated by the government in that year directs that history courses focus on the administrative records of the emperors and 'especially cultivate the spirit of patriotism and respect for the Emperor.'

The constitutional stipulation that, 'The Empire of Japan shall be reigned over and governed by a line of Emperors unbroken for ages eternal' (Chapter 1, Article 1 of the 1889 constitution) was given specific exposition in the Imperial Rescript on Education of 1890. In 1891, the Education Ministry's Fundamental Principles of Primary School Teaching expressly provided that the course in 'Japanese history shall consist essentially in the teaching of the main points of the fundamental character of the nation, and in the cultivation of the integrity befitting the citizenry.'

The concrete end result of this chain of direction from above on the 'spirit' of 'history' education was a state-vetted national history text for higher schools published in 1892, *Kōtō-shō-gaku kokushi*, by Higashikuze Michitomi. The introduction states point-blank that, 'This book . . . sets forth the main points of national history in order to arouse the spirit of loyalty to the

Emperor and love for the nation, as well as to foster morality and develop the intellect.'

The History Instruction Law, also issued in 1892, states just as plainly that such was the task to be accomplished by history education. 'Within the scope of general education . . . textbook instruction is not actually the direct goal, but is merely an instrument.' The law prescribes the sole character of instruction by recapitulating the same value system of the Meiji regime that was described in the previous section. It goes on to state that, 'As history courses are the most suitable means for molding the national spirit and also have the greatest effectiveness as moral education, in the primary school there is virtually no qualitative difference between morals training and history courses.

The equation of family-state morality and national history reached full stride in 1910, when the schoolbooks became the paradigm of the controlling ideology of the Meiji regime. Let us survey the major differences between the Japanese history course in the second series of state texts, and the history that was taught in the earlier periods of the school system.

During the time of translated Western textbooks, naturally, Japanese history was not given priority. Education consisted basically of morals, reading and writing, and the sciences. Leaving aside the actual teaching practices in the classroom, as far as textbook content is concerned, there never was a period of truly liberal education. In the first place, the discipline of history, as a means of shedding light on life or awareness or behaviour or socioeconomic factors, had basically not been formed, and hence was not something to be utilized. From the start, the history curriculum stressed only the monarchist-revival aspect of the Restoration, and not its aspects of the opening and Westernization of the country. For example, two books issued early on by the Ministry of Education, *Historical Summary*, Imperial Edition (*Shiryaku*, 1872) and *A Brief History of Japan* (*Nihon ryakushi*, 1875), confine themselves to the historical exploits of the emperors, starting with the 'age of the gods.'

From about 1881, along with the adoption of a more modern literary style, the contents progressed beyond the mere enumeration of the emperors. Still, history was limited to stories of the military exploits of the imperial line and the ruling elites, with virtually no perspective on socioeconomic change, or on the lives, thoughts and actions of the people.[18]

The state's second set of history texts differed in two key respects. First, the historical exploits of the emperors were painted over in monochrome approbation, eliminating such topics as Emperor Buretsu's brutality, 'Shōmu's Indulgences' and 'Godaigo's Misrule.'[19] The historical matter of the split between the Northern and Southern Courts, which disturbs the myth of the 'unbroken imperial line,' was disposed of by removing the Northern Court from the imperial genealogy. Kōgon-tennō (Emperor Kōgon) and Kōmyō-tennō in the first state texts became Kōgon-in (ex-Emperor Kōgon) and Kōmyō-in the second series.[20]

Second, the texts were not confined to the exploits of the emperors, but also included direct coverage of the lifestyle of loyalty on the part of the subjects, offering models of behavior for the modern citizenry. In contrast to the first series of state-complied texts, the story of Kusunoki Masashige and 'seven lives for the Empire' was added; the essay about the loyalty and filial piety of Taira no Shigemori was expanded from one to four columns; and new material was added to the episode of Sugawara no Michizane's 'Gift of Imperial Clothes.' Also, visual appeal was strengthened with the addition of an illustration of Chūshin Kamaashi (the bow-legged loyal retainer) proffering the shoes of the imperial prince, and illustrations of the loyalty of Wake no Kiyomaro and Sugawara no Michizane.

In Table 14.8, the contents of the *State-Compiled History Textbook, 2nd Series* (1911 revised edition) are classified by the central themes of the chapters. For a more detailed view, Table 14.9 is a breakdown of the 164 subheadings. It is immediately apparent that economic and cultural history, as well as the lives, attitudes and activities of the people, are virtually ignored.

Table 14.7   *Chapter themes in the state-compiled history textbooks (2nd series)*

	Chapter Vol. 1	Chapter Vol. 2
Emperor and imperial line	10.0	0
Loyal retainers	3.0	0
Ruling elites	6.5	7.0
Wars	2.0	4.5
Foreign affairs	0	2.5
Laws and political reforms	1.0	2.0
Other	0.5	1.0
Total	23	17

Table 14.8 *Subheading topics in the state-compiled history textbooks (2nd series)*

	Number of subheadings		Percentage of subheadings	
	Vol. 1	Vol. 2	Vol. 1	Vol. 2
Emperor and imperial line	20	0	23.6	0
Loyal retainers	5	0	5.9	0
Ruling elites	16	22	18.6	29.2
Civil wars, power struggles	22	16	25.9	20.5
Foreign wars	4	8	4.7	10.3
Foreign affairs	1	15	1.2	19.2
Laws and political reforms	10	6	11.8	7.7
Industry and economics	0	0	0	0
Thought and religion	3	5	3.5	6.4
Culture and science	1	1	1.2	1.3
Life of the people	0	0	0	0
Other	4	5	4.7	6.4
(Total)	86	78	100.0	100.0

The tables also furnish comparisons of the first and second volumes, the first running up to 'The Yoshino Court' and the second beginning with 'Ashikaga Yoshimitsu.' We see that the first volume is centered on the succession of emperors and the benevolence and virtuous authority of the imperial line; while the second deals chiefly with the record of the nation's brilliant achievements in the areas of foreign *wars and foreign policy.* This stems not from editorial policy but from the differing natures of the eras covered, and yet the priorities of the two volumes do correspond superbly to the two functions of the history texts. The first half taught mainly about what wonderful rulers the people were able happily to live under, while the second half concentrates on what shining results were achieved by the people of the nation (under the influence, naturally, of the emperors). That is, the first half tells us what sort of people we *are*, and the second what sort of people we *ought to be* – the sorts of deeds we have already performed and, by extension, should continue to perform.

In sum, the functions of the belief system that pervades these history texts were to first foster a stable sense of belonging among the people, and then to add onto it an active sense of devotion. The first (ascriptive) function begins with the opening passage:

Lesson One   Amaterasu Ōmikami

The Sun Goddess Amaterasu Ōmikami is the distant
Ancestor of the Emperors. Their virtuous authority is
exceedingly high and far-reaching, shining like the sun itself
in the heavens. The Sun Goddess is worshipped at the Ise
Shrine.

The Japanese Empire is the nation which the Sun Goddess
first bequeathed to the rule of her grandson Ninigino
Mikoto. When she handed the nation down, she said: 'This
is a land deserving to be ruled by my descendants. Thou
who are the Imperial descendants shall govern. Heaven and
earth shall forever be united, that the universe may
increasingly prosper.' The foundation upon which our nation
is established unwaveringly for all time was indeed fixed at
that moment.

(*State-Compiled History Textbook, 2nd Series*, Volume 1,
Revised Edition, 1911)

In Lesson Two, it is explained that in the fighting between
Emperor Jimmu and the other powerful clan leaders, because of
'his intentions for the people's contentment, the Emperor sub-
dued them.' Lesson Three, 'Military Lords of Japan,' recounts
an anecdote suggesting that the three imperial sacred treasures
possess the miraculous power of always bringing victory to the
Court. Later chapters cover such topics as the benevolent rule
of Emperor Nintoku (legendary, d. AD 399), the kindness of
Empress Kōmyō (701–60), and the divine will which dwelled
deeply within Emperor Godiago (r. 1318–39) who 'went so far
as to remove his clothing and bestow it upon people whom he
saw to be suffering during cold nights.' (Lessons Five, Ten,
Thirteen) There is no mention whatsoever of the brutality of
Emperors Yūryaku (456–479) and Buretsu (498–506). In the
modern era, for example on the issue of opening ports to foreign
trade, the reason why 'the Bakufu policy was not easily decided'
is said to have been 'perplexity about that measure' due to
Bakufu incompetence; whereas on the same issue, the Court's
indefinite postponement of imperial sanction is set down to 'the
Emperor's clear-sighted and beneficent anxiety about the future
prospects of the nation.' (Lesson Eleven)

The happiness and security of the citizenry who lived under

the kindness of such clear-sighted and beneficent emperors is vividly portrayed in the following passage from the state-compiled Japanese reader.

Kotarō's Village

Kotarō's village has one hundred fifty houses. Three of the houses have thatch roofs. One of them is the village hall, and the others are the school and the police substation.

Kotarō's father is the village headman. He is a very good person who takes good care of the village, and sometimes he comes to the school.

The schoolteacher is a very kind person who teaches the students very nicely.

The policeman is also a very kind person, and he makes the rounds from time to time. He makes sure that there are no thefts or fires or epidemics.

And so every family can safely go to sleep and wake up and do their work.

Aren't Kotarō and his family lucky to live in a village like that?

(*State-Compiled Japanese Textbook, 1st Series*, Lesson Four)

As for the second function of promoting the (achieved) value of devotion, let us survey the treatment of the contemporary, post-Restoration period. It is covered in five sections of the second volume of the state's history text: The Conquest of Taiwan and the Satsuma Rebellion, The Promulgation of the Constitution, The War of 1894–95 and the Treaty Revisions, The War of 1904–05, and The Peace Treaty and the Annexation of Korea (Lessons Thirteen to Seventeen).

Nearly all of the material consists of accounts of wars and foreign affairs. The People's Rights Movement, civilization and enlightenment, and the industrial revolution are entirely omitted.

The subtitles in those five chapters add resolution to the image of modern Japanese history that was instilled in the minds of the citizens from 1911 through 1945: Foreign Policy of the New Government – Conquest of Taiwan – The Satsuma Campaigns – Introduction of Public Discussion – The Imperial Household Act and the Promulgation of the Imperial Constitution – Convening of the Imperial Diet – Conclusion of the Friendship Treaty with

Korea – The Korean Uprising and the Treaty of Tientsin –
Outbreak of War with China – The Treaty of Shimonoseki and
the Retrocession of Liaotung – Subjugation of Taiwan – Treaty
Revisions – The Boxer Rebellion – Negotiations with Russia,
and the Anglo-Japanese Alliance – Outbreak of War with Russia
and our Army's Victories – Conclusion of the Peace Treaty –
Administration of Sakhalin and the Leased Territories – Protection of Korea and Preservation of Chinese Territories – Extension of the Anglo-Japanese Alliance, and the Agreements with
France and Russia – Annexation of Korea – Preparedness of the
Citizenry.

Aside from the closing essay on 'preparedness,' some 17 of
the 21 subtitles (81 per cent) concern foreign affairs, and six-
tenths of those (12 headings) are about wars and war-related
negotiations, disputes or ex-post-facto measures. Only four subheadings concern domestic affairs, and they are all about the
legal and political system. The areas of industry, economics,
society, labor, thought, discussion, science, the arts, education
and daily life are completely ignored.

Wars are always construed as our nation's 'righteous battles.'
Upon their conclusion with shining victory, the results of
'enhancing national prestige' and 'assuming an important place'
among the developed nations are emphasized. For example, the
section on the Boxer Rebellion concludes: '. . . is known around
the world as the Boxer Rebellion. Afterwards, our army ranked
among those of the great powers with many impressive exploits.
Hence as with the War of 1894–95, our military prestige was
enhanced and our nation assumed an increasingly important
place among the other nations of the world.' (Lesson Sixteen)
The same light spills onto such non-military foreign affairs as the
treaty revisions: 'After the War of 1894–95, our national dignity
was greatly enhanced,' leading to revised agreements with other
nations besides England. (Lesson Fifteen)

Under the morality of the family state, the state became more
and more a tight-knit in-group, which automatically made the
indifferent global society into a 'cold world.' Enhancing national
prestige and gaining international influence represented success,
making a name in the world, on the part of the nation as a
whole.

The annexation of Korea is made out as a deed of noble
intention:

Korea had been under our protection for several years, but as it was frequently a source of disturbances, the Emperor, for the sake of increasing the mutual welfare of Japan and Korea and perpetually guaranteeing peace in East Asia, perceived that it was necessary to annex Korea. Finally in August of 1910, he consented to a permanent transfer of all sovereignty from the Korean emperor. (Lesson Seventeen)

The concluding essay sets out the following expectations:

Prepardness of the citizenry

Thus our nation has gradually enhanced its prestige overseas, and has finally reached a position on a par with the great powers of the world. This derives from the great virtue of the Emperor and the selfless willingness of the citizens to courageously sacrifice themselves. In addition, it results from the beneficence over the generations of the unbroken Imperial line, the constant desire of the Emperor to promote the national interest and the welfare of the people, as well as the unity of the people of all generations in exhibiting loyalty to the Emperor and love for their country. It is therefore to be expected that we, the people who have been born into this glorious era, will properly comprehend the origin of this success, and discern the need for assuming additional responsbility for augmenting our dignity, and that each individual will complete that duty, and add more and more luster to our lustrous national history.

The overarching framework of the uniform history curriculum thus comes to rest. Having begun by preaching that our Japanese Empire is 'established unwaveringly for all time,' it concludes by preaching that the people must 'complete the duty' of self-sacrifice in order to 'add more and more luster to our lustrous national history.'

The dominant belief system presented so intensively in the state's revised history texts has a close structural affinity to the dominant value system presented so intensively in its revised morals lessons. It quite clearly points to the dual function of fostering a mentality of secure belonging, and instilling a zest for active devotion.

Notes

1 'Around 1884 teachers were free and the children too were quite free, enjoying themselves thoroughly as they practiced self-education. If guests came to visit the teacher, they would often go next door to the schoolmaster's house and have a meal in his parlor, and the children would immediately turn to studying on their own. If the meal went on for a long time, the children would have the good sense to go outdoors, and some might go to the nearby hillside or the river for physical recreation, and then return to the school in good time.

  'The situation was so extremely liberal that those who wanted to be most free would not even go to the school, but would eat their lunches along the way and study by themselves in the fields and then return home. The teacher respected the children's freedom, and the children respected the teacher's freedom. . . . At that time things were indeed free, and it was all right to take a holiday or go on a trip. If the next day was the *bon* festival, then they might take a three-day holiday, or if there was a performance in another village they might take the day off. The schoolmaster could act arbitrarily, as he did not receive orders from anywhere and did not have to seek any authorizations. It can be called the era when the teachers ran the world.' Karasawa Tomitarō, *Nihonjin no rirekisho*, pp. 46–7.

2 For example, Dewey's education theories were in wide circulation, through translations of such works as *The School and Society, The Child and the Curriculum* and *Democracy and Education.*

  The 'eight main trends of educational thought' which strongly influenced primary education in the Taisho years all took the standpoint that the child's development was the basic criterion. They were expounded in the following books (in Japanese): *Self-Education* by Higuchi Chōichi, *Autodidacticism* by Kōno Kiyomaru, *Free Education* by Tezuka Ganei, *Satisfy Everyone through Complete Stimulation* by Chiba Meikichi, *Creative Education* by Inage Sōfu, *Dynamic Education* by Oikawa Heiji, *Education for Everyone* by Obara Kuniyoshi, and *Liberal Education* by Katagami Chū.

3 See the preface of Karasawa Tomitarō's *Kyōkasho no rekishi.*

4 The Imperial Rescript on Education was drafted by Inoue Tsuyoshi, the head of the Legislative Office who also drafted the Meiji constitution, and amended and expanded by Motoda Nakazane, the emperor's tutor.

5 The Imperial Rescript on Education was summarized or reproduced in full at the beginning or end of every type of textbook after 1890,

along with an introductory note to the effect that every word in the book was based upon the Rescript's great morality of loyalty and filial piety. To illustrate the dominating influence that the Rescript had on education at the time, here are the contents of *Moral Training for Higher and Primary Education* (*Kōtō-shōgaku shūshin*) by Shigeno An'eki:

Lesson 1	We [Imperial] Reflect upon the Founding of Our Nation by Our Imperial Ancestors and the Depth of Their Vast Virtue
Lesson 2	We are Subjects who are Expertly Loyal and Expertly Devoted 'The Devotion of Life as a Loyal Subject' 'Devotion at the Ancestral Shrine in the Army Barracks'
Lesson 3	Unifying the Mind of the Multitudes and Completing the Beauty of the Generations
Lesson 4	The National Essence is the Source of Education and Resides Therein
Lesson 5	Thou Subjects Shall Be Devoted to Thy Parents 'The Fervent Filial Piety of Saburo Uemon' 'Ikeda Mitsumasa's Precepts of Filial Piety'
Lesson 6	Friendship toward Brothers and Sisters 'The Friendship of the Iwasa Brothers' 'The Obedience of Takeda Nobushige' 'The Friendship of Three Women'
Lesson 7	Harmony between Husband and Wife 'The Harmonious Care of Mr and Mrs Yamauchi' 'Mrs and Mrs Mihara's Chorus of Cheers'
Lesson 8	Trusting Companions 'The Fidelity of Takayama Egami' 'The Friendship of Hirato Gamō'
Lesson 9	Keeping Oneself Modest 'The Modesty of Itakura Shigenori' 'The Frugality of Ayabe Michihiro' 'The Thriftiness of Ii Naotaka'
Lesson 10	Exercising Charity toward the Multitudes 'The Kindness of Hoshino Yahei' 'The Merciful Love of Hosokawa Tadaoki'
Lesson 11	Developing the Intellect and Fulfilling One's Talents by Acquiring Learning and Practising Industry 'Ki Heishū's Virtuous Deeds'
Lesson 12	Enhancing Public Welfare and Cultivating Wordly Affairs

6 Fukuzawa outlined his objections in an article in the *Jiji Shimbun*, April 2, 1897: 'People in the world have a surprising amount of discrimination, and they also turn to others for assistance in making the appropriate choice in various situations. If the Ministry of Education were to carry out the authorizations in a strict manner, and with certain prejudices, and in the process were to mix in strong-willed inflexibility, then it would result only in the hindrance of the progressive development of education . . .'

7 From a speech in the Diet by Takada Sanae: 'The proverb has it that "The thief you catch will be your own child," but in this case it is different. Those who only yesterday heard their teachers and schoolmasters lecturing on ethics, and learned that such-and-such is good and such-and-such is bad, now see people who have grown from children into adults, people such as prefectural governors who are meant to be the representatives of the wise and virtuous Emperor, lined up and arrested on suspicion of taking bribes on the side. The allegations of profiteering by these gentlemen is indeed a very serious matter, for the implication that textbooks, which are such important vessels for acquiring wisdom and ethical discrimination, are the fruits of corruption clearly exerts a very bad influence upon the minds of our future citizens.'

The textbook scandal caused the resignation of the minister of education, and the prompt initiation of government textbook compilation, just before the Russo-Japanese War. The new policy halved the textbook fees which were borne by the parents and elder brothers of schoolchildren, a point which served as a persuasive pretext for state compilation.

8 In Tables 14.1–14.6: 'Syntheses and General Essays' include basic outlines of the moral foundations of good and bad, summaries and itemizations of moral points, etc. 'Other' in the Personal Values category includes such topics as apologies and courage. 'Other' in the Relations with Others category includes such topics as general social contact, humility and respect for elders. 'Other' in the Family category includes such topics as relatives. 'Citizens' duties' are primarily tax payment and military services. Lessons on elections and voting are placed under 'Citizen's rights'. 'Other' at the bottom of the tables includes such topics as love for animals.

9 Calculation procedures for Table 14.6:

Period I: *Taisei kanzen kunmō* was widely used for four grades (third through sixth), and *Shūshinron* was used mainly for grade six only. Accordingly, the ratio of relative importance is four to one. The former text has 56 chapters and the latter 16, and those figures produce nearly the same ratio. Therefore each chapter of the two books is given equal weight in the calculations ($100/72 = 1.39$ per cent).

Period II: *Shūshin jikun* and *Yōgaku kōyō* are totaled with equivalent weight of 50 per cent each. The former has a total of 50 chapters in five sections, hence each chapter is weighted at 1 per cent. The latter has a total of 20 lessons in five volumes, and each lesson is weighted at 2.5 per cent.

Period III: A special edition was used for grade one, containing some 34 lessons. To match these with the average number of lessons per year for the other five grades ($70/5 = 14$), the weighting ratio of a grade-one lesson to a lesson for the other grades is $0.4:1$ ($14/34$). Thus the weighting for each lesson in grade one is: $4/10 \times$

$$\frac{100}{(74 + 34) \times 4/10} = 0.48 \text{ per cent and for each lesson on grades}$$

two through six is: $\dfrac{100}{(70 + 34) \times 4/10} = 1.20$ per cent.

Period IV: The first-, second- and third-term state texts were generally used up to the sixth-grade level, and hence the third- and fourth-year higher school texts are excluded from the calculation. Each lesson is weighted as: $100/63 = 0.61$ per cent.

Period V: The first- and second-year higher school texts are excluded, for the same reason as in Period IV. Each lesson in the ordinary (primary school) texts is weighted as: 100/61 = 0.62 per cent.

10   The second series of state morals texts omitted such first-series lessons as 'The Freedom of Others' and 'Social Progress' (both from higher grade three), 'Competition,' 'Trust' and 'Money', and replaced them with such new lessons as 'The Ise Shrine' (ordinary grades two and six), 'The Founding of the Nation,' 'The Development of the National Character,' 'Supporting the Imperial Army,' 'The Union of Loyalty and Filial Piety' and 'Teachings of the Departed Sun Goddess and Imperial Ancestors' (all for higher grade two). (Karasawa Tomitarō, *Kyōkasho no rekishi*, p. 286.)

The first series of state texts for the study of Japanese were considered dull and dry, and were generally known as the 'i-e-su-shi readers' – i, e, su and shi being stressed in the opening section as sounds to be modified in correcting regional dialects toward standard speech. This suggests that the book was compiled along fairly rational lines of language instruction. The second-series Japanese texts were known as '*hata-tako-koma*' (flag-kite-top), the first page being filled with the national flag; nationalism frequently appears in the lessons in all volumes.

11   After the Meiji emperor, Lincoln was the person most frequently mentioned in the first series of state morals texts, but he completely disappeared in the second series. Meanwhile, the number of lessons about Sontoku (Ninomiya Kinjiro; see the following chapter) increased from four to seven, and he ranked with the emperor as the most frequently mentioned personage. (Karasawa Tomitarō, *Kyōkasho no rekishi*)

With Hideyoshi, the emphasis changes. For example, when petitioning for an imperial visit, he notes that, 'We made the daimyo swear allegiance to the Imperial line before the Emperor.' (*Jinjō shōgaku shūshinsho*, Vol. 4, Lesson 7).

12   The story of Kusunoki Masatsura is recounted in the lesson on 'Loyalty and Filial Piety': 'The Hojo clan collapsed and Emperor Godaigo went back to Kyoto, but soon the Ashikaga clan revolted. Kusunoki Masashige sought the Emperor's permission for his forces to fight the Ashikaga, and he succeeded in expelling Ashikaga Takauji to Kyushu. Later, when Takauji was preparing to invade the capital with a large army, the Emperor sent Kusunoki Masashige to fight them in Hyogo. Masashige believed that he could not survive the battle. He stopped along the way at the Sakurai post station and met his son Masatsura, and told him that 'Even if I die, you shall inherit my spirit and devote yourself loyally to the

Emperor. My primary bequest to you is filial piety.' Masatsura returned to Kawachi. At that time he was eleven years old.

'When Masatsura heard of his father's death, he broke into tears and tried to kill himself in his room. His mother stopped him, saying, "The reason why your father sent you back home was not to commit suicide. It was to raise an army in place of your father, so that you may serve the Emperor, was it not?" From then on, Masatsura obeyed his father's will and his mother's teachings, and never lost his sense of loyalty. As an adult, he served Emperor Gomurakami through many fine exploits in battle. When Takauji's successor, Shokō Shichoku, came to attack, Masatsura went to Yoshino with his younger brother Masatoki to say farewell to the Emperor and visit the grave of Emperor Godaigo. There, with his comrades, he wrote this poem along with his name on the wall of Nyoirindō.

> Knowing full well that we may not return
> By countless brave deeds shall we make our names

They then departed for the battle. Both brothers fought very bravely at Shijō Nawate, where they died.

Moral: The loyal subject does not stray beyond the gate of filial piety.

13 By the 1880s the phase, 'Loyalty is serving the Emperor with filial piety' (from Confucius' *Book of Filial Piety*), and the classical proverb, 'The loyal subject does not stray beyond the gate of filial piety' had come into use. Such preachings of similarity and affinity between the two ethics reflected what had long been the way of thinking throughout Japan. Not until the 1890s, around the time of the war with China, did textbooks assert the paradoxical concept that sacrificing one's life in the name of loyalty is the zenith of filial piety. The idiom *chūkō itchi* ('the unity of loyalty and filial piety') was first used as a lesson title in the second series of state textbooks, from 1910.

14 One of the two main value adjustments reflected in the textbooks, the confinement of Achievement-oriented aspiration within the specific limits of loyalty, is dealt with in the next chapter as part of the structure of Japanese Successism. This note sketches the background of the other major adjustment, in which passive energies were directed from communital Harmony toward national Devotion. On the level of ideology, the ethic of the family and the household was analogically coopted into the ethic of the family

state. But at the deeper level of the people's basic sensibilities, there were significant repercussions from three national policies.

The first was the institution of the regional administration system, which was provisionally completed through the large-scale amalgamation of towns and villages in 1888 and the promulgation of the new city-town-village system in 1889. Some 70,435 towns and villages were consolidated at a stroke into 13,347 entities. A man who was a middle school student at the time wrote the following reminiscence.

'One thing that changed after I left was that Higashi-tochii became one of the communities in the village of Shimoyonada. The local village administrator used to do his work at home, but from then on he went to work at the village hall and used an office. One time when I was back home, I had some errand that took me to the village hall. On one side of the main lobby there was a small entranceway with a little wooden tag nailed to it that said "Public Entrance." Inside, the officials sat on chairs doing their work, and the "public" would sit in front of them and state their business.' (Tsuda Sokichi, *Omoidasu mama*, 1949.)

The memoirs of Makino Chuken, who became governor of Fukui Prefecture in 1891, contain this story:

'One day I was told that a man was lying prostrate in front of the gate of the governor's residence and muttering to himself. When asked what he wanted, he said he was a farmer from a neighboring district, and that the day before, the governor had made an inspection tour of his dear native village. In the old days his village had not belonged to an important domain such as Echizen which comprised three hundred thousand *koku*, but now the official who governed a district of seven hundred thousand *koku* had come to visit his village, and this was such a blessing that he had come to express his gratitude. He did not want to come inside the gate, but simply stood there. In fact, the reason why I visited his village was to encourage the growing of indigo, which had recently been started there.'

The Meiji state thus absorbed a virtually intact, premodern mentality of deep-seated allegiance and affection toward the traditional 'natural' village order of one's native home. (For an excellent treatment of the psychological effects on the rural populace of the town and village consolidations, see Yanagita Kunio, *Meiji-Taisho-shi, Sesō hen*, Chapter 5.)

The second development was the consolidation of Shintō shrines, which was ordered by the central government after the Russo-Japanese War. The spiritual stronghold of the community, the locus of the patron deity of the village who was tended with offerings

261

during the annual festival of each particular shrine, was ordered closed in many places. The number of shrines went from 190,426 in 1906 to 137,136 in 1910 (Kamijima Jirō, *Kindai nihon no seishin kōzō*).

Third, occurring over a longer time interval, was the transposing from village to national scale of the *matsuri*, the Shintō festivals which played the role of 'enthusiastically unifying the communital sensibility' (Kamijima, op. cit.). The first festival that was simultaneously observed in towns and villages across the country was the grand celebration of the new imperial constitution – the very symbol of the consolidation of the Meiji regime – in 1889.

'The entire city of Tokyo is in an indescribable turmoil in preparation for the promulgation of the constitution on the eleventh. Everywhere they are setting up festive gateways and illumination, and planning parades. The joke is that nobody knows the contents of the constitution.' (*Diary of Erwin von Balz.*) The Yomiuri Shimbun reported on February 8,: 'As the Constitution Festival approaches, around the fifth inst. the price of national flags jumped some fourteen or fifteen sen in a single day. Most of the downtown flag shops were sold out, some of them claiming to have sold all of their stock but apparently holding some back for later sale.' The celebration itself was a lively affair. The elderly poet Tayama Katai recounted how even he, who was determined to ignore the racket of taiko drums and other instruments coming from all the surrounding neighborhoods, and remain in communion with his garden and the muse, was eventually coaxed out by neighbors and relatives to watch a costume parade with mock samurai and courtesans file through the snowy streets. (*Tokyo no sanjū nen.*)

The festive mood was not limited to Tokyo. During the constitution celebrations in cities around the country, the distinctive folk songs of various regions were for the first time performed in festive settings far from home. This symbolized the broadening and conversion of the role of the festival, and also fostered the convergence of the sense of belonging upon the national state. The enthusiastic participation of 'community members' in similar national festivals was repeated during the wars with China and Russia. Holidays and major festivals appeared time and again in the state textbooks for moral training, which is to say that the ruling elite made significant use of the new *matsuri* as one means for training the citizenry.

A change in worldview accompanied that separation from the 'natural' village order of the patron deities, and that coalescence of the function of the *matsuri* authorized from above. The unity of gods and people in traditional folk belief was *redistributed* into citizen loyalty toward a divinity concentrated in the hands of the emperor and his ancestors. The yardstick for that loyalty was Yasu-kuni Shrine. In folk belief, people became gods soon after death and provided divine protection for the peace of their native communities. But among the 'modern' Japanese, for the first time, one could receive the glory of becoming a god by dying in battle for the sake of the imperial state. These policies and movements, along with the analogical shift in ideology from a family ethic to a personal ethic, mobilized the true feelings of the people by tying them to a new 'home' – the state.

15 Textbook examples of those who were willing to die gloriously for their country, or send their children to do so, from Suematsu's *Kōtō-shōgaku shūshinkun*:

(a) From Vol. 1, Lesson 27, 'Loyalty' (see Note 15, first lesson)

Kiguchi Kohei   Died   With his trumpet   At his lips

(b) From Vol. 4, Lesson 3, 'Loyalty and Patriotism': 'In 1897, Kumamoto Castle was surrounded by the rebel army. Major General Tani, who led the defending force, wanted to send word of their plight to the distant troops of the Imperial Army, and he ordered Tanimura Keisuke to undertake the mission. Keisuke coated his body with soot and put on kimono, and left the castle under cover of night. Along the way he was twice captured by the rebels, and endured various hardships, but at last he reached the Imperial Army garrison and successfully completed his mission.'

(c) From Vol. 6, Lesson 9, 'Cool Courage': 'On 15 April 1880 at the Kure Naval Yard, while the No. 1 Diving Flotilla were practicing submarine maneuvers in the sea around the defense perimeter of the new harbor, submarine no. 6 unfortunately sank, and fourteen crewmen including Submarine Captain Sakuma lost their lives in the line of duty.

'Soon after submarine no. 6 submerged, damage occurred in the machine area, sea water flowed in, and the vessel tilted and gradually sank. Captain Sakuma immediately instructed his men to take preventive measures, but they were unsuccessful. Poison gas started leaking and it became difficult to breathe, but nothing more could be done. At that time Captain Sakuma was in the command tower, and by the faint light coming from the surface he wrote his will with a pencil in a notebook. In the will he apologized to his subordinates for sinking the vessel and bringing on their deaths, and he described his subordinates as working hard until the end. He recorded in detail the cause and the circumstances of the sinking, in the hope that submarine development would not be hindered by this accident. He also expressed his hope that the bereaved families of his subordinates would not be plunged into financial straits, and said farewell to his superiors, his elders, his teachers and his friends. When he stopped writing, he noted that the time was 12:40.

'The will was found in Captain Sakuma's clothing when the submarine was retrieved. No one can fail to be moved by his sense of responsibility and his humanity.'

(d) From Vol. 12, Lesson 8, 'Japanese Women': 'Kamitsu-kenuno Katana defeated the Ezo, but to no avail, for his soldiers scattered and slipped out of the castle under cover of night. Katana's wife said to her husband "My lord has achieved his objective, but now our name will be disgraced." She took up a halberd and several of her ladies held bows, and she struck them to make the bowstrings sing. Hearing this sound, the rebels thought that many soldiers were in the castle, and they ordered their men to leave.

'Nita Yoshisada fought with Sagara Shinno at Kanasaki Castle in Echizen, and lost his life along with the brother of Urifu Tamotsu. Tamotsu's mother lost two sons at that time, but she believed that she had no cause for grief. Saying, 'It is an honor for our family that two of our children have laid down their lives for the Emperor, and had I a third child, we would make another attempt," she showed no grief whatsoever. These people remained calm and collected during times of crisis, and they are fine examples of following the path that should be taken by our nation's women. Their moral strength is greater than that of men.

'Filial women devote their energies to serving well as father and mother to bunches of children. The constant devotion of Inō Kōken's wife to worshipping the ancestors, Matsushita Zenka's adherence to thriftiness, and the charity of the wife of Suzuki Imaemon all stand through the centuries as models of the morality of filial womanhood. We should imitate the morality of the wife of Yamanouchi Kazutoyo, who always gave foremost consideration to her husband despite her extreme hardships, and is celebrated in festivals on the battlefield as a wife who was the paragon of goodness. Kusonoki Masatsura's mother admonished her son, and the mother of the sailor on the battleship *Takachiho* scolded him, and these were part of a mother's care, in which kindness was set aside in the true spirit of devotion.

'As a rule the duty of a wife is to help her husband and manage the household affairs, and to teach her children and elevate the family name. This spirit must not be forgotten under any circumstances. Life may bring unexpected misfortunes or shocking reversals at any time. If one does not prepare by following this path resolutely during normal times, then in times of trouble one will become upset and confused, and behave disgracefully. The virtue of Japanese women lies in hewing to the morality of obedience and veneration, maintaining a firm inner purpose and never losing their composure.'

16   Excerpts from seven of the lessons on loyalty in *Jinjō shōgaku shūshinsho*:

(a)   Vol. 1, Lesson 27, 'Loyalty': See Note 15(a).

(b)   Vol. 2, Lesson 20, 'Loyalty':

To prevent	The Russian army	From escaping
The Imperial Army	Of Japan	Sank a ship
At the mouth	Of the harbor	At Port Arthur.
At that time	Our soldiers	Risked their lives
Struggling	Valiantly Serving	Loyally.

(c)   Vol. 3, Lesson 2, 'Loyal Devotion': 'Even though the priest Dōkyō was listening, Wakeno Kiyomaru fearlessly told the Emperor that he had received this teaching from a god at Usa Hachiman Shrine: "Those who cherish hopes of rising to the rank of Emperor must be eliminated." '

(d)   Vol. 4, Lesson 3, 'Loyalty and Patriotism': See Note 15(b).

(e)   Vol. 5, Lesson 3, 'Loyalty and Patriotism, Part I': 'Long ago the Mongol army attacked our country. Kono Michiari, one of the brave warriors who defended the Kyushu coast, had a very strong sense of loyalty and patriotism. When he left his native home, he vowed that if the enemy did not reach Japan within ten years, then he would go across the sea to fight them. He waited for eight years.

'His time came in 1281 when enemy ships approached the coast, and Michiari courageously set out with his men in two boats. As they drew near to a particularly large enemy ship, the enemy began shooting arrows at them, and Michiari was wounded in the left shoulder, but he paid no heed. He boarded the enemy ship and cut down several men, and finally he captured the man who appeared to be the general and returned to shore.'

(f)   Vol. 5, Lesson 4, 'Loyalty and Patriotism, Part II': 'Hojo Takatoki assembled a large army to destroy Emperor Godaigo, at a time when there were very few soldiers protecting the Emperor.

'Kusunoki Masatsura immediately responded to the Emperor's call, and the Emperor was extremely happy and asked him to subdue Takatoki. Masatsura said, "In any war there are victories and defeats. If there is news of a defeat, Your Majesty must not become worried. Even if you hear that I am the only one left alive, know that fortune will smile upon us." With that firm promise, he departed.

'Masatsura raised a small loyalist army and repeatedly harassed Takatoki's army with clever strategems. Soon many people joined the Imperial forces, and finally they annihilated Takatoki's army. The Emperor met Masatsura during his return from the Oki Islands to Kyoto, and praised him highly for his great success, and let Masatsura drive the Imperial carriage for their triumphant return to the capital.'

(g) Vol. 6, Lesson 6, 'Loyalty and Patriotism': 'The war of 1904–05 was a major war in which the Japanese Empire fought Russia and gained much prestige in the world. As soon as war was declared in February 1904, the people resolved to serve the nation with true patriotic spirit.

'There are many admirable stories of the courageous loyalty of the soldiers and sailors. They paid no heed to the cold or heat as they bravely fought, they performed their duty in a hail of bullets, and they begged to remain on the battlefield even after they were wounded. Especially, the wives of the soldiers gave them strong encouragement by taking care of their families so that their husbands would have no cause for worry. Even high-class ladies carried out the duties of women in wartime, by making bandages or serving as volunteer nurses to fulfill medical needs.

> Poem by the Emperor
> Whether standing with the army or not
> Caring for the country is not a divided path'

17   In an 'Opinion on the Textbooks Prepared by the Ministry of Education for Primary School Morals Training,' Higashikuze Michitomi, Nakano Fujimaro and Nomura Yasushi denounced the first series and urged that a second series be compiled. Their argument ran: 'The noble cause of loyalty and filial piety . . . is the spiritual belief inclination of our national unity,' and 'as the perpetual uniqueness of the Japanese race, it must be transmitted to all future generations,' but in the existing state texts there is a neglect 'on the part of those who have interpreted it, particularly with respect to the provision of an extremely deep impression of this noble cause.'

18   One primary school history text published in 1888 (*Shōgakkō-yo nihon rekishi* by Yamagata Teizaburō) was exceptional for its time in giving serious consideration to culture and manners. Its stated purpose was to present 'the elements running from the form of the establishment of our nation up to the point of the cultivation of today's enlightenment . . . by showing the general trends of the landmarks of our nation's past and present history, and also to enumerate the particulars of politics, manners, religion, wars, literature, the arts, foreign trade, etc.' For example, Chapter 9 on 'Customs in Ancient Times' describes the homes, food, clothing, cos-

metics, wedding ceremonies and funerary customs of the common people.

19 Karasawa Tomitarō, *Kyōkasho no rekishi*, p. 186.

20 Kōgen and Kōmyō were still regarded as emperors in the initial, 1909 printing of the second-series history text, but this was replaced after only one year with the 1911 edition, which was used until 1920. The revision was sparked when Diet member Fukuzawa Ikuzō posed a question from the floor to the effect that in a textbook designed to implant accurate ideas concerning the national character, it was a glaring error to teach the existence of both the Northern Court and Southern Court emperors. Maneuvering for a takeover of the government by the People's Party, he moved that the cabinet take responsibility for the problem. The incumbents had been shaken by the Great Treason Incident of the previous year, and their insecurity was used as a lever in the ensuing debate, which contained undertones of a campaign to strengthen and purify ideological controls. The result was a resolution to produce a text with 'no room for doubt about the continuity of the Imperial line,' and Chapter 23 of the first volume, 'The Northern and Southern Courts,' became 'The Yoshino Court.'

15 Successism as the Driving Spirit of Modernization

The Protestant ethic is regarded as the guiding spirit of Western modernity. It is said to have furnished the subjective impulse which welled forth and oriented the lives of those who forged a modern society in Western Europe and the United States of America. What was the guiding spirit of Japanese modernity, which was achieved so quickly? I believe that it was the cult of Japanese Successism (*risshin-shusse-shugi*) which provided the requisite subjective, inner drive.

'We shall rise in the world and make our names, striving with all our heart.' Every Japanese knows these words from *Aogeba tōtoshi*, 'Look Up with Respect,' which is sung during graduation ceremonies at every primary, middle and secondary school in the country. There are some who vehemently insist that 'Rise in the world and make our names' is part of the 'old morality' or 'feudalistic.' But clearly it is not what was taught to children of the farming and merchant classes during the feudalistic period. Under the ideology and the actuality of the feudal system, farmers' children were forever farmers, with no hope of rising above their lot.

The ideal that 'All persons should rise according to the wisdom of their natures' (as formulated in 1868 by Itō Hirobumi, the first prime minister of the Meiji regime) was revolutionary *in its time*. To a people whose careers had been cast from birth by their lineage, the concept that ability and achievement should determine one's position was an iconoclastic break from fatalism.

The singing of 'Look Up with Respect' predates the consolidation of the Meiji state. It first appeared in the Ministry of Education's choral songbook for primary schools in 1884, several years before the Meiji Constitution settled the power structure and the Imperial Rescript on Education suffused the curriculum with loyalty and filial piety.

Primary school had sweeping significance from the start. The Education System decree of 1872 stated, 'Among all of the people, nobles, samurai, farmers, artisans and tradesmen as well as women and children, on no account shall a village have a household without learning, nor shall any home have a member without learning.'[1]

The mental climate in the surrounding society made best-sellers of books such as *The Encouragement of Learning* (1872) by Fukuzawa Yukichi and *The Determined Spirit of the West* (1871) by Nakamura Masanao, and their many imitations and forgeries. (The latter was the translation of Samuel Smiles' *Self-Help*.)

It is no exaggeration to say that since the foundation of the Meiji state, the ideal of 'rising in the world and making our names' has been burned into the brains of every Japanese from childhood. Each generation has been ceaselessly exhorted by their teachers, by their parents and by opinion leaders to follow the ideal of *competitive ascent*.

What distinctive qualities were engraved upon Japanese modernity as a result of its propulsion by that ideal, as opposed to a Protestant-style ethic? What contradictions are inherent within that guiding spirit, and within the 'modern' Japanese society that was formed in accordance with it? These are the topics for investigation in this chapter.

A means for coexistence of hierarchy and energy

> Do not jeer at the student, the student
> Someday he may be a Cabinet member
>
> Do not jeer at the student, the student
> Cabinet and Diet members were students all

This is 'The Student's Song' (*Shosei bushi*) in the original version of 1873 (above), and a later version current in 1881. But by 1897, it was sung as:

> Do not jeer at the student, the student
> He shall be the young master in his home

This reflects the extent to which the image of society and the desire for ascent had by that time been deflected – and stunted – among the youth of Japan.

During the period when the system was being created, around the time of the Meiji Restoration, there was a certain realistic basis to Fukuzawa's agitation that, 'The peasants of today are the Diet members of tomorrow.' In fact, Itō Hirobumi, the first prime minister, had risen from peasant parentage, and Yamagata Aritomo, the third, from minor samurai status 'beneath the lowest officer.'

But when the hierarchy of the Meiji state was established, the opportunities for commoners to actually achieve their aspirations were closed off. A ladder of positional values was set in place, running from the emperor at the pinnacle down through the rungs of the Cabinet and the Diet, through petty officialdom and the police, with the commoners at the bottom. Had the erupting desire to rise in the world been allowed simply to run its course, the frustration at the bottom of the established order might have remained pent-up and smoldering. As it developed, the popular energies aroused by the creed of the universal chance for 'success' could take only two paths. They could either stagnate once again and ebb inward to the private sphere and 'degenerate the health of the nation' (as a writer of the time deplored), or else they could burst forth to destroy the disciplined order of the regime. Since neither of these situations seemed desirable to those who were in control, it was necessary to devise a means for the *coexistence of hierarchy and energy.*

The desire for ascension was to be steered into inductive channels which led into the disciplined order. The means by which this was accomplished was the fine-tuning of the *school system, especially as a route for advancement of public servants*, along lines set out by Mori Arinori.

Tokutomi Sohō's lament that 'To date there has been no avenue of enterprise; what is to be done to bring out the full talents of the people?' led promptly to the conclusion that, 'Therefore, aside from the government, there is no place at all for exertion of energy.'

As gateways for the advancement of high-caliber public officials, in 1886 the government set up seven elite, 'upper middle schools' around the country (soon to become known as 'higher schools,' the term still used today for secondary schools). These were quickly flooded with capable young applicants, and the notorious 'examination hell' made its appearance.

Few tests are as difficult as the entrance examination for the No. 1 Upper Middle School. . . . Each year more than 1000 take the test, but fewer than 200 are admitted. . . . Those who would settle for a setback in but a single examination are rare. Some have performed well and gained admission after one or two eliminations, while there are others who have not yet managed to attain their goal after seven or eight failures.

(From an article entitled 'A Guide to Schooling Away from Home,' 1890)

Kinjirōism: the base of the pyramid

As channels for safely inducting the erupting urge for advancement into the System, the elite schools and the associated route of bureaucratic advancement served to rescue no more than the highest stratum of commoners. Most people were stranded at the bottom, excluded even from ordinary middle schools, let alone the higher schools. (In 1895 only 4.3 per cent of boys and girls of appropriate age entered middle school. The figure was still only 18.5 per cent in 1935.)

The ruling class were faced with two requirements, to continuously draw out the active energies of the majority who could not progress beyond primary education, and to continuously draw those energies into the order of the established system. For these purposes, the model image of conformity which was officially sponsored for popular consumption was that of Ninomiya Kinjirō, the conscientious farmer.[2] It is no accident that Kinjirō ranked along with the Meiji emperor as the most frequently mentioned personage in the state-complied primary school textbooks for moral training.

The elite schools and the route of civil-service promotion, which were focused upon the higher stratum of the people, were the inductive channels of actuality. Kinjirōism, which reached

271

down to the lower strata, was the inductive channel of *ideas*. It was the base of the pyramid in the cult of Japanese Successism.

By 1881 the Meiji government was enamored enough of Ninomiya's moral precepts to assist a society which propagated his ideas, Kōshunsha, with a loan of some 15,000 yen. But it was in 1891, in the wake of the Imperial Rescript on Education, that Ninomiya Kinjirō was adopted in earnest as the model image of conformity for the masses. In that year Kinjirō (then officially known as Ninomiya Sontoku) was posthumously made a noble subject with junior fourth court rank; and a collection of his moral teachings was published as 'juvenile literature' (Kōda Rohan, *Shonen bungaku Ninomiya Sontoku*). 'Sontokuism' was popular throughout the country in 1906, when grand celebrations of the fiftieth anniversary of Ninomiya's death were organized by Hirata Tōsuke and his associates.

Sontoku ideology was the guiding spirit for both of the key national farmers' organizations of the prewar era, the Imperial Agricultural Association and the Industry Association. In addition to serving as the role model for the vast majority of farmers before the Pacific War, Sontoku furnished the ideology for employee management in the cities; permeated the ideas of the moderate wing of the labour movement (the Yūaikai or Fraternal Association); and cast a broad shadow through popular magazines like *King*, which were launched during the early Showa years. Primary schools throughout the country erected statues of Kinjirō as a youth, reading a book while carrying a load of firewood on his back. (American occupation officials were amazed and impressed by those images in 1945).

As late as 1959, in an attitude survey conducted in the city of Gifu (by the central government's Institute of Statistical Mathematics), Ninomiya Sontoku was most frequently named as an 'outstanding person,' especially among farmers, factory workers and common laborers.

The structure of successism (1): the process as an ethic

I will focus here on three distinctive characteristics of the cult of Successism which took shape among the upper and lower classes in modernizing Japan along with the consolidation of the Meiji regime. The first is its 'moralization' through an emphasis on 'right-mindedness.' The second is the conceptual void, in the absence of a fulcrum of transcendent values, of any critical viewpoint with regard to the System. The third is a bipolarity of reference groups, related to the assumption by the individual of the expectations of the home community.

We have seen how the opportunities for the anarchic model of success were closed off with the consolidation of the social hierarchy, and the interest of the aspirants was absorbed by the competitive upward ladder. At this point, the opinion leaders who had exhorted the youth to raise their hopes in vain responded by beginning a thorough shift of emphasis toward the topic of patient 'step-by-step' effort.

> Some of our vigorous youth will surely be set to dreaming when they hear, near at hand, talk of the situation around the time of the Meiji Restoration, or from afar, stories of success in America where those born poor may leap clear to the presidency or become millionaires with their bare hands. Yet in our country at this time, when the social order has been established and the educational system provided, it is difficult to attain a settled occupation without following the proper procedures and accumulating training.
> (Ishikawa Tengai, *Tokyo-ology (Tokyo-gaku*, 1909)

The magazine *Seikō* (Success), which was popular among ambitious youth of the time, invited submissions from its readers on the topic of 'My Credo.' The flavor of the essays selected for publication, in July 1907, is conveyed in these sample opening lines: 'It is of no benefit to cherish however lofty a goal, without devising a means to realize it.' 'My life's wish is to progress step by step in orderly fashion by means of a self-reliant spirit.'

Published from 1902, *Seikō* teemed with articles on the 'personal goals' and experiences of captains of industry in Japan and abroad, and of such figures as Alexander Hamilton and Herbert Spencer. The following exchange appeared in the 'Readers Ask Reporters' column.

Question: Sir, I aim to make very rapid progress overseas and I wonder which place would be best. At present I am

studying commerce, aged nineteen, in good health and averse
to physical labor, and in future I wish to become the head
of a large industrial concern. I hear America is promising,
and if that is indeed the case, is it possible to sail there to
further my present studies of commerce? – 'Carnegie,' Osaka
Answer: Since you wish to become the head of a large
industrial concern, it would be best after all to hold to your
present course of commercial study. (May 1904)

There was a corresponding shift in the treatment of the historical paragon of success, Toyotomi Hideyoshi. Out went the 'Taikō
cult' of admiration for the mature shogun, and in came the
ideology of the apprentice Tōkichirō.[3] The keynote article in a
1907 *Seikō* supplement on 'How to Rise in Today's World' begins
with a discourse on 'the Tōkichirō method': 'As everyone knows,
the key to success is to never neglect the details. Winning the
reliance of others depends not upon the skillful execution of
important matters, but rather upon taking care that the small
matters are carried out thoroughly.'

Similar examples are legion, but let us cite just one more
typical piece of advice, from one of the many success manuals
published during the final Meiji years, entitled *One Hundred
Success Stories*. Says the wealthy entrepreneur and industrialist
Yasuda Zenjirō, 'The way in which the peasant's son has finally
reached the summit of power . . . has never been by getting rich
quickly, but by having followed in sequence each of the steps of
the system.' (Otsuki Ryū, ed., *Seikō hyakuwa*)

In the end it was this Tōkichirōism, with its 'care that the
small matters are carried out thoroughly,' that attracted all of
the attention, while the resonances of the Taikō Hideyoshi image
of 'skillful execution of important matters' were relegated
entirely to the shadows. Kinjirōism was akin to Tōkichirōism:
'When handling the master's sandals, do a first-rate job with the
sandals. When handing the horse's bit, do a first-rate job with
the bit.' In short, be a first-rate farmer or worker.

With the arrival at placing emphasis on 'right-mindedness,' we
find in the above-cited *Seikō* keynote article this quotation from
Baron Shibusawa Ei'ichi: 'The essence of rising in the world
consists most importantly in respecting the old and familiar ways
of loyalty and filial piety.' Th 'how-to' boom had rather quickly
changed into a moralistic 'character-building' boom.

As the actual route of ascent from the bottom becomes more specifically defined, the idealism which serves as the motivator for social energies must become more abstract. For example, this item from the second series of state-complied primary-school Japanese textbooks:

Undaunted Spirit

When raindrops drip down from the eaves
Striking endlessly never pausing
They bore a hole even through stone.
For we who have been born human
Once our spirit is firmly fixed
Immovable, untempted by anything
Diligently advancing, we shall
Attain whatever goal, with adamance
We will soon overcome all adversity.
Even a sapling will diligently serve
To erect a stout tower, even a swallow
Will persevere across an ocean of waves.
All the more, having been born as people
Having once set our sights and fixed our purpose
Undistracted, unwavering, neglecting nothing
Dashing boldly forward, heedless of obstacles
We shall soon move the weightiest rock.

There is a spiritual kinship between that and the texts which served as instruments of training for the upper echelons of the System, such as these lines from a No. 1 National Higher School dormitory song:

Once aroused, we shall achieve
The great exploits of life . . .

The difference is in the functions which they served within the social system. The latter verse is a relatively realistic ideology, motivating the singers to rush happily forward along the upward route which was in fact open to them. The former, by furnishing the illusion of limitless ascent, ensures that the rising energy of ordinary people at the bottom is combusted within the confines of the official hierarchy, and that any perception of obstacles or dissatisfaction is turned inward as *self-punishment*. As a mechanism for channelling energy in directions advantageous to the oligarchy, this ideology takes on additional fictitiousness.

Another essay on 'My Credo' from a *Seikō* reader:

> 'A life of fulfillment!! It is my credo that a wasted day is surely a dying day and a wasted year a dying year. There are two types of people in the world, those who are dying every day and those who are living.

That is the functional equivalent of the following teaching of Benjamin Franklin, which was cited by Max Weber (in *The Protestant Ethic and the Spirit of Capitalism*) as the classic, near-perfect exposition of the capitalist spirit:

> It must be emphasized that time is money. If a man who earns ten shillings per day for his labor spends half a day taking a walk outside or sitting idly indoors, even if he spends a mere sixpence for diversion and relaxation, we must not think that he has consumed only that small amount. We must realize that he has expended an additional five shillings, or rather, has thrown them away.

The structure of successism (2): lack of a critical standpoint

I have posited Kinjirōism, the quintessential image of the Successism on the popular level, as the functional equivalent of the Protestant ethic during the formative period of Japanese capitalism.

The decisive difference between Kinjirōism and Protestantism, as has been hinted above, is that Kinjirōism lacks a transcendent value standard which would enable a radical critique of traditional morality or status-quo values. Such a value standard need not necessarily transcend the present world, for it can exist within such constructs as secular humanism. Yet at the least, a radically critical viewpoint must have at its core a conception which *transcends the existing system*.

The worldview of Successism rested on the assumption of a

predetermined harmony between the pursuit of individual ambition and the prosperity of the state. The preface to *One Hundred Success Stories* begins as follows:

It is a truism of all times and places that success benefits the individual and also benefits the nation. When many people succeed the nation will be rich and strong, but when few succeed the nation will become poor and weak. The significance of the necessity for success does not encompass merely the ups and downs of a single person or family, but extends more broadly to the causation of the vicissitudes of the nation as a whole. While we must all strive mightily and work for success, and indeed that is one's *duty* as a person, the laurels of glory will fall to those who advance not only personal profit, but also the profit of the nation. The reality of society is that many who do not succeed finish out their lives cloaked in distress and misery. Alas, may we succeed.

The anecdotes collected in that book have happy endings, couched in realistic terms which frankly express the idea of pre-determined harmony. 'After overcoming all sorts of difficulties over the 25 years up to today, it has become one of the leading electrical equipment factories in Tokyo, having succeeded to the point where it contributes one thousand yen in income tax and more than eight hundred yen in business tax.' Thus the acqui-sition of wealth or status or power is evidenced, first and fore-most, by *capability with respect to the state*, and this capability, it goes without saying, is part of the duty to be of service at the will of the 'absolute divinity,' the emperor.

This same sense of predetermined harmony between the indi-vidual pursuit of profit and the process of realizing ethical value was in evidence during the formation of the modern age in the West. But if we venture to ask whether the content of the ethical value embraces a universal which transcends contemporary his-torical and national systems, a vast disparity is opened up between Japan and the West.

Consider the story of Abe Go'ichi, who rose from dire poverty to make a name for himself in the business world. In return for having helped his father build a barge and enter the marine transport business, he received a battered sailing ship that held two thousand *koku* (about ten thousand bushels of rice), which he repaired and christened *Success*. Soon after he set sail the boat met with disaster, but fortunately it was insured, and he ended up with three thousand yen. He placed the entire sum in the Dai-Ichi Bank as a 250-year long-term deposit, with a written undertaking that it could not be withdrawn before the full term. With compound interest calculated through to the middle of the twenty-second century, the principal and earnings will amount to 1,208,411,179 yen. That money is to be applied to the national defense, to the preservation of old temples and shrines, to educational scholarships and to public works, with the remainder to comprise the Abe family estate as well as capital for the Hōbi Bank. (From *One Hundred Success Stories*)

The earmarkings are a superb expression of Meiji ideals, while the contract barring withdrawal for a quarter of a millennium fairly oozes with the unwavering faith placed in the imperial state by successists of that era.

In Kinjirōism as in Protestantism, the private impulse to obtain wealth, status and power was systematized and spurred onward by its justification in an ethical standard, and by being deemed meritorious in the name of a sanctified, inviolable, absolute divinity. However, in the case where the absolute divinity is in fact the ruler of the system which comprises the status quo, the value structure thus established is inherently and perpetually enclosed within that system.

In order to rapidly effectuate an advanced capitalist production capacity, the ruling class settled on the promotion of top-down modernization. Dispensing with a thoroughgoing bourgeois revolution, they instead gobbled everything up for themselves by relying upon the remains of the feudal system. The perfect ideology for this purpose was none other than a Protestantism from which the fangs of anti-establishment criticism had been extracted. Protestantism without protest. Such was Kinjirōism.

The structure of successism (3): bipolarity of reference

The last two sections have contrasted Kinjirōism, which was the spirit of success existing in the lower tiers of Japanese society, with the Protestant ethic, which was the guiding spirit during the formation of the modern age in Europe. We have seen that they had in common the organization of daily life according to a process involving behavioral ethics, while they diverged with respect to the existence of a value standard which extends beyond the established social system.

We should also consider the fact that Japanese Successism benefited from a particular, powerful motive force which was not present in Protestantism. This was the shouldering by the individual of community expectations, centering around those of the *ie*, or extended-family household.[4] The individual's rise in society was always spurred on by an awareness of the constant, expectant gaze of his 'home' in the background, as indicated by such ubiquitous expressions of the time as 'Honor the family name' or 'The hope of the village.'

The other side of the concept of identity with the community is illustrated by one of the injunctions which students memorized from the state-compiled morals textbooks (second series): 'Lest one member of a household be unvirtuous and bring dishonor upon the family name, each member of the household must maintain the duty of proper behavior.' (This awareness was also channeled toward the state. For example, in a well-known story from Meiji primary school readers, 'A Sailor's Mother,' a commanding officer gives a lecture on the 'collective shame' which obtains at all levels. 'The shame of a sailor is the shame of the ship, and the shame of the ship is the shame of the Empire.')

The Calvinist doctrine that a momentary lapse will lead to hell served to drive people to compulsive achievement, via surveillance from within by the *conscience*. In parallel, the Japanese precept that individual dishonor leads to dishonor of household and community had the same effect, via (mutual) surveillance from the outside by *the eyes of others*. In positive terms, the Calvinist was guided by a consciousness of *principles* and the Japanese by a consciousness of *expectations*; or in negative terms, the one was coerced by a consciousness of *guilt*, the other by a consciousness of *shame*. The irrational core of the purposeful, rational spirit of modern capitalist society in Western Europe was an internalized belief in a transcendent spirit, whereas in Japan it was a practical motivation to 'embellish the brocade of home and community.'

That this was taken as the ideal in Successism is aptly portrayed in a lesson which appeared in a common primary school reader of the 1890s, 'The Success Banquet.' There was once a poor widow who toiled ceaselessly to send her son to school. Fulfilling his mother's fondest hopes, he was very successful and ultimately gained acceptance in 'high-class society.' On one occasion he held a banquet in his home. In the *tokonoma* alcove stood the obligatory aesthetic centerpiece, but for this occasion it was a crude old spinning wheel. In response to the questioning glances of his guests, he explained that it was his mother's, and that it was thanks to her spinning that he was able to attend school. A little later he led in an old woman of humble bearing, and introduced her as the most important guest of the banquet, his mother. 'How joyful was the heart of this aged mother who by raising her child well and supporting his education had enabled him to achieve such good fortune.'

Thus the cult of Successism was marked by a *bipolarity of reference*, or two poles of conformity. It was inclined simultaneously toward the 'center' (Tokyo, the metropolis) and the 'home' (mother and the native community). These two poles of conformity operated in tandem to furnish goals and means. Success in the 'center' was furthered by the use of connections (for information and 'pull') from 'home,' even as this success in the 'center' was pursued as the route to recognition and admiration 'at home.'

Such were the outlines of the image projected upon the inner world of the individual by the dual structure of the controlling mechanisms of the Meiji regime – the bonding of the modern bureaucratic system with traditional community discipline. Those who would adapt within this *double-framed* structure were inevitably under the influence of this bipolarity of reference.

The ideal of Successism lay within the reality of this paradoxical union, between the inclination toward the value of constantly rising and soaring toward the 'center,' and the inclination toward the value of constantly returning to and reposing in the 'home.'

Systemic functions (1): papering over contradictions

Having defined the structural characteristics of Japanese Successism, we may turn to the functions it served within the social system. Clearly, as the above accounts have indicated, it patched up various contradictions within the imperial state. In more positive terms, it also laid the subjective groundwork for the promotion by the oligarchy of a 'top-down industrial revolution,' in order to serve their goal of rapidly developing industrial capacity without radical political reform.

After the Russo-Japanese War of 1904–5, it was impossible to ignore the disturbance and slackening of the traditional village order, known as the 'rural peril,' which was exacerbated by the spread of modern capitalist production. Referring to the village social structure with the landlords at the apex, Sumiya Mikio noted that, 'Since it was precisely this community order which was the foundation of the emperor system, the disturbances could not be allowed to take their own course.'⁵

The Boshin Rescript, issued in the name of the emperor in 1908, responded to the rural peril by exhorting conformity high and low to the community spirit and to a work ethic of diligence and frugality. Home Minister Tokonami Takejirō followed with policies to activate 'rural improvement' campaigns, and to foster institutional competition among village, county and prefectural entities. Many new national organizations were formed at the village level, including industrial and agricultural cooperatives, youth groups, the Women's Patriotic Association, Village Societies on Military Affairs, a firemen's association, and credit unions, as well as branches of Hōtokusha, the society which Ninomiya Sontoku himself had founded to spread his teachings. This process can be regarded as 'a rearrangement of local society in order to strengthen the control structure of the emperor system, in response to various symptoms of shakiness and decline in the communal order.'⁶ Thus the traditional community was reordered into functional groupings so as to stave off disintegration, and it was common knowledge that the guiding doctrine for almost all of the new organizations was Hōtokuism, as Ninomiya's philosophy had come to be known.

From the beginning, then, Hōtokuism was stage-managed in order to bridge the contradiction between the two mainstays of the Meiji regime, the traditional community order and modern capitalist production. Before long, it was also called into service to cope with the internal contradictions of capitalist production itself. An explication in *Seikō* of 'the true meaning of the Hotoku teachings' stated:

> With Sontoku's concept of 'mutual concession' it is possible to maintain harmony between selfishness and altruism, and also to resolve the current issue of socialism. Through the principle of mutual concession, the rich will take care of the poor, and harmonious relations between rich and poor will yield happiness. In short, Sontoku's teachings are an excellent method for resolving contemporary social problems.
> ('Local Administrations and the Teachings of Hōtoku,' March 1907)

A year earlier, during the celebrations marking the fiftieth anniversary of Sontoku's death, Suzuki Tōzaburō, the president of the Dai-Nippon Soy Sauce Brewery and the sponsor of the event, spoke on 'The Capability-Yield Method for Employees':

> Being utilized is the lot of employees. It is necessary to regulate yourselves according to your lot. Arriving at six in the morning and working until six in the evening is the duty. As for the 'mutual concession,' arriving on time and leaving on time is the ordinary standard, and the concession consists of diligence in arriving earlier and working later than the standard.

We have seen Baron Shibusawa's assertion that loyalty and filial piety are the only route to success, which is to say that only those who are 'right-minded' will succeed. In the same essay he goes on to state the converse: 'We have no sympathy for the socialists who, as they slide from laziness into hardship, cry earnestly for equalization of wealth.'

Articles in *Seikō (Success)* magazine attributed the 'causes' of poverty, or of 'failure' to become an official, to a person's own 'mental posture,' while remaining blind to systemic contradictions.

Causes of poverty

(For study by the poor as techniques for becoming rich)

1 Because they have no means and only their plans are large
2 Because they think the world has an obligation to support them
3 Because they don't tote up their expenses on an abacus
4 Because they reject the maxim that after suffering comes happiness, and are easily cheated by swindlers
5 Because they too often seek happiness through high spending
6 Because they don't know that even a loose farthing or two, when saved, becomes precious
7 Because they endanger their present position by rushing impatiently to seek happiness
8 Because in trying to be well-liked they are foolishly impressed by the loose talk of their friends
9 Because they work for personal stimulation while neglecting undertakings for personal achievement
10 Because the child of thrifty parents so often becomes great in temperament only

(April 1904)

Causes of failure to become an official

- I pay constant attention only to the clock
- I speak only of complaints
- I am always inferior in everything
- I ask too many questions
- I have been harmed by immoral books
- I only imitate the habits of those of higher class

(November 1904)

The visage that comes to mind for each of those lines is a harried one, shaped by the premises that social conditions must be taken as a constant, and that personal 'mental posture' is the only determinant variable of success. The plucky countenance of the aspirant from Restoration times, informed by thoughts of the system itself as a variable, is long forgotten.

Systemic functions (2): impetus for national prosperity

The cult of Successism, especially at the common level where it was centered on the Kinjirō image, functioned to paper over the structural contradictions of the imperial system. This was negative in one sense only. On the positive side, it served as a driving force for the rapid industrialization and capitalization of Japanese society, through the top-down industrial revolution. For Kinjirō-ism, as we have seen, was by no means a simply feudal idea.

> There are some rural youth who are quite disappointed that they cannot make a name in the world as farmers. I don't think about this, for questions of whether it is true that one cannot make a name as a farmer, or of what will or will not result from tireless exertion, are causes for insufficient effort. In any case, I say that the way in which to make a name in the world is to achieve a record rice harvest. I will reap ten *koku* from each *tan* [fifty bushels from each quarter-acre]. Even if I fail I will be happy.
>
> (*Agricultural Association News*, June 1919)

The Imperial Agricultural Association seized upon this 'confession' of a rural youth to hoist the familiar slogan of 'Japan's Number-One Farmer.' While this case points up the hidden anxieties and the urge for ascent among rural youth, it also illustrates how Kinjirōism functioned to immediately channel those impulses within the established system.

In the magazine emporia during the last few years of the nineteenth century, on display alongside such staples as *Taiyō (The Sun)* and *Bungei kurabu (Literature Club)* was the popular new monthly, *Shonen sekai (Boy's World)*. In each issue, this magazine introduced a number of model boys whom the editor had presented with medals of honor for, among other factors, 'distinguished devotion and diligence as a shop or factory apprentice.' Here are some examples from the August 1895 issue (Volume 1, Number 15):

No. 32   Master Takei Manpei
He helps his father plant and harvest rice, and also attends to household chores, he devotes his spare time to study at

the village moral training institute without neglecting his scholastic preparations, and he is lauded by the community for his piety and determination. (Attested by his middle school teacher and the head of his moral training institute.)

No. 33   Master Kurozu Zenkichi
He works hard and diligently the whole day through, and journeys a great distance to and from home without the slightest complaint or weariness, is never absent even if his clothes are soaked and his feet muddied by storm or flood, thoroughly obeys his teacher's instructions and faithfully assists his friends at school. . . . (Attested by his primary school headmaster.)

No. 34   Master Kondō Moku
Even while wholeheartedly pursuing household duties and reading, he hews to his commercial work, and pays no heed whatsoever if friends come to invite him out. . . . (Attested by his private school headmaster and the village mayor.)

Along with the Imperial Agricultural Association slogan of 'Japan's Number-One Farmer,' these models impart to Japanese commoners of all stripes the motivation for each person to enthusiastically persevere in the individual duties of one's present position within the system.

Internal contradictions (1): the competitive ethic and community reliance

While the Cult of Success indeed functioned admirably to stitch together the structural contradictions of modernizing Japan and to promote the policies which served the goals of the regime, it contained within itself several unavoidable contradictions.

The first of these is the paradox posed by that basic attribute of the success ethic in general, the *universalistic* logic of competition, as against that most remarkable peculiarity of the *Japanese* cult of success, the *particularistic* attachment to the home community. This contradiction is necessarily connected with the *bipolarity of reference* which was described above.

Kinjirōism, as we have seen, was promoted and diffused in a carefully controlled fashion as a means of coping with the rural dislocations arising from the spread of modern industry. Nevertheless, it accelerated the erosion of the community mentality in rural areas, through its latent ethic of competition.

During the Meiji and Taisho years the ideal of the 'venerable farmer' took on a subtle function (or dysfunction), which is aptly described by Yanagita Kunio:

> The ancient term *rōnō-seinō* [venerable and industrious farmer] must originally have referred to people with long experience and deep understanding of agricultural activities. The source of our difficulties is that it was later applied to the type of people who excelled in the cultivation of particular crops and took top prizes at country fairs.[7]

Yanagita continues:

> Without any warning to those living alone in the cities, the countryside had progressed. While it was not quite Tokyoization, at the least the cherished hometown had become a rougher place. Yet unaware, they nursed hopes for a return to the past. Those who went back seeking a restful interlude were disappointed.

The remembrances of the migrants, who had borne with them the hopes of their families and communities, were thus betrayed.

Successism was demolishing with its own hands the source of the motive energy upon which it was supposedly founded, the home community. On the other hand, since ties to 'home' were utilized for advancement in the 'center' (as described earlier), the competitive principle could not be fully carried through, for it was functionally checked and hindered by the ubiquitous nets of assorted 'cliques.' Entanglements in factionalism gave rise to derivative forms of hostility, frustration and mistrust.

Internal contradictions (2): public ideology and private motives

The second contradiction within Successism was between the ideology of contributing to the national community, and the reality of the individual (bearing expectations from home) selfishly pursuing happiness. Bluntly put, claiming virtue for private happiness in the name of the public good was sheer hypocrisy.

Imamura Seinosuke was a typical hero of Meiji success stories. The account of his career in *One Hundred Success Stories* ends as follows. On a night when he was young and poor, the oil lamp on his street stall burned out, whereupon a geisha who happened to be watching from an upstairs restaurant laughed and applauded. At the time Imamura could barely hold back tears of despair, but:

> in 1888 he founded the Imamura Bank with capital of 250,000 yen, and his capital then grew to twice that amount. . . .
> He later engaged the very geisha who had ridiculed his lamp for an evening of wild and prolonged merrymaking, and he finally dissolved the bitter tears from that night so long before.

In actuality, the motives behind Imamura's strenuous personal efforts extended far beyond that incident, a key factor being the ambition to restore his family's fortune. Yet it is significant that in a success story aimed at the masses, the writer should deliberately stress his vulgar vengeance as if it were something particularly thrilling. It reveals another of the faces of successism: a naturalism of delayed and ethically refurbished cravings.

While this aspect of the motivation to succeed was somewhat of an open secret among the successful themselves, it was all the more ironically reflected in the chilly gaze of the commoners who had been pushed off the ladder of success. In 1912 a worker in an artillery factory who was asked by a magazine reporter about the 'purpose of life' had this to say:

> People are all the same, they eat, that is they eat sweets as much as they can, and they look for entertainment. A man

wants a pretty wench and a woman wants a handsome
husband and that's all there is to it. The learned professors
keep on glossing it over, with their quibblings that we can't
even understand. But deep down in their guts they know
it. They just can't admit it because of their status. They think
they can put on airs and act so smart, and we think they're
hilarious.

('Spectrum of Views on Life, from Government Ministers to
Rickshaw Pullers,' supplementary edition of *Seikō*, April
1912)

Internal contradictions (3): desires pursued and desires suppressed

The third contradiction is between the affirmation of desires (the
pursuit of happiness) implied by the purpose and motivation for
successism, and the extreme restraint involved in the ladder to
success.

Fundamentally, as we have seen, the cult of Successism did not
serve to deny the pursuit of worldly cravings. On the contrary, in
the eyes of the individual, Successism in part represented a
means of satisfying those desires to the maximum, by following
the route approved by the system.

Irregardless, those on the road to success focused their concern
entirely on efforts which would serve, studies which would serve,
connections which would serve for success, while purposefully
and completely avoiding any concern with other values.

A young lawyer's 'Worldview during Baptism by Fire in the
Real World' included the judgment that, 'Anyone who wishes to
pursue his studies after he is out in the world would be unwise
to take a wife.' For during his concentrated study of the law, 'a
wife would disturb me by serving tea, bringing warm clothes and
so forth' ('A Spectrum of Views . . . ,' op, cit.).

Another writer in the same supplement, a dental student,
spoke up for matrimony: 'A wife is the energy for one's endeavors.' But the keystone of his argument was that, 'since she is
far away in the country, working to help maintain my parents'
household,' he is left alone in Tokyo with no heart for frivolity,

and thus his endeavors are 'energized.' Such were the frank, if rather extreme, views of successists on marriage, the household and women.

A classic juxtaposition of the naturalistic motivation of Successism and the self-restraint of the upward path occurs in the novel *Yadorigi (Mistletoe,* 1909), which is based on an actual diary. At one point the young protagonist expresses the purpose behind his intent to succeed (emphasis added): 'In the Iwate Middle School there is a guideline to success. Intangible assets, unlimited glory, *happiness, enjoyment*, all are there.' To further his goals he later prepares a Self-Examination Note, a set of vows, sealed with his own blood, to 'Eat nothing between meals, never more than two bowls of rice per meal. Never drink or smoke throughout life,' etc. (Tokutomi Roka novelized the diary with virtually no dramatic embellishment after the writer, Ogasawara Zenpei, took his own life.)

For the *Yadorigi* diarist, who managed to attend an elite school, life went on under a spartan regimen. Meanwhile, the character model set forth for farmers' children, who could not rise to the surface without literally following Ninomiya Kinjirō's model of 'gathering firewood, braiding rope and making straw sandals,' was so stoic as to be lamented even in the *Imperial Agricultural Association News*:

> It is quite deplorably sad to see rural youth seduced by the dictum of thriftiness and more thriftiness, and ending up with atrophied minds like so many small beans. A young man works every night braiding rope in order to save his pennies, another collects horse manure from the roads. How desolate in spirit they must be. Then their elders take notice and offer praise and they become the paradigms of local gossip, and they redouble their efforts in the same direction.
>
> (By Kumagai Shigesaburo, March 1911)

As the writer had partially foreseen, this sort of 'desolate' frugality tended on the one hand to constrict the entrepreneurial spirit, and on the other to tame the domestic markets, and soon turned into persistence for the unfettered growth of capitalism. This is one reason why the diminutiveness of the spirit of Kinjirō-ism is reflected in the diminutiveness of Japanese capitalism itself.

Thus Successism did not even suggest a new value standard

for rising above worldly cravings, but instead relied on such primitive desires and drew energy from them, thereby making extreme repression a compulsory part of the process. This gave rise not simply to frustrations, but also to the dissatisfaction of suppressed desires, which constantly precipitated out as a sense of *unease* that something was unnatural in one's present way of life, of alienation from the essential 'natural' way of life as human beings. This is one basis for the paradoxical Japanese convention that to directly affirm 'natural' desires is to go 'against the grain.'

Seikō magazine occasionally ran 'consultations' between readers and the editors, such as this from the April 1904 issue (emphasis added).

> *Question*: I am inspired by *Seikō* to maintain the drive to succeed, to fight my way forward and to cultivate my own destiny. Day and night I have no thought other than this self-discipline, and I idolize the learned elders here in my village. But *for some reason I have a feeling of a kind of 'loneliness' in my heart*, an almost unbearable anxiety about my destiny, and I can't settle down to my studies. I seek your advice on *what I should do to reach a place of spiritual calm*. I was a devoted reader of the Bible but I gave it up, as I could not settle on the ground of faith. I have profound trust in the novels of Tokutomi Roka and others. I am exhausted from crying and crying and crying and crying. I beg you to please be kind enough to give me your advice. – Hamada
> *Answer*: You are suffering from your own weak points, having aroused your drive for success to the point of excess which leads to weakness. You should carefully read and study the biographies of heroes and great men. In your case *novels should be strictly avoided*. You should never have laid eyes upon them.

Internal contradictions (4): universal ideas and limited chances

The fourth contradiction is that between the universality of successist ideas and the limitations on the actual opportunities to succeed. As we have seen, all of the people were encouraged to succeed from primary school onward. But since the fundamental meaning of success was to rise to a *relative* position within the social system, it was unrealistic to ignore the assumption that in the end, the majority of the people *would not* succeed.

Even in magazines devoted to the mission of encouraging success, evidence of disappointment was frequently visible between the lines. An example from *Middle School World*:

I am a graduate of a private college. Upon obtaining my diploma two years ago in July, I immediately set out to find work and finally obtained a position that November. At present I remain engaged in that work, but things in the world don't go as I expected. Before graduating I was full of big talk about doing this and doing that, about all the learning I had acquired and the great efforts I would make, about setting the world on fire and struggling to grasp the laurels of success. I was very much pleased with myself. But when at last I went out into the world I did not find my ideals or my ambitions, for I was 'in a world that is not as I expected.' I am working for no reason other than to eat.

The disillusioned writer also recounts what he was told when he visited one of his professors to talk about finding another job:

[Pupils who continue their mental training while supporting themselves] all become frustrated along the way. The interesting thing is that their frustration always follows the same pattern. To put it simply, since the young graduates want, like you, to continue their training, they find a job that pays 20 or 30 yen and they also study diligently, especially at the start. But unlike their school years, now they have social expenses, usually including clothing, and they have to eat a great deal of nourishing food because they use so much energy working as well as studying. They must dispense with luxury, and they claim their salaries are insufficient. Before long they are fed up, so they put on their sandals and go out and find another job. After a while they again feel dissatisfied and they look for a side job. The initial plan, to focus on their own education and work only as a means to survive, is inverted, and there is no time for studying. They end up thinking, 'This is no different than if I had gone back home. No, actually it would be easier to live at home,' and finally they do return to their hometowns. Back home, their brains come to a halt, and very few manage to rise substantially in the world.

('Initial Battle in the Real World,' *Chūgaku sekai*, March 1908)

Idealistic encouragements such as 'You'll be happy even if you fail,' or 'Why not become the number-one farmer?' existed precisely in order to deal with this inherent paradox of Successism, as devices to forestall rebelliousness or dispiritedness on the part of the dropouts, the losers, and the groups who from the start had no hope of success.

But the cult of success was primarily a wellspring of motivation to pursue the fulfillment of worldly desires, and to the extent that this motivation latently persisted, it was hard for the dropout or the loser to say 'I am happy' when there was no hope of ever fulfilling his wordly desires. That would require an immense amount of norm consciousness. Similarly, the hope of becoming 'the number-one farmer' could not be embraced by just anyone. The syllogism that a greater investment of labor will yield a greater return was to some extent valid in the context of self-sufficiency amid the simple 'natural' economy. But the spread of the commercial economy unavoidably brought new pitfalls, such as the ruinous difficulty of competing through individual diligence, and the peril of serial collapse brought on by webs of interdependence.

As for those who were unable to realize their goals, most entrusted their dreams of success to their offspring (this shows the Japanese parental zeal for education to be in part a postponement of despair). Yet some among them must have entertained at least slight misgivings as to whether the System was really committed to their happiness.

This concludes our examination of the paradoxes inherent in Japanese Successism, to wit, the contradictions between:

1 the universalistic competitive ethic and the particularistic reliance on home and community;
2 the ideology of contributing to the nation or the public and the reality of selfishly pursuing happiness;

3 the affirmation of desire as motivation and purpose, and the negation of desire along the path; and
4 the ideological universality of successism, and the actual limitation of opportunity.

In their respective ways, these contradictions gave rise to distrust and doubt concerning the way of life which was commended by the dominant values and beliefs of the modernizing Japanese system – the first by way of the keen awareness of the dismemberment of the traditional community; the second by way of the awareness of the structural hypocrisy of the cult of Successism; and the third and fourth by way of the accumulated dissatisfaction of suppressed desires, among those still battling for success as well as those who had left the field.

In the political, literary and criminal spheres, it should be possible to trace a geneaology of forms of resistance, contrariness and delinquency that shined forth from the depths of these suspicions, as the negative images of the several dimensions of the successist world. But we will leave these where they lie, having completed our present task of analyzing the structure, the functions and the internal contradictions of the subjective *motive force* behind the social system of modernizing Japan.

Notes

1 Though universal in nature, the education system took some time to diffuse completely. Attendance reached 50 per cent around 1885 and 90 per cent in 1902. By law, school was compulsory for 16 months from 1872, for three years from 1880, and for four years from 1886.
2 Ninomiya Kinjirō (1787–1856) is also known as Sontoku and as the creator of Hōtokuism. He rose from poverty, worked vigorously as an agricultural engineer to resuscitate depressed villages, and was eventually given charge of land development in the Tokugawa clan domains. Ninomiya and his disciples actively propagated his ideas, which emphasized that the benefits received from heaven, society and the earth should be repaid through filial piety, diligence, thrift and cooperation.
3 Taikō was a title taken by Hideyoshi late in life. Tōkichirō was

his name as a young retainer of Oda Nobunaga, who noticed his attentiveness to detail and promoted him, eventually to the height of power. The fabled example is that in anticipation of Nobunaga's return from a journey, Tōkichirō would warm his sandals by placing them inside his kimono.

4 The linkage of the individual to the *ie*, either as a family member or as a resident worker, had long been reinforced by the Tokugawa administrative system, under which all Japanese were legally beholden to the heads of their respective *ie*.

5 Sumiya Mikio, 'Integration and Disintegration of National Vision' ('Kokuminteki vijon no tōgō to bunkai,' *Shidōsha to taishū*, Chikuma Shobō.

6 Kimbara, Sumiya et al., 'Ideologies and Political Roles of Lower-Level Leaders,' in 'Kokuminteki vijon no tōgō to bunkai'.

7 Yanagita Kunio, *Meiji Taisho shi, Sesō hen*, Chikuma Shobō, 1963.

16 The History of Modern Japan in Image

1 Generations, eras and historical consciousness

People create history, and they are created by history. 'Generations' pay a key role in this cycle. The eras mold the generations and the generations mold the eras.

The image of an era which is harbored by a generation is a complex tapestry, in which the warp is the character of the era itself, and the weft is the life experience that the generation encountered in the era. The images of the eras define historical consciousness, and it is upon this ground that each generation proceeds to mold the ensuing eras.

What sort of images do the several generations in contemporary Japan harbor toward the various eras they have lived through? A survey conducted in 1963 probed the popular mind with two simple questions designed to elicit that imagery:

1 (a) Which one of the following eras do you think is the best? Please choose only one.
(1) Meiji (2) Taisho (3) Early Showa (4) The War Years (5) The Immediate Postwar Years (6) The Present
(b) Which era do you think is the most unpleasant? Again, please choose only one from the following.
(1) Meiji (2) Taisho (3) Early Showa (4) The War Years (5) The Immediate Postwar Years (6) The Present
2 What color do you think is the best to represent each era? For each era, please choose the one color from the list below that you feel is the most appropriate.

These questions were one segment of a nationwide survey conducted by Nippon Television. The sample number was 3,000, of

	Meiji	Taisho	Early Showa	War years	Postwar years	Present
Red						
Pink						
Yellow						
Brown						
Green						
Blue						
Purple						
Gray						
Black						
White						

which 2,639 responded. Table 16.1 is a breakdown of the repondents by age, occupation and locale.

Analysis of the survey data tells us much about the images of

Table 16.1 *Characteristics of the poll respondents*

	(Age)				
	20s	272	Professional/Technical	113
	30s	347	Management	79
Men	40s	271	Office worker	251
	50s	207	Shopkeeper	170
	60–	178	Sales clerk	95
			Service/maintenance	60
	20s	361	Factory (skilled)	75
	30s	348	(unskilled)	123
Women	40s	312	Transport	32
	50s	186	Craft/apprentice	75
	60–	157	Laborer	92
			Agriculture	564
			Housewife	707
			Student/unemployed	203
Major cities		505		
Towns/smaller cities		1230		
Rural areas		904		

the modern eras that are held by the Japanese of the 1960s. It also reveals the transition of those images over the generations. (In this chapter, a 'generation' spans an interval of ten years, which happens to correspond roughly to the duration of each of the eras in twentieth-century Japanese history.)

2 Modern history in the minds of the people

The purple era (Meiji)

Meiji (1868–1912) was named the 'best era' by 5.6 per cent of people over twenty years of age (about 3.3 million people if extrapolated to the entire population). It is less popular than Taisho and Early Showa, and most of its proponents are senior citizens (over sixty). (See Table 16.2.)

It seems fair to say that the idea that there was a better era before we were born is virtually non-existent in present-day Japan.

Analyzing the Meiji nostalgists by occupation, we find that most are retired and hence unemployed, with service, transport and craft the next most numerous. This is the old urban middle class. On the other hand, the proportion naming Meiji as the 'worst era' is a mere 0.3 per cent lower than for any other era. On the whole, then, Meiji evokes a faintly favorable feeling.

Purple is the color which best represents Meiji in the popular mind.

Murasaki bushi, *'Purple Song' was one of the most popular songs in the closing years of Meiji (c. 1901): 'The rustling of a purple hakama/With a white ribbon.' Purple was the color associated with the Meiji Romanticism movement of the 1890s and its flagship literary journal, Bungakukai. It was the fashionable color at the turn of the century.*

Purple was rarely chosen, however, by respondents over sixty who actually lived in the Meiji era. Its predominance among the younger strata suggests that, rather than representing the actuality of the era, 'purple Meiji' is an *abstracted, crystallized image* within the historical awareness of later generations.

From ancient times purple was the color used to signify the rank of high nobility in such things as headgear at the imperial

Table 16.2   *Shading of popular images of modern Japanese history*
(attitudes of various generations toward various eras)

1900 1910	1920	1930	1940	1950	1960	Present	Ages at 1945	The year of birth
Meiji	Taisho	Early Showa	War time	Post-war time	Present	20	2	1943
○		○	●●	●●	○ ○⊘	(20s)		
			●●	●●	⊘○○			
			●●	●●	○○○	30 —	12	1933
○		○	●●	●●	○○○	(30s)		
		○	●●	●●	○○○			
			●●	●●	○○○			
			●●	●●	○○○	40 —	22	1923
	○	○ ○	●●●	●○	○○○	(40s)		
	○	○ ○	●●	●○	○ ○			
		○ ○	●●	●○	●○○			
○	○ ○	⊘○	●●●	○○	○○	50 —	32	1913
	○ ○	○○	●●	○○	○○	(50s)		
		○○	●●	○○	○			
			●●	○○	○	60 —	42	1903
○○	●●○	●○○	●●●	○○	○○	(60s)		
○○	○	○	●●	○○	○○			
○			●●		○○			

A circle indicates selection as 'best era' by 5 per cent of males.
An asterisk indicates selection as 'worst era' by 5 per cent of males. (Data for females was nearly identical.)
The thick diagonal tracks respondents' birth years; the thin diagonal tracks their 20th years.

court. It is a refined and classical color, imparting a perspective of distance and aspiration. On a more concrete level, it is the primary color of Meiji costume in woodblock prints and post-cards. These were potent media in their time, supplying for example the ubiquitous images of the 'reign of Meiji' in village homes.

Okajōki ('Steam Train'), *the painting by Hiroshige III of a crowd at Shimbashi Station, is one of today's most widely current visual records of Meiji manners. Some 25 of the 30 people in this scene are wearing purple (13 coats, 4 pairs of trousers, and 8 other items). Likewise, in Yōshū Shūen's classic woodblock print, 'The Rokumeikan Ladies Charity Society', we can make out the clothing colors of 55 persons, 39 of whom are attired entirely or partially in purple.*

Because we know that Yōshū made the print just before a Rokumeikan charity bazaar at which it was placed on sale, we may conclude that it is not a work of realism. A more realistic woodblock image of the manners of the time, Mizuno Toshikata's *Group of Contemporary Women*, depicts six women, not one of whom is wearing anything purple. The fact that purple is the key tone of 'Meiji' garb in block prints seems to be significant not as data on the actual manners of the time, but as a sign that the *sensibility of the era* was receptive to the hue, and as a source for the *stereotyped image* of Meiji among later generations.

Those aged respondents who saw the Meiji era for themselves most often chose white rather than purple, and a fair number of the women among them chose red, pink or green. Also, among those naming Meiji as the 'best era,' the color most commonly assigned to it is pink, followed by white and green. (See Table 16.3.) These patterns suggest that two key factors of nostalgic longing are at work. First, the women to whom Meiji looks pink or green no doubt see it as the good old days when their generation was in the bloom of youth. Second, 'white Meiji' is probably an image of majestic masculinity, related to the icon of Emperor Meiji's white horses.

Generally speaking, two factors operate either separately or in tandem to produce nostalgic feeling for a past era: a yearning for *bygone youth*, and a longing to return to *the era itself*. This distinction will come out again in the ambivalence displayed by those who grew up in the 'dark era' toward the period of their youth.

The Yellow Era (Taisho)

Unlike Meiji, Taisho does not evoke any one predominant color. Relatively speaking, yellow is the color most frequently chosen for the Taisho era (1912–26).

The golden hue of Taisho might be interpreted as an image of

299

Table 16.3 *The spectrum of history in popular consciousness (most numerous color responses)*

	Meiji	Taisho	Early Showa	War	Postwar	Present
All respondents	Purple	Yellow	Blue/Green	Black	Gray	Pink
(Age)						
Men 20s	Purple	Brown	Blue	Black	Gray	Green
30s	Blue	Blue	Blue	Black	Gray	Green
40s	Purple	Yellow	Yellow	Black	Gray	Green
50s	Purple/Yellow	Blue	Green	Black	Gray	Pink/Green/Yellow
60–	Blue	Yellow/Green	Blue	Black	Black	White/Yellow
Women 20s	Purple	Yellow	Blue	Black	Gray	Pink
30s	Purple	Blue	Yellow/Pink	Gray	Gray	Pink
40s	Purple	Yellow	Pink	Black	Gray	Green
50s	Purple	Pink	Blue/Green	Gray	Gray	Green
60–	White	Yellow	Green	Black	Black/Gray	Pink
'Best era' respondents	Pink	Pink	Pink	Black	Brown/Gray	Pink
'Worst era' respondents	Black	Yellow/Black/Gray	Brown	Black	Black	Black/Gray
Age groups responding most strongly (fewest 'don't know' answers)						
Men	50s	50s	40s	40s/30s	40s/30s	30s
Women	(20s) 60s	50s/40s	40s	30s	20s	20s

pecuniary values prevailing in a 'nouveau-riche nation.' Or it might mean simply a bright and rather frivolous age. It also calls to mind an idiomatic expression, 'yellow voice' (kiiroi-koe) in which yellow means shrillness, as if to describe an urban culture gone slightly hysterical. A reckless use of yellow is indeed apparent in the contemporary postcards. Then there are the romantic paintings of Takehisa Yumeji, in which yellow is one of the most heavily used colors (the other is flesh color). Amid the somber scenes of 'Yoimachigusa,' his famous poem which has become a perennial popular song, the only vivid coloration is yellow. The point is not that Yumeji created the image of Taisho, but that he held sway over an era by appealing profoundly to its sensibility.

People in their fifties have a particular image of Taisho: for women it is mostly pink, for men blue or green. It was the season of their youth.

The 9.2 per cent who named Taisho as the 'best era' consist mainly of those in their fifties, followed by those over sixty. Most are public servants or professionals, on the whole a rather intellectual group. A miniscule 0.5 per cent (13 respondents) saw Taisho as the 'worst era.'

The blue era (Early Showa)

For the Early Showa years (1926-c. 1935), the four colors of blue, green, yellow and pink come out with nearly equal frequency. It would be well to conclude that this very *profusion or confusion* of color is the tone of the era. Early Showa stands out (along with Taisho) as an indistinct era in modern Japan.

This is because historical consciousness does not function retrospectively. Before an image of this era could harden, it was painted out by the overwhelming blackness of war. In the popular sense of history, Early Showa is not a clearcut era with a character of its own. It dissolves against the preceding upsurge of Taisho on one side, and paves the way to the upheaval of war on the other. It is really more an interval than an era.

Those in their twenties seem to view Early Showa as a period of preparations for war, the time when fascism came to the fore. Blue comes first among both sexes in this age group, but *gray* comes second among the men. Brown is the second most common choice for women, and the third for men. Those in their thirties and forties, meanwhile, show a distinct trend toward yellow, in continuity with Taisho. The older brackets tend to blue and green, tipping the leading choices overall to blue and green (colors which overlap each other in the eyes of the Japanese).

The color blue is something distant, the color of ocean and sky. The setting, perhaps, for a people's dreams, dreams which in their eyes are wholesome and boundless: crossing to the Continent, mastering the seven seas, unfurling themselves throughout the world. With verses like, 'Boom, boom, boom (don to, don to, don to)*, cresting across the waves,' the hit songs in the late 1920s took up a common theme of oceans and harbors and sailors and exotic ports.*

The significance of blue and green might be interpreted in any number of ways. But given the fact that, out of the 522 people who chose those colors, 126 call it the 'best era' while only two feel it was the 'worst,' we may safely assume that it is not the blue of sickly melancholy as in English, or the green of immaturity as in English, but rather a coloration that carried some sort of affirmative meaning.

Some 19.1 per cent of the adults polled (extrapolating to some ten million people) feel 'best' about Early Showa. Setting aside the responses of 'no best period,' 'don't know,' and 'The Present,' we find that more than 50 per cent of those who long for a past era selected this one. Those aged 40 to 59 are the core, with relatively large numbers of business managers, shopkeepers, laborers and wives of blue-collar workers. Pink is their main color for the period. The 21 respondents (0.6 per cent) who feel 'worst' about this period color it brown or black. Five are unemployed and the others have agricultural or old-middle-class occupations – the major victims of the Depression years.

The black era (war years)

Just over half of the respondents named the War Years as the 'worst era' (52.2 per cent).

In particular, the unusually large proportion of public servants and their wives (63.3 per cent and 68.4 per cent) who say 'worst' evokes a state of mind that is bent various ways. Surely they would not feel victimized if they had been in the lower strata at the time and had now risen to important jobs. It must be the remorse of those who were already in key positions and were responsible for leading the war effort. Or is it that pretense has become second nature to them in the postwar world?

Stronger still in their negative reactions, corresponding to the depth of their experience, are 'housewives' without husbands (68.6 per cent).

Twenty-two respondents (0.8 per cent) said the War Years were the 'best era' (extrapolating to about 480,000 of the adult population). Nine of them (two-fifths) were adolescent boys during the war.

Each generation displays nostalgia for the era of its youth, as noted previously and illustrated in Figure 16.1. Hence the peaks of 'best era' feeling for Meiji among those over sixty, for Taisho among those in their fifties, Early Showa in their forties, and the Present in their twenties. It is only those now in their thirties who lack good old days of their own. Having passed their youth amid

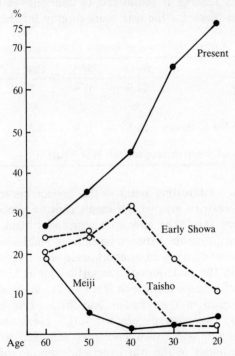

The chart is based on figures for women; those for men are nearly identical.

The War and Postwar eras, favored by extremely small numbers of respondents, are omitted.

Figure 16.1 *Generational variation of 'best era' choices*

the 'worst era' (see the thin diagonal line in Table 16.2), they see today's mass-society, when they are over thirty, as 'the best'.

After black, gray was the color most frequently chosen to characterize the war years. More than 80% of the color responses in this category (responses other than 'don't know,' which was chosen by 19 per cent) are concentrated in black and gray. Other colors add up to only 14.3 per cent, with red in the majority. The proportions choosing black or gray vary in several interesting ways according to living standards and gender. While the upper-class image of the war years is overwhelmingly gray, with only 24.3 per cent for black, black is the most common response among those at or below the middle-class level. (See Table 16.4.) It seems to reflect a gap in sensibility, between the class to whom the war signified restricted enjoyment and endangered assets, and the classes who were exposed directly to the shadow of death. This reading is reinforced by the shift in the dominant image from black for the war years to gray for the postwar era.

Table 16.4 *Class breakdown of images of wartime experience*

	Black		Gray	Red		Purple		White
Upper class	24.3	<	51.4	2.7	<	8.1	=	8.1
	∧		∨	∧		∨		∨
Middle and lower classes	34.8	>	30.9	7.5		1.5		0.9

Percentages of color choices for the War Years

The other interesting point is the gender contrast. Whereas black far outstrips gray in the men's choices, among women in their thirties and fifties gray comes first and black second. This must be the difference between battlefront and homefront experience, or between battlefront and homefront images. The pattern continues in the male-female proportion for red, the next most common color response, which was two-to-one in all age groups. Among women in their forties and fifties, brown is the third choice. The two patterns which emerge, black and red among men versus gray and brown among women aged 30 to 59, sketch varying meanings of the war experience among different demographic groups.

Returning to the quite different image of the War Years among the (relatively few) upper-class respondents: aside from their preference of gray over black, we find substantial minorities choosing purple and white. Those colors, it will be remembered, were the pallette of Meiji glory. From this we may well guess where these respondents stood during the war.

The gray era (immediate postwar years)

The years just after the defeat of 1945 were named as the 'best era' by only fourteen persons (0.5 per cent, corresponding to 310,000 in the entire population). This is even lower than the number who chose the war years.

The proportion who named the postwar years (from 1945 to about 1955) as the 'worst era' is 37.3 per cent, second only to the war years. This choice is strongly marked by urbanites, as well as by people in their twenties (who were babies or children during the war). Occupational groups who feel the postwar years to be worse than the war years include company managers, as well as commercial stallkeepers and unskilled factory workers.

The managers, in all probability, are people who suffered through the postwar dismantling of the industrial system, and are now leading players who claim responsibility for the current wave of prosperity. The other two groups would be people without property or special skills who, upon demobilization and repatriation to the ashes, endured severe privations.

In the people's historical consciousness, the basic image of the years just after the war is not the blue of emancipation, hope and rebirth. Nor is it the red of revolution, upheaval and fanaticism. It is gray, the color of fatigue, disappointment and ruin. Gray or black were the choices of some 62.8 per cent of the above occupational groups, or nearly 80 per cent when the 'don't knows' are excluded.

The backdrop for the popular image of the postwar years is not the vision of a fresh start for a democratic Japan, nor the brightness of jazz and lipstick. Rather, it is smoldering ruins, black markets, power failures, food hunts and rundown shacks. Those are basically *continuations of war*, a point which appears all the more clear against the pink sensation of the next era (today's society).

What does August 15, 1945 mean to the people? Does it mean the moment when the war ended? Does it not mean civilian uniforms, disabled veterans, missing persons, repatriation problems, commodity shortages – in short, crisis? In the day-to-day awareness of the people, the war did not simply grind to a halt on the day of the surrender. During the next few years the installment payments for the war came due in their own lives: the dismemberment of the family, the hollowing of control structures, the collapse of morality, dislocations of space and pace in daily life, women stepping out into society.

The common people never struggled for the liberation which anyway came. In their real feelings they seem to regard the end of the war and the crumbling of the militarist regime not as a purgation, via an unequivocal color such as black, but as a less clearcut diffusion of gray, washing out some of the fundamental blackness of the War Years.

The third-ranking color after gray and black, which is to say the first color with chromatic value, varies according to socio-economic status. At the upper and upper-middle class level it is brown; for the lower-middle and upper-lower classes it is red; and for the lowest class it is blue. We may thus glimpse three minority images of the postwar era, and infer their contexts. At the top the leading image appears to be the incendiary destruction of material wealth. In the middle is the image of a shakeup of the system, as promoted by the labor movement and others among this most doctrinaire stratum of society. At the bottom, where there were no handsome assets singed brown, where filling the stomach came before running up the red flag, there is a sense of the breakdown of civilization in general on the level of physical survival. 'Silently gazing at the blue sky' ran the words of a leading popular song at the time.

The pink era (the present)

For 55.6 per cent of the people, the 'best era' is the present. In all age groups, in all types of communities, in all educational and occupational groupings, the years leading up to 1963 were the finest of the six modern eras. Clearly, all is right in a tranquil world.

However, if we lump Meiji, Taisho and Early Showa together into a single prewar era, it garners more 'best' votes than the present among *men over fifty and women over forty*. And so we must wonder if today is in fact the most comfortable time for all. Broken down by age and gender, the results make it out as a most especially happy time for *women in their twenties* (74.5

per cent). Yet it does not follow that women are enjoying the present era more than men, for above the age of thirty it is men who are proportionally more enamored with the status quo.

By occupation, office workers (70.9 per cent) and technicians (69.2 per cent) are particularly enthusiastic: salaryman heaven. The wives of all white-collar types seem to agree.

The color which symbolizes the present in the popular mind is pink: the color of happiness, the color of dreams, the color of desire, the color of sex. It is the overwhelming choice of women in their twenties and thirties. Among men in their twenties, forties and fifties, green comes first, followed by pink.

It deserves mention that of all the colors on the list, pink was the only one written in the katakana script (reserved for loan words). *Pinku* differs in nuance from the old-fashioned words *momo-iro* ('peach') or *bara-iro* ('rose'). Thus we may detect an afterimage of Americanization in the lens chosen for this era.

Besides pink, the colors most frequently chosen were green, blue, yellow and white. Here again are the colors that were jumbled together for Early Showa, but with the addition of white. What are we to make of white? Does it mean simply, 'bright era'? Is it a symbol of freedom and peace? Does it reflect the white buildings and sidewalks of the new urban culture? Or does it symbolize the *transparency* of a modern mood of vacuousness?

Images of the present as the negative colors of black and gray amounted to just 1 or 2 per cent each. This seems trivial enough, but a breakdown by living standards reveals a significant consistency. As the economic level declines, the pink Zeitgeist quickly deflates, while the black/gray shadow steadily expands. (See Table 16.5)

The Present is the 'worst era' according to 63 respondents (2.4 per cent, extrapolating to about 1.4 million adults). Let us close

Table 16.5 *Socioeconomic variation in the 'mood of tranquility'*

	Pink %		Black + Gray %
Upper class	27.0		0.0
Upper-middle class	20.6		2.1
Lower-middle class	17.9		2.7
Upper-lower class	13.0		4.3
Lower class	5.5	<	6.6

with a look at the distribution of this unhappiness within the population. First, the percentage rises among the elderly, to 4.5 per cent of male and female respondents over 60, and particularly among widows and spinsters (9.4 per cent). Second, there are relatively high percentages of professionals (8.3 per cent) and intellectuals (university or college graduates, 3.8 per cent). Third, the occupational categories of unskilled blue-collar (6.5 per cent), transport (9.4 per cent), and craft (5.5 per cent) stand out, underscoring the lower-class trend noted above.

The composition of these three groups suggests three flaws in today's prevailing mood of prosperity. First is the predicament of a generation left behind, with intertwined issues of dislocated value consciousness, abandonment, and material insecurity. Second is an undercurrent of spiritual dissatisfaction (or existential frustration). The third problem is poverty itself, be it relative or absolute.

3 Colorful and colorless eras

In the intellectual view of history, the defeat of 1945 stands out as the major dividing line of the post-Restoration century. The history of modern Japan thus falls first and foremost into two main periods, which are then subdivided as shorter eras.

This is not the case at the level of the day-to-day feelings of people in general. For them *the end of the 'postwar situation' in the 1950s is more decisively meaningful than 1945*. For that is the point at which color returns to the historical scene (see Table 16.6). Regardless of popular sentiment, of course, the turnabout of 1945 is conceptually decisive. Common opinion sometimes holds that the world is flat.

Table 16.6 *Images of historical periods in popular consciousness*

	Old Japan	The dark time		Today
Meiji	Taisho – Early Showa	War	Postwar	Present
Purple	Yellow / Blue / Green	Black	Gray	Pink
	Colorful eras	Colorless eras		Colorful era

But if history is approached as currents in the life experience of a people, with the realization that the popular historical consciousness running through various generations will mold the history of the future, then the images of modern Japanese history which have precipitated in the hearts and minds of the people are indispensable to a grasp of the nation's past or future.

PART THREE

THE SOCIAL PSYCHOLOGY OF MODERNIZED JAPAN

17   The History of Bestsellers

Time segments of the postwar social psyche

Seven veins of bestsellers

When I happened across a list of the bestselling books in Japan for each year since the war, I was soon helplessly engrossed in analyzing it from various angles. Here is a report of some of my observations.

What interests me is not simply which books were most often read, but rather the *desires and interests* which led readers to choose them, and especially the patterns of change in those interests. I avoid classifying the books into their formal disciplines (literature, history, social sciences, etc.), in favor of categories which reflect thematic areas of appeal. The data does not allow us to probe the inner workings of the individual reader's mind, so a highly detailed analysis would have little significance. But on the general level, we may say that the mass readership of a book such as *Twenty Years of the Whirlwind* indicates that the public had an interest in the historical times in which they lived; or that readers of *Techniques of Memory* were interested in practical knowledge. Thus it is possible to portray with some accuracy the general areas of concern among the reading public. Along that line, the list of bestsellers from 1946 through 1962 breaks down into seven repeatedly displayed main *themes of interest*:

A   *Contemporary history and society*: Sociology, economics, recent history, reportage, literary works dealing with problems of contemporary society, etc. (e.g. *Twenty Years of the Whirlwind*, Remarque's *Arc de Triomphe*).

B   *Unfamiliar worlds*: Primitive, ancient and medieval history and historical novels. Travelogues and exotic literature (e.g. *Riddles of the Man'yōshū*, *The Realm of the [Parsee] Towers of Silence*).

C   *Philosophy of life*: Essays and literary works dealing with

313

issues of human life, biographies, etc. (e.g. *Notes on Living, The Human Condition, Jean Christophe*).

D *Love and sex*: Literary works dealing primarily with issues of sex and love, interpretive or explanatory essays, etc. (e.g. *Season of the Sun, Wisdom on Sex Life*).

E *Children and education*: (e.g. *The Years of Boyhood, I Am a Baby*).

F *Humor and wit*: Novels or essays whose main appeal is literary style or light 'entertainment' (e.g. *Professor Ishinaka's Manners, The Director of The Toilette Department*).

G *Practical knowledge*: How-to and similar books (e.g. *Improving Your Brain, Gaining Power in English, The Citizen's Encyclopedia*).

A single book often straddles two or more categories. For example, *The Human Condition* falls into A, C and D, and *Wisdom on Sex Life* falls under D and G.

For the purpose of this discussion, books which reached first or second place on an annual bestseller list are assigned three points; those reaching third, fourth or fifth place are assigned two points; and those reaching sixth through tenth place are assigned one point. Figure 17.1 shows the annual totals in each area of interest.

An overall pattern of three distinct time intervals can be recognized in Figure 17.1. Figure 17.2 is a mathematical reduction of Figure 17.1 which filters out the random influences of particular factors that affect only a single year, to clarify the relief of the patterns of transition.

Figure 17.2 reveals the following:

1 The postwar trends of bestselling books form three definite periods: Period I, 1946–50. Period II, 1953–58. Period III) 1959–??.

2 Interest area A (contemporary history and society) declines in a stairstep pattern from Period I through Periods II and III, and by the early 1960s it had virtually disappeared from the top ranks of bestsellers.

3 Interest area C (philosophy of life) is the key factor in Period I, containing almost all the bestsellers, but it declines in importance thereafter. The pattern is notably

Year	1946	47	48	49	50	51	52	53	54	55	56	57	58	59	60	61	62
A	7	9	10	9	8	5	3	4	4	4	6	1	7	2			1
B			3	2	1	4	8	2	1	1	3	2	3	2	4	5	8
C	11	13	17	14	12	5	6	11	5	6	4	6	6	3	1	1	5
D	3	1		5	8	6	5	14	10	7	8	11	9	4	3	2	4
E						4							1	5	5	4	
F			1			1	2		5	7				6	4	5	
G	1	1			1	1	1		3	1		2	3		9	10	10

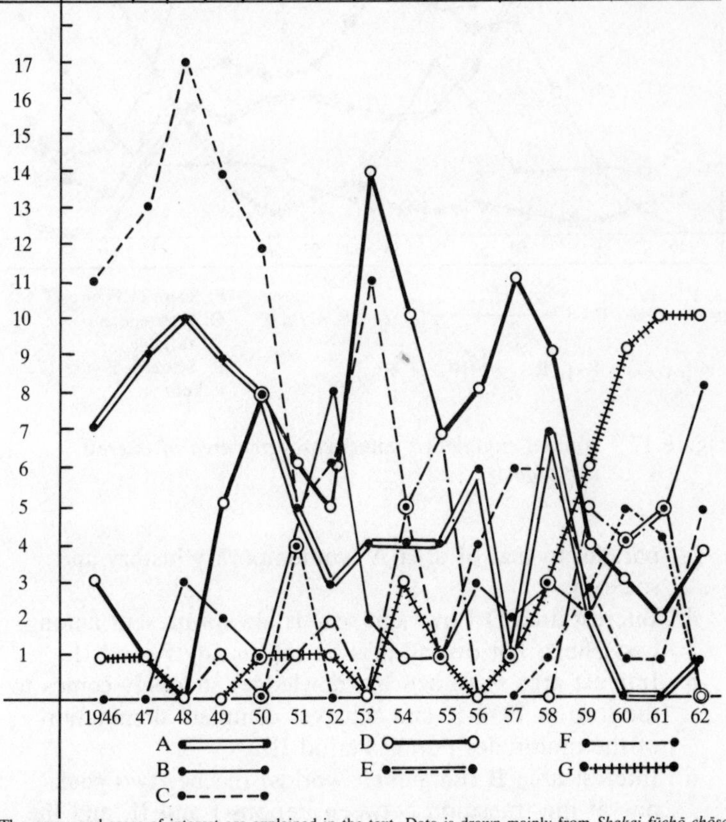

The scores and areas of interest are explained in the text. Data is drawn mainly from *Shakai fūchō chōsa shiryō* issued by the Cabinet Survey Office, and materials from the Shuppan News Company upon which it was based. Various other sales surveys exist; due to varying survey methods, there are some differences in ranking.

Figure 17.1 *Annual cumulative scores per area of interest*

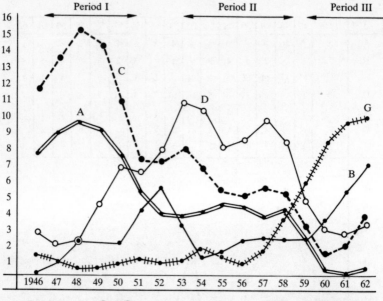

$$Q_i = \frac{P_i + P_{i-1}}{2}, \quad R_i = \frac{Q_i + Q_{i+1}}{2} = \frac{1}{4}[P_{i-1} + 2P_i + P_{i+1}]$$

$$R_{46} = \frac{1}{4}[3P_{46} + P_{47}], \quad R_{62} = \frac{1}{4}[P_{61} + 3P_{62}]$$

P: Score in Figure 17.1
Q: Intermediate variable
R: Score in Figure 17.2
i: Year

Figure 17.2 *Annual cumulative point scores per area of interest (simplified)*

parallel to that of area A (contemporary history and society).

4 Interest area D (love and sex) is always present among bestsellers, but overall it is on top during Period II.
5 Interest area G (practical knowledge) suddenly comes to the fore in 1957–8, and achieves complete domination of the multitudes during Period III.
6 Interest area B (unfamiliar worlds) reaches two peaks, one at the transition between Periods I and II, and the other in Period III.

The three periods which show up in Figure 17.2 correspond almost exactly with the major changes and periods in the political and economic spheres (Figure 17.3).

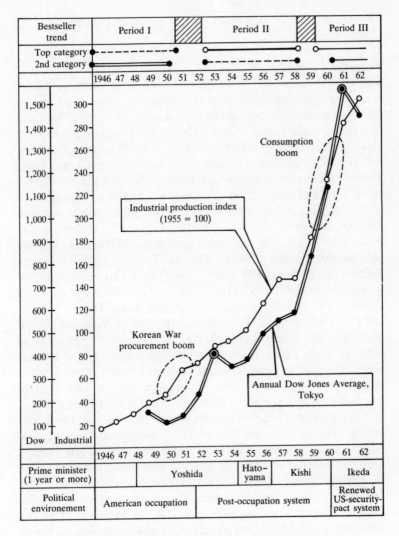

Figure 17.3 *Economic indicators and political environment*

The three historical phases of the postwar psyche (1946–62)

Period I (1946–50)

The several years after the defeat of 1945 were a time of fundamental questioning concerning the *meaning* of the times and of life in general. The bestsellers of that sort are typified by *Love is Like a Falling Star* (Ozaki Hotsumi), which together with *Twenty Years of the Whirlwind* (Mori Shōzō) monopolized the top two positions among bestsellers for 1946, 1947 and 1948. There were many books which dealt both with the search for the reality and meaning of the times we had lived through and were living in, and with the ways that we ought to live our own lives in our time; that is, with issues of both worldview and philosophy of life. They included both fiction – *Windblown Grass* (Miyamoto Yuriko, 1947), *Arc de Triomphe* (Erich Maria Remarque, 1946–8), *The Setting Sun* (Dazai Osamu, 1948), *Not without Hope* (Ishikawa Tatsuzō, 1948), *The Naked and the Dead* (Norman Mailer, 1950); and non-fiction – Nagai Takashi's *Leaving This Child Behind* (1948–9) and *The Bell of Nagasaki* (1949), and *Hear the Voices under the Sea* (University of Tokyo Press editorial staff, 1950). Further variations on that type of interest are represented by novels of ideas such as Sartre's *Nausea* (1946) and Dostoevsky's *Crime and Punishment* (1958), and even in Mitchell's historical novel *Gone with the Wind* (1949–50).

Among philosophical and intellectual books, the torch was swiftly passed from the 'progressive' works of Miki Kiyoshi (*Philosophical Notes, Notes on Life*) and Kawakami Hajime (*Autiobiography*) in 1946 and 1947, to the 'conservative' writings of Tanabe Hajime (*Introduction to Philosophy*), Amano Teiyū (*Paths of Living*), and Ko'izumi Shinzō (*A Commonsense Critique of Communism*) in 1948 and 1949. In literature, too, the same years saw Sartre and Miyamoto Yuriko give way to Yoshikawa Eiji's novelizations of the lives of Toyotomi Hideyoshi, Shinran and Miyamoto Musashi, and the satirical *Professor Ishinaka's Manners* (by Ishizaka Yōjirō).

At the end of this period, interest in worldview and in philosophy of life begins to wane. On one hand there was the shift to objective volumes of current knowledge and information such as Mori Shōzō's *The Postwar Situation* (1951), and *Words We Use Today* (1951). On the other hand were books providing insight on the human situation from standpoints not necessarily linked to present conditions, such as *Shinran, Miyamoto Musashi* and Tanizaki Junichirō's *The Makioka Sisters* (1949–50).

Politically, the last years of Period I run from the 'red purge' of 1949 into the Korean War and on to the end of the American occupation in 1951. Those three years saw the serial demise of a number of intellectual magazines (*Bunka Hyōron, Sōgō Bunka, Chōryū, Sekai Hyōron, Jiyū Hyōron, Ningen, Tenbō, Nihon Hyōron*), as well as a foretaste of Period II with the founding of the magazine *Fūfu Seikatsu (Married Life)* in 1949, and the appearance of books such as *Lady Chatterley's Lover* (1950) on the bestseller list.

Period II (1953–8)

The first year of the second period in bestseller trends, 1953, was the year that the circulation of the girls' magazine *Heibon* exceeded one million copies, and the curtain was raised on the era of television in Japan.

There was some carryover of the dominant vein of Period I, such as *The Diary of Anne Frank* (1953), Julius and Ethel Rosenberg's *Death House Letters* (1954), and Victor Frankl's *A Psychologist Experiences the Concentration Camp* (1956). But if one book is to be cited as the symbolic bestseller of this period, it is *Taiyō no kisetsu (Season of the Sun)* by Ishihara Shintarō.

In 1953 the leading bestsellers included *The Second Sex* by Simone de Beauvoir and *Human History: The Golden Age of Women* by Yasuda Tokutarō. Thus Period II began with a main-current of works taking up the issue of gender in various senses, against historical and social backdrops.

But beginning in 1954, with Itō Tadashi's *Twelve Chapters about Women*, the topic of sexuality in the setting of private life diverges into three streams. The first was a vein of adult-style material. Its prelude in 1954–5 included *Naked Writings* (Satō Hiroto), *The Fruit at the Top of the Vine (Uranari*, Watanabe Kazuo) and *My Old Man* (Fukushima Keiko). It continued in 1955 with Ishikawa Tatsuzō's *On One's Own Hole*, climaxed in 1956–7 with Ishikawa's *Resistance at Age 48*, Mishima Yukio's *A Misstepping of Virtue*, and Tanizaki Junichirō's *The Key*, and played out with Matsumura Shōfū's *Female Sutra* in 1958.

The second stream was a series of sexual love stories. The

forerunners were Mishima's *The Sound of Waves* and St Laurent's *Caroline* in 1954. It climaxed with *Season of the Sun* in 1956, and flowed on through *Elegy* (Harada Yasuko), *A Misstepping of Virtue* and *The Key* in 1957, to *The Sunstruck Slope* (Ishizaka Yōichiro, 1958). The third stream consisted of works of psychology such as *Desire* (Mochizuki Mamoru, 1955) and *Heterosexual Neurosis* (Katō Masaaki, 1956), and flowed toward the Period III flowering of how-to books with *The Brain* (Hayashi Takashi, 1958).

The dominant spirit of Period I – critical appraisal of the war and the system in general – echoed only twice in Period II before fading out entirely: *The Human Condition* (Gomikawa Junpei) and *The Wall of Humanity* (Ishikawa Tatsuzō) reached the first and third positions for 1958. In its place, also in 1958, came *Introduction to Business Management*, paving the way for the Period III 'management boom.'

Period III (1959–   )

In late 1958, Tokyo share prices began rising to unprecedented heights. In 1959 the home-appliance boom reached full stride and there was an acute labor shortage. The heady atmosphere continued in 1960 as the mass media pulled out all the stops for the gala wedding of the Crown Prince and 'Mitchy.'

The veterans of the early-Period II 'bloody Mayday' labor movement and Anti-Subversion Law opposition dispersed and melted into the system, some by way of the intermediate 'people's route' symbolized by 'singing saloons' and folkdancing. Likewise, by 1963, the veterans of the spectacular struggles of Period III, the demonstrations against the Police Duties Law and the Ampo uprising, were for the most part lying low within the daily frameworks provided by the system.

If Period III were to be symbolized by a single volume, it would be the biggest seller of the postwar period, *Gaining Power in English* (Iwata Kazuo, 1961), which sold more than a million copies within four months of publication.

Amid the flood of how-to literature which suddenly rose up and swept the public, the main theme of Period II, sexuality, was intensified in *Wisdom on Sex Life* (Shakkoku Ken, 1960), while the philosophical mood of Period I was transmuted in *Guide to Expository Writing* (Shimizu Ikutarō, 1959). The shifting style of concern had abstracted, or inverted, the substance of love and of thought into 'techniques of presentation,' and channeled them into 'standard' manuals of accomplishment.

Four of the top ten bestsellers in 1960, six in 1961, and seven in 1962 were of the how-to type. Among the top twenty, the figures are four, ten and eleven. Their titles can be read as a catalog of the desires of the modern Japanese.

- *Improve Your Mind* (1960–1); *Techniques of Memory* (1961), *Practical Memory Techniques* (1961), *Gaining Power in English* (1961), *Authentic English Expression* (1961), *English for Adults* (1962), *How to Study a Foreign Language* (1962). *A Primer on Mathematics* (1960), *Gaining Power in Mathematics* (1962). *Guide to Expository Writing* (1959), *Techniques for Practical Writing* (1962).
- *The Benefits of Green Juice* (1961), *Attaining Stamina* (1962), *Wisdom on Sex Life* (1960), *I Am a Baby* (1960), *I Am Two Years Old* (1961).
- *Collected Japanese Songs* (1959), *Collected Japanese Folk Songs* (1960). *Introduction to the Japanese Economy* (1960–1), *The Japanese Company* (1961), *The Business Cycle* (1962), *Economics for Drinking under the Cherry Blossoms* (1962), *Your Own Car* (1962). *The Citizen's Encyclopedia* (1961), *The Encyclopedic Dictionary of Japan* (1962).

From how to raise children to how to live longer, from study techniques for schoolchildren to success techniques for company employees, what was demanded was ready, instantly applicable knowledge.

Meanwhile, as if to compensate for a sense of closure brought on by all that prosaic, quotidian realism, there is a distinct strain of yearning for the exotic, for unusual experiences, and for distant epochs. *The Inca Empire* and *History of Japan, Volume 2: The Asuka and Nara Periods* in 1959; *The Realm of the Towers of Silence* and Inoue Yasushi's historical novels *Dunhuang* and *The Blue Wolf* in 1960; and the very popular Chikuma Nonfiction Collection centered on a volume called *The World's Worst Journeys*. On the lighter side of exoticism were *Dr Manbo at Sea* (1960), *Try to See Everything* (1961), and *South Pacific Siesta*

Trip (1962), as well as Joy Adamson's *Born Free* and *Living Free* (1962).

Perfectly blending those two central, contradictory areas of interest was the 1962 bestseller *Divination Made Easy*, in which an unabashedly 'mysterious' narrator in the form of a 'small yellow moth' furnishes instant advice on the course of life, using a ten-yen coin (right out of people's daily lives . . .). Here was a surplus utility, as a harmless, trendy conversation piece for everyone, including readers who didn't believe a word. Other books of the same line were *Palmistry* (1962) and *The Hypnosis Handbook* (1959).

In the world of Period I bestsellers, a burning romanticism crossed swords with 'contemporary' reality. Actualistic analysis was enriched by a romantic spirit soaring beyond realism.

In the world of Period III bestsellers, the trivialized realism of the how-to books, shorn of all romance, coexisted with romanticism in the form of exoticism, separated from reality and disempowered. When the two streams were commingled, it was no longer within the sweep or crucible of social and historical tension. As *Divination Made Easy* clearly symbolizes, what was sought was a means for quickly inferring and conforming to a destiny that is somehow predetermined.

From fundamental inquiry concerning the 'meaning' of life and our times, to the quest for daily happiness and techniques of living. Today, eighteen years after the war, have we regained our mental soundness, or have we lost it?

(1963)

'One-point luxury' of mind

The flourishing of the how-to manual in the world of bestsellers corresponds, in one aspect, to an abandonment of the concept of success in life as a question of 'character,' and a new perception of success as a question of 'technique.' In prewar Japan, success in life was always more or less connected with 'character' and 'mental training.' After the war these concepts lost their ethical embellishments and have come to be thought of as questions of pragmatic technique within specific areas. Its social foundation is that the standard by which one person chooses and judges others has become a partial, specific skill, or a superficial 'mood.'

The result is that modern people concentrate their concerns entirely on the creation of their own partial, specific skills or superficial 'moods,' and consequently the inner zone has been forgotten about and hollowed out. If an episode of pure love or devotion happens to appear in this forgotten region, the void is flooded by brilliantly vivid emotion. The outstanding popularity of the current million-seller *Gazing at Love and Death* should be viewed in this context. (This is a collection of letters between a young woman, Ōshima Michiko, who suffered from cancer-like sarcomas, and her Platonic lover, Kōno Makoto, up to her death.) The publisher has been tirelessly promoting it in the mass-circulation weeklies and on television, and given the nature of the modern bestseller, that is no doubt an important factor behind its explosive success. But all of those efforts serve only to *amplify* the fundamental appeal which the work itself contains for the interests and desires of the reading public.

The theme of the love of a person confronting death has many precedents in the history of bestsellers, including *Love is like a Falling Star* just after the war, *The Diary of Anne Frank* in 1953, the Rosenbergs' *Death House Letters* in 1954, *Memento of Love* (Tamiya Torahiko and Tamiya Chiyo) in 1957, and *Mementos of Love and Death* (Yamaguchi Kiyoto and Yamaguchi Hisayo) in 1962. It is noteworthy that the situations of these novels progress more and more into the sphere of personal life, as the key element of the hero or heroine's confrontation with historical and social conditions gradually wears thin, in step with the intensity of the postwar situation.

According to a survey of readers of *Gazing at Love and Death*, female students are 'moved to know that there can actually be such an earnest form of love,' while young men are encouraged that 'I too might be able to achieve something if I try hard enough.' This suggests that there are two sorts of readers of this book: those who read it mainly as a love story, and those who read it mainly as a death story.

For the first type of reader, this book corresponds to the motif of a contemporary popular song verse which in fact turns up in a letter written by Michiko:

> And there amid the morning light
> Discovering my body gone cold

> Will that someone
> Shed some tears for me?

(from 'When the Rain Stops in the Acacias'). The fervent question on which many modern young women staked their entire existence was whether or not to believe in the dream of genuine love, or rather, of being genuinely loved. The book gave them just the 'answer' they needed, and the one they were dreaming of.

For the second type of reader, the death motif is taken up not in its existential context, but merely as a symbol of the 'worst situation' in life. It vividly describes for young men the dream that 'happiness' is possible in any situation, no matter how unhappy. Just as the youth of wartime Japan had their minds adjusted to their allotted destinies for the first time by gazing constantly at death through the resolution that 'life lasts 25 years,' so through anticipating the 'worst situation' in advance, people are able to sound out the 'bottom' of the abyss of insecurity, and thereby discover peace of mind.

That sort of 'spiritual preparation' was furnished in prewar Japan as a permanent enshrinement, on the basis of the perpetuity of the family (*ie*) or the 'indestructibility of the land of the gods.' In the Yamaguchis' *Mementos of Love and Death*, the axis is salvation by a Christian God. But in *Gazing at Love and Death*, 'god' no longer exists. 'So many people urge me to believe in God. But my feeling is that believing only in Makoto is enough. There the 'love' of these two people in itself becomes the basis of subjective salvation which can endure whatever troubles turn up in this world; it is the functional equivalent of 'god.'

This Feuerbachian feeling is again expressed by Michiko in a poem that is presented as 'feelings which I happened to record in my diary.' Appearing as it does at the beginning of the volume, it clearly serves as a key image in the book.

> Two cups on the orange-crate tea table
> One dim light on the low ceiling
> And a stereo, out of place in a room like this
> Bringing in beautiful dreams
> To two people listening silently, shoulder to shoulder
> Just once, I'd like to have a day like that

The scene typifies what Terayama Shūji calls one-point luxury. In fact the stereo is a symbol of the 'love' of the couple, who have entrusted their entire salvation to that single item.

In this way the book serves as Scripture for modern young men and women who are seeking a ray of light at the 'bottom' of countless pressures of discrimination and competition, without being able to believe in god or nation or social solidarity.

This book of love-in-stereo is playing beautiful sentimental dreams, so 'out of place' on the bookshelf of contemporary Japanese youth beside *The Complete Company Rankings, Machiavellian Management, Add Boldness to Your Life* and the other prosaic how-to bestsellers. The drearier the cups and the tea table, the more the 'luxurious' stereo becomes a necessity of life.

(1964)

18   Revolution of Nostalgia

> It takes forever to get home.
> – Anna Domino
> ('Home,' *Mysteries of America*, 1990)

In the old days, wrote Yanagita Kunio, a child had a mother whether or not the real mother happened to have died after giving birth. Even the unfortunate orphan would grow up in the village, and might re-establish the family name. For surely the community included relatives and old friends of the parents, as well as an ethos for rearing the forlorn child within the village. But with the mobility and employment patterns of modern times, the household has been isolated from other elements of society, and the duty of childrearing has fallen squarely and solely upon the shoulders of the parents. On one hand, this has led to orphans being left out of the normal means of existence. On the other, 'for one who wishes to die, it has led to the seemingly cruel necessity of first having to kill those who are most dear' (*History of Customs and Everyday Life in the Meiji and Taisho Periods*).

Nowadays there is a vague notion that family suicide is something 'characteristically Japanese.' But this view was not held as recently as fifty years ago. The typical perspective of older books dealing with suicide goes as follows: 'Outbreak of Joint Family Suicides – The joint suicide of the entire family is a phenomenon that deserves special mention amid our nation's history of mainly individual suicide.'

On the evening of May 29, 1925, on the Hasegawa plantation in Sorachi, Ishikari, Hokkaido, one Tanaka Yoshi, 43, took his own life after killing his five children, aged up to 15. His action was later said to have initiated a vogue for family suicide in Japan. News of the incident was widely transmitted, and within the year there was a spate of imitators – a used-goods dealer in Nagoya, a confectioner in Tokyo, the bereaved family of a bank manager in Nagano – and before long there was a 'fad' of several incidents in Kobe. It is significant that the phenomenon first occurred in a new agricultural settlement, then spread to the cities. The distribution runs clearly through locations where the traditional pattern of person-to-person bonds had disappeared during the process of modernization.

Parent-child suicides have in fact occurred in Japan since ancient times, but the rapid proliferation of such behavior dates from this century. The so-called 'uniquely Japanistic' phenomenon of family suicide is actually a tradition born in *modern Japan, during the process of the breakdown* of the traditional village world and the extended-family system.

Concealed within that tragic episode from the past is a clue toward an understanding of the deep currents flowing beneath certain phenomena on the surface of mass society in *present-day* Japan.

In the shadow of the breezy, weekly-magazine catchwords of 'homemaking' and 'homebuilding,' it is possible to detect the weighty, earnest prayer of the mass of emigrants who abandoned their homes and villages, and who wish, consciously or unconsciously, to *create a new Home*. Today's 'homing era' is, at root, a premonition of the destruction of the social, domestic and mental frameworks of the Japanese *dekasegi* pattern – the established practice of 'working away from home.' Conceived now as a place to find 'peace of mind,' home (which includes the hometown or village) is no longer assumed to be the place which one leaves and will return to, but is changing into something which one constructs for oneself. Traditionally, 'home' means the point of origin, the given place that one comes *from*, which means that 'creating a home' is a contradiction in terms. The growing acceptance of this paradox among the Japanese demonstrates that an unconscious Copernican revolution has occurred in their concept of Home.

In the background, of course, is the tangible final phase of the collapse of the traditional community and extended family system in the farming villages. This might appear at first glance to accelerate anomie in the cities. But the situation was not so simple. What actually underlay the absence of commonly held values and morals in the big cities was the *dekasegi*-patterned social, domestic and mental structure, which in turn was based on the very stability of the rural community structure. It might even be argued that the collapse of the traditional family and community will *put an end* to anomie in the cities.

The modernization process in Japan has differed in this respect from that of West European societies. In England, for example, modern cities were molded by influxes of permanent residents, whose rural communities had been dissolved by the enclosure movements up to the eighteenth century and other historical processes. In Japan, on the other hand, through much of the modernization process (up through the 1950s), the rural community and family systems remained stably in place, and the workforce for modern industry in the cities was made up in large part of temporary migrant (*dekasegi*) laborers who were based in rural districts. Up to about 1960, many residents of industrial cities viewed the city as a 'temporary residence' or a 'home away from home,' for they still felt that the bases of their lives were the *inaka* (home villages). As a result, the morality of modern civil society never matured, and anomie was characteristic of the urban society. In other words, the strength and stability of the value system and social order of the rural community worked in the other direction in the big cities, as the basis of anomie.

At any rate, the ultimate dislocation of the old community is heightening the *sense* of anomie among urban migrants from those home communities, even if it does not directly intensify, nor relieve, the *state* of urban anomie. The same condition of urban anomie comes to be sensed more acutely and unbearably than ever. The resulting interplay of the sensibilities of disconnection and distress might, as one possibility, amplify the condition of anomie into real despair; or it might, as another possibility, provoke attempts to overcome the general anomie by redirecting the system as a whole toward the building of a new societal Home for the future. The third way out is the vague compromise of quietly constructing a 'small home' of one's own amid the crowds of the massed society, while cynically accepting the anomie of the 'outside world.'

Meanwhile, the number of people working away from home was growing at an extraordinary rate in the early 1960s, as shown in Tables 18.1 and 18.2. In Akita Prefecture (part of the Tohoku region where *dekasegi* is rather common), the number of migrant workers during the winter nearly tripled in just five years.

These figures seem to discredit the idea that the *dekasegi* pattern is breaking down, but they do not tell the whole story. There are three background factors which demand consideration:

Table 18.1   *Temporary migrant workers from Akita prefecture*

1958	15,005
1961	21,349
1962	29,085
1963	39,433

Source: Prefectural Survey.

Table 18.2   *Members of households engaged in agriculture, forestry or fishing, working seasonally away from home (nationwide)*

February 1960	179,000
December 1961	186,000
December 1962	351,000

Source: 1964 Labor White Paper.

the changing nature of 'working away from home'; the pronounced decline of farming as the sole or primary occupation in rural households; and the downward trend since 1960 in the number of agricultural households.

First, the qualitative change in working-away-from-home is that there has been a clear reversal of the *headquarters* of life. The new type of *dekasegi* typically means working 'away from home' for six or more months each year, and returning to the village for the rest of the time and surviving on *unemployment* insurance. While the form is the same as before, in substance, the wages earned in, say, the construction industry have become the mainstay of household finance. Working away from home is no longer a means of gaining supplemental income, or reducing the cost of boarding at home, but is rather the key means of survival.

The apparent explosive growth of *dekasegi* in the early 1960s actually corresponds to an overall breakdown of the '*dekasegi* structure' of society, of lifestyle and of mentality. It is a work pattern which *tends to deny itself*. Its nature is shifting away from work which is done away from home, and toward a sort of *seasonal commute* to work from what might be called a bed-village.

Second, agriculture is the primary occupation of fewer and fewer 'farm' families. The number of households in which non-farm work is the key source of income (i.e. agriculture is the secondary occupation) grew rapidly and steadily, and came into the majority among 'farm' households by 1970 (Table 18.3).

Third, the number of rural homes engaged to any degree in agriculture is declining. For nearly a century after modernization

329

Table 18.3 *Role of agricultural work in farming households*

	Sole occupation	Primary occupation (more tham 50% of income)	Secondary occupation (less than 50% of income)
1950	3,086	1,753	1,337
1955	2,106	2,274	1,663
1960	2,078	2,036	1,942
1965	1,218	1,082	2,365
1970	843	1,820	2,739
1975	616	1,259	3,078

Unit: 1,000 households.
Source: Ministry of Agriculture and Forestry.

began in the 1860s, despite the outflow of farming *population* to the cities, there was never any significant decline in farming *households*. The younger sons were typically absorbed by the industrial economy of the cities, but the first son stayed in the village to take over the farm. But by the early 1960s, more than 50,000 households were quitting agriculture each year (Table 18.4).

Table 18.4 *Farm household terminating agriculture activities*

February–November 1960	38,766
December 1960–November 1961	62,642
December 1961–November 1962	59,780
December 1962–November 1963	57,370

Source: Ministry of Agriculture and Forestry.

Since the beginning of the 1960s, on average, well over one hundred *families* per day have abandoned the home community and flowed into the masses who have no home at all to return to. Hamlets with no people – ghost villages – began to appear from that time all over the archipelago, particularly in the mountain districts.

Nowadays, even when the household head or his parents are minded to cling fast to the fields, the successor generation often gives up cultivation. In a considerable and apparently increasing number of these cases, although the children may have expressed some intent to return to the land after the death of the parents or grandparents, when the generational succession actually occurs, the whole family gives up farming.

Thus the village home is fast losing its significance as the'lifeline in an emergency,' as the 'place of refuge.' The hometown and the extended family are losing their down-to-earth function as Home. The 'non-returning fathers' of the Tohoku region have become a social problem – the wives and children left behind are deprived of their means of livelihood, and the incidences of illness, neurosis, suicide and family suicide are rising. This is frank testimony to the complete *reversal of the meaning of the Old Home* in the minds of those who work in the cities, from ultimate life base to heavy burden.

As the process of breakdown of the Old Home in the traditional village accelerates, among the urban masses of laborers and white-collar workers, the conceptual role of the hometown, even as something 'to feel in the distance,' is fading out. Their path of retreat has been cut off. Many of them have responded by choosing to build a humble home amid the massed society. Naturally the physical substrate for this New Home is not the fields, mountains and forests of rural society, but rather, in line with the modern economy, monetary wealth and its pursuit.

At the moment of this desperate *leap from the home of the past to the home of the future*, the timely erection of the Ikeda government's 'income doubling' program, a vision of the welfare state, furnished solid spiritual support for the mass of humble homebuilders. In many cases, even as they cynically mouthed their mockery and scorn and their mistrust of government blarney, a furtive, phantom expectation had been illuminated in their heart of hearts.

But for this vision, the energies built up by the loss of the Old Home, by the blocking of the path of retreat toward the past, may well have worked to amplify the general level of desperation and intensify systemic anomie; or else they may have flowed torrentially toward the creation of some new Home as a premise for total reform of the System. In the end, the fact is that most of the potential energy was swiftly sucked into the erection of a 'small home' for the future.

In retrospect, how orderly and consistent were the LDP-Ikeda government programs: the plans to upgrade rural infrastructure and create a series of new industrial cities, 'income doubling' and the welfare state, expansionary financial policy, and of course the constant 'forward-looking' posture.

The extraordinary surge in share prices between 1959 and 1961 (coinciding with the moment of completion of the mass-societal condition in Japan) was propelled by a rush of virgin shareholders into the market. Real estate and durable goods also exploded with new activity. This passion for building assets – the obverse of the anxious prayer of the 'lonely crowd' for a New Home – was well served by an economy awash in fiat money.

The 'homing era' corresponds to the breakup of the classic *deka-segi* structure of society, daily life, and sensibility. But insofar as it is predicated on a cynical affirmation of massed society in the 'outside world,' and especially in the workplace, it is merely a *daily dekasegi*, going from the 'small home' set up in the suburbs to work in the city.

The movement to establish economic foundations reflected the need for a spiritual resting place, to resolve the underlying insecurity and isolation of the masses who had lost the Old Home. Listen to the theme song of the leading television 'home drama' of the early 1960s:

> It's a small town
> It's a small house
> It's a small garden
> But we have plenty of dreams
> Dreams, dreams, at number 10 Dreamhills Street

A deluge of feeling poured to and from a huge audience through that tiny house and garden. This was precisely the shunted (forward-looking!) channel of the stormy cathexis which surged toward the lost native Home. It can also be tracked in the lyrics of popular songs, such as this hit from 1961:

> Struck by the rain, in the acacias
> This is how I would like to die
> The dawn will break, the sun will rise
> And there amid the morning light
> Discovering my body gone cold
> Will that someone
> Shed some tears for me?
> – *Akashia no ame ga yamu toki*, ('When the Rain Stops in the
> Acacias', 1961)

Uncertainty of the existence of someone who would shed tears for one's *dead* self. The urban query. 'Love' as a sign of lost community.

The million-selling document *Gazing at Love and Death* (letters between a dying girl and her close friend, published in 1963) provided precisely the 'answer' sought by the poignant questioning of the contemporary young who could not yet believe in a Home, who have no Home in the sense of a group that would incline its diffuse concerns and affections toward one's personal fate. It supplied a vivid image of actuality to their *nostalgia* for the no-longer-visible community of affection.

The concurrent successes of prosaic how-to books and of books about 'pure love' actually reflect two aspects of the same process. It was not only *Gazing at Love and Death*, but also *Wisdom for Your Sex Life* and *How to Double Your Assets* which were songs of the new nostalgia, of the search for a functional equivalent to the lost Home.

> Hello, darling baby, it's your life,
> Hello, darling baby, here's to your future
> This good fortune is your Daddy's wish
> – *Konnichi-wa aka-chan* ('Hello, Darling Baby', 1963)

Singing along with this smash-hit song were countless people who, like the singer herself, in fact had no such family. It is a song of *new homesickness*. The songs which sang over and over of the dreams of the happiness of love and marriage and family, along with the many television 'home dramas' and weekly women's magazines, were paeans to the lost spiritual home of today's lonely young.

> I want you to love me, to love me
> To love me like a native home
> I want to love you, to love you
> To love you like a native home
> – *Furusata no yō ni* ('Like a Native Home')

Here is the perfect logical expression of the directional shift of affections during a transitional era: the revolution of nostalgia.

19   The Typology of Unhappiness

Introduction: Personal-advice columns and the problems of modern life

The social background of personal problems

To track the configurations of unhappiness that are expressed at the level of everday life by people in our time, this chapter takes two complementary approaches. I utilize the particularities of various cases, repeatedly unraveling the operation of their underlying cycles of cause and effect, to throw into relief the universal problematic condition which permeates them – human self-alienation, or the state of living in estrangement from one's essential human nature. At the same time, I take the opposite tack of clarifying the specific routes along which that universal condition casts its shadow as the 'life problems' of individuals.

The goal is to describe the constellation of factors which mark the paths by which the root condition of human self-alienation prescribes people's life routines.

It would be a mistake to equate the problems of unhappiness and alienation, or to assume that alienation necessarily leads to unhappiness, or is its sole source. For example, the unhappiness of the handicapped or the infirm arises basically from sources unrelated to the issue of alienation. (It is nevertheless true that many of the specific hardships they must endure in modern society, such as deprivation, loneliness and insecurity, ultimately derive from the social structure.)

Nor should the *phenomenal forms* of alienation – dissatisfaction, loneliness, insecurity, boredom – be confused with alienation itself. For alienation is an *objective* situation which transcends personal awareness, while those forms of unhappiness are its subjective results.

If the unhappy are not necessarily alienated, neither are the alienated always unhappy. It is well known that some alienated people are happy persons who seem quite 'secure and comfortable.' But as we move on to observe the energies which are directed to the conquest of alienation, and to pursue their real sources, the state of alienation is revealed to be a *problem* in those people's lives.

Moreover, versions of 'security and comfort' are not the only reflections of the state of alienation, even among those with material wealth and positions of influence. Since the unhappiness of alienation leaves basic human desires unsatisfied, the happiness of an alienated person is always threatened by the shadow of inner anxiety and boredom. As we will see later, there is no escape from this paradox. We will examine this phenomenon of *happiness consisting in unease and ennui* as one of the types of modern unhappiness.

The significance of personal-advice columns

An active volcano is by no means an 'average' sample of the earth's surface, but by analyzing the lava which it spews forth, we obtain excellent clues for understanding the inner structure of the earth's crust. In the natural sciences, extreme or exceptional cases often provide *strategic data* for a clearer understanding of the mass of ordinary cases. As strategic scientific data on the types of unhappiness in modern Japanese society, I have selected the letters published in the personal-advice column of a mass-circulation daily newspaper.

Cases that apepar in the advice column tend to articulate causes and factors of unhappiness which in ordinary life lie vaguely dormant, or are incompletely expressed, or cancel each other out. Also, in describing those causes, the anonymous contributors tend to go into matters which they are unable to confide to their friends, colleagues or neighbors, much less to an opinion pollster. For these two reasons, the personal-advice column serves, like lava from a volcano, to expose intact the various causes of unhappiness which are hidden away behind the walls of domestic 'private affairs,' and belied by the calm, quotidian expressions of modern life.

Only a few people write in to the advice columns, and only a handful of letters are selected for publication, but each of them has hundreds of thousands or even millions of avid readers. Some read purely out of curiosity. But many readers are consciously or unconsciously superimposing a more-or-less similar situation which either they or someone they know are confronting. A single letter can elicit many inquiries to the newspaper office from people wanting to know 'if that wasn't my daughter (brother, etc.) who wrote in.' Behind the single dissatisfaction, the single antagonism, the single irritation, the single tedium which appears in the advice column, there are tens or hundreds of thousands of similar sentiments which do not appear (the existence of which may not even occur to the actual writer).

Limitations of the data

Personal-advice columns were selected not because they are perfect data, but rather because in comparison to other sources, they seem top be one of the most appropriate for the topic at hand. I have given due consideration to the limitations of the data at the outset, so that the method of analysis could be adjusted as far as possible to take them into account. Quantitative data would be judged by the criteria of attribution ratios and distributive bias. For a critique of our *qualitative data* the key question is: to what extent does it *cover the basic types and factors?*

Some types of problems are more easily expressed in the advice column than others. Specifically, man-woman problems and dissension within the home seem to be the preferred topics of the letter writers as well as the editors. This in itself presents no obstacle to our inquiry, because we are not trying to draw quantitative conclusions about the proportions or distribution of various types of problems. However, certain types of problems are *entirely avoided* in the advice columns, and this category does constitute a limitation which affects our study. Here, then, is a survey of topics which are generally recognized as types of unhappiness, and which do not appear in personal-advice columns.

1. The problems of people who cannot write in: infants, imbeciles, the seriously ill, the illiterate, those in such extreme poverty that they do not encounter newspapers.
2. The unhappiness of intellectuals: they generally scorn and ignore the advice columns.
3. Topics which are moralistically taboo: especially sex.
4. Problems of political and religious minorities: those who are shut out by the ideological stance of the publishers.

5 Issues related to fundamental values of the social system.
6 Highly specialized or individualistic problems: sufferings related to areas of advanced expertise, for example.
7 Trifling adversities which cannot be solved by seeking 'guidance': one's foot was trampled on the train, or the neighbor's cat stole the fish from the kitchen.

Categories 2, 3 and 4 are not completely absent from the advice columns. There are quite a few letters from teachers, technicians and students. Concerning sex, the advice columns of the major newspapers occasionally cover some rather racy issues. A few letters about political and religious minorities are published. Categories 6 and 7 basically lie outside the scope of our consideration. Of course even if a person is alone in his or her distress, there may be some social significance to the case; and even trifling discontentments can lead to important consequences, perhaps numerous enough to be worthy of sociologically informed correctives. In such cases these types of problems may actually be taken up in the advice columns. That leaves us with categories 1 and 5.

To compensate for category 5, it is not sufficient to consider only those factors and causative cycles which are raised by the writers and the respondents. We must also analyze the underlying *latent causes and linkages*.

To compensate for category 1, we must look carefully at the circumstances not only of the writers, but also of the secondary characters who appear in their letters. In some cases it is necessary to *shift the focus of analysis* to them, and reconstruct the factors and linkages which are expressed by the writers. This technique enables coverage of the problems of many people who do not write in for themselves.

Using this methodology, let us categorize the *dramatis personae* in the letters sent to the leading personal-advice column, and see which social strata they belong to.

The cast

The main characters in this study are 468 persons who appear in the 304 letters on personal problems that were published during the year 1962 in the Yomiuri Shimbun (the largest-circulation daily newspaper). A 'main character,' who may have been

Table 19.1 People figuring in letters in the personal-advice column (Yomiuri Shimbun, Tokyo edition, 1962)

Gender and Marital Status	Male		158
	Unmarried		72
	Married		71
	Divorced/widowed		8
	Unknown		7
	Female		308
	Unmarried		112
	Married		150
	Divorced/widowed		39
	Unknown		7
	Gender unknown		2
Age	0–4	13	
	5–9	19	} 32
	10–14	19	
	15–19	37	} 56
	20–4	56	
	25–9	77	} 133
	30–9		94
	40–9		34
	50–9		20
	60–		17
	Unknown		82
Occupation	Professional/technical		17
	Management		8
	Clerical		53
	Sales		28
	Service		17
	Factory workers/labourers		45
	Farming/forestry/fishing		36
	Housewife		132
	Primary student	22	
	Middle student	11	} 55
	Secondary student	13	
	University student	9	
	Unemployed		36
	Unknown		41
Education	Middle school		24
	Secondary school		27
	University		16
	Unknown		401
Employment	Employer		10
	Sole employee		24
	Family business member		47
	Employee (including 28 public officials)		158
	Unknown		229

Region

Tokyo		216
Hokkaido	3	
Tōhoku	63	} 226
Kantō	100	
Chūbu	60	
Unknown	22

(The Tokyo edition excludes western Japan)

included via the above-mentioned shift of analytical focus, is a person who can be seen to play a central role in the problematic situation which a letter describes. Those involved as assailants or onlookers, however, are excluded, because the roster is limited to those who in some direct sense bear the weight of unhappiness. Table 19.1 shows the demographic distribution of the tragic players.

Table 19.1 is not an indication of the ranking or the percentages of the problems explored here. It shows only which areas of society are covered and which are excluded by the data. Geographically, almost all the data reflect situations common to eastern Japan (central and northern Honshu). But the inclusion of only three people from Hokkaido and none from western Japan does not mean that none of the problems or types of unhappiness faced by the people of those regions are covered. The only things 'left out' would be types or factors which are *exclusive* to them, and such regional peculiarities are of negligible import to the purpose of this inquiry. After all, the circumstances and forms of alienation do not fundamentally differ in eastern and western Japan, as they would in, say, East and West Germany.

While there are relatively few university students, managers, and divorced or widowed men, again, for the purpose of *this type of inquiry*, eight or nine cases are enough to provide basic coverage.

Table 19.2 is a breakdown by outward appearance of the types of complaints expressed in the published letters. To fill in the background beyond the published letters, Table 19.3 furnishes statistics on all of the people who wrote in for advice to the newspaper office during the year.

1 Types of Modern Unhappiness and Their Social Underpinnings

This section analyzes the key factors and the causal linkages of twelve cases, which were selected from the 304 published letters because they are *qualitatively representative* in the senses described above. The data which are arrayed and analyzed separ-

Table 19.2 *Types of complaints in the personal-advice column (Yomiuri Shimbun, Tokyo edition, 1962)*

Romance	Unrequited love or broken heart:		
	Women (concerning men)	17	
	Men (concerning women)	4	
	Other romantic problems	10	
	(Total)		(31)
Marriage	Past marriageable age	39	
	Marriage opposed by parents or others	12	
	Unease or dissatisfaction with fiance(e)	20	
	Other problems related to getting married	10	
			(81)
Married life	Infidelity: of the husband	26	
	of the wife	10	
	Husband's drinking, gambling, violence, idleness, drug use, etc.	28	
	Other husband–wife problems	16	
			(80)
Family	Wife's problems with mother-in-law or other in-laws	23	
	Remarriage, second wife, children from previous marriage	19	
	Parent–child relations (support of parents, succession of family trade, etc.)	29	
			(71)
Livelihood	Economic problems	68	
	Personal relations at work	9	
	Other problems	12	
			(89)
Juvenile problems	School admission or examinations, finding employment	15	
	Misconduct, discipline, etc.	30	
			(45)
Other	Illness, physical handicap, appearance	46	
	Neurosis, mental handicap	22	
			(68)
	General malaise, ennui, blockage	23	

Note: Many of the 304 letters published during the year mention two or more problems, hence the grand total exceeds 304.

ately in this section will serve as material for synthesis and overview in Section II, but that is not the only purpose of this

Table 19.3   *Letters sent to the personal-advice column* (Yomiuri Shimbun, *Tokyo edition, January–November 1962*)

Writers		Male	Female	Total
Students: Primary/middle		39	112	151
Secondary		118	178	296
University		34	21	55
Age: (excluding	10–19	138	201	339
students)	20–9	580	1,271	1,851
	30–9	292	750	1,042
	40–9	112	262	374
	50–9	64	128	192
	60–	271	581	852
Total, Jan.–Nov. (letters are not tallied in Dec.)		1,716	3,566	5,282
Monthly average		156	324	480
Projected annual total		1,872	3,890	5,762

Note: These figures do not match those of Table 19.1, which is based only on the letters selected for publication.

presentation. The reader will surely agree that the causes and correlations which are discovered through these particular cases are significant in themselves, because they are quite resonant with universal meaning.

1   Deficiency and dissatisfaction

Case 1 (3.28): I am writing about the family of my younger sister who lives in Niigata. A few days ago her husband died suddenly at the age of 36, leaving her with three children in the eighth, sixth and first grades. He was a driver for a wholesale firm, but there was no retirement fund, and they gave her only 20,000 yen as a condolence gift. They have always been poor and she has been working as a laborer to make ends meet. She wrote us saying she has no idea what to do. Many relatives live nearby and the funeral was a proper affair, but no one could offer any help. They just talked about what a shame it was and drank up. She says she applied for government assistance, but meanwhile she still owes 20,000 yen in monthly payments on the television, which she doesn't want to sell because of the kids, and her youngest who just started school has his heart set on a knapsack and new clothes. I am afraid that nobody will loan money to a fatherless family until the children are able to work. It worries me no end. Please give some wise advice for my bereaved sister.

– A housewife in Akita

When an unexpected calamity rips apart the fabric of one's life plans, one comes face-to-face for the first time with the true forms of the various realities hidden in the depths of the life routine. (See Figure 19.1.)

Causes and corollary factors

1   The central complaint of the letter is the hardship of the bereaved household of mother and children, and the writer cites two groups of factors as the direct causes. One is the lack of guaranteed income, with no retirement fund and a mere 20,000 yen (about sixty US dollars) in condolence money from the employer. The other is increased expenses: for the funeral, which was obligatory under the country-style custom of the 'gathering of the clan,' for monthly television payments, and for the new student's school equipment.

2   Among the latent factors of the situation, the husband's 'sudden death' is the primary cause. The work of a 'driver' entails considerable chance of an accident, and there is also a series of relevant social factors, including the driver's job conditions. The data at hand, however, are insufficient to fully clarify this point.

3   That the surviving family were immediately at wit's end was due to a lack of financial reserves to deal with an emergency, despite the fact that both parents were working. This points up the problem of the sparse resources of a driver (the husband) and a laborer (the wife), and the problem of the deteriorated state of working conditions in smaller businesses, as well as the background issue of the 'two-tiered' Japanese economy.

4   That the future livelihood of the surviving family is not guaranteed is connected to two problems. One is the societal and local manpower surplus which makes it difficult for the widow to find a satisfactory job. The other is the problem of which the letter writer implicitly complains – the inadequacy of social guarantees for fatherless families.

5   The funeral expenses were inevitable under the rural custom of gatherings on ceremonial occasions. *Alongside this requirement*, the television payments are also a major burden,

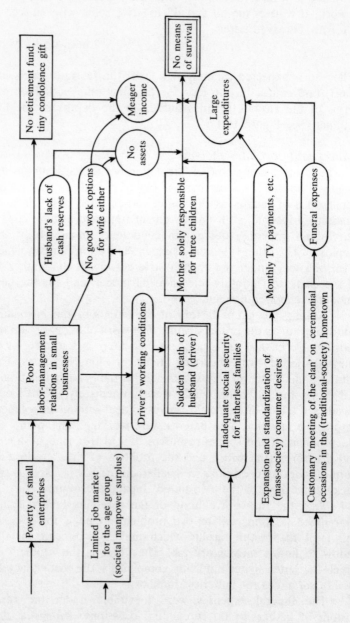

Figure 19.1 *Causal linkages of case 1*

pointing up the pressure exerted on the lower classes by the expansion and standardization of modern consumer desires. This smooth coexistence of a factor from traditional society and a factor from mass society indicates the dual burden which is imposed by the disequilibrium of the processes of modernization and urbanization.

Similar cases

6 Very few of the published letters complain specifically about hardships of life. However, economic and material deficiencies cry out as direct or indirect factors in many cases of ignorance, loneliness, uneasiness, misconduct and illness. Such letters appeared during 1962 in the Yomiuri Shimbun advice column on 1.14, 1.31, 2.7, 2.14, 2.23, 3.1, 3.10, etc.

7 In particular, the extreme difficulty of finding another job for people in this age group with family dependents blocks all means of escape. One letter tells of a person wishing to escape from the terrible conditions of one job, who was introduced to four other places only to find that they were all even worse (6.7).

8 As a result, the fact that a man works for a small business is cited as the official reason for the breaking off of an engagement (3.3), and in one case an engaged man who had 'obscured' that fact worried constantly that his 'clumsy explanation would lead to the misery of cancellation' of the marriage plans (5.25).

9 On the employer's side, meanwhile, conditions are such that one wife complains that she is 'running around like crazy every day, working without a break at the office to manage the accounts, disbursements, receipts and loans, and returning home to cook, wash and prepare the bath for the boarding workers,' and that she is 'afraid that I will use up my youth (this way) without ever having the time even to read a book' (9.7). (The respondent comments that there are many similar letters.)

10 But in situations like the fatherless family of Case 1, there are few opportunities to find work even in that sort of small business, and most must manage a livelihood through even worse means of day labor or part-time work done at home. In one such case, a woman who is raising two children on her daily wage of 541 yen as a crossing guard complains that while she waves the flag every morning and evening for the safety of (other people's) children, she has no time to attend the parent-teacher

meetings on behalf of her own children. She skewers the hypocrisy of the customary 'thank yous' from government officials and newspaper editorials by asking, 'If this is such a valuable job, why is there only an unreliable daily-wage payment?' (12.29) (The answer supplied by the resondent epitomizes one aspect of the contemporary personal advice column: 'the problem is not that the job pays a daily wage of 541 yen. The problem lies in your own life plan. You should brighten your spirits and seriously pursue the prospects for remarraige.'

11   At first glance, the 'premodern' issue of economic poverty would seem to be a theme which lies outside the essential area of concern of a discourse on 'alienation.' Yet we see here that in the shadow of the prosperity of the 'affluent society,' life has come to be driven precisely by the necessity of 'material' reproduction. In a world where work and other routine duties have been reduced to little more than pain, concern for what is essentially humane within the process of living has been worn down and buried away. It must not be forgotten that the majority of the population today is living in these conditions.

Case 2 (7.11): I am the second daughter among six children, and I have been married ten years. My parents live in Tokyo with my eldest brother and his wife, their child, and my youngest brother. My father, who is 57, neither drinks nor smokes, and is a hard worker who never took a day off from his company until he retired. Although I am only a middle school graduate, he is a strong believer in eduction. My two elder brothers finished university, and my two younger brothers are attending public high schools. My brother, my elder sister and I are all married and living happily. Our only worry is that our father has a habit which we have to keep secret. He never has affairs with women, but he loves to put on young women's underwear, and his habit has gotten worse as he has gotten older. My brother and my mother often discuss his behavior, and once they decided to burn about ten pieces of underwear. After that Father didn't speak and hardly ate for two days. My father gives his retirement pension to the family, and my brother takes care of expenses for food and clothing and gives Father 1000 yen as pocket money each month. He keeps on collecting red underwear. We don't know whether he buys it out of the pocket money or not, but that isn't what worries us.

– Y'ko, Fukushima

Beneath his business suit this father nurses an urge that is probably unknown to the colleagues who have socialized 'intimately' with him for decades. The neighbors probably don't know either. This letter gives us the first glimpse of the odd interior scene at the depths of the standardized personality of an ordinary, upright salaryman such as can be seen everywhere. (See Figure 19.2.)

Causes and collorary factors

1 The respondent accurately points out that this 'bad habit' is a type of 'safety valve.' Lack of academic credentials is the biggest handicap that the modern Japanese salaryman can bear. The various human urges and desires which were suppressed and distorted over the years in order to provide his children with an excellent education – 'neither drinks nor smokes' and 'never took a day off from his company until he retired' – seem indeed to have thrived in a damp, dark space hidden from the light of day.

2 The ability to educate five children and the payment of a retirement pension suggest that the father did not work for a small enterprise. During his lifetime of service, he probably watched the spectacular advance of many younger men who were university graduates. As he endured the countless daily humiliations which were expressed in manners of speech or in the expressions or glances of those around him, he would consciously or unconsciously have stored up much resentful energy. When his underwear collection was burned, this family man 'didn't speak and hardly ate for two days,' a telling indication of the enormity of the urges which had been wrestled inward and bottled up.

3 From another angle, scholastic and career records aside, the situation also entails the experience of a person who is alienated from the means of social production, who exists as a structural component of a bureaucratized organization, a victim of the emotional exhaustion brought on by standarization of living schedules and behavior patterns. In that sense this father's abnormal escape pattern may be seen as the functional equivalent of the normal or subnormal, socially approved escape patterns – the pachinko and mahjong parlors, the racetracks, the bars.

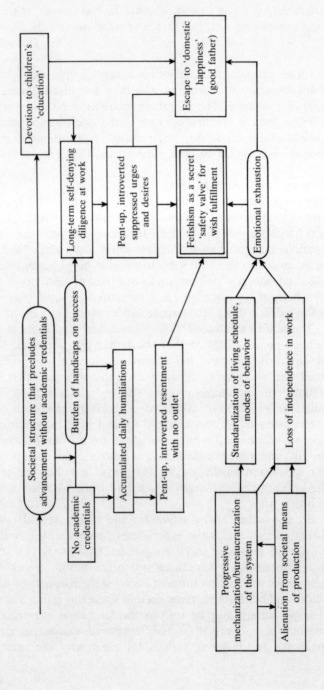

Figure 19.2 *Causal linkages of case 2*

Similar cases

4   The case which most strongly resembles this one appears in
a letter from a female high school student:

> My father demands absolute obedience from his children in
> a completely feudalistic way. He is constantly nagging and
> scolding . . . Even the dishes for the evening meal are
> prepared after he comes home, according to his particular
> instructions. Yet he supports us very well and pays for
> everything we need including school expenses. He delivers
> heavy mental blows to my mother and the rest of the family,
> yet he himself is extremely reliable and hardworking. On
> top of a full day of work he also tends the fields and does
> other business, sometimes getting only three or four hours
> of sleep. And just as regularly, every evening he drinks and
> gets drunk and repeats the same sermon about how children
> should obey their parents, and how even though he works
> so hard he gets no sympathy from the family, and so on.
>
> (10.24)

In this case, the accumulated dissatisfaction which was suppressed during the long years of struggling for livelihood, as well
as the emotional exhaustion and frustrated self-respect, are being
diffused toward the family who are included as a part of the
father's ego. But the family, especially the younger generation,
does not acquiesce to being a part of the father's ego, and this
is a source of further frustration. (The types of influence which
the long-term struggle for livelihood exerts upon human nature
are explored below in Cases 10 and 11, and in their 'similar
cases.')

Case 3 (8.31): I am a 34-year-old middle school teacher,
presently hospitalized with what has been diagnosed as
nervous heart disorder.' The head doctor says it verges on a
case of neuropathy, and he thinks it is caused by an
accumulation of multiple stresses. In that regard, after middle
school I entered the naval academy, but then the war ended
and I had to start over. I managed to pass the entrance
examination for the Keio University medical course, but my
father was unsympathetic and the relatives who were
supporting me were also opposed to my wishes, and so I

gave in and enrolled without enthusiasm in the science course at Waseda University. I wanted to share the experience of the medical students, so I attended psychology lectures and accumulated credits toward a teaching certificate, and although the profession did not really excite me, eleven years ago I embarked on a career as a teacher. At the beginning I worked vigorously, but for the past few years the quarrels between the authorities and the teachers' union which have enveloped the workplace have sapped most of my energy, and frayed my nerves so badly that I had outbreaks of paroxysmal tachycardia. The doctors at the hospital have been kind enough to explain the medical appliances to me and lend me some medical books, and this has rekindled my unfulfilled dream of studying medicine. Of course at this point it would be virtually impossible to switch over and become a medical student. I feel trapped.

– N, Tokyo

Nervous disorders, which afflict one in twenty-five people, are a concentrated expression of the dissatisfactions and discord which smolder in modern society. (See Figure 19.3.)

Causes and corollary factors

1 As the writer himself is well aware, there is an accumulation of several sorts of frustration and unwillingness. First came the interruption of plans due to the loss of the war – part of the intangible damange inflicted on the generation in between the adults who were marched off to war, and the children who were evacuated and malnourished.

2 Next, in starting over, his medical studies were precluded by the 'opposition' of his father and relatives. At that point, he was unable either to fully realize his original ambition, or to adjust his plans to be satisfied with the life of a technician, as his father and relatives wished. Joining the science and engineering faculty in name only, to receive the support of his relatives, he pretended to 'belong to the medical course' by attending psychology lectures, taking the half-baked compromise route of accumulating credits toward a teaching certificate. The result was that he could neither meet the expectations of his 'father and relatives,' nor fully realize his own aspiration, and took up teaching without being able to feel any passion for it.

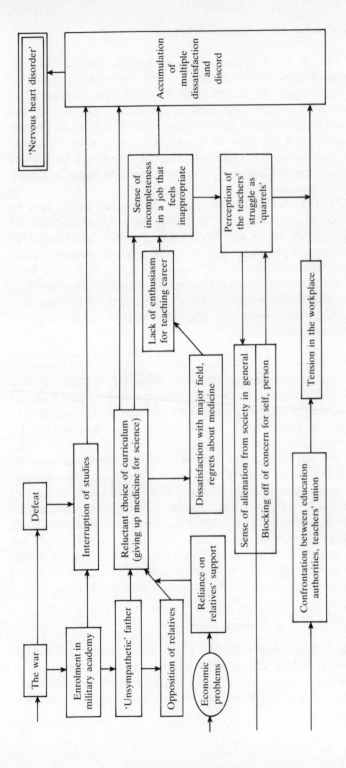

Figure 19.3 *Causal linkages of case 3*

3   Then he was 'enveloped' in the 'quarrels' between the education authorites and the teachers' union. Most likely, the writer
once again opted for compromise, seeking neither to ingratiate
himself with the principal and head teacher, nor to win the
respect of fellow union members. As the fundamental polarization of the struggle grew more and more acute, such a noncom-
mittal attitude became untenable, the pain of self-schism became
unbearable, and consciously or unconsciously he began in earnest
to seek a way out.

4   Further, due to his half-baked educational experience, he
is unable to understand the true purpose or significance of the
struggles involved in the basic idea of education. Instead he
perceives such phenomena only at the level of 'quarrels' which
come from somewhere on the outside and 'envelop' him. Since
he is incapable of active participation based on his own internally
driven will, as the struggle intensifies, his feelings of unproduc-
tiveness, powerlessness and isolation deepen and he becomes
utterly exhausted.

Similar cases
5   The more common situations of unwilling employment in a
given profession due to pressure from parents or guardians are
of two types. The first is those who are reluctantly compelled to
continue the family trade, usually shopkeepers or farmers (7.17,
10.3, 6.2, 9.26, etc.).

6   The second common type of unwilling employment results
from being forced to carry expectations of success. For example,
a university student with a father who was a landlord but lost
his holdings in the postwar agrarian reforms, entertains doubts
about the 'success' that his father is expecting of him, wondering
'if there is any choice but to repay my father for not making me
work and allowing me to study full-time, by fulfilling his hopes'
(5.4). (Other types of occupational dissatisfaction are explored
in Cases 8 and 12, and in the 'similar cases' under Case 7.)

2   Loneliness and antagonism

Case 4 (6.6): Housewife, 39. I have three children, the eldest
a girl in middle school. I got married fourteen years ago
through an arrangement which I left up to my elder brother.
Six months later my husband started gambling, sold all my

kimonos, and ran up debts all over the neighborhood. I thought about leaving him, but I dreaded returning to my family and living with my elder brother's wife, and while I was hesitating a baby came along. He is addicted to gambling. He works less than half of each month, pawns everything from the mosquito nets to the yukata, and drinks. He sold the house that his parents gave him and we moved to Tokyo to live in my sister's house, and then he gambled away half the proceeds from the house. After we came to Tokyo he plunged into the bicycle races. When I came home from the hospital after giving birth to our second child, the chests of drawers and the sewing machine that I used for piecework were gone. Even my tailor's board and scissors had been converted to cash for his gaming. When I ask him to work he turns nasty and beats me. Now the children and I are working and just managing to survive. I'm planning to leave and look after the children myself.

– A housewife in Tokyo

This problem, along with the wife/mother-in-law conflict which comes up in Case 5, is quite typical fare in the personal-advice column. To top it off, the 'answer' is an outburst that, 'Your husband is a perfect scoundrel and a good-for-nothing,' complete with a report that *foreigners* say that, 'Because Japanese mothers spoil their sons, many Japanese men are no good.'

The truth is that from the day when she left it to someone else to arrange her own life, she had already waived her claim to happiness. (See Figure 19.4.)

Causes and corollary factors

1   Her unhappiness began when the most decisive choice of her life, the selection of a husband, was 'left up to my brother.' The respondent gives strong emphasis to the need for stricter upbringing of boys. But there can be no solution unless the girls themselves are brought up and educated in a way which instills a solid sense of self and the ability to plan their own lives. Hence we must harden our hearts and take a look at the *responsibility of the victim*.

2   Another aspect of 'marriage arranged by someone else' is its premise of indiscriminate optimism about human relations, to the effect that when people live together, no matter who they

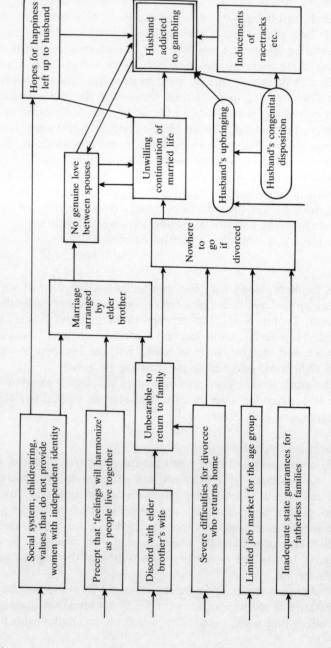

Figure 19.4 *Causal linkages of case 4*

are, 'their human feelings will come into harmony.' One aspect of this conception is that it helps to foster a Japanese form of humanism, different from that of the modern West. For that very reason, this conception needs to be reorganized as a model for relationships between mutually *self-reliant* people.

3 The third cause of the 'marriage arranged by someone else' was probably that, given the antagonism between her and her elder brother's wife, it was no fun at all for this 25-year-old to remain at home. As for the brother, he seems to have selected a mate not with a view to the happiness of his younger sister, but rather as a means of quickly disposing of his wife's sister-in-law. Of course a choice which is motivated mainly by the desire to quickly escape one's current situation, be it marriage or leaving home or moving to the city or finding or changing employment, is rarely made well.

4 As for the husband's gambling, as the respondent said, his upbringing is probably part of the problem. Likewise his congenital disposition. And we should not overlook the role of the bicycle races and other betting venues as proximate causes. But the letter tells us that he began gambling several months *after getting married*, which suggests that for him too, married life was unsatisfying or disappointing. Three points come to mind. First, given the above-stated circumstances of the marriage, there was no genuine, inward feeling of love on the part of either husband or wife. Second, the matchmaker, being the brother who wanted to quickly marry off his sister, painted a fine picture that set the husband up for disappointment. Third, judging from the wife's character as displayed in her letter, she would have 'left it to him' to furnish the happiness she was hoping for, making no concerted effort toward the joint building of a successful marriage.

5 The final problem is that for women who have such cruel husbands, the reality is that they have nowhere to go if they divorce. A divorced 'returnee' is generally unwelcome among her original family, for financial reasons, for reasons of appearance, and perhaps also because of intrafamilial tensions. Meanwhile, the state offers no security for divorcees and their dependents. Going back home as a 'reject' is unbearable, but if she leaves home and ventures into the limited job market for this age group, she is not likely to find pay and conditions that would suffice to raise children. Suffering from both 'premodern' and

'modern' alienation, these women find themselves welcomed neither by family, nor by civil society, nor by the state.

Similar cases

6   As noted above, the woman who suffers from her husband's
behavior is one of the main themes of the personal-advice
column. Dozens of them turned up in the data examined for this
study. Though on the surface there are a great many types and
variations, the situations have one basic element in common –
the feeling that she 'can't take it any longer.' The nature of the
charges runs from gambling (2.21, 3.26) to drinking (6.18, 6.27,
8.4, 8.28, 9.12), violence (4.19, 6.18, 8.4, 11.2, 11.22), wasting
money (5.3, 9.4, 9.21), laziness (4.4, 4.25, 8.6, 9.12), and drug
abuse (7.6). But womanizing is the most common issue, amounting to half of the wives' complaints (1.15, 2.1, 2.9, 2.26, 4.13,
5.3, 5.9, 5.23, 5.26 and many more). There is also the voice of
an old woman who put up with her husband's violence and girl
friends for forty years, and wants to separate 'now that our six
children are grown' (11.22); in all probability, this phenomenon
shows up in the advice column as merely the tip of a giant
iceberg.

Case 5 (10.17): I am the eldest son among four children,
presently a *ronin* waiting a year for another attempt at
entering university. Besides my father (47) and mother (42),
my father's mother (70) lives with us. The continuing conflict
between my grandmother and father and my mother troubles
me so much that I can't study. My late grandfather was a
man about town who didn't support his household.
Grandmother sent Father's younger sister to the country
and lived along with her son, and she worked so hard
teaching and doing side jobs at night that she has chronic
heart trouble. Father, who is a doctor, divorced his first wife
because of bad relations between her and Grandmother, and
then married Mother. He is more devoted to Grandmother
than to Mother, with whom he has never gone out since
they were married. When he goes out on calls, he tells
Grandmother only, and as soon as he returns he goes to
her room to talk. I have never seen him and Mother talking
together. He hates the idea of visiting Mother's family, and
when one of her relatives has died he says 'we'll just send a

couple hundred yen.' When we children asked to attend the first anniversary of the death of her father, he turned up his nose and in the end he didn't let us go. Mother never goes out except for shopping. She gets her grocery money from Grandmother, who is likely to say, 'Today's food is rather shabby, you must have used the money for something else,' or to turn to Mother and say casually, 'This is awful,' or something equally rude. Mother always puts on a cheerful face, but I feel so sorry for her.

– 'A' in Tokyo

Each of the moral imperatives of traditional society – submission, gratitude, filial duty – were fundamentally bipolar obligations, between persons of superior and inferior position. In a social system with no basis for the development of morals to guide the multi-dimensional relations of civil society, at some point in a multi-position relationship, the morality inevitably breaks down. When this happens, the strain of sacrifice shifts along the normative line of least resistance, from male to female, from parent to child, and thus the same patterns of unhappiness are passed from generation to generation. (See Figure 19.5.)

Causes and corollary factors

1   In the beginning there was the 'man about town.' In this situation, in Grandmother's day as well as in the 1950s and 1960s, few wives put up serious resistance or opt for divorce. Most of them, like Grandmother, entrust their wounded love and life-purpose to their children. Fortunately, in this particular case the son is repaying his mother's affection through his sympathy with her sufferings. Unfortunately, this is the starting point of a chain reaction, reminiscent of the tedious tragedies of Japanese naturalist literature. What the mother should demand from her husband is demanded from her son, what the son should provide to his wife is provided to his mother, and hence what the wife should demand from him is once again demanded of the son. Filial love is assigned the role of compensating for conjugal love, resulting in the proscription of real love between husband and wife, and one of the two women must be sacrificed. So goes the recurring, alternating cycle of unhappiness.

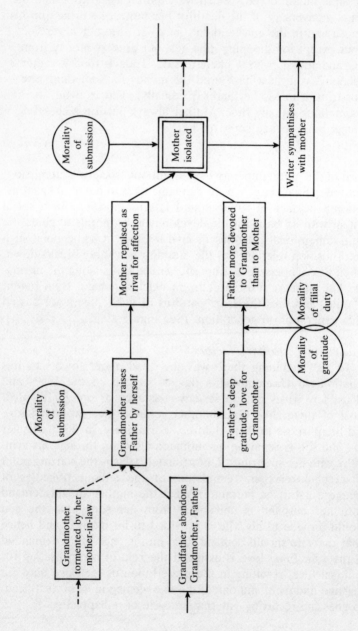

Figure 19.5 *Causal linkages of case 5*

Similar cases

2 Problems between wife and mother-in-law (or father-in-law or sister-in-law), invariably appear once or twice a month, even in 1962. Twenty-three cases were published through the year (1.11, 1.26, 2.15, 2.20, 3.29, 3.30 . . .). But lately, it is not necessarily the wife who is the victim. This is particularly notice-able in cases which involve the dissatisfaction of a husband who started out 'intent upon a salaryman's household' but along the way was forced to take over the family trade (2.15, 7.17). (Among rural as well as urban women of the middle and lower classes, the stereotype of 'the status of the salaryman's wife' passes for a symbol of happiness.) The converse is the parents' complaint that their son can't find a wife who will come to the farm (7.7), a turnabout in the mother's position. There was also a case of distress over a son who left home because his wife insisted on living away from his parents (7.17).

Case 6 (7.21): Five years ago I moved to Tokyo as a live-in apprentice at a kimono sewing workshop. Up to now everyone has always said that I am 'a gentle and docile person,' and now I am trying hard to become friends with my senior and junior colleagues. One woman who started working with us a year ago, M'ko, has a very perverse attitude, perhaps because her family was poor and she has been working since childhood. She tells the mistress bad things about us, only some of them true, and as a result several people have quit because the mistress became hostile to them. Experienced workers train the new people, and I have been assigned to train M'ko. She is simply impossible – if we watch her she flares up, and if we praise her she mocks us. I have tried to talk with her on several occasions, but it only makes her more perverse, and she says I am crazy. I should add that in our house there are no newspapers because the mistress thinks we would learn bad things by reading them, and she won't let us listen to the radio because of the electric bill. I have thought about consulting with the teachers and the mistress about M'ko, but I'm not sure they would think well of me for it. Every day I worry about what to do.

– A'ko, Tokyo

The romantic intellectual is typically disillusioned by the true pettiness and vulgarity of the masses, and surely there is a kernel of 'injury' sustained in the process. (See Figure 19.6.)

Causes and Corollary Factors

1 As the central factor of her problem, the writer cites the existence of her 'perverse junior,' M'ko, focusing the blame on a personal 'villain' who is near at hand. As background, she hypothesizes M'ko's impoverished childhood, and also complains about the secondary factor of the treatment she herself receives as a live-in apprentice to a kimono maker.

2 The three main characters – the 'victim' and the 'victimizers' at hand – each bear their own series of problems. First is M'ko. Knowing of the 'poverty' and the resulting hardships of her upbringing, we can glimpse, hovering behind the modus operandi of the tattletale, a cultivated distrust of others and bottled-up feelings of resentment, resulting from the cool indifference of 'the world' and the accumulation of countless routine humiliations. This sort of personality contains a cycle which induces defiance toward those around her and intensifies her distrust and malevolence. The progressively deepening isolation brought on by that cycle produces a longing to be valued by someone, expressed through her repeated tattling to the mistress. She turns to this twisted mode of behavior because she is at a loss for what to do in order to be loved.

3 Next, the personality of the mistress. Behind her penchant to take every piece of M'ko's tattling seriously lies a hypersensitivity to mundane details (begrudging even the cost of electricity for the radio) and a general distrust of humanity (one 'learns bad things' from reading the newspapers). These attitudes combine with the tension between M'ko and her colleagues to produce a workplace atmosphere of moldering mutual distrust. As we have no way of knowing the mistress's life history, we cannot infer the factors which molded her character.

4 Finally there are the problems of the writer herself, who spends her days worrying about something so trifling as being called 'crazy' by a malcontent. This points clearly to the factor of the lack of physical or mental refuge within the closed-off sphere of existence of the live-in apprentice system.

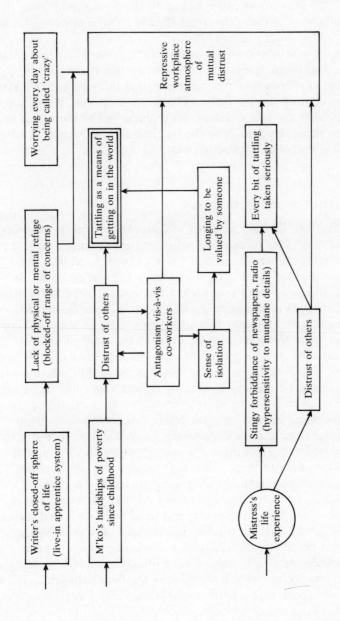

Figure 19.6 *Causal linkages of case 6*

Similar cases

5   A 35-year-old spinster dormitory manager complained, in a
slightly spiteful tone, about the slightly spiteful attitude of a 40-
year-old spinster resident (10.27).

These cases stand among many in the personal advice column
that display an ignorant antagonism in which the victimizer is
simply condemned as the victimizer, and the victim simply sym-
pathized with as the victim. This permits no resolution, for in
most cases the real cause of the problem lies in the actual situation which *envelops both* the 'victimizer' and 'victim' at hand.
Case 7 is another typical instance.

3   Anxiety and fretfulness

Case 7 (1.5): I am a 19-year-old entrance-exam *ronin*, living
with my elder brother and sister and my parents. I have a
relatively timid nature, and I don't get on at all with my
strong-willed father (59). He doesn't like me and is forever
scolding me. Once in a while I talk back, but he won't listen
to my side of the story at all. He just claims, 'Whatever I
say is right.' He may be entitled to see me as a mere child,
but I am no longer a child. I don't even want to see his
face, so I stay cooped up in my room. He knows nothing of
the reality of the university entrance exam situation, but he
seems to be displeased with my present *ronin* life, and I am
reduced to cowering in my own home. My mother is a
traditional woman who just listens quietly to whatever my
father says, and since his salary is small and the house is in
the red every month, she is preoccupied with survival and
has no time to think about my situation. My sister shows
some understanding of my problems, but she is reaching
marriageable age and I can't rely on her. My brother is in
the third year of university, and until he is graduated the
household finances will be very strained, and poor Mother
must borrow against Father's retirement pension. I have
trouble studying because I keep thinking that if I were to
go straight to work, it would ease the financial burden and I
could speak to my father as an equal. This frustration makes
my days even darker.

                                                    – A *ronin* in Yokohama

With the weighty contradictions and inequalities of the entire social system upon their shoulders, within the cramped space of the family home, fellow human beings bump up against each other's anxieties and irritations and grow hateful and hostile toward one another. (See Figure 19.7)

Causes and corollary factors

1　According to the writer, the central factor is the 'difference in character' between him and his father, and the secondary factor is his situation as a *ronin* in a straitened household.

2　The respondent shifts those problems aside and offers a reinterpretation. He says the writer's delusion of victimization is 'overanxiousness' caused by the characteristic sense of dependence of the 'youngest child,' and by the impatience and neurosis induced by *ronin* status (a pscyhologistic reduction).

3　Both writer and respondent overlook one crucial factor: the anxiety of a father who is approaching mandatory retirement. This increases his frustration with his son's entrance-exam failure, and also casts a nervous pall over the whole household, which only exacerbates the impatience and 'neurosis' of the *ronin* son. Behind the father's anxiety are the problems of the mandatory retirement system and limited social security for the elderly.

4　Another factor in the father's anxiety and the household's nervousness is that 'the house is in the red every month.' This is connected to the problem of a salary level (or the gap between that and the level of desires) at which even a 59-year-old man cannot support a wife and three children.

5　As the writer's sphere of concern is restricted to his state of limbo between examinations, he is unable to make new friends. Former friends have likely gone either to university or to work, and various complexes and differences of interest are now interposed in the relationships; at the least, these have lost the intimacy of high school days. This causes him to focus exclusively and hypersensitively upon intrafamilial relationships and, as the respondent points out, leads to 'overanxiousness,' increased frustration and neurosis.

6　The writer is trapped in 'the reality of the university entrance exam situation.' The problem which underlies that reality is the particularly Japanese response to the society's population surplus: a social structure in which it is impossible to advance without a diploma. This corresponds to the factors out-

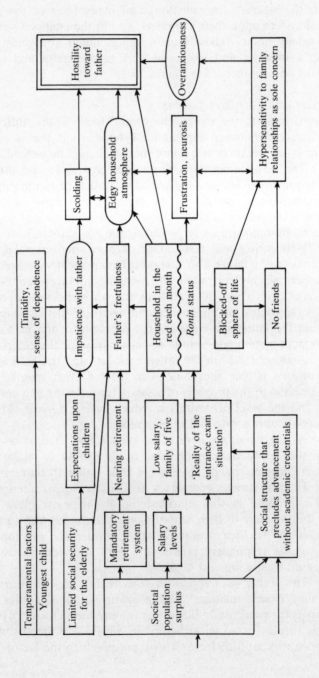

Figure 19.7 *Causal linkages of case 7*

lined in paragraph 3. Meanwhile, education has lost its original function. For the provider, it has taken the form basically of a 'resource,' and for the recipient it is like an industrial certification mark that enables one to be sold at a slightly higher price.

Similar cases

7　No other cases involving the mandatory retirement issue appeared during the year. On the general plane of the employment situation affecting the family, the uncertain future of certain age groups is frequently mentioned, as in the Case 1 issues of the difficulty of changing jobs and the deficiency of social guarantees.

8　The problem of worry and fret over the entrance exam turned up many times. Here is a typical section from a student's letter:

> but lately, my feelings for K'ko are taking priority over the studying battle. Sometimes I feel that I am exacerbating my own suffering and there is no solution. I have searched through books but found nothing. I suppose I am acting irresponsibly toward my parents. . . . Please tell me what I should do in order to extinguish my feelings for K'ko.
>
> (1.10)

At the time in life when they are newly awakening to fundamental concerns about the meaning of love and existence, when they should be readying themselves to pursue their own individual courses for future careers, the young are forced to devote almost all of their waking time to the acquisition of the most non-fundamental, non-individual sorts of knowledge and techniques. While they are solving scores of standardized, externally posed 'practice questions' for the entrance examination, their concern with but a single genuine, inner question is seen as the sort of disturbing factor which must be disposed of. Any undisposed remnant of the real question will lead to nothing but feelings of guilt and inferiority that one is *not yet sufficiently standardized*.

> *Case 8 (8.23)*: I am a 28-year-old graduate of a first-class university, working in a regional company. The trouble is that I have fallen off the success route. When I entered the company I failed the test for the executive track, and now

I get the same salary as high school graduates, despite my diploma. If I play my cards right, after thirty years I can be a local section chief. I got this job through a recommendation from my elder brother-in-law who is an executive of the company, but I have fallen far behind due to my feminine tendency to prostrate myself. This character has allowed me to get along without being disliked by my superiors and colleagues, but after seven years of service I am growing impatient. It's wretched living in the dormitory, and lately I'm afraid that if I drink my resentment will spill out in a drunken frenzy. As for marriage, I want to choose a 'good partner,' and so I broke off with a switchboard operator with whom I was deeply involved. I want to lead an active, manly life. But at the moment I have a marriage offer through my brother-in-law from a woman who just wants someone who will promise himself to her forever. I am constantly depressed from telling myself how miserable I am.

– Y, Gumma

Believing the myth that the stairway is 'open' and everyone has the chance to reach the executive tier, young people conform to the unitary standards of the system, only to have their ambitions and goals snatched from them. (See Figure 19.8.)

Causes and corollary factors
1   The writer himself complains of frustration and feelings of inferiority due to having 'fallen off the success route,' and he posits his own 'passive character' as the sole cause.
2   Before turning to the problem of 'falling off' the success route, we must first consider the fact that, regardless of efforts to conform, the 'success route' is unquestioningly assumed to be monistic. Here we encounter the stereotyped image of 'success' in contemporary Japanese society, and the fixed, unitary nature of the success route: from a 'first-class university' to the 'executive track' in a 'first-class company.' During the war people were appraised under a unitary standard by which it would be said, for example, 'In the army he'd be field-officer material.' Values became pluralistic for a time amid the postwar anomie, but with the establishment of the monopoly capitalist system they soon reconverged into monism, giving rise to a similarly conceived

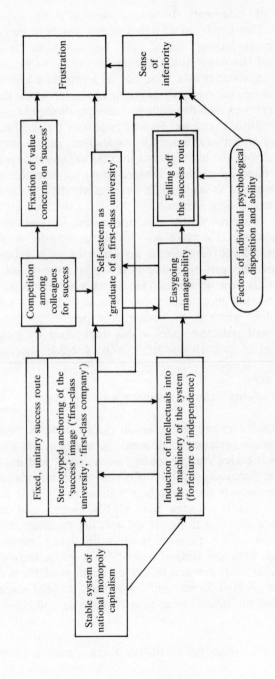

Figure 19.8 *Causal linkages of case 8*

standard of judgment: 'In a company he'd be section-chief material.' This condition stretches across not only the sense of frustration at having 'fallen off,' but also the background elements of the competition among colleagues to succeed, and the futile self-esteem as a 'graduate of a first-class university.'

3 Likewise, the easily manageable character which the writer himself perceives includes both personal psychological issues and issues of *societal character*. To wit, as part of the stabilization of the system of national monopoly capitalism, means were established to absorb the intelligentsia into the organizational machinery. The majority of them seem content to take the route of promotion as docile white-collar workers who have been emasculated of their independence.

4 The pressures of the competition for success produce a warped value sense in which even love is turned into an expedient for ascent. Moreover there is no sense of guilt about it, no concern for the cast-off woman: this man's complaint reflects only upon his own 'weakness.' He displays nothing other than a desire to become more audacious. Thus he forfeits his sensitivity toward values which might be found in areas of life other than 'success,' and puts the spurs to his impatience by locking his entire range of concern into the notion of selfish 'success.'

Similar cases

5 The following letter is reminiscent of this case:

> now I have a respectable position thanks to Mr S, and I am receiving his guidance in all areas. In addition, Mr S's mistress is taking care of me in various ways, and has given me some financial assistance. Recently Mr S introduced me to a woman with the suggestion that we marry. The problem is that at almost the same time Mr S's mistress said outright that she would like to fix me up with her daughter. For my part . . . it's not a question of which one I like, but if I am to marry, then the mistress's daughter is the better choice. But in that case, I would betray the feelings of Mr S who has been so kind to me, and I am afraid it could severely jeopardize my future. I can't concentrate on anything.
>
> (11.11)

6 Uneasiness about falling off the success track is involved in

many academic-career problems. A typical example is the young public official who 'found a job because all I wanted was to escape from studying for the examination,' and 'after I found a job, for the first time (I developed) a desire to attend university' (6.1).

7   Another newly employed high school graduate, who succeeded in obtaining a long-dreamed-of job in a 'large enterprise,' reports his pent-up unhappiness: 'Inside the large enterprise my dream has vanished. I can't find satisfaction as a man by working my whole life in such a marginal position.' (11.24) Aside from the actual problem of marginalization for lack of the surface criterion of 'academic credentials,' there is the issue of the value perspective in which he is unsatisfied 'as a man' with his marginal duties.

They are convinced that they have been aiming toward their 'personal' happiness and ideals, and have accordingly chosen and planned and striven for their own lives. But the truth is that the happiness and ideals do not spring from the depths of their own humanity. They are merely the institutionalized values which serve to march people into the system's control mechanisms.

Case 9 (10.20): I am a 27-year-old woman, employed in a financial institution and living with my elderly parents. Up to now I have had several marriage offers which I did not accept because I am hoping for a situation in which both my parents and I can be happy. My parents would rather see me remain single and working than reluctantly married, but I know that my neighbors and co-workers say behind my back that I am an old maid who is aiming too high. I'm beginning to feel a bit awkward at work. It's hard to put up with, and it's reached the point where I can hardly keep up a cheerful attitude. Where I work, women must resign when they marry. I have begun learning tailoring in order to improve my earning power, and during the next semester I intend to prepare for a teacher's license at the school's main branch in Tokyo. To do so I will have to leave my present job. I am wondering how to go about finding work in Tokyo, and what to do about my house and my parents, especially since the help-wanted notices in the newspapers all offer salaries that are less than half my present earnings.

– R'ko, Nagano

369

In a society which creates fixed stereotypes of the images of happiness or success, those who do not match them are commonly perceived as unhappy or as failures. The currency of those attitudes causes even people who are not necessarily unhappy or failing to suffer feelings of frustration, irritation and inferiority. (See Figure 19.9.)

Causes and corollary factors
1 The writer describes her problem as follows: she has stayed single beyond the conventional marriage age because she must support her elderly parents. Therefore she must have independent earning power, but her present job has become insufferable and she cannot find a suitable new position, and does not know how to proceed.

2 First of all, the underlying situation is that the burden for supporting an elderly couple without means falls entirely on the shoulders of the family, which in this case hinders the marriage of the sole, family child.

3 Meanwhile, single women are forced into an unbearable position by the prevailing social attitude, which holds that they are failures in life because 'happiness for a woman' lies only in the home and family.

4 The writer's inability to find a good job, and the fact that many employers force women to resign at marriage, point to the problem of surplus population, and also to the issue of the woman's position as 'office flower.' The latter point involves not only the problem of the attitudes of managers and other colleagues toward working women, but also the question of how to practicably handle the burdens of housework and child rearing.

5 Also in evidence are a sense of blockage caused by the stagnancy of rural society, where people gossip maliciously and there are few chances for marriage; and a complementary impulse to escape to 'the city' which, while it may not be the promised land, seems at least to hold some 'possibilities.'

Similar cases
6 Many women wrote of their frustration at having sacrificed their youth for their families and 'missed the boat for marriage' (1.6, 2.27, 5.7, 5.14, 8.8 . . .). There were also some complaints from eldest daughters who took care of their siblings as 'substitute parents' after being orphaned, only to find themselves

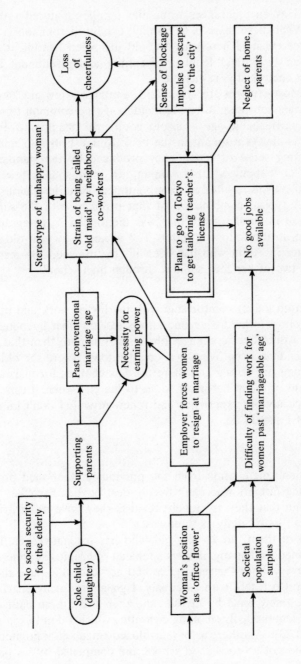

Figure 19.9 *Causal linkages of case 9*

treated as encumbrances when the families matured (10.31 et al.). What these martyrs to 'family' exhibit in common is a sort of sorceress-style heroism ('I could just keep bearing it all on my own . . .'), and feelings of futility and resentment at not having been 'justly' rewarded.

7   Most of them are around 30, although a few are 24 or 25. The unspoken premise of old-maidhood (the common terms are 'past marriageable age,' 'unsold goods' or 'daughter over 30'), which is always resonant in the background, brings to mind the frustrating sense of redundancy produced by the standardized image of 'happiness for a woman.' In more than a few cases, this frustration resulted in disappointment by unscrupulous men.

8   A typical combination of that problem with the sense of blockage in rural society that was mentioned in paragraph (5) appears in the following letter. The writer, a 26-year-old eldest daughter in Akita who has been jilted, furnished the resources to put two of her four siblings through high school:

> I am no longer comfortable with my life at work and in the
> dormitory, where everyone knows exactly what happened,
> so I would like to change jobs. . . . But more than that,
> rather than keep living in a country town where the old
> customs are strong and there are few chances for marriage,
> I think it might be better to go to the city where I can
> enrich my life experience and renew myself. I don't know
> what I should do.
>
> (9.1)

9   Among men, aside from the previously mentioned problem of young farmers who can't find brides, boys in their late teens complain that they are lonely because they have no girlfriends. We shall look briefly at three cases.

One of them, an 18-year-old who has just moved to Tokyo and joined a company, depicts a tableau of insipid dreariness: 'At work everything is unreasonable and nervewracking and there is nobody I can talk with as equals. I go home to my apartment, have a lonely meal by myself, and then waste time until about ten, absentmindedly smoking cigarettes which I don't even really like' (4.23). Another, a 19-year-old postman, disappointed that he could not go to a good school and compelled by his parents to go to work, says he is unable to see what makes life worth living (8.15).

The third case, from Tokyo:

Lately I've been reading magazine articles that give advice on how to choose a marriage partner. There are all kinds of ways to judge people, from facial features to physique, how you walk, how you hold the handstraps on the train, handwriting and so on. I always turn out to be the extreme left-wing type who should be given a wide berth . . . I've become totally pessimistic, wondering what bad thing I did to deserve to turn out this way. I'm a fairly warmhearted person but it seems that everyone thinks I'm cold. What can I do to make women like me? Please tell me the simplest, most effective way.

(8.14)

Here again, we find *anxiety and fretfulness about not being standardized* as a 'commodity' in the marketplace of love, in parallel with women who worry about being 'unsold goods.' These cases have in common the paradoxical condition of the commoditization and standardization of youth in modern society.

Entering the standard company by way of the standard school record, obtaining the standard position by way of the standard course, having the standard household after marrying at the standard age. . . . The key assumption, unspoken yet pervasive, is that only those who 'hold the handstraps' in the standard way will be happy, will be full-fledged, valued persons. It causes people to worry and fret that they have not standardized themselves. They respond by fàiling to follow their own internal desires, and by molding themselves in conformance to a uniform standard imposed from the outside, in the name of public opinion or some organization. They work harder and harder toward that end, and day by day their lives become less and less their own, and the quality of life becomes poorer. Finally they manage to 'succeed,' and what they have at the moment when 'happiness' is achieved is the lethargy and ennui of not knowing 'what I should live for.'

4   Lethargy and ennui

Case 10 (10.26): My husband is 42, I am 32, we have been
married ten years and we have no children. He has a
respectable position as a civil servant. Together we have
worked our way up from the bottom, and now we own our
house and land outright. But as our life has become secure,
he has acquired a great many young female acquaintances,
including many office ladies and college students who are
children of good homes. They call him up and visit him at
the office, and they go out together to films and restaurants.
Sometimes I receive gifts from his friends 'for your wife,'
and I'm sure they wouldn't give them without a reason, so
they must be in return for presents from him. In the ten
years we have been married he has almost never taken me
out to the cinema or anywhere else, and he has never once
bought something for our relatives even when they have
daughters of marrying age. I am growing aggravated,
especially since I think I am very careful about household
expenses. But if I say something about it he turns sulky and
says I'm too suspicious, so I can't do a thing. I do know
many people whose husbands are worse, but I feel like I'm
just the caretaker for his house, and I'm tired of sacrificing
myself to his egoism.

– M'ko, Tokyo

The standardization of living schedules and behavior patterns has
different meanings for the husband and for the wife. As the
zest drains from their lives, emotional dissatisfaction builds. (See
Figure 19.10.)

Causes and corollary factors
1   Starting with the husband, we may surmise, as did the respondent, that there was an accumulation of emotional dissatisfaction
during the years of living as a frugal civil servant, and as he rose
in position and his life became secure, the level of his desires
also rose, to the point where he was no longer satisfied with his
wife as a woman.
2   The wife has devoted a decade to maintaining the 'house.'
This seems to have lead to a sensual and mental stagnation that
makes her seem boring to her husband. At the same time, due

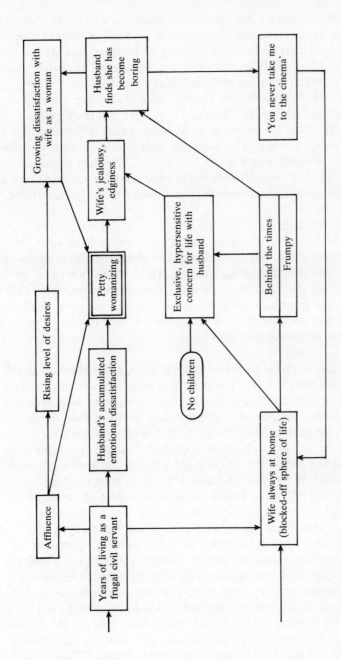

Figure 19.10 *Causal linkages of case 10*

to the closure of her sphere of concerns, with no children, she is so hypersensitively focused on the details of their life and his behavior that he finds her nagging and bothersome. Hence he is all the less likely to 'take her out anywhere,' she stays cooped up at home, and the cycle continues.

3 Having found the security of a stable life after years of working 'up from the bottom,' they have lost their purpose, and the resulting weariness and ennui has taken different forms for him and for her. The story of their future is clearly plotted, there is nothing left to actively create. The only solace she can find for her present situation is to remind herself that there are some people who are unhappier, 'whose husbands are worse.'

Similar cases

4 Many letters reported that after years of hard work, at the moment when they had managed to make their lives secure, the husband began playing around (12.18, 6.20, 9.5 . . .), or the wife left (10.1, 1.20), or the daughter began misbehaving (1.24). Besides troubled family relations, another problem which may occur at such moments is the feeling of lack or loss of purpose, as the following case illustrates.

Case 11 (3.1): I am the first son among five children and I am now 28. When I was 12, just after the war, my father died and his large wholesale lumber business went bankrupt, and my mother was contemplating family suicide. Under those circumstances, I left high school after one year and went to Tokyo. Without a sponsor, I had a very hard time finding work, but I finally got a live-in job with a monthly salary of 500 yen, and now after more than ten years of steady diligence, I have earned the respect of my employer and my fellow workers. During that time I have refrained not only from alcohol and tobacco but from any type of frivolity, and as a result I have been able to marry off my two elder sisters, to see my younger sister through junior college and marriage, and to help my younger brother to attend university, find work in a first-rate company, obtain a small house and get married. I was finally able to put up a proper grave for my father, and I have brought my mother up from the country to live with me. But now, in my own heart I feel that I have gone terribly wrong. I have talked

with my employer, my mother and my brother and sisters,
but they can't understand how I feel. Recently I find
everything distasteful and have no desire to keep living.
Since I had only a smattering of learning, I can't figure out
what I ought to do, so I turn to you for advice.

– Y, Tokyo

He who has been striving toward goals that were thrust upon
him by external circumstance grows used to thinking of his own
life as a means for those goals, and consequently loses the ability
to set subjective, internally driven goals by which he can plan
his life. Once the original goals are fully realized, he loses sight
of any purpose that could give meaning to the days of his life.
(See Figure 19.11.)

Causes and corollary factors

1   The factors which compelled the writer to struggle include
the upheaval of the immediate postwar period, the Japanese
family system, discrimination by academic credentials and discrimination against single parents, the society-wide surplus labor
pool, and the limited resources of small businesses. Most of these
problems have been discussed in the analyses of previous cases.
Here we encounter a complainant who stands at the point of
having surmounted these difficulties.

2   By struggling for many years, the writer has managed to
mend his family's fortunes and secure their lives. For him the
past is but a succession of days of dull, tasteless labor. He has
no memories of a youth colored with beauty and exuberance
which might satisfy his spirit. The gratitude and admiration of
his elderly mother and adult acquaintances cannot compensate
for the sense of emptiness concerning his lost youth.

3   For the future, there is not a single goal which can serve
as spiritual inspiration. During the days when he worked so hard
and singlemindedly to resuscitate the *family* and establish his
siblings in the world, there was no opportunity to set subjective
goals or make plans to enrich the content of *his own* life. Now
the writer finds himself at a complete loss as to 'what I should
live for.'

4   He is also deprived of the consolations of interpersonal
understanding which could fill in some of his emptiness. Behind
the communication breakdowns with his employer, his mother

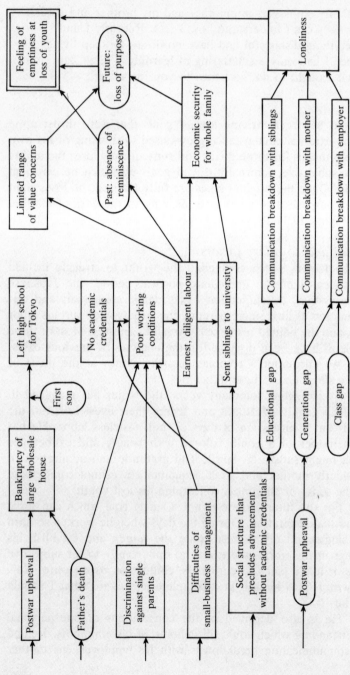

Figure 19.11 *Causal linkages of case 11*

and his brother and sisters, lie the class distinctions and the generational and educational gaps of contemporary society. These in turn spring in various ways from the same societal factors which compelled the writer to work so hard.

Similar cases

5 This case has aspects in common with Case 9 (daughters who serve the family and 'miss the boat for marriage') and Case 2 (the skewed character of the father who worked hard for many years to support the household). The falseness of the moment when security is grasped appears in the instances cited as similar to Case 10, and also in a letter from a 57-year-old father who, having sent his first son to university and seen him into a 'first-rate company,' complains that he has 'lost his vigor' (4.18).

Case 12 (7.5): I am a 35-year-old housewife with five sons, the eldest in the first year of middle school. I have been married fifteen years, and my husband is an exemplary person without a single fault. He brings his salary straight home, speaks little, and gets on well with the neighbors – a truly good man. But I have felt that I was completely happy only once in these fifteen years. That was the time when my first son was born and my husband came home from work and lay down with me on the floor and told me everything he felt about that day's event. He so seldom talks about anything but simple household matters. When he comes home in the evening he watches his favorite television programs, paying no attention to my likes or dislikes, simply enjoying himself alone. There is never the slightest spark of interest. Our life is dry as dust. I constantly feel unsatisfied, as if there is a huge hole in my heart. Must I keep on living this way just because I'm married to this kind of man? Is it selfish of me to think about how happy I would be, even if we were poor, if we could only chat and laugh together?

– A housewife in Iwate

It may be only natural that the respondent, having dealt with so many complaints from miserable women, answered: 'To have such a superb man as a husband, and then to complain about him while failing to humor his personal quirks, is the way to use up a woman's luck.' The writer's situation must surely seem enviable in the eyes of women who 'missed the chance for marriage,' women whose 'marriage fell apart' on them, women who have been widowed, women who 'cry' about their husband's unfaithfulness or violence or vices, women without children, women who are tied to old-fashioned households where they live amid the antagonism of mother- and sisters-in-law, women who must perform hard labor in order to survive. Yes, she who has attained the status of 'salaryman's wife' seems to have painted a montage of the images of 'happiness' in the hearts of all those women. And yet for that very reason, the ennui which by rights she is not supposed to endure – feeling 'unsatisfied, as if there is a huge hole in my heart' – indicates that what we have here is a symptom of a still larger, more fundamental problem. Through her situation we are able to glimpse the deeper-lying wellsprings of unhappiness in modern society. (See Figure 19.12.)

Causes and corollary factors

1   In this case, since there are almost no individualistic or particularized factors worth mentioning, the general situation of the white-collar worker and his wife is directly mooted. Let us first pursue the conditions which are common to husband and wife, and then seek the divergences between the husband's and the wife's means of coping with those conditions. First, there is the shared condition of emotional exhaustion and lack of excitement with life – a sense of meaninglessness and ennui – corresponding to the basically stable and secure lifestyle, the predictable future (i.e. the nonexistence of a future which ought actively to be created), and standardized living schedules and behavior patterns.

2   Behind those elements lie other issues: the loss of creativity in work, due to alienation from the societal means of production; and the reduction of the human being to 'a cog in a machine,' through organizational bureaucratization and mechanization. These two syndromes are mutually reinforcing.

3   In addition, on the husband's side, the nature of interpersonal relations in the workplace and the competition for status and prestige, together with the fact that work has lost all semblance of independent activity, build up a sense of futility and fatigue. As a result, with his personal temperament also in play, he probably looks to the home for nothing more than peaceful mental and physical retreat.

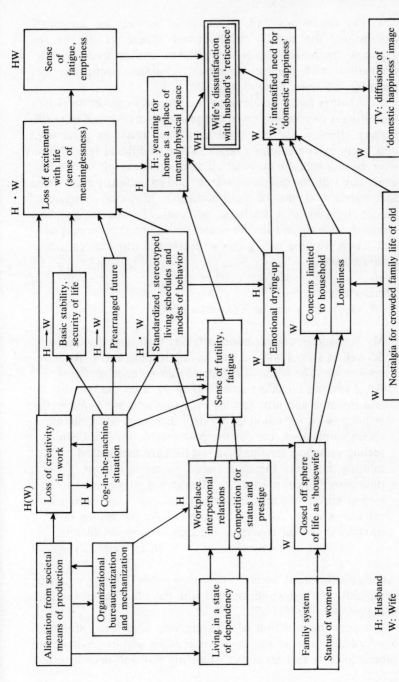

Figure 19.12 *Causal linkages of case 12*

H: Husband
W: Wife

4 On the wife's end, meanwhile, besides the emotional exhaustion, the tightly circumscribed sphere of life of the Japanese 'housewife' leads to loneliness and an exclusive pre-occupation with domestic personal relations, intensifying her need for 'domestic happiness.'

5 Another factor accelerating the process would be the wife's background disposition: given the provenance of Iwate in north-eastern Honshu, she may well have been raised in a crowded and lively extended-family home of the traditional type. More-over, having seen the husband off to work, she is left face-to-face every day with the television screen, and its endless variations on the standard theme of petit-bourgeois 'domestic happiness.' Hence the matured husband and wife harbor images and demands with respect to 'the home' which are at cross-purposes, and this is why the wife grows so frustrated with the 'reticence' of her husband.

Similar cases
6 A salaryman's wife in Yokosuka wrote:

> My husband is a sober-minded family man, and the children
> do well at school without our having to push them. *We have
> no worries. The house is equipped with modern appliances.*
> After making breakfast and washing up, I do the laundry
> and cleaning and just wait for everyone to come home in the
> evening, with television as my only diversion. My daily life
> seems so pleasant, but for the past year or so, I've been
> feeling somehow lonely. I started to learn mechanical
> knitting, but since there's no need for me to take in
> piecework, I lost interest. . . . In short, I pass my days
> feeling bored. My husband says it's a luxury, and shrugs it
> off with a smile. As for me, I can't shake the feeling of
> wanting to live an enjoyable life that is *more worthwhile*.
> (6.25; emphasis added)

Another wife, aged 24 and living in a public housing complex, complains, 'I've grown dissatisfied with day after day of ordinary commonplace life' (11.15).

Consider the situation of a young wife who feels inferior to her husband because she is one year older and her mother has tuberculosis: 'I feel no regret, since my husband does love me, but then I went and said I want to leave him, though I didn't mean it' (8.13). Then there is the middle-class household without a trouble in the world, where one day the high school-age son suddenly announced, 'I can't stand this house any more' and said he wanted to live on his own; when the mother asked him why, he replied, 'Father and Mother and my older brothers are all simply wonderful people, and that's why I hate it here' (8.7). Of course young women and adolescent boys will display their particular sorts of whims, but it is hard to deny that at the same time they reveal the furtive guilt and shadowy boredom which haunt 'happiness' in our time.

8 An engineer writes that he has changed jobs ten times, for he is unable to 'go through the motions' of work that is unsatisfying in order to be guaranteed basic affluence: 'I wish I had a job where nobody holds me back and I can act on my own power to make a life worth living' (6.23). An 'office lady' reports that she is unhappy with her work, and nurses a dream of 'devoting my life to education in a remote area' (8.24). Clearly, they are driven not by dissatisfaction with rank or remuneration, but rather by the craving for a job worth living for, 'a job where I can work with all my might.' And clearly, their attitude cannot be dismissed as simply the 'neurosis' or 'sentimentalism' of certain individuals, for it touches on the fundamental condition of today's society and person. Granted that they are exceptional, perhaps even a bit abnormal. But what that really means is that they are more keenly cognizant, more honestly engaged with their situation than are the mass of 'wholesome' types, who manage to channel the feelings of personal non-fulfillment that lie deep in their hearts into the distractions of the daily routine, or into comparisons with other people.

II Macrosystem frameworks of structural linkage among types of unhappiness

In the preceding analysis of the various phenomenal forms of 'unhappiness' and their social underpinnings in contemporary Japan, we have adhered strictly to the data of individual cases, and laid bare the universal problematic conditions which lie beneath them. The purpose of this study of unhappiness, as reiterated earlier, is not any sort of search for quantitative distributions or proportions. Accordingly, as we move on to a synthesis of the analytical results of the first section, it is necessary to adopt a special methodology, one that is not simply additive.

The technique that is used here can be called the montage of distributive causal linkages. Suppose for the moment that the cause-and-effect linkage $A \rightarrow B$ is discovered in Case 1, and that the cause-and-effect linkages $B \rightarrow C$ and $B \rightarrow D$ turn up in Cases 2 and 3. We could then determine that the 'montage' $A \rightarrow \boxed{B \Longleftarrow \begin{matrix} C \\ D \end{matrix}}$ describes circumstances which are realistically possible. That is:

$$(1): \quad [A \rightarrow B] + [B \rightarrow C] + [B \rightarrow D] = \left[A \rightarrow B \begin{matrix} \nearrow C \\ \searrow D \end{matrix} \right]$$

For example, if in one case unemployment brings about discord within the household, in another case domestic discord is the cause of delinquent behavior, and in a third case domestic discord causes a nervous disorder, then we may assume that the montage:

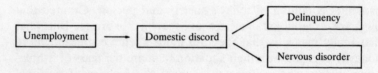

describes a linkage which *may actually occur*.

Similarly, an additional set of cases where, say, the causal linkages $E \rightarrow A$, and $A \rightarrow E \rightarrow F \rightarrow D$ are observed, would allow us to expand montage (1) to:

$$(2): \quad A \rightarrow B \begin{matrix} \nearrow C \\ \searrow D \end{matrix} + [E \rightarrow A] + [A \rightarrow E \rightarrow F \rightarrow D] = \begin{bmatrix} A \rightarrow B \rightarrow C \\ \updownarrow \quad \searrow \\ E \rightarrow F \rightarrow D \end{bmatrix}$$

By incorporating case after case in this fashion, we may continue to broaden the montage of realistically likely causal linkages.

We shall apply this technique below to construct diagrammatic frameworks which describe the overall system of structual linkages among the diverse forms of 'unhappiness,' and among the main background factors which influence them, in the society of present-day Japan.

1 The framework of conditions typical to smaller enterprises and 'backward' sectors

This and the following subsection are devoted to making representative models (see Figures 19.13 and 19.14) of the 'structural conditions' of the strata which make up the 'two-tiered structure' of the Japanese economy. In doing so, we should not lose sight of the original purpose and scope of this chapter, which is to track and elucidate, by way of an analysis of the various contemporary forms of 'unhappiness' and their social foundations, the particular forms of being which *alienation* assumes in present-day Japan. Now this may give the impression that we are determined to 'look only on the dark side.' Certainly there are various 'bright sides' of contemporary Japan. But with respect to such truly bright circumstances, shall we simply pay lip service to reality through some conjunctive parallelism such as, 'But on the other side of the coin . . .'? Is it not better, and more appropriate to the resilient nature of human beings, to unflinchingly describe the 'darkness' as it is discovered by thorough investigation?

People manage to endure the darkness of the night, not because there are bits of light here and there from stars and lamps, but because they are able to believe that in due course morning will come. Petty brightness, which is all that can be found by merely pointing up the 'flip side' of a dark situation, is not a true light.

1 In the two-tiered Japanese economy, the fundamental elements defining the conditions of the lower strata are relative or absolute poverty, and the resulting actual or latent chronic non-fulfillment of desires. (See 1:1, 1:3, 1:9, 1:10, 6:2, 11:1.) *Note*: 'x:y' refers to the analysis in Case x, Paragraph y, above.

In the background here is the economic imbalance of Japan as an eccentrically developed country where, within the single nation, there exist both a fully matured 'advanced imperialist nation' and, under its domination, a 'backward colonial nation.'

2 This situation, in conjunction with the deficiency of the social-security system, also works to bring about a general state

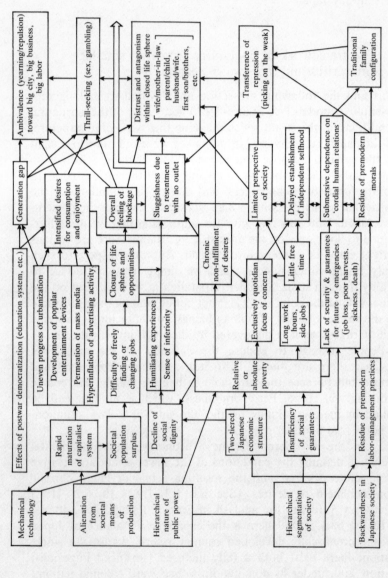

Figure 19.13 *Framework of conditions typical to smaller enterprises and 'backward' sectors*

of insecure livelihood, due to a lack of guarantees for the future or times of emergency (1:3, 1:4, 1:10, 4:5, 7:3, 7:7, 9:2).

3 In addition, these realities drive people into reliance upon the 'affection' of relatives, husband, parents, etc., and hence reinforce the retention and reproduction of premodern morals and relationships as important foundations of society. While those morals and relationships serve in the short run to appease deficiencies and frustrations on the physical and spiritual planes, in the larger picture they tend to make the overall conditions in these strata still more inferior and unstable, as can be seen in the retention of lopsided labor-management practices in small and middle-sized businesses (1:1, 1:3, 1:5).

4 The paucity of free time due to long working hours (sometimes compounded by side jobs), together with the abovementioned chronic non-fulfillment of desires, tends to restrict the field of personal concerns to daily routines and issues of physical survival (1:9, 1:10, 6:4, 11:3).

5 Lack of free time plus exclusive focus on quotidian life *limit the scope of one's viewpoint on society*, and at the same time *obstruct the establishment of independent selfhood*. These factors further reinforce the retention of premodern morals, as well as reliance upon and submersion within old-fashioned human relations (1:9, 4:1, 1:3).

6 In today's Japan, where economic value has become a synonym for value in general, and the amount of economic value one possesses is widely accepted as the measure of one's worth, economic hardship brings with it low levels of esteem and social prestige. For the financially poor, this occasions humiliating experiences and a sense of inferiority in various aspects of daily life (1:8, 6:2).

7 The escape route from those circumstances is effectively blocked off by the serious difficulty of independently finding or changing jobs, which derives from the society-wide population surplus. This leads to *closure of the range and opportunities of life*, which further strengthens the blinders of daily routine and limits the perspective upon society at large (1:4, 1:7, 4:5, 6:4, 7:7).

8 The energy of the anger built up by chronically unfulfilled desires and daily humiliations, and exacerbated by restricted spheres of life and narrow social perspectives, generates an

387

amorphous resentment with no outlet, which leads to a state of sluggishness and vaguely sensed emotional blockage (6:2, 10:2).

9   The stagnating energy of locked-in resentment, reinforced by residues of premodern morals and human relations, promotes various forms of *transference of repression* (tormenting of the weak). Also, within the dark, damp interior of the closed life sphere, it creates a bed of mistrust and antagonism – as between wife and mother-in-law, father and son, husband and wife, first son and younger brothers, those going out to work and those cooped up at home, new employees and old hands, etc. (4:6, 5:1, 5:2, 6:2, 6:3, 6:5, 7:3, 9:6).

10   Inter-generational antagonisms are also supported by the effects of postwar democratization, centering on the educational system; and by the rapidly advancing urbanization of communities. (2:4, 3:5).

11   Meanwhile, diffusion of the mass media and hyperexpansion of the advertising industry, along with the development of popular entertainment devices, have had two types of effects which heighten intrafamilial tensions. One is an unevening of progress, with urbanization proceeding while old cultural elements are left in place. The other is an intensification of desires for consumption and enjoyment, which helps induce such behavior as drunken frenzy, gambling, extramarital affairs and wasteful spending by husbands (or wives); and delinquency among teenagers and young adults (9:9, 4:4).

12   A mood of uneasy ambivalence has taken root with respect to modern mega-organizations – the big city, big business, big labor unions – consisting in simultaneous feelings of yearning and repulsion (9:5, 9:8, 4:3).

13   The collapse of the traditional morals of apportioned contentment, and the permeation of politically conceived equality, have set free the billions of desires which comprise the foundation of society. Further spurring on the equalization of desires is, again, the spread of mass media and massive advertising. However, economic wealth, which in today's Japan is the basic means for quenching desires, is by no means equally distributed, as noted in (1) above. The accumulation of unfulfilled desires that result from this contradiction between goals and means, ideals and reality, aspiration and opportunity, is naturally a potential source of active reform of the existing deficiencies and inequalities. But the conversion of that potential into realization

would require liberation from the spell of obsession with quotidian affairs, and the acquisition of a direct perspective on the sources of personal unhappiness.

2 The framework of conditions typical to white-collar workers in 'advanced' sectors

1 The living conditions of this class of people are characterized by basic material stability and security, supported by the fully mature capitalist system, and dependence upon authority and 'big capital.' The key factor in their security is that centerpiece of 'Japanese-style labor-management relations,' the practice of lifetime employment. Since this stable security stems initially from the incorporation of their personal lives into giant organizations which are bureaucratized and mechanized, the various problematic aspects outlined below are inherent in their situation.

2 In most cases, while the future is materially secure, the future path has been predetermined by the organization to which they belong. For them, the 'future' is no longer an area which they themselves must actively choose or create. It is merely an extension of the past along installed rails (12:1, 10:3, 8:3).

3 As with all components, their behavior must be as precisely measured and predictable as possible. Aside from a few people in special positions and occupations, the great majority settle into standardized living schedules and modes of behavior and stereotyped mannerisms which suit the requirements of capital and organizations. Life becomes rigorously commonplace, with today a repetition of yesterday and tomorrow a repetition of today (2:3, 9:9, 10:1, 12:1, 12:6).

4 The componentization of the large organization, whereby everyone becomes a cog in a machine, involves the forfeiture of independence in the sphere of work. Aside from the few in special positions and occupations, it is impossible for people to give free rein to their own individuality and creative power within their respective jobs. Moreover, even in situations where their individuality and particular creative powers are fully encouraged, the purpose of the work itself guarantees that these do not issue from their own internal volition, but rather are imposed by capital and public authority in the name of the organization. Hence

it is quite difficult for them to find anything really worthwhile in their work (12:8, 12:2, 2:3).

5   The 'seriality' of modern civil society brings about not only divergence and competition among and within classes, but also the *externalization and fetishization of 'social' rules and affairs*. That is, 'society,' insofar as it consists in countless, essentially contradictory interests, comes to resemble an integral calculus of the complex power relations among them; and since its workings will never concur entirely with the aims of any of the individuals or groups of which it is composed, for the individual, 'society' becomes emblematized as some sort of transcendental, distant power that is controlled by an 'invisible hand.' (The movements of the stock market provide an excellent model of this point. Ironically enough, at this core of the modern economy, which may be fairly called the concentrated embodiment of its abstract rationality, all sorts of irrational divinations and jinxes are thought to stalk the streets even today.)

This phenomenon, along with the organizational cog-in-the-machine syndrome, causes a relative localization of the sphere of life which individuals are able independently to foresee or to manage, and accordingly engenders a sense of alienation from society at large (3:4, 9:9).

6   The basic conditions of life which are outlined above lead to chronic emotional impoverishment among this class of persons (the leading causes being forfeiture of independence in work, and standardization of schedules and behavior) (2:3, 12:1, 12:2, 12:6, 9:9, 10:1).

7   The emotional impoverishment tends to elicit two basic styles of response among contemporary people, a 'street style' and a 'home style.'

8   The first style reflects overinflated desires for consumption and enjoyment, which stem from the basic stability and complacency of life, along with the predictability and non-creative nature of the future.

This goes hand-in-hand with the contradictions between production and consumption created by mass production under capitalism. To wit, the goal of expanding 'ultimate demand' stimulates large-scale advertising activities and the development of devices for popular entertainment, and that process further inflates desires for consumption and enjoyment, to the point where they continue to swell even as the goods and fun are gulped down. Sex and other thrills emerge as the means of 'resistance' to this cycle, and the streets are flooded with versions of eroticism and gambling (2:3, 9:6, 10:1).

9 The second style consists of a craving for 'domestic recreation,' generated from emotional impoverishment and the sense of alienation from the larger society. On one hand, this is connected to nostalgia for the traditional family configuration; on the other, it is built up by the images of 'domestic happiness' that are dispersed by glossy weekly magazines and televised soap operas (12:4, 12:5, 9:9).

10 The gap between these two styles of reaction to emotional impoverishment fosters dissatisfaction and antagonism in the home, e.g. when the husband is intent on taking to the streets and the wife is determined to stay at home (10:2, 10:4, 12:5, 4:6).

11 Competition for rank and status among colleagues and neighbors, combined with relative localization of the independently manageable life sphere, and alienation from society at large, lead to general feelings of distrust toward others and toward 'society' as well as to egoism and submersion in private life. These in turn generate considerable antagonism and loneliness, both at the workplace and in the neighborhood (7:5, 9:9, 6:5, 2:2, 3:3, 8:5, 12:3).

12 Such strife in domestic and social human relations, and the anxiety-producing efforts which are habitually made to head it off, lead to various types of nervous disorders and associated illnesses (3:3, 3:4, 2:2, 2:3).

13 Forfeiture of independence in work, lack of a future demanding active creativity, and standardized schedules and behavior – along with a lifestyle of basic stability and security – result in loss of excitement about life, and consequent feelings of ennui and emotional blockage (9:9, 12:1, 12:8, 2:3, 12:6, 12:7, 11:5, 10:3).

14 The foregone nature of the future, and localization of the sphere of active engagement, bring about a sense of powerlessness concerning one's personal destiny (viz. fixed retirement age, job transfers, recession, etc.). This in turn reinforces the feeling of blockage, and also leads to unease and restlessness about a 'future' which seems impervious to one's own energies (7:1, 8:3, 8:4, 8:6, 8:7, etc.).

15 Competition at work and in the neighborhood for status and prestige naturally creates anxiety and restlessness on the part

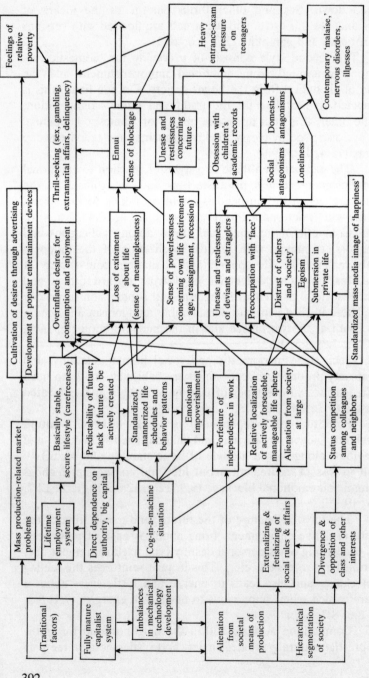

Figure 19.14 *Framework of conditions typical to white-collar workers in 'advanced' sectors*

of those who fall behind, while the stereotyped images of 'success' and 'happiness' spread by the mass media only intensify their misery. Furthermore, those who differ simply because of individuality are inculcated with feelings of inferiority (and anxiety) which are tantamount to a sense of defeat (8:2, 8:7, 9:9, 12:5, 2:1, 7:8).

16 Among 'deviant' types, this sense of inferiority and 'defeat,' and their anxiety about the future, tend to intensify expectations and concern about the children's life paths, and especially their scholastic records. Thanks to such intangible yet heavy pressure, children of this stratum often go on to lives marked by general feelings of blockage and ennui, adherence to values shaped by stereotyped images of success and happiness, anxiety and restlessness about the future, as well as loneliness and distrust in various forms (2:1, 3:6, 7:5, 7:8).

17 The general sense of lethargy or ennui that is widely apparent in this group includes a potential for maturing, via the agency of their very keen desire for 'a life worth living' and their skepticism toward the set of values promoted by the system, into the power to go beyond the system of the status quo. Yet the conversion of this potential into realization would require that they bring forth from within themselves an energy of tenacious resolve, by confronting the multi-storied realities of their situation.

3 Conclusion: the macrosystem framework of contemporary conditions of alienation

To properly grasp and position the various patterns of 'unhappiness' in the daily life of the people, they must be elucidated as an aggregate of (1) the 'objective' fundamental structure of society; (2) its 'subjective' consequences in the minds of individuals (dissatisfaction and frustration, loneliness and antagonism, anxiety and fretfulness, lethargy and ennui); and (3) the constellation of intermediary factors linking those two.

Figures 13 and 14, above, portray such constellations of linkage in two representative situations of modern Japan, based on the data used in this study. Extracting from those diagrams only the factors which are fundamental and/or general, we may venture to portray the overall structural linkage of the sociology of 'unhappiness' in modern society (Figure 19.15).

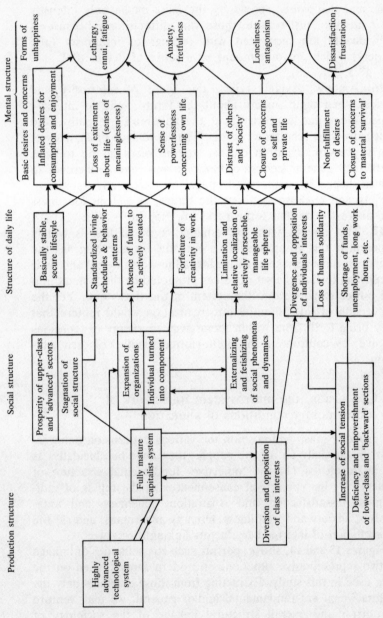

Figure 19.15 *Macrosystem framework of the sociology of 'unhappiness' in modern society*

20　White-Collar Split

I　The segmentation of the new middle class

The new elite and the gray collars

The old middle class has dissolved, and been replaced by the new, white-collar middle class. This is a commonly accepted truism about the social structure of Japan. But in fact, that 'new' middle class has begun to dissolve once again. Two complementary trends have become clear in the white-collar world since the 1960s: at one end, a relatively small number are precipitating into a new elite, and on the other, the bulk of those who wear white collars can no longer be clearly pegged above or below blue-collar workers, in terms either of income or prestige.

In the United States, blue-collar wages began to outstrip white-collar salaries during the 1950s. In 1956 male clerical workers there were reported to be earning, on average, only two-thirds as much as workers in electrical power plants and machine factories, and their social status tended to be a notch lower than that of skilled blue-collar workers. A decade later, hundreds of thousands of white-collar workers had lost their jobs as a result of automation, and the figure is growing.

In Japan, the demise of the white-collar worker has not taken on such drastic proportions. But in the middle and lower echelons of the offices, there is a pervasive sense of anxiety and of 'quiet demise.' The conventional categories of white and blue are losing their meaning, as a new gap emerges between the so-called New Elite, and the 'gray-collar' workers who are difficult to distinguish from the blue-collar class.

While awareness of the split is keen enough in business circles and among the workers themselves, it has also been noted by many outside observers. A typical comment (from Ebata Kiyoshi): 'In this era of mass production of university graduates and mechanization of the office, a top/bottom split is occurring *within* the graduate group, between white-collar managers and

395

the majority of ordinary office workers.' Morimura Minoru concluded that:

> Being a salaryman is no longer a 'carefree occupation.' Swept
> off his feet by technical innovation and tossed about by the
> storm of the office revolution, he can quickly sink to the
> lower level for life. For having once assumed a lower-level
> position, it is very difficult to climb to the upper level. . . .
> No matter how much office experience is accumulated, the
> ladder stays out of reach.

The new dictum everywhere is, 'Only Top Managers and
Specialists Survive.' Book titles and magazine headlines are
flooded with phrases like Advancing to Qualified-Salaryman
Rank, The Specialist Route, Marketable Skills, and Professional
Salaryman. The clear implication is that those who do not heed
the bywords are 'stragglers' who cannot escape ruin, who will
either lose their jobs or be frozen at the lower level. Tens of
thousands of young and middling salarymen are devoting most of
their free time to studying – with a zeal they never displayed in
their student years – to acquire credentials as accountants, patent
attorneys, real estate managers, small-business consultants and
the like, or to gain a working knowledge of English or computers.

For accountancy certification, the success rate in the national
examinations of 1967 was 25.5 per cent in the first stage, 7.1 per
cent in the second stage, and 32.1 and 25.2 per cent in the third
stage (given twice). If these rates are assumed constant, then
even among university graduates who are exempt from the first
stage, only one in fifty attains certification; for high school graduates, the figure is one in two hundred!

A section chief from a large corporation who passed the
accountancy examinations, profiled in Oya Yasuo's essay on 'The
Specialist Route,' studied for an average of four hours every
evening after work. My own encounters with people preparing
for the exams suggest that this is not at all exceptional. One of
them described his motivations as follows:

> I've seen men older than myself who expected to become
> section chiefs when they reached 40, but they didn't make
> it, because something changed, for example a new division
> chief came in. I've realized that being a salaryman is not a

pleasant fate, that the organization is a cold place. You work like crazy, then when you're 40 you're stabbed in the back. What can you do? The point is, you have to have a skill of your own, you have to get some kind of competence that will make them scout you out. I'd like to quit when I'm 30. I think 30 should be the retirement age. But setting up my own business would be unrealistic, that's only a dream. So what should I do? . . . Constant self-examination and constant effort, that's the only way. Endless self-examination and effort. . . . They tell you the union will get us higher pay. None of that for me. The way I see it, we owe our lives to the company. I'd like to see the wage system based on job capability, not on the 'market basket' guarantees that the union stands for . . . I'm studying to be an accountant so that I can work in a company job with my own motivation.

His is a very convoluted account, revealing a whole set of issues clustering about the axis of the disintegrating white-collar situation – standard of living, day-to-day frame of mind, ideology. In this chapter I shall wade into the various facets of awareness of that disintegration, and attempt to justify some *working hypotheses* that may point the way toward more rigorous research into the changing white-collar mentality. This first half will anatomize the process of segmentation, and the latter half will examine the ways in which people respond to it.

The three causes of segmentation

The splitting of the white-collar class is the result of three well-known factors: the ongoing revolution in office technology; the devaluation of academic credentials; and the widespread adoption of modern management methods.

First, the mechanization of what was traditionally the substance of middle- and lower-level office jobs – calculating, posting, recording, copying – is turning more and more white-collar workers into machine operators. Such menialization is also occurring in technical and sales-related jobs, as we will see below.

Second, there is rampant inflation of the established currency of success, the university degree, due to the explosion of higher education. In 1931 there were 70,000 university students in all Japan; by the late 1960s, the enrollment of a single institution,

Nippon University, exceeded that figure. Hence a diploma no longer guarantees membership in the elite. As the salaryman-oriented literature repeatedly emphasized, 'the floors are littered with discarded university graduates.' In other words, while office mechanization reduces the *demand* for intellectual workers, the explosion of graduates increases the *supply*, so the market value of the educated man inevitably drops.

The third factor, the management revolution, is closely related to the first two. What an enterprise really needs now is a relatively small number of program managers and outstanding technical specialists, and a relatively large number of terminal operators, leaving an overabundance of intermediary white-collar types. The red carpet is rolled out for a few talented individuals who take up 'glamor' positions, and the run-of-the-mill graduate is treated with growing indifference.

The classic Japanese organization, with its cardinal principles of *lifetime employment* and *promotion by seniority*, has been not so much a pyramid as a bell-shaped structure. Now, in the wake of technical and managerial innovation, it is taking on the shape of a gourd (see Figure 20.1).

The tremendous vogue for American-style management

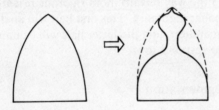

As the organization changes from bell-shaped to gourd-shaped ...

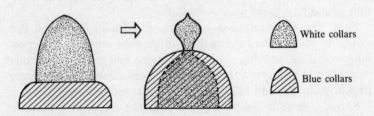

... the blue collar-type base balloons

Figure 20.1 *The changing organizational structure*

methods in the 1960s and 1970s was not a passive response or a passing fad. The actual requirements of the Japanese industrial system forced the emulation of the competitive American model, despite resistance within the management camp itself, not to mention the unions.

'Abolition of the section chief' and 'middle-management reductions' are not yet so widespread as the mass media have made them seem. Salaried office workers are still far less prone than blue-collar wage-earners to snap judgments in commodity terms. Yet it makes good copy precisely because it is a plausible result of obvious trends. The media are at once feeding upon and reinforcing a certain psychology in the white-collar class, a heightened sensitivity toward the career pattern. 'At 30, it's not the salary but the diploma that counts,' they say, for at that age the concrete goal tends to be a middle-management post, section chief being the first step up the ladder. All signs point to serious disquiet, if not despair, in the private thoughts of the younger salaryman.

The axis of segmentation

Where exactly is the turning point? In terms of individual salaried workers, where is the line drawn between he who rises into the New Elite and he who sinks into the mass of 'salaried laborers'? Let us consider in turn the three broad categories of white-collar work – specialist and technical occupations, managerial and clerical occupations, and sales and service occupations.

In the specialist/technical area, a clear division is gradually emerging between the scientists and top engineers who function as 'brains' in the planning and development of technical systems, and the technicians and ordinary engineers who function basically as operators. In the field of computers, for example, the systems engineers who are the brains on the manufacturer's end, and the planners who are the brains on the user's end, have settled into specialized roles which are essentially different from that of the ordinary programmer. Meanwhile, beneath the programmers is a group consisting almost entirely of operators and keypunchers. The operator's job may be temporarily complicated during the development and introduction of new technologies or machines, but the situation is soon sorted out by the console manager, and the ordinary operator settles into an increasingly monotonous routine.

The traditional image of 'engineering work' included both the aspect of the creator of the technical system and the aspect of the operator of that system, in undifferentiated form. Now, as technology grows more complex and layered, the two sides of engineering are polarizing into different kinds of work.

In the management/clerical sphere the same sort of conceptual fission is apparent. 'Office work' used to imply both the function of controlling and managing the overall corporation (including the office structure itself), and the function of implementing the policies and procedures of the corporation. The individual career path typically involved both aspects, and the seniority system meant, at least for university graduates, a *gradual* expansion over the years of responsibility in the former function. Now the circle is dividing, as the control function breaks up into specialized professions (accountants, tax specialists, patent attorneys and the like), and the implementation function breaks down, especially through the development and diffusion of machinery, into simple labor.

The sales and service job category was at first comparatively immune to this cleavage, but the germ has progressed. A 'salesman' never really bothered to realize that he was both planning and executing his strategies. Yet now there is an evolving professional corps of sales engineers, copywriters and market researchers, working as the 'brains' who generate ideas and sales plans, in contradistinction to the bulk of sales 'receptionists' working at counters or traveling to customers.

In each category, then, the two aspects of white-collar work which were previously undifferentiated and latent – the 'brains' and the 'hands' – are in the process of splitting apart. Taking the spotlight are the brainy elite who hold the glamorous jobs of the moment. Sinking silently into the shadows are the main group of increasingly menial white collars.

The suffering of the new elite

The requirements of society aside, in terms of the life plan of the individual member of the white-collar class, the prerequisite for 'survival' is to become part of the 'brains,' a member of the New Elite of society's system of labor. The brain being a highly specialized organ, arduous effort is required. But admission into the elite is not necessarily the end of that story. The suffering involved in being part of the 'brains' became apparent to me as I talked with some systems engineers, paragons of the new elite of bright specialists. As they spoke, they were naturally full of confidence and aspiration, but there were also telling intervals between the words, and moments of sobering verbal reflection.

Computer systems engineers at the user end (in companies which lease mainframe computers) seem particularly susceptible to high-altitude professional stress. One of my informants worked with a computer leased from a major American maker. Three months after it was installed, an improved operating system came out, and the system that his company had adopted up to that point had to be rearranged. In principle, of course, the new operating system was designed for continuity with the old one, but on the user's end, where fairly sweeping changes had been devised to serve the company's particular purposes, the manufacturer's version of continuity was not so useful. Much of the load was shifted onto the shoulders of the brain workers at the user's end. To the extent that fixed systems are used, such difficulties may be avoided, but at the risk of their becoming obsolete and thus working against the principle of maximum profit: 'Computers progress with amazing speed, they have a momentum of their own.'

He was quick to point up the loftiness of his position, claiming that 'programmers aren't actually specialists, systems engineers are different,' but in virtually the same breath he confessed that, 'What I learned for sure after I took this job is that I hate systems. I can't stand the feeling of keeping up with machines, as if human beings are just being scrapped. . . . It's miserable to be under the whip of technological progress.'

If his experience is a guide, then in fields which are undergoing intensive innovation, there is the basic stress (and at the same time the exhilaration) of grasping the technical revolution by the horns; plus the stresses deriving from conflicts between the profit-seeking nature of the company and the generational momentum of the technology, as well as from conflicts between the corporate purposes of the manufacturer and the user. Systems engineers engaged in product development at the *maker's* end might breathe a little easier, being able to hold the reins, as it were, but then again there is always an intense competition in which

401

they must struggle either to catch up to the industry leaders or stay ahead of the challengers, or perhaps both. At either end there is a constant feeling of being driven. Thus for today's technical specialists, model 'brains' though they may be, the sense of being passively controlled by the technological revolution is often stronger than the sense of being actively in control.

Asked whether they intended to stay indefinitely in their jobs as system engineers, most of my informants replied that at a certain age they hoped to become management generalists within the company, or independent consultants, or to set up their own software firms: 'A specialist has to have stamina. In computers, especially, your twenties are when you have the aptitude.'

The axis of segmentation moves upward

For those brain workers, then, the stress of the elite position seems to remain strong as long as they are workers in the universal sense, part of the social system of labor. Though they are perceived as the elite, they themselves tend to believe they will join the elite only when they become embodiments of corporate purpose, either by setting up an independent company or by attaining a high management rank. The significance of becoming independent (granted that their confidence that 'One usually succeeds' actually holds true) is that they would be able finally to take their specialist's knowledge into their own hands, as entrepreneurs, and completely escape from the proletariat (here, the 'new middle class'). In this sense, they would for the first time feel that their elite status is permanently guaranteed.

This is the key point for understanding the true nature of the elitism of the New Elite. They themselves view a career as a specialist as no more than a 'step.' We might say that the initial process of entering a promising company is a 'hop,' and rising into the brain ranks is a 'step,' but only by managing successfully to 'jump' to independence does one actually join the real elite in contemporary society.

One reason for the suffering of the 'brains' in the technological system is that today's more-or-less constant process of innovation (besides intensifying the meniality of lower-level work) is ceaselessly converting brain-level work into something akin to the labor of the 'hands.'

Looking back to the segmentations of the old middle class, it is possible to trace a *rising of the dividing line*, linked mainly to the process of technical innovation. From the prewar years through the immediate postwar era, the dividing line for Japanese farmers was generally reckoned as possession of one *chō* of land (2.45 acres). Those above the line had basic security and could perhaps move further up, while those below the line basically had to choose among bankruptcy, side jobs, or abandoning the farm to join the industrial proletariat. Later, amid the technological innovations of the late 1950s and early 1960s, the line rose to one and a half *chō*, and by now it has likely passed two *chō*.

The new middle class is experiencing a similar phenomenon, although its segments and dividing lines naturally have somewhat different forms and meanings. With the old middle class, those who managed to substantially differentiate themselves from the tenant-farmer proletariat, those reaching the 'stairway,' were the ones who owned the actual means of production; hence the axis of segmentation depended on the scale of production, and the rise of the axis corresponded directly to changes in that scale. In the new middle class, the means of differentiation from the blue collars is for one's work to have a brain-like character; hence the dividing line has to do with the presence or lack or degree of that character, and the rise of the axis of segmentation accords with changes in the dimensions of that brain-like character.

Another difference is apparent between those rising axes of segmentation. For the old middle class, a simple quantitative increase in landholding, i.e. capital, was what sufficed to reach the ascendant stratum, which means that no matter how much toil and trouble were involved, the logical structure of the process remained simply linear. But with the cadets of the elite who hail from the new middle class, we find for the first time the possibility of arrival in the ascendant stratum through the process of making a jump, of exchanging one's specialization or talent for capital.

403

II Modes of coping with the split

Three patterns of response

Given that a gulf is opening up among them, and the status-level location of that gulf is rising, how do individual white-collar workers go about planning their lives?

To begin with, of course, there is widespread adoption of the goal of staying on the bright side of the shifting chasm, by rising resolutely into the New Elite. This is what drives the tremendous wave of enthusiasm for acquiring new qualifications, skills and talents, for these are seen as conditions of 'survival.' Another reflection of this mentality is the management-science boom. There is the 'specialist route' on one side and the 'generalist route' on the other, but these are really two faces of the same coin of survival.

It is noteworthy that this general aim seems clearly to exist, and to function as an ideology of life, among a group that is many times larger than those who actually have the relevant opportunities. Witness the flood of people taking the accountancy exams – one or two orders of magnitude greater than the number who pass – and the countless readers of bestselling 'management science' publications who are neither entrepreneurs nor their heirs.

At the opposite extreme there is a large crowd of 'dropouts.' They are the white collars who either lack the spirit to join in the status competition, or reject it out of hand on the basis of their personal beliefs. In terms of modes of response to the situation, some of them are carriers of resistance to the system, either inside or outside the labor unions; while the majority simply prefer to devote their attention to the rewards of life in their humble homes, away from the workplace.

In which strata and segments of the actual white-collar population are these respective modes of coping generated and distributed?

In objective terms, the mode is likely to be prescribed by the relative status of the individual white-collar worker.

In subjective terms, meanwhile, the factor of one's personal inclination toward the extant social order is no doubt strongly operative. This assumption is fleshed out in Figure 20.2 (which represents no more than a rough working hypothesis).

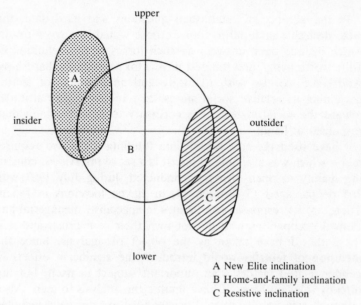

A New Elite inclination
B Home-and-family inclination
C Resistive inclination

Figure 20.2 *Distribution of inclinations*

To verify this hypothesis, it would be necessary to analyze the correlations of these inclinations, through a survey which includes yardsticks for quantifying relative status and attitudes of resistance toward the system; as well as questions designed to qualitatively (or quantitatively) detect the three sorts of inclination. In lieu of such a perfect survey, I will make do with what approximate data as can be found, and draw some provisional inferences which will serve not so much to prove as to enrich the hypothesis.

Classification of the three types

There have been a fair number of surveys focusing on the home-and-family type, and a thorough search turns up a few that profile the resistive type. But those whose inclination is to join the New Elite have virtually never been specifically covered by questions contained in attitude surveys. For although this is a key element in the mentality of the large white-collar population, with significant structural implications, and it is certainly spreading to considerable breadth and depth, it is nonetheless a phenomenon which has only very recently materialized.

In the absence of established questions and hard data, the most desirable material for our purpose would be survey results which include open answers on such topics as the definition of a life worth living, and the best means for overcoming hardships. And since we also wish to locate and analyze sets of factors pertaining to relative social status, and to underlying attitudes toward the social system, it is necessary to have the individual responses at hand.

I have used the sole set of data fulfilling these two requirements which was available to me. It is a set of interviews, consisting mainly of open answers, conducted during July 1967 with 785 people aged 15 through 44, in eleven locations in Japan. There are 94 responses from males in specialist, managerial and clerical occupations who do not own their own firms, and it is these that I have taken as the object of analysis. Since the inclusion of females would introduce the significant effects of gender-related factors – an important subject in itself, but not directly relevant here – I have limited the analysis to men. Also, although sales/service-related occupations are normally included in the white-collar category, I have removed them from the analysis because the majority of those types who were surveyed are shopkeepers or tradesmen (such as barbers), who as a group lead lives which are quite different from the typical white-collar worker.

I begin by classifying respondents in terms of their status and their inclinations (Table 20.1) using the following precedures. Income and education are taken as the criteria for the objective factor of social status. Since the goals of the present jobs can be easily if roughly estimated, and since the data (especially for income) is not very detailed, rather than adopting a finely gauged methodology, I have used the following simple procedure. For income, three points are assigned for annual incomes over 800,000 yen, two points for incomes over 500,000 and under 800,000 yen, and one point for incomes below 500,000 yen (these being the only classifications in the survey). For education, three points are assigned to graduates of university (or a 'higher school' of the pre–1948 educational system), two points to high school (or former middle school) graduates, and one point to middle school (or former primary school) graduates. Income and education scores are simply added together for a rough quantification of social status (the combined scores range from two to six).

Table 20.1   *Classification of respondents by status and inclination*

Objective status	Subjective Inclination						
	I	II	III	IV	V	X	Total
6	10	2	1	7	1		21
5	7	5	2	14	4		32
4	10	1	2	5	2	1	21
3,2	2	2	1	10	1	1	17
x	2			1			3
Total	31	10	6	37	8	2	94

Categories I–V and 6–2 are explained in the text.
Category x is those whose income level is unclear.
Category X is supporters of the Clean Government Party (Kōmeitō).

To classify inclinations toward the System, I have devised five
categories on the basis of political-party support as well as the
individuals' stated demands or wishes with respect to the parties.

   I *Conservative*: (1) Liberal Democratic Party supporters;
      and (2) those without party affiliation who answered
      'conservative.'
  II *Neutral*: No party affiliation, and neither conservative
      nor progressive.
 III *Social-democratic*: (1) Democratic Socialist Party
      supporters; (2) those without party affiliation who
      voiced good will toward the DSP; (3) supporters of both
      the DSP and the Socialist Party; and (4) SP supporters
      who criticize it from a rightward perspective (e.g.
      demanding that it become 'more moderate' or 'more
      mature').
  IV *Socialist*: (1) SP supporters; and (2) those without party
      affiliation who do not fall under category III or V.
   V *Communist*: (1) Communist Party supporters; (2)
      supporters of both the SP and CP; (3) those without
      political affiliation who voiced good will toward the CP;
      and (4) those who criticized the SP or CP from a
      leftward perspective.

The purpose is not to gauge actual party support, but rather
to identify degrees of affirmation or denial of the present system.

White-collar workers tend to support the Socialist Party in such large numbers that the discriminatory function deteriorates, so I have devised the 'Social-democratic' and 'Communist' categories and assigned them the broadest possible range. These are merely aliases which suit the present narrow purpose, and they basically signify rightism and leftism with respect to the Socialist Party.

Distribution of the three types

To locate the actual patterns of the basic inclinations, I searched for indications mainly in the open answers which the 94 respondents gave to questions about 'a life worth living,' 'hardships' and 'means of overcoming hardships.'

A *Indicators of the New Elite Inclination*: A life worth living involves 'rise in status,' 'increased accomplishment in the company job,' 'being noticed by superiors,' 'company-related study,' etc. Means of overcoming hardships include 'rise in status,' 'becoming an entrepreneur,' 'gaining recognition for my abilities,' 'selling myself dearly to the company,' 'developing my abilities,' etc.

B *Indicators of the Home-and-Family Inclination*: A life worth living involves 'watching the children grow up,' 'having a happy home,' 'family trips,' 'remodeling and beautifying the house,' 'coming home early sometimes and playing with the children,' 'having the children somewhat inclined to build a home when they grow up,' etc.

C *Indicators of the Resistive Inclination*: A life worth living involves 'union activity,' etc. Means of overcoming hardships include 'multiple opposition movements,' 'changing the capitalist society,' 'getting the Socialist Party into power,' etc.

The patterns of these indicative responses are summarized in Table 20.2, and graphed in Figure 20.3.

Several provisional conclusions can be drawn. First, the initial hypothesis (Figure 20.2) is shown, in a very broad sense, to be correct. Second, area A (New Elite inclination) turns out to be considerably larger than area C (resistive inclination). Third, the reform-minded segment of white collars is mostly of the home-

Table 20.2 *Classification of the three response patterns*

	I Conservative	II Neutral	III Social-democratic	IV Socialistic	V Communistic
6. Upper class	A, AB, AB B, B, B	A B	B	B, B, B B, B	BC BC
5. Middle class	A, A, AB	A, A	A	B, B, B, B B, B, BC	BC
4. Lower class	A, AB, B AC, AB, B	B	B, B	B, B, C	BC
3,2. Lowest class	AB	B		B, B, B, BC	

AB, BC, and AC signify that the same respondents showed two inclinations.
The X column and x row of Table 20.1 (five respondents in all) are excluded from analysis. Among the remaining 89 respondents, based on the recorded data, 41 exhibited neither inclination A, B nor C. Hence this table shows the relative positions of the remaining 48 respondents.

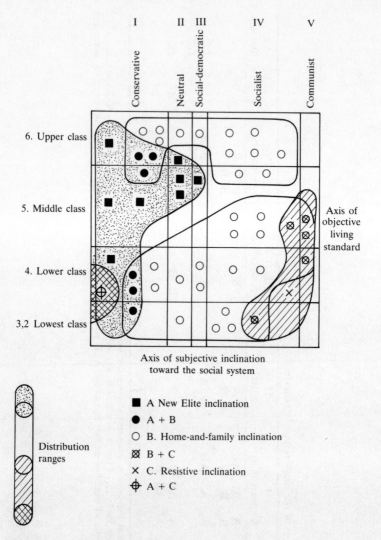

Figure 20.3 *Distribution of the three response patterns*

and-family inclination, which shows up notably more often than in the conservative segment.

But the most interesting phenomenon that shows up in Figure 20.3 is the prominence of the New Elite inclination among what is often called the upper-middle class. In this area, inclinations toward higher status, company-related study, development/recognition of abilities, rising in the company, and 'trying my hand as an entrepreneur' are very strong. From another angle, the home-and-family inclination here is indentedly weak; the context of this shortfall is worth a moment's inspection, before we return to the picture of those aspirants to the elite.

The two types of home-and-family inclination

The upper-class and lower-class home-and-family devotees who surround that indentation seem on the surface to express the same domestic tendency. But the verbatim data shows that they are actually rather different. The upper-class domestic types said things like this:

- *Mr A (late twenties, office worker in a large company, university graduate, Liberal Democratic Party supporter)*: A life worth living: 'Seeing the children's faces.' Hardships: 'Hardships? I don't have any . . . [thinks for a moment] Nothing comes to mind. . . . Right now, I'm very happy.' Interviewer's remarks: 'Young couple living in an enviable apartment, pretty wife and cute three-month-old baby, easygoing attitude and good temperament. Probably no hardships would turn up even with searching inquiry.'
- *Mr B (early forties, specialist in government employ, university graduate, Socialist Party supporter)*: A life worth living: 'Since everything is going smoothly in my life and my work, what I live for is to raise the children.' Hardships: 'I have no problems. At work and at home, my own feeling is that everything is going well.' (The reason for his politics: 'Because our union backs the Socialist Party.')

Compare with the following quotations from lower-class home-and-family types:

- *Mr C (early forties, office worker in a small company, old-system middle school graduate, Socialist Party supporter)*: A life worth living: 'Well, in my case, at any rate I have to keep supporting the family.' Hardships:

'Well, prices are high, you know, I suppose it's the same
for everyone.'

- *Mr D (late thirties, office worker in a medium-sized
  company, old-system middle school graduate, Socialist
  Party supporter)*: A life worth living: 'Just working and
  educating the child, you know, we've only got the one.'
  Things desired: 'When you come right down to it, a
  house.' Important things: 'What's important? Why, it's
  only the child, that's the only thing I'm living for.'

The nuances are indeed very different, pointing up a 'contented'
home-and-family type and a 'humble' home-and-family type.
These states of mind seem to reflect *fulfillment* in working life
and *frustration* with working life.

The marginal elite as the apex of ideology

In the intermediate area, where there is neither complete fulfillment nor thorough frustration, an enthusiastic inclination toward
'work' is most easily born.

This is the likely vicinity of the axis of white-collar segmentation. It is here that there is the actual chance, via one's own
frantic efforts, of 'survival' as one of the elite, and at the same
time, lacking the same, the potential of failing to rise into the
elite. These are the sort of people who most ardently devote
themselves to acquiring qualifications and skills, and to voluntarily attending on-the-job training classes and seminars, and
these are the main supporters of the recurring 'booms' in management science and specialization. In short, this is the white-
collar marginal elite.

The modern revival of do-or-die ideology

There was once another sort of marginally successful group in the
Japanese middle class. The segmentation of the old agricultural
middle class left some farmers on top, some on the bottom, and
some along the somewhat flexible boundary, and there were identifiable differences of mentality. The upper stratum adopted a
relatively modern sensibility as they developed a modernized form
of agricultural enterprise. In the lower stratum there was the
additional aspect of a breakaway from the traditional sensibility,

as a result of their proletarianization. The middle layer of farmers, those straddling the axis of segmentation, were in a situation where they might 'rise upward' if they strove desperately as family units, and at the same time without such effort they could easily fall into an untenable position. In order to justify their endless self-exploitation of family labor, the middling farmers tended most strongly to retain the dyed-in-the-wool agriculturalist ideology.

A similar phenomenon is apparent in the marginal elite who straddle the contemporary white-collar axis of segmentation. In the vicinity of the dividing line, among those who must strive frantically if they are to reach elite status, the radical 'do or die'-style ideology is most markedly visible. Scrambling for a few hours each night to 'study for the company job' on one's own volition, and thereby effectively extending one's work time, is a form of self-exploitation which is directly comparable with that of the earlier generation of small freeholding farmers.

For today's salarymen, as for yesterday's farmers, the reality of life at the edge produces a subjective sense of fulfillment, an inversion of insecurity into a new 'life purpose.'

In terms of the modern Japanese experience, this intensity of ideology could be viewed as a transmigration of agriculturalism into urban mass society. Agriculturalism in its original form was justified by attaching a special meaning to the work of its carriers, through the venerable idea (and political slogan) that 'farming is the base of the nation.' 'Transmigrated agriculturalism' glorifies its white-collar workers as shining lights of the new age and leaders of innovation, based on the idea of the 'age of specialization.' The effect in either case is to outwardly enhance one's significance, and inwardly spur the desire for exertion.

The difference is that, as opposed to the reactionary bent of agriculturalism, which consists in part of nostalgia for the bygone time when farmers were truly 'the base of the nation,' the mentality of the New Elite inclination has a *futuristic* bent, in that it contains the dream of a coming era when the white-collar class is actually the backbone of society.

Hence today's code-of-battle attitudes – the vogue for 'grit and determination' and the revival of the 'samurai spirit' – are not to be dismissed as simple reactions or anachronisms. The ideology may range far and wide for bases of legitimacy, but it's roots lie in the inevitable reality of the *contemporary* white-collar condition in Japan.

21   Desires and Uneasiness of the Marginal Elite

The life design of the new specialist

The white-collar 'class' is coming apart, along a seam that stretches across the spectrum of technical, managerial and sales occupations. The segmentation, as was detailed in the previous chapter, is occurring along an axis between workers who serve as 'brains' and those who serve as 'hands.' In short, creative decisionmaking and control are increasingly the preserve of well-paid, sometimes 'glamorous' specialists; while the jobs of the majority of technicians, general office workers, and sales and service staff tend to become more machine-oriented, less interesting, and harder to move up from.

This chapter explores the sorts of self-awareness, and the nature of the ambitions and anxieties that are embraced by the new breed of specialists and specialist candidates. My investigation took the form of roundtable talks with groups of veteran and aspiring systems engineers, chartered accountants (certified public accountants) and copywriters. These particular types of professionals were selected as representatives of the three basic types of white-collar work (technical, managerial, sales), and also because they are widely viewed as exemplars of today's so-called New Elite. (A recent issue of a leading business magazine aimed at white-collar readers identified the five most 'elite' occupations as Electone organ demonstrators, copywriters, computer programmers, small-business consultants, and chartered accountants.)

I shall first present records of my interviews of the three groups, and then proceed to discuss some of the trends and issues which are pointed up in the discussions. The actual interviews were frank and informal conversations, lasting several hours each. I have substantially compressed them into the following verbatim excerpts, which focus on the interviewees' descriptions of their motives for choosing their present professional courses, their plans for the future, and their job-related dissatisfactions and problems. (The interviews were conducted in neutral conference rooms at various locations in Tokyo.)

1 Chartered accountants

A: Auditor for a public corporation, age 44
B: Management consultant, 30
C: Accounting staff member in a rubber company, 24
D: Business staff member in a pharmaceutical company, 28

A: I've been working in the corporation for 20 years, and recently my superiors encouraged me to freely choose my position, so I made what I thought was the best use of that opportunity.

– Is accountancy certification necessary for your work?

A: It will help with my work, but I think it was actually a step beyond my scope of service. Moving as far as possible into the business circles, you know . . . The truth is that I had my future in mind. In management jobs we usually retire at 55.

D: I entered my company ten years ago, after I finished high school, and I've been doing office work in the business section. Recently I was transferred by the company, and I'm studying at my own expense, in order to get managerial credentials.

– Privately?

D: On the quiet to my company. (Laughter) Eventually I hope to join the roster of a 'talent bank.'

– If a good chance comes along, then, you'd make a change?

D: For now, I'm sitting tight with my present company. I see the talent bank as a means of security once I'm past the fixed retirement age. . . . But if everything goes well, I think I might leave the company for a management opportunity somewhere else.

B: After I graduated from Chūō University, I worked briefly in a foreign-owned accounting firm, then spent two years in someone else's office, and now I'm on my own as an independent management consultant. I think my character just isn't suited to company employment. I'm a qualified tax specialist, but a tax specialist has fairly low standing in a company, and the range of activities is limited, so I thought it would be a good idea to get the accountancy credential. My ideal for the future would be to set up a management consultancy with about 100 employees. Not just tax specialists and accountants – I'd want to have lawyers and personnel specialists and market researchers as well, so that we'd be able to handle any kind of management problems that might come up.

C: After finishing high school, I went through the commerce department night school at Chūō University while working in my present company. For me, the reason for seeking acountancy certification is not to get a high salary or to be able to go independent. I've seen men older than myself who expected to become section chiefs when they reached 40, but they didn't make it, because something changed, for example a new division chief came in. I've realized that being a salaryman is not a pleasant fate, that the organization is a cold place. You work like crazy, then when you're 40 you're stabbed in the back. What can you do? The point is, you have to have a skill of your own, you have to get some kind of competence that will make them scout you out. I'd like to quit when I'm 30. I think 30 should be the retirement age. But setting up my own business would be unrealistic, that's only a dream. So what should I do? . . . Constant self-examination and constant effort, that's the only way. Endless self-examination and effort. for me. The way I see it, we owe our lives to the company. I'd like to see the wage system based on job capability, not on the 'market basket' guarantees that the union stands for . . . I'm studying to be an accountant so that I can work in a company job with my own motivation.

– In your work as accountants, do you have any dissatis-factions, any particular problems?

B: There are some contradictions between the logic of the accountant's position and the policies of the company. To be specific, there are problems with things like reserve funds and dating of audits. One problem I see is the practice of auditing only with prior notice.

C: For accountants, I think it's getting to be difficult now to carry on without some practical understanding of management.

D: When you do the audit, it is indispensable to understand the operational structure and the internal control system, especially to figure out the flow of the books. But it is rather difficult . . .

B: Then again, sometimes you don't want to see things clearly, because you'd learn too much about one of your clients who's cooking the books. You're drawn into conspiracy with the businessmen, you're right in the middle, and if something goes strange, you're completely stuck. I think that was the story in the Sanyō Special Steels scandal, for example.

D: There are a lot of entrepreneurs who don't have a sense of social responsibility, and don't see the need for auditing. Their feeling is that no one has the right to invade the 'privacy' of a private enterprise.

B: In Japan, an accountant's prestige is not yet very solid, and the compensation and benefits are insufficient, so I think we're in a bit of a weak position. To strengthen our footing, and to prevent collusion with individual firms, I think we need to form a chartered accountants' union.

2   Systems engineers

E: General-operations staff member in a computer company, age 29

F: Teacher in a computer science school, 27

G: Student at a systems-analyst training school, 23

H: Computer-center staff member in an advertising company, 26

E: My major at university was business administration. I've been aiming to be a management consultant, and I started with computers because from now on I think they'll be important weapons for the management consultant.

F: I finished an electronics engineering course and then spent two years in the navy, which I quit, well, for various reasons, and then I joined the school.

G: While I was taking a computer class at university, someone said I should become an operator, and that's how I got involved.

H: I did maths at university, and since I wanted to go into advertising, I joined an agency branch. From there I was transferred to headquarters.

 – What is the age distribution of the students in computer science schools?

E: From 18 to about 50.

G: The older people come because their compaies are introducing computers. The younger ones are mostly in their twenties, with about a fifty-fifty breakdown between people sent by their companies and people who come to get the skills on their own initiative.

– What kind of jobs, what kind of status do they tend to have?

E: They come from all kinds of companies, all kinds of occupations. Most of them are regular company employees.

G: They do programming for the first year and then get into systems in the second year, but only about one person in ten goes on to systems.

H: At my company, they take in graduates of Fuji Gakuin (a junior college) as operators, send them to night school for four years, and after about five years they put them in programming. After two or three years of programming, they put them into systems, but only those who show aptitude.

– So they are mostly women . . .

G: They are mostly women, but most women stop at the operator level, or at the highest, in programming.

E: I think they're aiming to be programmers. They're no good in systems.

H: Programmers aren't actually specialists. Systems engineers are different . . .

– All of you are in systems engineering. Tell me, do you really have the feeling that you're on the cutting edge of the era?

H: What I learned for sure after I took this job is that I hate systems. We're using a General Electric computer (imported), and about three months after it was installed an improved version came out with a completely changed operating system. I can't stand the feeling of keeping up with machines, as if human beings are just being scrapped.

G: I think it's because the users are arbitrarily making too many modifications.

F: The maker and the user have different points of view, don't they?

G: You're forced to keep studying, and that's true on the maker's side, too. Computers progress with amazing speed, they have a momentum of their own. What's more, a system design usually takes about a year, so by the time that job is finished, things are very different from when it was started.

H: It's miserable to be under the whip of technological progress.

– The maker's side is the driving side?

G: We all constantly feel *driven* to try to catch up with IBM.

– Do you intend to continue as specialists for the long term? If at a certain age you were given the chance to switch over to the generalist track to become, say, a department chief, which would you choose, the lifestyle values of the specialist or the status of a management job?

E: I'd take the management job. From the start I've been interested in human-relations problems.

G: As long as I were on the maker's side, I'd want to remain a specialist. On the user's side, I'd go with management.

F: If I were with a user, after going a certain distance I'd switch over and become a generalist. Or else I might try my hand as an independent management consultant. I've known of many successful cases from the school.

E: A specialist has to have stamina. In computers, especially, your twenties are when you have the aptitude.

D: If the seniority system doesn't change, it's not just us, but the companies who won't be able to survive.

3   Copywriters

J: Planner in an advertising company, 23
K: Homemaker, 24 (female)
L: General-affairs staff member in a publishing company, 19 (female)
M: Manufacturing staff member in a machinery company, 26
N: Designer in a printing company, 26

J: I graduated in English literature, and I'm with a ten-person production company that does subcontract work for Hakuhōdō [a major advertising firm].

K: After high school I spent about five years as a typical female office clerk. But a woman has to have some kind of skill, in case her husband dies early, for example. . . . I feel that I need to have some means of self-support, so I'm taking a course in small-business management, and I'd like to combine that with something related to copy. I've always liked writing poetry and haiku.

L: I joined the general-affairs section of my company, but the job contents are boring. I hate being used by others. I'd like to use my head, and the writing aspect of copywriting attracts me. I think it would be wonderful to penetrate into people's minds.

N: I did economics at university, and now I'm in my third year with a securities printing firm. Most of the customers leave the designs up to us, and I was interested in being a copywriter. I've liked writing poetry ever since I was a child, and I prefer writing in the third-person rather than the first-person style. I wanted to be a journalist, but I was turned down by about six publishing and newspaper companies. (Laughter) So I went with a printing company, since at any rate it had to do with words in print. For the future I'm not set on being a specialist copywriter. If possible, I'd like to get into publishing. I'd like to be an editor writing captions for publications.

M: I moved to Tokyo after graduation from a technical high school, and I work during the day as an engineer in a large factory. My job is mechanical design, but it's dull. There's no creativity. Since I've always liked writing poetry and fiction, I went to school and studied scenario writing. I got interested in copywriting as a way of connecting my engineering work with my love of writing. I was lucky enough to have a hand in a good piece of work which won a publicity conference prize, and that has given me a genuine desire to continue.

J: I don't like work that isn't creative. I always want to observe myself, but you can't observe yourself if you're alone. I need a dialogue process to observe myself in.

At first I wanted to be a *rakugo* performer (old-style comedian). Then I thought I'd like to be an announcer, but an announcer does nothing but read scripts written by others. I always want to rebel. Rather than doing any single thing, it's diverse activities for me. I want to do a variety of things. I'm aiming for diversified management of life. Diversified management based on a solid product.

K: At first I thought I could be a copywriter even if I were married, that I could work as a freelance and the two would be compatible. Then I took some classes and heard that from now on the freelance route won't work, so I'm wondering what to do. But more than pursuing a profession, what's right for me is to live a happy life doing something that interests me.

L: If it seemed possible, I'd like to follow a profession. But I don't think it would work as a freelance. Having come this far, it seems that I have some kind of dream. But I don't necessarily have my heart set on being a copywriter.

M: If I have the chance, I'd like to take up a profession. The problem is the chance. It's hard being freelance, so rather than going the entrepreneurial route, I'd like to become a company employee. At any rate, I want to have people, not machines, as my partners. The copywriting world is something that has a wonderfully modern appearance, but in fact the thing is that you work with regular people, down-to-earth types.

J: Look at what we're doing. We're not the sort of people who sit and talk behind closed doors, are we?

M: The hard thing about going it alone is not just the creative aspect – you need to have some position in a company. You can't make it without understanding production processes, and you have to know about marketing, too. Individual talent by itself is not enough.

N: That's where we're different from designers. A designer expresses his own individuality. A copywriter has to express not just his own individuality, but the individuality of the product and the company as well.

– While you work as copywriters, do any of you harbor a secret desire to step out in the literary world, like Kaikō Ken or Yamaguchi Hitomi [copywriters-turned-successful novelists]?

N: I do have that feeling.

M: Certainly I do.

J: The down-and-out literary types who do it because they like being able to write – I think those days are over. From now on I think you have to approach it like an art director, as teamwork between the idea types and the technical types and the marketing types.

N: We're focusing here on specialists, but actually you could say that a copywriter is an anti-specialist.

M: Take someone like me, I'm restless if I can't be doing at least two things.

N: You run into a lot of people who are very full of themselves, who don't really want to be set in a frame. If it were possible to work freelance I don't think we'd see quite so much of that. It's because before they started, they imagined it would be more freestyle. I think that has something to do with it, but anyway, you can't make it without working in a company.

– What kinds of things would you like to work with?

421

N: Liquor. You get to project a mood.

M: Mechanical products. I can put my engineering experience to good use.

K: Rather than some 'thing,' I want to do work that gives people a sense of value. If life becomes affluent, then the same old product takes on enhanced value. New markets can be cultivated by delivering that new sense of value.

– Say in one case you have a product that really has more value than other products, and you sell it by telling everyone about that extra value. And say in another case you have a product that is in fact inferior to other products, or has about the same value, and you sell it by making it appear to have value. In which case do you really feel your worth as a copywriter?

N: In the second case, naturally.

J: The second case. Let's be honest about it – the copywriter's job is to make clothes for a corpse, to put the makeup on the corpse. To decorate the dead man for all we're worth.

K: Giving character to things that don't have character.

Life as a business

These three roundtable talks suggest that the new specialist has rather widely varying characteristics. For one thing, this multiplicity itself is an outstanding characteristic of the new specialists as a group.

Overall, the accountants seem to be the group for whom the traditional white-collar temperament, centered around corporate office work, remains the strongest. The tendency toward a radical life design, filled with urgency and zeal to cultivate a career, is naturally strong among older people who are dissatisfied with their prospects in the organization, as well as among younger people who feel handicapped in some area such as education. In the context of the white-collar split outlined in the previous chapter, the accountants most classically embody the condition of anxiety about relative eclipse and the imperative to struggle for 'survival.'

The systems engineers, on the contrary, display the confidence and ambition of those 'on the leading edge,' even as they talk of their misgivings and disaffections. In this sense, they are the group who best represent the enthusiasm of the new specialists *as the elite* of today.

While those two groups are trading on specialized skills, the copywriters epitomize the talent-intensive new professional, and they show some resistance to the term 'specialist.' On the other hand, they are the group who best typify the emergent elite in that they espouse the most extreme, clearcut form of the philosophy-of-life of the new professional operating in today's environment.

The outstanding conceptual pattern which these different groups have in common is a way of thinking that views *life as a business*. They constantly talk in terms of the 'marketability' of their skills, the 'diversified management' of their careers, the 'basic merchandise value' of their lives. This attitude squares with the ambient intellectual climate, typified by this paragraph from a book aimed precisely at those belonging and aspiring to the New Elite:

The operative goal of [the 'pro salaryman'] is career development, the constant expansion of a life centered on work achievements. For him, the 'client' is society. His objective is to sell the 'wares' of his abilities and his work. His daily wages are the 'proceeds.' The enterprise of his career is founded and opens its doors for business when he accepts employment or enters a company. Before choosing his job, he should conduct market research by examining various companies, in order to effectively merchandise his aptitudes and skills. His acceptance of employment or entry into the company marks the start not only of business dealings, but also of career development activities. Career development requires constant new investment (buying books, taking in nourishment). When he rises to the chief clerk's position, his sphere of activities is sharply expanded. By becoming a specialist he increases his knowledge and skills in particular fields. Those are the moments when 'business expansion' is undertaken. . . . And when his operating goals and the client's purchasing policy diverge, he quits the company. He cultivates a new client and changes jobs.

Morimura Minoru, *Supesharisuto jidai (Age of the Specialist)*

423

There, in a nutshell, is the mentality of the new breed of specialists.

Posture toward the opened system

If working life is likened to the management of an enterprise, then the nation has replaced the company as the sphere of operations. The cracking of the traditional protective barriers – lifetime employment and seniority ranking – has brought on an era of 'trade liberalization.' Since the individual's rivals are now to be found outside as well as inside the company, the skills and experience and secrets of success which circulate only within one's own company are no longer enough. One has to acquire 'international competitiveness' to deal with the expanded system. Inevitably, a new set of fears and expectations is born.

How are the candidates for elite status coping with the advent of the open system? Their basic strategy for 'international competitiveness' lies precisely in preparing for the chance to make an 'overseas advance,' either independently or with the aid of a talent scout. The watchwords are 'negotiable skills' and 'scoutable abilities.'

They know that the times have changed, and in their image of the career situation, the ever-present anxiety about failure is overshadowed by a keen sensitivity to the new opportunities and dreams that have opened up. Their demands have shifted away from the life-maintenance posture which the unions pursue, and moved toward aggressive expectations of rewards commensurate to abilities, qualifications, and talents.

The mentality of liberation and its refractions

In terms of patterns of consciousness, the accumulation of 'marketable skills' represents a liberation from the spell of the single company. 'If the seniority system doesn't change, it's not just us, but the companies who won't be able to survive.' Behind that statement lies a double layer of audacious confidence: the demand for adequate compensation, plus the idea that 'even if the company goes under, I'll survive.'

That posture is most sharply apparent among the super-elite systems engineers, who are the most convinced of their special status. In contrast, the accountants and copywriters find themselves 'liberated' from the specific company whether they like it or not. This attitude breaks down further into (1) a turnabout of the sense of dependency, as seen among the accountants who say they can no longer expect lifetime assurance from the company; and (2) a revulsion against life within the company, as seen among the copywriters who resent being managed.

Other realities intercede to refract their sense of liberation. As things stand, those two groups can bring their abilities to flower only within the frame of the company. The accountants face the dilemma of an inescapable reliance on the company and an inherent professional standpoint of independence from the company. For the copywriters the paradox is that they entered the profession cherishing dreams of independence and individual expression, only to find that their working life has no meaning until it is absorbed into the image of the individuality of a product or a company, and their attitude accordingly shades into cynical defiance and self-abuse.

(1968)

22 Hell of Eyes: A Case Study of an Alienated Youth

The City is not a panorama of buildings, bridges and streets. Nor is it a static structure of several classes or a dozen districts. The City is a giant, teeming set of countless lives of individuals, each of whom is aiming to *live unlimitedly*.

Nagayama Norio is one young person who actually lived in the modern Japanese city. This chapter unfolds along the axis of NN's documented life story, but it is not about him. It is instead an attempt to define some part of the *actual significance of the City for one human being*, and to describe aspects of the urban situation which are thrown into relief when a young man tries to live unlimitedly.

I Wind and shadow trail: a blank identity

Metropolis envisioned: the city as somewhere else

In 1965, upon his graduation from the Itayanagi township middle school in Aomori prefecture, NN went up to Tokyo as part of a group of local young people who were seeking work. He carried a Boston bag which contained: 'Two white shirts, two pair of work trousers, one pair of street trousers, two plain shirts and two sets of underwear and socks, all packed by his mother, as well as several middle-school textbooks which he himself had chosen.'[1]

The number of fresh middle-school graduates flowing into the Tokyo-Yokohama metropolis that year was 48,786 (along with 62,229 high-school graduates). Conversely, of the 54,242 persons including NN who graduated from middle school in the Tohoku region, some 33,526 or more than 60 per cent found employment outside their native prefectures; 20,876 of them flowed into Tokyo-Yokohama.[2] NN's three elder brothers were already working in the Tokyo area.

NN found work at the Nishimura Fruit Parlor in front of Shibuya Station. A supervisor recalled: 'He was a very diligent worker, our records show he was one of the best we had at the time. At the start we were a little concerned about the high absence rate in his school record, and his character was rather gloomy, but we put those down to the influence of his impoverished family background, and gradually we stopped worrying about him.' Another colleague said he was 'unusually short, with a pale complexion . . . the type who did his work without saying anything.' It is also known that NN was the first among the new crop of employees to let his hair grow out and wear neckties.

Toward the end of his training class, the new employees were asked, 'Who pays your wages?' After several answers of 'The owner,' NN was the only one to earn the instructor's praise by answering 'The customers.' This point had in fact been covered in the training text. The boy who was an indifferent school student had turned into one who carefully did his homework, which suggests what high stakes he had placed upon going up to Tokyo.

NN and his six siblings were raised mainly by his mother, amid such poverty that he was mocked by his classmates, sometimes for being 'stupid.' He often had to miss school because he could not quit working at such jobs as newspaper delivery, and he gradually lost interest in the classes. Although he managed to complete all three years of middle school, he was present less than half the time; during the entire second year he attended only 32 days of school.

NN 'suddenly became interested in school and began wanting to attend after the end of the third-year winter vacation, when there began to be evident excitement among his classmates about going on to high school or finding work. One snowy evening, he appeared at the home of his teacher S to ask, "Will I be able to graduate?" S told him that he could if he came to school every day, but there was no chance if his poor attendance continued. He then pleaded tearfully, with his shoulders hunched and neck trembling, "Whatever happens, I want to graduate. I want to go to Tokyo to work." ' After that, he never missed a day.

NN was staking his life on the anticipated liberation of Going Up To Tokyo.

Later, when he was a laborer in the Tokyo area, no matter

how hard he had just worked, NN would instantly grow angry if served mugimeshi (a mixture of boiled barley and rice, usually considered a poor person's meal). 'Mugimeshi makes me remember my Aomori years, it gives me a feeling that I just can't stand.' If he happened to walk along a lane with a filthy open sewage ditch: 'Those alleys remind me of my Aomori years, which automatically gives me a feeling of self-hatred.'

NN's highly inflated expectations for 'going up to Tokyo' were based not on the reality of Tokyo itself, but on an intense, persistent *hatred of his home.* Predictable though it may seem, the evidence of his orientation toward escape from the poverty and stagnation of his village highlights the city's *Etre pour autrui* or existence-for-others, its substance as a *mirage* projected from outside. Going-up-to-the-metropolis comes first and creates the image of Tokyo, rather than the other way around.

Two points should be confirmed here. First, the village which NN hates so much is not a village of the original communital model, but a village whose matrix has been eroded and dissolved by the operative modes of the modern industrial system, a village which is *a community destroyed* through the remote effects of the City. (Here I shall forego a concrete demonstration of this point through detailed analysis of NN's attitudes toward his family and village.)

Second, as implied by the quotations above, NN's hatred for the home is of a sort which must reside in internalized *self-hatred.* It infects the very core of his identity.

Some examples of how NN speaks of his family: 'From my second year of middle school up to the spring of my third year, the person who calls herself my mother would bring two men with her into that house and give me two or three hundred yen and chase me off to the nearby movie theater . . .' 'And when it was getting to be time for me to go up to Tokyo, that lady who calls herself my mother and my two younger sisters were bubbling about how once I was gone from that tenement house they would "make [festive] red rice and celebrate." ' And:

> The child who would instantly
> Cry when he felt resentful
> Became an adult, a hateful adult
> . . . .

Became a man whose heart was heavy with loneliness
Became a man who feels no love
You ask why?
Why must you ask?

A social structure which rends the fabric of connections among family members and neighbours prescribes a child's experience in a certain way, stamping the grown-up with a certain *character*, something that is hardly possible (if not impossible) to overcome even when one is able to recognize it. Here we may peep into this cruel mechanism.

Early on, when the family moved from Hokkaido to Itayanagi, they lived at first in a single room that was separated from a saloon by a single sheet of plywood. The child NN drilled a hole in the plywood and peeked through it every evening, and when the saloonkeeper covered the hole, he would promptly drill another.

Kamata Tadayoshi, who researched the details of NN's life, wrote as follows about this episode: 'What was this matter of obstinately continuing his peeking, despite repeated warnings? He had discovered what amounted to an utterly "different world" from that of household life, a place that produced a hubbub night and day . . . He bored through the plywood and sat next door, clutching his empty stomach and constantly staring at the spectacle of their "different world." '

NN was inordinately fond of films. It is true that there happened to be a cinema across from the house where he spent his childhood. But over and above that, might it not be because a film, like the hole in the plywood, is a means to *set the spirit free from life*?

For the majority of villagers who are a bit better off today than NN was, the television tube now serves as the little peephole that bores through the walls of region and class. It draws the spirit into a 'different world,' toward a reference group quite separate from the membership group. It produces a *visual orientation* toward Somewhere Else, Away from Here.

Peeping. Dreaming. Freeing the mind from life. A means of 'escape' from inescapable reality. But at the same time, a means which promotes awareness of the self as, at best, something deficient, and discloses reality as something flawed, problematic.

It may indeed serve as a safety valve to keep things 'under control,' but at the same time it builds up an unchecked energy of negation in the minds of those of us who live in a negative reality.

Later, in prison, NN wrote this poem:

Beneath the glittering lights of the splendid silver chandelier
Upon the red carpet, the virtuous people of the world
Enjoy themselves, a warmth suffuses the pleasant chatter
In the chamber where hearts steep in mellowed homemade
   cognac

Flowers blooming with French accents and various perfumes
The women in chic white dresses, the men in white tuxedoes
Seven musicians play their Wurlitzers to melt the hearts
Of ladies and gentlemen wearing smiles as they dance

For me on my side watching the dream, there is . . .
An aluminum cup, a grimy table on black tatami, a slatted
   board on the toilet
The dialogue I hear is the fighting rhythms and frightful words
   of yakuza

Were it all smashed away with the dignified jailer's devil face
Then would I see the dream that wipes you all away
For I need no words of sympathy, and I need the time to
   dream.

He describes the scene of that 'different world' glimpsed, as if projected on a screen, through the peephole of a dream which wears away a bit of the wall of class division, and sings of his love for the 'time to dream.'

While Kamata approached NN from the viewpoint of 'peeping,' Terayama Shūji stressed 'running.' The youth peeps, then quickly runs – rejecting the liberation of the imagination, believing instead in the release of direct action.

For NN just after he had gone up to Tokyo, the capital must have been a 'different world' of virtually unlimited possibility – in the same sense as the saying among the fishermen of Minamata that Kumamoto is 'a fine city as long as you don't go there.'

Why did his small travel bag contain textbooks from the middle school classes he had usually skipped? Later, NN tried two or three times to complete part-time high school, revealing the passion, so intense as to be steadily cool and calm, of his resolve to 'remake his life' when he went up to Tokyo.

Golden eggs: the paradox of commodity manpower

We have outlined the repulsive force of the home village which thrust one young man toward the city, and the form it took as feelings of negativity in his particular life.

Rural Japan in general has been serving as a pool of 'latently surplus population' throughout the process of modernization, silently delivering cheap manpower for the purposes of the metropolis. The villages have been 'domestic colonies' of the nation, stagnating in poverty as their remote communities erode and dissolve. This social climate has produced a fundamental split in the mentality of villagers, leaving them stamped with characteristic self-negation.

NN expresses and embodies not the average value, but a single *limiting value* of the *existential meaning* of that social structure. The phenomena of dualized consciousness and self-hatred could be further dissected, to describe less outstanding configurations among migrating young people in general, such as a vague country-bumpkin complex, or a converse sense of village solidarity and anti-Tokyoite-ism, or hypersensitive self-consciousness about speech and dress and hair style, and the corresponding, characteristic internal colorations.

From our perspective along the line of repulsive force, NN's extremeness allows him to serve as a sort of litmus paper – a highly sensitive receptor, a revelatory medium for understanding the logic of the City he enters.

Let us consider the city which absorbs him in terms of its *attractive force*. For the moment we turn away from NN's peculiarities, to survey the general situation which awaits the tens and hundreds of thousands of people arriving over the years.

In 1965, the year NN went up to Tokyo, some 448,000 middle-school graduates sought work nationwide, while the number of vacancies open to them was 1,668,000 – 3.72 times higher (for high-school graduates the factor was 3.50). On average, three to four job offers awaited each middle-school graduate in Japan. Of course greater Tokyo was the area with the highest demand

and, as is well known, Tohoku was its major supplying region. In 1970 there were 22.84 jobs per applicant in Tokyo-Yokohama – 216,843 middle-school-grad openings and 9,494 such jobseekers. In short, NN and his fellow Itayanagi graduates had a surfeit of big-city admirers.

Repulsion on one hand, attraction on the other. No contradiction whatsoever, no problem, on the surface.

On the inside, the youth who quit the village and beat paths to the city clearly embrace hopes of liberation. They aim to live life to the fullest. The city supposedly demands and welcomes young people, but that is a lie, or at least not the whole truth. What the city demands is not youngpeople, but only *fresh manpower*. What the city welcomes is *not* free human beings who are determined to live unlimitedly.

Each unit of 'fresh manpower' is an individual seeking to open up his or her life, all the more for being young. It is precisely this gap between the needs of youth and the needs of the city which lies at the core of the so-called 'migrant youth problem' that is much discussed in officialdom, the mass media and academia.

In contrast to the urban influx described by Engels and by Yokoyama Gennosuke for the early stage of capitalism, in the case of the Japanese city from the 1960s onward, what awaits the new arrivals is not a bare subsistence wage. Sustenance and the reproduction of flesh (and labor) are now guaranteed, and with perseverance one might well be able to operate a respectable home. If only these boys and girls were content to be nothing more than 'manpower.'

In the logic of the city, which demands and welcomes the young immigrants only for the material value of their lives, as 'golden eggs,' the aspirations to freedom cherished by those 'eggs' are something surplus, an embarrassment, an uninvited guest.

A golden egg is a fine thing for its 'owner,' but not at all for the embryo that lives inside it. When the eggshell is made of gold, the inner process of maturing and breaking out of the shell will be discouraged. The living being will be left to rot and petrify within the hard physical casing.

Newly arrived middle-school graduates were known as 'golden eggs' in 1960s Japan because they were cheap and efficient manpower. The ambient image of working youth from the countryside as 'naive, eager and tenacious' is a tacit condition of the job offer. The deeper significance of the metaphor is the *eyes* which expect them to behave in conformity to this image.

As 'golden eggs' they are welcomed, indulged, and handled very gingerly by the employers who are short of help. But only so long as they resemble motivated domestic animals, and fill the bill as patient, hardworking young manpower. In the eyes of the employers, nothing is so unwelcome and provocative as the desire of these young people to live unlimitedly. 'After I've taken such good care of him, how arrogant can he get?' 'Don't they teach morals anymore?' 'I can't understand today's young people.'

From the moment they arrive in the city, the young rural emigrants are caught in the contradiction between their class-stipulated existence-for-others and their existence-for-themselves. They are stuck in a glue secreted by the eyes of others to restrain their flight to individual freedom.

Phantom populace: a migrant mode of existence

Aside from the police and cheap mass-consumerism, there is no particular system in place to deal with the troublesome, dreaming heart that has attached itself to the 'fresh manpower' flowing into the cities.

There is a hidden, swelling group of the spiritually unemployed who have lost sight of their destinations, who wander in the void of the big city, vanishing into the crowds on busy streets or the lonely television audience in cheap apartments.

As for the fruit parlor where NN showed so much zeal upon arriving in Tokyo, he abruptly put it behind him after six months, for a trivial reason. After a dressing-down from the dormitory supervisor for having skipped cleaning duty, he simply walked out with nothing but the clothes on his back.

He would leave another job within the year, seven within three years. The pattern would later be connected with NN's crimes, as the news reports in various media parroted the catch-phrases of 'repeated job changes,' 'rolling stone,' 'downward slide,' etc.

Yet job changes were by no means rare among young people. Just over half the nation's 1967-graduate jobseekers made a change within three years (52 per cent of middle-school and 54 per cent of high-school graduates). Nearly half of those made a

Table 22.1 *Reasons for job changes by recent graduates in Tokyo, 1964*

Reason for leaving	High school graduates			Middle school graduates	
	Manuf'g work %	Retail work %	Office or technical work %	Manuf'g work %	Retail work %
Family circumstances	28.3	30.2	37.9	22.8	16.8
Ill-suited to job	26.4	15.9	15.3	17.5	14.1
Invited to apply elsewhere	11.9	23.8	10.3	13.6	14.6
Resumed schooling	8.2	6.3	12.1	4.3	1.6
Lost confidence at work	4.4	1.6	1.7	2.5	4.3
Illness	4.4	6.3	3.4	4.0	9.2
No desire to work	1.9	1.6	3.4	4.6	1.6
Misconduct	1.9	3.2	3.4	7.0	11.4
Relations with co-workers	1.3	–	5.2	3.2	5.9
Homesickness	0.6	1.6	–	8.3	11.9
Conditions different than contracted	3.1	–	–	0.1	–
Other	2.5	3.2	3.4	3.4	5.4
Unknown	5.0	6.3	3.4	8.7	3.8

March graduates who left jobs in the listed sectors between April and September.
Source: Tokyo Metropolitan Bureau of Labor.

change during the first year. In NN's own graduating class, of the twenty who took work outside the prefecture, more than half made four or five changes over four years, one left a trail more checkered than NN's, and the whereabouts of two were unknown to the hometown families. Quitting and changing jobs had become part of the normal pattern of life for young people.

Table 22.1 shows that the reasons for job changes tend toward family circumstances, incompatibility, and receipt of other offers. In NN's initial category of middle-schooled retail workers, homesickness and misconduct are relatively high on the list. A glance at this table gives the impression that the quitting and changing are fairly 'selfish' movements, and even evokes some sympathy for the plight of the bosses.

But some other official statistics present a very different picture (Table 22.2). Poor conditions, misleading contracts, and bad equipment or environment are the main reasons cited for changing jobs, although those categories are absent or rare in Table 22.1.

Table 22.2 *Reasons for job changes by young workers in Japan, 1964*

	%
Job unsuited to physical capacity or interests	27.5
Salary, hours or other conditions unsatisfactory or different than contracted	23.5
No future	18.2
Bad equipment or environment	12.5
Relations with superiors or co-workers	10.5
Family reasons	7.8

Source: Ministry of Labor

Clearly, Table 22.1 was based on a survey of employers, while Table 22.2 was based on data from the young workers themselves. The debate over which set of figures is 'objectively' correct may be set aside for our purposes, because the glaring subjective difference between the two is the crucial point. We may assume there is some conscious lying on both sides, but over and above the issue of good faith it seems very likely that the employers, and for that matter adults as a class, really *do not know* the true reasons for the departures.

Apart from those subjective reasonings on either side, we may take as a neutral index the correlation between rates of job departure and the number of regular days off. A glance at Table 22.3 is enough to see that job shifts do display at least one sort of objective pattern. In the crystal clarity of its relation with departure rates, time off is miles ahead of such items as aptitude tests or suggestion systems or personnel policies;[3] the cleverest management techniques do not seem to make a difference. Even wage levels do not match up as well as time off. We are left with a telling clue to the nature of the desires and dissatisfactions of young employees.

Table 22.3 *Job changes and number of weekly holidays in Japan, 1965*

Weekly holidays	Rate of departure			
	<10%	10–29.9%	30–49.9%	>50%
Less than one day per week	24.3	16.7	12.1	46.9
One day per week	45.8	21.2	13.5	19.5
More than one day per week	66.7	20.2	4.4	8.9

Unit: % of companies surveyed.
Source: Ministry of Labor.

Wind and shadow-trail: a blank identity

The reason for NN's first job change was put down to a 'trivial matter.' In fact it was not just NN but the majority of job-changing youths who left their employers and the surrounding adults with that sort of impression. Might there not be a reason to be found within this very 'lack of reason'?

On one hand, the willingness to make a substantial life change for a 'trivial reason' might be connected to moments in their city lives of *a diluted sense of social existence*: a sensitivity to the randomness of existence, the uncertainty of relationships, the instability of social identity.

On the other hand, the inability of the adults to come up with anything more than the enigmatic 'reason without a reason' to explain those moments of vague indeterminacy suggests a yawning gap of incomprehension between the inner climate of the young and the social atmosphere.

These two hypotheses seem to contradict each other. If the employees have no particular reason for changing, then there is no gap in perception. If there is a gap, it would be due to 'some reason' in their minds. For the moment we may say that these are two poles of interpretation, and that either both situations or an intermediate situation may exist. But a connection may be found between those situations which stand in rather different dimensions, by returning to the situation of one of the young people who flowed into the city.

There is no remaining clue to infer the meaning or lack of meaning for NN himself of the first job change. More suggestive are the circumstances surrounding his departure, the next year, from a live-in job as a clerk in an Osaka rice shop, where he had worked very responsibly for half a year. Upon being scolded for accidentally breaking a fluorescent lamp and allowing some fragments to fall into the rice, he quit 'on the spot.' That is how the storekeeper remembers it. But based on the recollections of NN's mother:

At that time NN wrote to ask for a copy of the family register, which was sent. He answered immediately with a letter asking, 'Mother, was I born in Abashiri Prison?' He complained that he was teased by his co-workers because of his birthplace (incidentally the site of that notorious prison), in connection with a scar that came from a burn at the age of three. The closing line of the letter was, 'It's all over for me, I think I'll die.' The mother immediately went to the welfare commissioner's office to obtain a letter saying that no such thing was true, and sent it to him. But that letter came back marked 'addressee unknown' and then for a time there was no news at all from NN.

This pattern matches the latter of the two interpretations. Other people take a casual attitude toward an event and soon forget about it. But the youth feels suddenly assaulted and is reduced to desperation.

Concerning the trauma of that incident, there are two facts which should be noted. First, afterward NN limited himself to marginal jobs for which a family register was not needed, and drifted around; this may or may not have been an 'unconscious' choice.

Second, again after that time, NN was persistently obsessed with the idea of escaping the country as a *stowaway*. I present only a few of the many known details. For example, when discovered in his second attempt to stow away, he tried to commit suicide by cutting the veins of his wrist with a knife, saying,

437

'Anywhere is fine, it makes no difference as long as it's not Japan.' Later, his first murder victim was a man whose appearance on the scene interrupted his stowaway dream, and NN acted reflexively in order to protect a secret which was central to his plan.

Hence it appears that on the occasion of the family register incident, for NN the concrete imagery of liberation shifted from escaping the village by 'going up to Tokyo,' through the desperate turning point of 'It's all over for me, I think I'll die,' to escaping from the country (the totality of the village and the city) as a 'stowaway.'

When NN took his first job, he was 'very positive and enthusiastic about his work' and at the same time immediately let his hair grow out and began wearing a necktie, which is to say that he displayed a burning desire to plunge into a new existence as a young man of the city. It was nothing more than a conspicuously strong version of the desire felt by any of the young people flowing into the city.

From now on, whenever his personal history entered the discussion, NN would find his desire for freedom clearly proscribed by the others in the city, through something connected to his past home village. Those fragments of the reality of his past home village would dog him, no matter how hard he struggled in his career, like a tin can which had been affixed to his life in advance.

Before investigating that mechanism in detail, let us turn to the framework in which NN began to live as an urbanite who was, as it were, shut out by the city.

Later he made these notes under the title of 'Provincial Tokyoite': 'Tokyo is closed to me / It's quite a detestable place / I have the handicap of not knowing life anywhere else . . . / And just occasionally, just a wisp of my hometown / Right now I'm defective, but over the years I'll forget all about it / But still, I'll never be a Tokyoite / Somehow, it will show / Yes, the feeling is there, it's my speech with the local accent.'

NN's experience with his family register should be regarded as an extreme case of the experience of the many immigrants to the city. They routinely experience various negative identities such as provincial speech. They are compelled, by precisely the people whose standard of values they wish to match, to negate the hometowns which have decisively stamped the cores of their selves and identities.

As people who are doubly shut out, from the hometown and from the city, they are not so much marginal persons as they are people living in the *gap* between two societies. There is a void in their transition between conformance groups, and hence their social existence is shadowed by a deep-seated sense of uncertainty.

As noted earlier, two of NN's twenty classmates who went to work outside the prefecture were out of touch with their family homes. Indeed there are many thousands of urban immigres, mainly in their thirties and forties, who have thus gone 'missing.'[4]

A survey of NN's own written vocabulary to find what he compares himself to, what sort of concrete images he projects himself into, turns up several items that clearly spring from the identity of an *uprooted person* – a balloon (taken away by the wind), a flower petal (fluttering over walls on the wind), ash, etc. These are similar in emotional quality to a set of typical images in Japanese popular songs from about 1920 onward – water plants, rootless plants, scattered flower petals, fallen leaves, stray birds – lyrics made popular in part by the many home-forfeiting urban immigres who took joy and solace in song.

'I flew away . . . I flew away into the blue sky with no heaven and disappeared, like a balloon that is somehow possessed. But I left a dark trail of my shadow.'

Someone who is anchored in a social identity and smoothly engaged in social relations, whether happy or unhappy, is highly unlikely to compare himself to a balloon.

Later, when asked by a presiding judge about the reason for one of his crimes, NN answered, 'I don't know . . . Even now, I myself . . . don't know why . . . why I had to do it.' Other circumstantial evidence indicates that this was not a perjury designed to reduce his prison sentence. (At the time he expressed determination to accept capital punishment.)

A person's existence is so much the sum of his social relations, that the dissolving of those relations virtually dissolves his very existence. The trauma which NN evidently suffered in connection with the family register seems to have destroyed what psychologists would call his self-integration.

Despite such an extreme dilution of the sense of existence, the consequences of one's own actions still impinge upon others, and one's own future is still much determined by the consequent attitudes and reactions of others.

NN's actions and the social repercussions of his actions were indeed something of *his own*, and yet they were something alien from himself, which he could perceive only in terms of the 'the trail of my shadow.'

II A mind consumed: personal existence of social structure

The hell of eyes: the self as someone else

Much has been said about the yearning for love and the insatible loneliness of young urban immigrants. While those writings may not be mistaken, the full depth of such feelings can be grasped only by considering their linkage to desires and dissatisfactions which, at first glance, are directly opposite.

Charting the path from loneliness to love, or from indifference to caring, and using it as an abstract generalization, leads to strange, superficial conclusions which lose the reality of loneliness or love. This sort of process leads theoreticians, as well as practitioners trying to work with young people, around in circles. It even leads young people themselves around in circles, so that they no longer understand what it is that they really want.

We may approach a more realistic protrayal by observing a survey of the work-related dissatisfactions of young people who have migrated to the city of Tokyo (Table 22.4). The first two

Table 22.4 *Types of dissatisfaction of juvenile newcomers in Tokyo*

	Men	Women
Lonesome due to lack of friends	10.9%	9.9%
Unable to find girl/boyfriend	8.7	5.2
Little free time	19.3	24.9
Little pocket money	10.9	14.1
Cannot attend part-time school	2.9	8.9
Dissatisfied with work or workplace	10.0	9.9
Lack of recreation or cultural facilities	7.4	9.9
No room where I can settle down in peace	20.3	36.6

Source: Tokyo Metropolitan Government report

items, 'lonesome due to lack of friends' and 'unable to find girl/boyfriend,' correspond to the well-known longing for relationships, and the loneliness of being unable to attain them.

That sort of unhappiness does actually exist, but far more frequent are complaints of 'no room where I can settle down in peace' and 'little free time.' These are apparently longings for solitude which follow the opposite vector from that of 'longing for relationship,' and emerge as straightforward requests for privacy and freedom *from* relationships.

Of course most people would invite some of their friends into the 'room where I can settle down,' and would spend some of their 'free time' with companions. Expressed longings for solitude and for freedom from relationship may be seen as complementing rather than contradicting the longings for love and relationship.

While wanting to escape from *some* kinds of intense relationships, they desire *other* kinds. The lesson of this table is that within the daily mentalities of the young people surveyed, the repulsion *from* relationship is much more strongly sensed than the desire *for* relationship.

Turning again to the data of NN's experience, we may proceed to infer the framework underlying that polarized relational disposition. For one thing, the birthplace issue, which brought on the turning point in NN's life in the city, typifies a framework which might be called 'the spell of the past.'

By what means does the past bind the present and the future? The family register in and of itself is simply a scrap of paper, without any inherent power. What invests it with the tremendous power to totally derange the life of a human being is the practices of others who ascribe a certain significance to the paper record of his past (Abashiri = 'child of criminals' = evil, e.g.), and accordingly ridicule him, repeatedly deny him the chance for emploeement, and *limit his future.*

The past is not a living thing which works to block off a person's life path. The agency of blockage, the thing which enthralls the present and the future, is the practices of others, and especially *the eyes of others* which are persistently directed at the person. They turn the past into the person's 'present' and 'future.'

What drove NN to desperation was not the family register, but the social structure which uses the family register to discriminate. Some will protest that this is a leap in reasoning: Yes, there were co-workers who occasionally teased NN about his birthplace, and yes, there may also have been NN's own overactive 'imagination,' but no, that does not mean there is a general problem with the social structure. Such refutation is superficial, for surely the frame is a necessary part of the picture. If in our society there did not exist any framework of discrimination via the family register, then how on earth could it be the germ of 'teasing' by his co-workers, or of an 'excessive' emotional reaction?

It is the same with the 'facial injury' which became the germ of another 'joke.' Later, when he was in prison, NN wrote:

> I have grown up now to be a caged animal of a non-human person . . . I lapse into a repentant state of mind, I want to escape, but I have reconciled myself to the fact that it is absolutely impossible to get away. I have gotten a scar that is deep, deeper than the depths of the sea. The scar on my face has turned into the real thing.

> The looks and actions of others which say that a person with a scar on his face may be a criminal, can indeed program him as a criminal. I have heard about a 'yakuza' who wears the trademark dark glasses, and who in fact has a congenital ailment which requires him to wear dark glasses. He does not wear dark glasses because he is a yakuza, but it just may be that he is a yakuza because he wears dark glasses. That circuitry, which can so program the entire life of a person with a certain aspect, consists of the eyes of someone else, the gazes and acts of others.

> It has died out now, but in the old days there was a flourishing trade in Bohemia. They would capture children, and cut off their lips and compress their skulls, and keep them shut up in boxes day and night in order to obstruct the maturation process. Through this method, and others of the same sort, they would turn the children into fascinating freaks, freaks who would be the objects of wondrous reports.
> (Sartre, *Saint-Genet*)[5]

For a long time before NN was incarcerated in the Tokyo prison, he had been a prisoner of the eyes of the others in the city . . .

the knowing looks which predefine the entirety of a human being through some sort of outward appearance, be it the concrete appearance of a facial scar or the abstract appearance of a personal history sheet. NN exists in relation to others *in the form of* a facial scar, in the form of someone born at the site of a notorious prison.

Concrete superficiality consists of clothing, hairstyle, possessions and the like. Abstract superficiality consists typically of birthplace, school record and diploma. Urban existence-for-others, in the form of these superficialities, is what blocks off people's existence at the fundamental level.

Human existence consists of little more than the totality of the social relationships which one is actually involved in. The eyes which are fixed upon one's superficialities play the role of *deflecting every relationship* that a person in the city seeks to form, and thus, steadily and surely, they determine the shape of one's destiny.

Insofar as NN sought to 'live life to the fullest,' to live as a free subject always attempting to step out beyond himself, those looks in the eyes of others were nothing less than hell.

The NN of a much later time, in prison, wrote:

This must be happiness, this situation of writing so leisurely as I wish. Maybe it's not much, but up to now I have never had the chance to look back at things, never had enough time to think, so for me it's happiness. Now I am not under anyone's eyes, not distracted by fury toward anyone – because of that I am fully enjoying my own sense of happiness. Here in prison I have no complications or entanglements. To die in this state . . . I would feel that life is something which has a marvelous significance. I must say that for a human being, having the time to think . . . is happiness. It's true! *Now* I am blessed!

Thus does NN now come to acquire what he and many others like him so keenly yearned for: 'a place to settle down in peace' and 'free time.' A refuge from that hell of eyes which rudely scrutinize, classify and label him into someone utterly alien to himself.

Needless to say, the 'happiness' and 'liberation' are ironies. His prisoner's existence, under constant surveillance, subject to ultimate classification and labeling, thoroughly defenseless, was his first and his last place of refuge. What an eery light that casts on the condition of alienation as a *prisoner of relationships* in the city.

Style and diploma: the performance of the surface

The impulse to evaporate and transform is widespread in today's city, even among long-term residents, and it is surely a form of prayer for escape from the hell of eyes.

Still more routine is the attempt to manipulate the gaze of others, by acting out surface aspects of our selves. This is a means of achieving some measure of transcendence.

NN's life history before he became a habitual criminal, combined with testimony from those who knew him, reveal two focal points in the molding of his character in the city. One is his repeatedly exhibited *zeal for further schooling*. The other is his *taste for high-grade goods* related to personal adornment.

Even people who were sympathetic toward NN were put off by his fondness for display, his chic ostentation. What is the existential meaning of that exhibitionist urge?

Immediately before going up to Tokyo, not knowing that his mother had packed underwear for him, NN attempted with some of his job-seeking companions to steal from a local clothing store. The items involved, undershirts and drawers, appear to have been for the purpose of living in the capital.

In another instance of walking out of a job after a petty dispute, NN left a milk shop in the Suginami district, where his diligence had earned him the trust of the shopkeeper, leaving behind virtually all his possessions. Aside from such common items as underwear and bedclothes, they included high school textbooks and a high school identity card, as well as a hair drier. The milk dealer recalled:

When he was with us he had a passionate love for learning and worked very hard. Especially English and math, he never stopped begging for instruction in them, and we spent a lot of time together going at it. There were two older shop workers, and they were always saying how well he worked, always looking out for him. After he started high school, he told us how delighted he was to have been chosen class representative. We used to talk about how he had turned out better than anyone ever expected . . . He planned to finish at the part-time high school and go on to university night school, and live with us until he graduated. He said that himself.

Under the arbitrary branding and classification practiced by adults, enthusiastic love of learning is the mark of a 'serious young man,' while stylish ostentation is the mark of a 'frivolous young man.' In fact, both are embodiments of the same basic undertaking: the taking on of the surface behaviors by which the city passes judgement upon young people, and the attendant separation from existence as the self.

NN smoked Pall Malls even when he was working as a day laborer. He recorded a conversation that he had with the wife of a man he worked for one day. 'She said, "You like to smoke unusual cigarettes, don't you?" and I said, "Well, yes, it's a little something for show." "How old are you?" "I'm 22," I answered, and she kept probing. "Are you a university student, then?" I took a deep drag on my cigarette, and while exhaling I answered, "Used to be . . ." '

Before long NN would print up and carry calling cards with the title of 'university student.'

First were the new undershirts and the middle school textbooks. Then the hair drier and the high school textbooks. And finally, imported cigarettes and the calling card of a university student.

So long as the city used superficial aspects to discriminate among people, he would play the game on the superficial basis. One may stage concrete superficialities, such as hairstyle and cigarettes, and one may stage abstract superficialities, such as a diploma or a title. Such is the bag of tricks for squirming through the hell of eyes.

Like most 'well-adjusted' young people, NN was merely taking exactly the direction that the city demands of people, which was to give himself a facelift. A bit of effort in the clothing and hairstyle departments, a bit more in the labeling department. His props and his costume were convincing, but he played out *the role which was demanded* with a bit of *impetuousness* (Pall Malls, forged title), and it was just that which left a whiff of aberration.

Personal existence of social structure (1): a mind consumed

To understand the process of surface projection, both concrete and abstract, which NN utilized to get by, we should take up a further question. What is the significance for human beings of the strata and the classes which make up the structure of social reality in the City?

NN's diaries contain a curious parable.

> Once upon a time, and forever after – I was riding on the back of a whale, and while we were traveling merrily around the world, I ran out of food! For days I was dizzy, thirsty, tired, hallucinating about food . . . I was really in a fix. Finally I decided to talk to the whale. 'Would it be all right to eat you? You see – ' and the whale used ultrasonic waves to answer my brain waves, and all he said was, 'Nothing else to do.' I wanted to talk some more . . . I was hesitant at first, but then I ate some tiny pieces, really tiny pieces from his back. He didn't make a sound. The whale didn't say a thing. And every day we continued on our way. A worldwide journey without end! By the time I realized how sinful it was to eat him, I had already eaten one third of the whale. I apologized to the whale. The whale . . . didn't say anything. The whale was a corpse . . . From that day on I was all alone. And by the time I perceived the meaninglessness of living, I was cutting my own throat with the knife that I had been using until then to torture the whale. At the moment when the last drop of blood drained out of my brain, I understood that the whale was my own mind . . .'

What was NN trying to say here? The fragment just before the parable begins: 'What I want now is a thinking mind . . . A thinking mind is something that can work out the possibilities for the future in only an instant . . .'

In a poem which he worked on continuously in parallel with that story, NN writes of his time as a laborer in Yokohama.

> A laborer thinks only of today
> That's the full-fledged laborer, I was told

But the butt of jokes will think about next year
So no laborer talks about it seriously
Shouldering the loads along, tromp-tromp over the earth
TACHIKAWA MISAWA YOKOTA ATUGI [sic]
Just read those letters and the job goes well
Knowing any more would be bad luck, I reckon . . .

Such dismembering of the future, or dismembering of the 'thinking mind,' has much to do with the normative existence of a coolie within the economic process. The fundamental reality for the temporary laborer is that he is made to 'come here, go there' as the capital flow demands.

Writing a little earlier on the topic of happiness, NN says, 'Now I am talking about happiness in the physical sense . . . As for "mental" happiness, it can only be talked about within a decent life. For the poor, mental happiness is just a secondary problem . . .' Then he interjects, 'Ah, but even so, what agony mental poverty was for me!'

It is likely that 'mental' poverty refers not simply to knowledge and 'culture,' as opposed to physical conditions, but is related to the totality of NN's existence as a human being.

NN's loathing of mugimeshi was mentioned earlier. When this rice-and-barley dish was served in the Tokyo prison, he would eat just a little and flush the rest down the toilet. 'It's not whether I like it or not. Mugimeshi is just plain awful, it stinks of poverty.' There were some who criticized him for that, and for his love of finery, with comments such as, 'He keeps talking about poverty and so on, but he was pretty luxurious.'

We saw earlier that NN connected his hatred of mugimeshi directly to his childhood. 'All I remember of my youth is poverty.' The real source of the 'stink of poverty' was not food, but an atmosphere that left indelible, intolerable memories.

Mugimeshi does not have an inherent, physical 'stink of poverty.' There are executives and professionals who think it delicious and claim they eat it regularly. It is even used in the traditional cuisine of Kyoto. When rich people choose mugimeshi, for reasons of health or taste or whimsy, it does not stink of poverty. It only stinks of poverty when, for the person who has no other choice, it embodies the totality of a certain situation. What NN really hates is the all-pervading 'stink of poverty,' not his food.

NN's initial experience of poverty was the physiological hunger of his childhood in Abashiri and Itayanagi. After he migrated to the city, that physiological hunger was satisfied, for the moment at least, because he was a 'golden egg,' a fresh young laborer. What was by no means satisfied was the hunger arising from societal discrimination, the negativity of personal identity within society, or what might be called *existential hunger*.

His childhood experience of hunger was traumatic, for it is said that due to insurmountable poverty, his mother deserted four of her eight children, including NN, for a winter. (That all four survived is considered a 'near miracle.') The experience of being *abandoned*, as a type of *experience of relation*, left a decisive mark on NN's memory. He writes: 'It is impossible for me to conceive of kindredness. To explain in a word why it has turned out this way, the answer is that everything, everything, everything, everything is because of poverty. Ignorance is born from poverty. *And the thing called human relations is destroyed.*'

NN learned in many ways how poverty destroys and dissolves not only the family group, but also labor groups and various other social relationships. Later, in prison, he came across the following passage by Bongar, in English, which he copied down and memorized by recitation: 'Poverty kills the social sentiments in man, destroys in fact all relations between man. He who is abandoned by all can no longer have any feeling for those who have left him to his fate.'

Poverty is not a problem only on the material level of life. It is a total condition which crushes one's pride and dissolves one's future in all sorts of concrete social milieus, which snatches away the 'thinking mind,' which stamps every aspect of one's lifestyle with the 'smell of poverty,' blows apart interpersonal relations, dries up feelings, and designates a person's very existence as some sort of *shortcoming*.

What NN sought to describe in his parable of eating the whale was very likely his resentment of the fact that *poverty is something more than poverty*, that over and above the economic category it is a category of *social ontology*, that poverty eats one's mind.

'The serene child within me who died long before the ax cut my neck' (Sartre, *Saint-Genet*).

Personal existence of social structure (2): the invisible ghetto

Migrants from rural areas who flow into the cities tend in general to make up the urban lower class, as Lipset and Bendix concluded from a survey conducted in Oakland.[6] Sociologists such as Kurasawa Susumu have justified the same hypothesis for Tokyo, where the majority of immigrant job seekers are initially emloyed as laborers or, at best, as sales and service workers (see Table 22.5), and more than 80 per cent work for small businesses. Comparisons of presently held occupations show that urbanites with rural roots are disproportionately likely to be employed in blue-collar, sales or small-business jobs.[7]

Table 22.5 *Initial jobs of people moving to Tokyo to find work, 1960–1*

	%
Freelance	0
Business proprietor	16
White collar	19
Sales or physical labor	62
Other	3

It is true, of course, that this sort of class wall is not insurmountable. One of NN's brothers, the next-elder third son, had through his own efforts completed part-time high school and graduated from a university night school, and was working in the mid–1960s for a publisher of educational materials. It was this brother's example that inspired NN to plot his own future course along the high school-university-salaryman path.

NN tried more than once, but failed to follow through for a high school certificate. Completion of a part-time high school course requires higher-than-average effort, as can be inferred from the remarks of one of his teachers: 'He seemed to be a bright and serious pupil. He stopped attending after the holiday week in May, and as is often the case each year in part-time high schools, he was dropped from the roster.'

NN later wrote, 'Among those who study hard in the hope that they can manage to live a splendid life, there are some who succeed, but those people are up against virtually impossible chances so something is bound to make them stumble (like my next-elder brother).' (We do not know how the brother 'stumbled.')

I once participated on a research team which included people working in many different occupations. For the purposes of our study we had to place the occupations of contemporary society into various categories. Following standard sociological practice, we drew up such categories as self-employed and employee, and white collar and blue collar. One participant who had moved through many occupations suggested the categories of 'jobs that require curricula vitae' and 'jobs that do not require curricula vitae.' We learned a great deal from that practical classification.

For example, because of discrimination, Koreans living in Japan often fail to find work as employees, or else they give up the idea from the start, and tend to become entrepreneurs. From an abstract sociological point of view, they are taken to be non-employees and hence self-employed, or in other words, non-proletarian and hence petit-bourgeois. But the reality of their situation has nothing to do with a 'rise' in class. They became entrepreneurs only because in the Japanese system they were unable even to become proletarian employees.

This problem is by no means limited to Koreans. The numerous housewives who do piecework for companies in their homes (classed in official statistics as 'self-employed'!), elderly and middle-aged people who have lost their jobs, those who come from families of burakumin 'outcasts', and the many people whose curricula vitae contain some sort of 'stumble,' together make up a substantial portion of the 'entrepreneurs' in Japanese cities.

Those who are unable even to become 'self-employed' take up 'jobs that do not require curricula vitae.' Capital always requires a steady flow of dismissible labor, and naturally they change jobs repeatedly. Between them and the 'jobs that require curricula vitae' there is an invisible barbed-wire fence that can seldom be crossed.

The requirement of a family register and curriculum vitae has the automatic effect of proscribing a person's future with his or her past and present, with irrevocable effect.

Laborers have the freedom to choose a particular job each time, and they have the freedom to reject the job and walk away. But each of these 'free choices' is confined to the set orbit of the job-switching route, which runs only through an invisible ghetto.

The sons of the rich casually slip on sweaters and stroll along the Ginza. NN puts on a 'dapper' necktie. It is he who stinks of poverty. Tagging along behind every attempt to escape, chaperoning them home to their allotted existence, the barbed-wire framework of class and status always exists.

In his former, childhood years, NN had been strictly separated by a sheet of plywood from the 'different world' he peeped at. During adolescence, his aspiration toward that 'different world' would be embodied in an irrepressible impulse to go up to Tokyo. And as soon as he went up to Tokyo, NN climbed Tokyo Tower, accompanied by his next-elder brother T. He later noted that the view from on high over the grand city in which he had just arrived and especially of the nearby Tokyo Prince Hotel with its splendid pool and garden, was burned into his vision.

He would soon realize that between him and that splendid garden stood another, virtually insurmountable barrier. Not a sheet of plywood, not a geographical gap, it was the invisible wall of *class*.

On October 10, 1968, three and a half years after going up to Tokyo, having lost all shred of hope except the dream of being a castaway, NN wandered through Ikebukuro, Shinjuku, Shibuya and Roppongi, then 'watched other people having fun in a bowling alley beneath Tokyo Tower,' then went into the garden of the Tokyo Prince Hotel, i.e. into that symbol of The Capital which he had acquired immediately upon his arrival, and prowled around. Challenged by a security guard who was making his night rounds, grabbed by the collar and knocked to the ground when he tried to escape, and fearing discovery of the pistol he had hidden for use as a castaway, he shot off two bullets. The guard died around noon the next day. NN took flight all over the country and shot three more people to death. The mass media were full of panic-stricken stories about 'the serial murderer.' Six months later, on April 7, 1969, he was apprehended by a city policeman while trespassing in an English school in the Sendagaya district of Tokyo. He was 19 years old. Among the items he was carrying, aside from the pistol, were a Rolex wristwatch, a Ronson lighter, a metal comb, a student identity card from Meiji Gakuin University, and two pawn tickets. Among the possessions found in his three-tatami (60-square-foot) apartment in Nakano ward were a savings passbook with a balance of zero, a Sheafer fountain pen, a Parker ballpoint pen and an American-made Boston bag.

III   The chain of original sin: modern society and the person

The Bohemian box shapes the flesh of maturing youths with solid physical constructs. The hell of eyes shapes the minds of maturing youths with the looks in the eyes of others. Unlike the box, the eyes shape people's *inner selves*, and therefore must erode people's free will. But by what devices? In NN's case, the devices were the performance trap, and the anger trap.

The performance trap was discussed above. Facing watchful eyes that define the self entirely in terms of superficiality, a person attempts to turn the tables and manipulate the others' gazes by developing and staging his or her own surface aspects. 'Genet, being flotsam in a society which prescribes existence according to possessions, wanted to possess in order to exist' (Sarte). Rolex, Ronson, barber's comb, university ID.

This process of performances operates by means of the free will itself. That is the instrument through which the city tailors an individual to the pattern it prefers. People will recompose themselves to resemble the pattern of the city they may hate, because they exist within the context of relations to others. Then, following subjective schemes designed to manipulate the vision of others, they turn into odd clowns who cover their bodies with whatever clothes the city seems to demand.

The anger trap: Later, in prison, NN read Franz Fanon's *Black Skin, White Mask*, and copied a section out of it, underlining one particular passage and writing next to it (in English), 'Fanon! Aren't you a God?' The passage reads: '*the impossibility of being understood as one would like.*'

In the hell of eyes, as one's words and actions are mercilessly reinterpreted and misinterpreted by others, as an unbridgeable gap is opened up between identity for oneself and for others, the frustration of being 'always misunderstood' accumulates within the self.

At this point most young people swallow the resentment and

assimilate themselves into the performance of the role demanded by the social system. If that is the primary alienation, then the secondary alienation consists in the anticipatory seizing of a defiant attitude, with the aim of breaking through precisely that primary alienation.

'Children of the poor tend naturally, upon reaching puberty, to develop a consciousness of their own selves from the social standpoint,' writes NN:

> During that period, they reach the poor person's fork in the road of determining the course of life. On one side is the easy path, the process of accepting the universal fate of those born into the laboring class and becoming a worker, without plunging into stormy seas. The other path leads through a survey of the difference between your own condition and the living conditions of the upper class, and on to a mad dash in which *anger is put before discretion*. You turn into a so-called juvenile delinquent and are eventually convicted of a crime, and without ever having known the normal happiness of youth, you have determined your fate for good.

Anger is the key element which defines that fork in the road.

In NN, case, if we examine each of his crimes separately, it is possible to interpret them as 'defensive' acts, or as acts to which he was 'driven by necessity.' But such ready resort to such unfeeling *over*defensiveness also points toward a *latent* motive of generalized malice or resentment or anger toward 'other people.'

Or it may be that no really reasonable reason existed for each individual offense. But then again, the reason may have existed within the very lack of reason. NN notes, 'When chance occurs repeatedly, it becomes hard to speak of chance.' 'A lunatic killed someone – But there is no reason why – *It is* a horrible thing. I suppose I never noticed that malice had developed to the point of causing murder.'

The anger, or malice, had precipitated so thickly within NN, as so much generalized gloom, that he virtually lost all specific sight of it. 'My gloom is heavy, and even though I know what it is, it is impossible to talk about it inside my mind. Even if I want to be frank with myself, the self that is my own self cannot speak.'

A 'gloom' like some foreign matter incorporated unwillingly

from the outside, something about which there is nothing to be done, which has precipitated and somehow coagulated within the interior of NN's mind. That 'foreign matter' within NN's soul would grow of its own accord, to occupy the nucleus of his self-volition.

NN went on from the just-cited passages to write of his resentment for his parents and siblings. 'I had no purpose – that's what everyone is saying. Is that it after all? But for me, there was a purpose. . . . In order to get even with you all, I gave up my youth. Maybe it was revenge on all those around me. And at that I succeeded.'

NN became a man of resentment. Revenge was the overall purpose of his life. He closeted his own existence within that relational imperative. He became a *free will obsessed* by that foreign matter.

'I will die – that will be my happines. And that will be my life, but . . . I will die with a smile . . . because I achieved my purpose.' And then: 'Oh, such gloom! How ugly I am!'

The gloom is *someone else*, alien to him and yet still inevitably the core of his own self.

When NN defines his own existence through the anger which he could not govern, we find that he was able after all to possess an unshakable social existence. 'This Case No. 108 is a case of my existing. Without me there would be no case. Because there is the case, there is I. It must be that I exist.' 'It is for me that this cage of a room exists. . . . I hear it is usually a punishment chamber. The room exists for me! It's something to be grateful for, isn't it? Through these circumstances I am able to know that I exist.'

Proof of existence through evil. Yet it was nothing but an existence as one who should not exist, an in-human existence.

That in itself was not a problem for NN, whose talk of 'success' shows that he was set upon having just such an existence. The failure of NN was that that evil existence was also nothing more than one which had been skilfully prepared in advance by the system, complete with the appropriate structure and supporting personnel, as a sort of anticipated 'waste' or excretion.

The city is a giant, vigorously functioning digestive system. Every year it swallows several hundred thousand fresh young people and absorbs and exhausts their manpower. The excess matter, the *undigested* matter is congealed and excreted.

The ways in which the city beckons young people in, and shuts them out, were described in the first two sections of this chapter. The 'undigested matter' is especially the *free will that aims to soar* which has become attached to the labor commodity. The city does succeed in decomposing and absorbing the better part of these free wills which aim to soar. For the undigested portion, the will which turns to juvenile delinquency in the digestive tract, a sturdy container is specially prepared. What NN was able to acquire was none other than an existence designated for that special container.

The holes which NN really drilled were in four living skulls, those of a young security guard and two young drivers, and an aged shrine night-watchman, who like NN were weaklings and victims of the system.

At the instant when NN's bullets hit each target *at close range*, he actually missed the target forever. Here lies the awesome trap of the system. His bitterness came out later, when he understood *after the fact*. 'I cannot think of myself as a fearful person. There is something I am burning crazily for, and self-restraint doesn't work.'

Negativity is an indispensable moment for breaking through. Anger and other negative feelings are prerequisites for overcoming and reforming one's present existence. But when emotions such as anger come upon us too directly and vividly, they block off our will to transcend and we are pulled back into immanence by a power too strong to contend with. They prevent us from stepping back from the conditions and clearly grasping them in their entirety. Anger binds us in the spell of the *simple negativity* of our conditions. It is confined to antagonists of the same rank. It oversimplifies. Meanwhile, the flexible structure of the contemporary control system contains various institutions for ridiculing and absorbing such defenseless negativity.

'I can remember now how around the time between sixth grade and middle school, I would stop playing and go deliver newspapers, telling myself that I was different from the others, and crying and crying . . .'

Some people are poorer than others, and some people are held in much more contempt than others. For that reason poverty and humiliation are typically experienced in *isolation* as things which create a *disparity* between oneself and one's fellows. As long as it is so direct, the experience is one of resentment and anger toward one's fellows. The capacity for transcending this aggregate of hellish traps cannot be found within anger itself.

Later, in prison, grieving over his former 'ignorance' and craving 'knowledge,' NN greedily devoured works of philosophy, literature, economy. By that time the knowledge he was seeking was no longer the abstract 'education' which he had once wanted to display.

He wrote out Bacon's 'Knowledge is power,' not as a student would copy a quotation out of a textbook, but in the context that, 'When I attain knowledge destiny lies irrevocably before my eyes.'

'My heart aches with sadness that so many things will happen after my doings are finished . . .'

None of us can scoff at the failure of NN's venture of 'leaping before he looked.' The 'trap of anger' is none other than the reverse side of the 'trap of not getting angry.' It is the indifference of those people who do not get angry that drives the many NNs into desperate isolation.

'From now on you will be able to taste the agony of those who are wounded. And just as all of you never once made contact with me, when you feel the necessity for being rescued, there will be no one who will help.' NN aimed that anathema directly at his kin, but it comes home to each of us.

Through indifference, the outside world of society punishes the indifference of the family: the hell of the chain of abandonment. Then what is the outside world for we who are 'the outside world?' It is the world outside the world, the underworld. It consists of us ourselves, but in particular it is all of the resentments which are repressed, cast out, and constrained to existence as the *sous-homme* or 'sub-person' (which NN calls himself).

The words which NN used to turn away his mother, who had come to meet him in prison, pierce beyond his family through us all: 'After you have discarded the powerless!'

In the poor villages of old Japan, lives which a family would not be able to nurture were forced out beforehand in the 'abortion grove.' Modernity has moved that patch of woods into the city hospital.

In traditional community society, surplus population was disposed of through such practices as *obasute* (leaving the old in the mountains to die). Civic society provides the amenities, leaving its elderly members to die silently in closed rooms or institutions.

In baseball, the forced out eliminates a runner without directly tagging him, by blocking off his path of survival. There's a runner on first base, the batter's hit is thrown to second, and automatically *either* the man on first *or* the batter is picked off. Two runners are trying to live and there is only one base for life. The opposing team can select at will which one it wishes to kill.

Back in Abashiri, when NN's mother set out to remake her life by abandoning four of her children, the situation was logically the same: *someone* must starve. But she was not playing baseball with her family. The station platform where the child NN kept running and running after his mother was not the baseline of a tidy stadium. What is the meaning of the game, in human terms?

The 'near miracle' of NN and his siblings surviving the winter deserves a second look. It must be seen as *attempted murder*. And not just the normal sort of murder. The murder most cruel among all murders is when the rules of the game force a mother to kill her own child. There is the human meaning of the game.

And there is the *actual human meaning* of the array of precise statistics in modern social science. Surplus population, social selection, degree of maladjustment, dropout rates, probability of 'pathological' phenomena . . . The abyss of numbers.

The logic of modern civic society dismantles the straitened villages and families, dissolves their communites, and chooses its own victims. 'It is the parents who are bad.' 'It is the sons who are bad.' 'It is the neighbors who are bad.'

'We respectfully request capital punishment,' declared the family of one of NN's victims to the court.

On the day of that hearing, NN recorded in his diary, 'This is like my own feeling just before I committed the act.'

That sentence echoes ominously with denial that the world will be restored to tranquil equilibrium as the ceremony of execution closes the chain of retribution.

The deserting parent cannot be forgiven any more than someone who has murdered can be forgiven. Yet NN's mother was not particularly heartless. If I or you had been in the place of this mother clutching her seven children, what choice would we have had? At that crossroads, her path might in fact have been nearly the best choice. Irregardless, *from NN's standpoint*, this mother cannot be forgiven; at least, not so long as he remains immanent within his circumstances.

In our society, within the endlessly linked chains of causal relation, each of us, who at various times and in various situations *cannot but* claim that 'there was no other way' and cluck that 'troubles never end,' is in fact the one who cannot be forgiven by the somebodies we have discarded.

(1973)

Notes

1 All quoted pasages concerning Nagayama Norio (NN) or attributed to him, all excerpts from his writings, and all specific facts about him and his family and associates are from the following books:

Nagayama Norio, *Tears of Ignorance (Muchi no namida*, Gōdō Shuppan, 1971).
Kamata Tadayoshi, *A Will to Murder (Satsujinsha no ishi*, San'ichi Shobō, 1972).
Nagayama Norio, *Canaries who Forgot the People (Jinmin o wasureta kanariatachi*, Henkyōsha, 1971).

2 Employment statistics in this chapter are from various Ministry of Labor reports, unless otherwise noted.
3 1967 White Paper on Youth.
4 Midoro Tatsuo, *Dekasegi*, Nihon Keizai Shimbunsha, 1965, pp. 137–9.
5 Quotations from *Saint-Genet*, by Jean-Paul Sartre, are from the first volume of the Japanese translation by Shirai and Hirai.
6 Seymour Lipset and R. Bendix, *Social Mobility in Industrial Society*, 1959.
7 Kurasawa Susumu, *Urban Society in Japan (Nihon no toshi shakai* pp. 189, 190, 198).

PART FOUR

THE CHANGING MENTALITY OF CONTEMPORARY JAPAN

23 Generational Composition of Contemporary Society

The mentality of the Japanese was very fruitfully explored by two identical, wide-ranging attitude surveys conducted in 1973 and 1978 by NHK, the public broadcasting organization. Utilizing data from those surveys, I shall devote two chapters to analyzing some of the variations within the contemporary national mentality. This chapter covers the most telling *generational* variations among the whole population while the next chapter focuses on the attitudinal changes occurring during the 1970s within the *younger generation*.

The surveys, entitled 'The Mentality of the Japanese,' entailed interviews with 5,436 persons (in 1973) and 5,400 persons (in 1978), who were selected from the population of Japanese citizens aged 16 and over, by random two-stage non-artificial sampling. Usable responses were obtained from 4,243 persons (78.1 per cent) and 4,240 persons (78.5 per cent), respectively. The full contents and results of the surveys are reported in *Nihonjin no ishiki*, 1975; and *Dai-ni nihonjin no ishiki*, 1980, both edited by Nihon Hōsō Kyōkai Hōsō Yoron Chōsasho, and published by Shiseidō. (Parts of the present chapters were originally drafted for those reports.)

Changes in mentality from generation to generation are a natural feature of modern society. In attitude surveys, these variations commonly take the form of smooth, or nearly smooth, increases or decreases. A fascinating aspect of the NHK survey results is that in several key areas, the changes show up as radical U shapes or inverted-U shapes, and sometimes as more complex patterns. It is those particular areas which we shall examine here, in order to trace in detail the consciousness shifts among the several generations of contemporary Japan.

461

1 Dissastisfaction with life

Questions about the basic degree of satisfaction with life were one area which elicited intricate patterns. Figure 23.1 charts the proportions of people who said they were 'dissatisfied' or 'somewhat dissatisfied' with their overall lives, that is with both the material and the spiritual aspects of life. Women exhibit relatively little variation by age, but among men there are two conspicuous peaks, in the early-twenties and early-thirties age groups.

To zoom in on these crests of dissatisfaction, Figures 23.2 and 23.3 break down the rates of men's material and spiritual dissatisfaction, in the contexts of personal life and of society. On the personal side (Figure 23.2), material dissatisfaction peaks among those in their early thirties and remains high in the late thirties and forties; while spiritual dissatisfaction peaks sharply in the early twenties and is also high in the late teens and late twenties. Material is generally stronger than spiritual dissatisfaction among all age groups, but the opposite is true among teenagers, and the two are about even for those in the early twenties. Thus dissatisfaction tends to be materialistic for men in the prime of life, and spiritual for younger men. In the social sphere, though, both types of dissatisfaction are strongest among those in their early-thirties (Figure 23.3).

What the two peaks in Figure 23.1 reflect, then, is a gener-

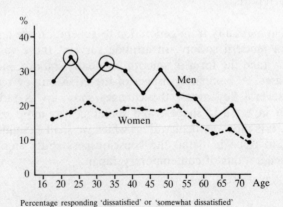

Percentage responding 'dissatisfied' or 'somewhat dissatisfied'

Figure 23.1 *Rates of overall dissatisfaction with life*

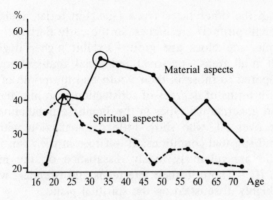

Percentage of negative responses to the following questions:

Material aspects: 'Are you living in affluence in terms of clothing, food, housing, etc.?'

Spiritual aspects: 'Are you living a fulfilling life, with a sense of pride and peace of mind?'

Figure 23.2 *Rates of dissatisfaction with personal life (men)*

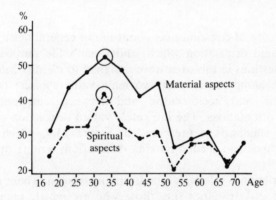

Percentage of negative responses to the following questions:

Material aspects: 'Do you live in an area with well-kept surroundings, that promotes a life of safety and comfort?'

Spiritual aspects: 'Are you able to speak candidly and feel at ease with most of the people in your neighborhood, and at your workplace or school?'

Figure 23.3 *Rates of dissatisfaction with societal life (men)*

ational difference, between bearers of dissatisfaction in the personal-spiritual sphere; and dissatisfaction in the personal-material and the social spheres. Moreover, that personal-spiritual dimension of discontent is much the most intense – enough to bring the peak of overall dissatisfaction into the early-twenties range,

463

even though the other three types (social-material, social-spiritual, personal-spiritual) are highest in the early thirties.

Meanwhile, the older age groups exhibit higher degress of satisfaction in all areas – personal and social, material and spiritual – compared to those in their youth and the prime of life.

In sum, in terms of degrees of satisfaction with life, there are three broad generational types in the Japanese population: I – Those over 50, who show little dissatisfaction with their material and spiritual conditions; II – Those in their thirties and forties, who are relatively highly dissatisfied on the material plane; and III – Those in their late teens and twenties, who are relatively highly dissatisfied on the spiritual plane.

2 Basic values

Near the core of consciousness about life in general lies a fundamental value orientation which guides one's life purpose. The survey questions in this area were designed to identify four basic standards, along the axes of two main value choices: between 'self-centric' and 'socio-centric' and between 'emotional' and 'rational' orientations. The intricately varied disposition of these life-value standards is presented in Figure 23.4, which charts both the first- and second-ranking orientations among men and women.

The variation is relatively simple among women. Those in their teens and early twenties (i.e. those who are mostly unmarried) tend toward the Love value orientation; those between the late twenties and late forties (mostly married homemakers) tend toward Utility; and after the age of fifty the Love orientation is again dominant.

The complexity lies again with the men. In the late-teen group, the Love orientation is most frequent, followed by Pleasure, and in the early-twenties group Pleasure ranks first. From the late twenties, as with the women, the concentration is in the Utility orientation (at about 40 per cent), and this continues through the early fifties. In the late-fifties the weight shifts toward Right, and in the early sixties Right and Love are about even. Then in

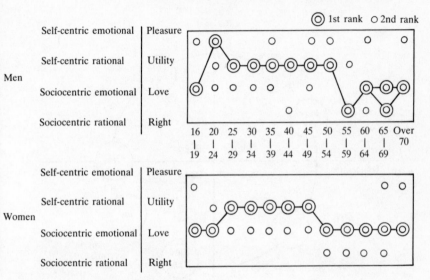

Terms of orientation reflect choices of the following positions:

Pleasure: 'Live for today, enjoying freely'
Utility: 'Lay solid plans, build an affluent life'
Love: 'Live in harmony with close ones'
Right: 'Cooperate with others, do right in the world.'

Figure 23.4 *Generational variation of basic value orientation*

the over-seventy group there is a reversion to the original Love orientation.

Represented graphically along the two main value axes, as in Figure 23.5, these trends display a very interesting circular movement. The increase in self-orientation from the teens into the twenties can be seen as the establishment of a contra-social 'ego.' The shift from emotional to rational orientation during the early and late twenties seems to correspond to the heightened responsbilities of marriage and pursuit of an occupation. The linkage with working life is underscored by the continuance of this rationalism precisely through age fifty-five, the normal retirement age.

Next, during the several years following retirement age, comes the largest augmentation of the Right orientation. This period, in which withdrawl from direct activity tends to be accompanied by enhanced prestige and new social responsibilities, seems to bring on a moralism based on a sense of distance from the field of play. In relation to the idealism of the youthful period before

465

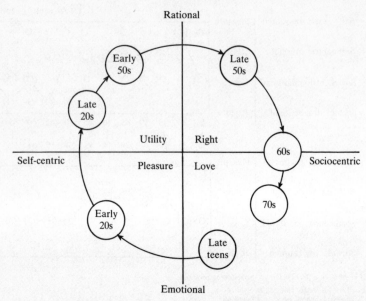

(See Figure 23.4 for explanations of Pleasure, Utility, Love and Right)

Figure 23.5 *Phase shifts in value consciousness through men's lives*

the age of heavy life responsibilities, this later stage might be called a 're-ideologizing' of one's attitude toward life. Of course, the later, moralistic 'ideologicality' frequently follows a vector running opposite to the attitudes of youth.

Finally, past the age of seventy, when a man has retired in turn from the sphere of social concerns, we may surmise that he once again desires a passive, gentle harmony with those around him, as he awaits a quiet death (reunion with nature). The passive character of the Love orientation ('live in harmony with close ones') in this old-age period is made clear by an analysis of men over sixty, broken down into those who lead solitary lives and those who do not (Table 23.1).

Among solitary men, the more self-centric Pleasure orientation is more common than the Love orientation. While it might seem natural that self-centrism is common among solitary persons, the fact is that among solitary late-teenagers, the Love orientation is most frequent. Hence the Love orientation in the over-seventy group, in contrast to that in the youngest group, may be generally

Table 23.1   *Life orientations of solitary and non-solitary men over 60*

	Non-solitary %	Solitary %
Pleasure	24.6	32.4
Utility	19.0	17.6
Love	27.4	29.4
Right	25.8	17.6

(Terms of orientation are explained in Figure 23.4.)

regarded as a turning toward 'perfect harmony' within life relationships that have already obtained.

Figure 23.6 shows that the arch-shaped transition of rationalism during men's lifetimes substantially corresponds to the patterns of response in two other categories: the Efficiency orientation on the axis of efficiency vs sentiment, and the Work orientation on the axis of work vs leisure. (That the Work orientation peaks rather more clearly in the youngest of the three generations can be explained by the normally strong correlation between academic credentials and Work orientation, along with the historically greater frequency of higher education among the younger generation.)

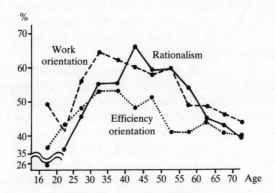

Rationalism: Those with Utility or Right orientations (see Figure 23.4).

Work orientation: Those taking one of the following positions on work and leisure: 'Take some leisure time, save most energy for work' or 'Work is life's purpose, all energy is devoted to it.'

Efficiency orientation: Those whose responses to three questions on human relations indicated that priority is given to 'efficiency' over 'personal character' or 'feelings.'

Figure 23.6 *Variation by age of rationalism, work orientation and efficiency orientation among men*

3   Relations between the sexes

Sexual mores

This is one of the three categories – along with religious attitudes, and feelings toward the emperor – in which generational differences are not only the most striking, but also consist mainly of 180-degree reversals. Quite interestingly, all three of these outstanding cleavages are connected in their own ways with *taboos*. The implication is that substantial social strains go along with the generational consciousness differences in present-day Japan. An analysis of this phenomenon would no doubt be interesting, but here we shall do no more than point out its existence.

We shall approach the topic of change in sexual mores by observing the transition by age of attitudes toward premarital sex (Figure 23.7). Among women, the largest segment of almost every age group holds that marriage is prerequisite to sexual relations. The only exception is in the early twenties, where more than half responded that marriage is not necessarily required.

With men the variation is much sharper. Those over thirty-five are inclined against premarital sex, but only about 20 per cent of those in the teens and twenties take this attitude, dipping to barely 10 per cent in the early twenties. Conversely, the majority in the teens and early twenties decouple the idea of sexual relations from that of marriage.

That the turning point does not occur in the early thirties, at a point that would be related to a change in the stage of life (marriage and children), hints that the shift does not depend upon a simple advance in age, but rather upon a generational change. For if stricter attitudes due to older age and parenthood were the key factor, then one would expect those now in their teens and twenties to assume the same attitudes as the present mature adults; but Figure 23.7 suggests, on the contrary, the existence of a *chronological* factor. To wit, those who most strongly believe that marriage is necessary for sexual relations were born between 1900 and 1935, while those most frequently taking the opposite view were born mostly after the war; and those born beteen 1935 and 1945 are the transitional generation who are rather split on the issue.

A similar question from a recent worldwide survey of young

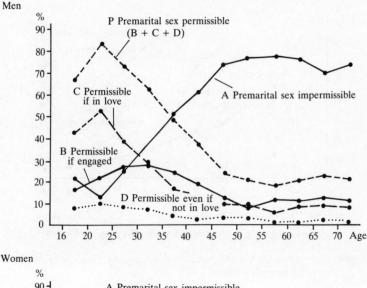

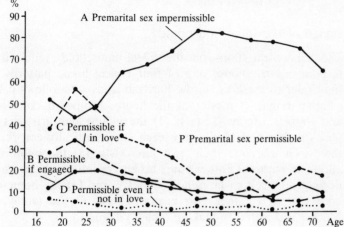

Figure 23.7 *Generational variation of morality concerning premarital sex*

people, conducted by the Japanese prime minister's office, provides a comparison of Japan with other countries (Figure 23.8). Those in Japan who believe marriage is prerequisite to sex are proportionally more numerous than in Europe; fewer than in India, Brazil or the Philippines; and about the same as in the USA.

469

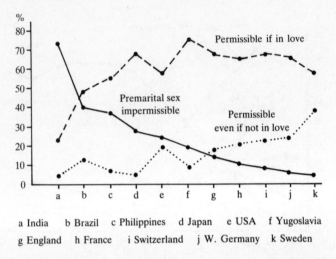

Figure 23.8 *Attitudes toward premarital sex among youth (age 18–24) of various nations*

Image of the ideal household

The survey questions on the 'ideal household' required the respondents to choose one of four typical home patterns. We shall refer to these as (1) the husband-leads-wife-follows pattern ('Father reigns as master of the house, Mother backs him up and wholeheartedly serves'); (2) the independent-partners pattern ('Father and Mother are each enthusiastically absorbed in their own jobs and their own interests'); (3) the outer/inner-allotment pattern ('Father pours his energy into working, Mother dedicates herself to household duties'); and (4) the home-centered pattern ('Father also pays attention to the family, and Mother is devoted to making a happy home').

Figure 23.9 indicates that, in terms of these ideal images of the home, there are clearly three generations: I – those over sixty-five (born mostly in the Meiji era, up to 1910), where the husband-leads-wife-follows pattern is most common; II – those between twenty and sixty-five who favor the outer/inner-allotment pattern; and III – those in their late teens (born mainly in the late 1950s), who seek the home-centered pattern where the husband participates in domestic life. A closer look at the trends in the youngest group reveals that while the home-centered pattern ranks first, the outer/inner-allotment pattern is also rather

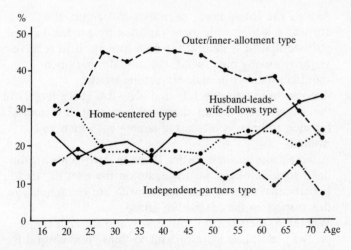

Figure 23.9 *Ideal household image*

common (the difference between them is not statistically significant), among men as well as women.

Division of housework

Support for the idea that men should *not* participate in housework might be supposed to decline in proportion to youth, and to be weaker among women. Yet Figure 23.10 shows that neither is necessarily the case. The variations are quite complex:

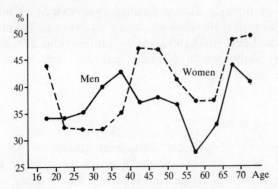

Percentage endorsing the statement that 'Male household heads should not help in the kitchen or with minding the children.'

Figure 23.10 *Attitudes on division of housework*

471

1 Among the (Meiji-born) over-sixty-five group, this
   attitude is strong with some variation by gender, i.e. the
   attitude that 'it is natural for men to help' is in relative
   majority among men, while the attitude that 'men
   shouldn't help' is in majority among women.
2 Among those between fifty and sixty-five (born largely in
   the Taisho era), the 'modernistic' view that 'it is natural
   for men to help' is increasing among both men and
   women.
3 Among those in their forties (born in early Showa), the
   'men shouldn't help' idea is again on the rise; the trend
   is particularly strong for women, who are comparable in
   this respect to the Meiji-born group.
4 Women in their thirties (the first group through the
   postwar education system) tend to think 'it is natural for
   men to help,' in contrast to the previous decennial
   generation, but the men are opposed in numbers greater
   than their immediate seniors.
5 Those in their twenties generally support a housework
   role for men, apparently reflecting the solid rooting of
   postwar education patterns.
6 In the late teens, males go along with the previous group
   in thinking they should help, but females increasingly
   put on an outward show similar to couples in their forties,
   claiming 'male household heads shouldn't help.'

This way of thinking among females aged sixteen to nineteen
corresponds with their relatively strong tendency to aspire to the
'dignified husband' (husband-leads-wife-follows) household ideal,
which they supported in numbers exceeded only by the late-
sixties age group (Figure 23.9).

Women and work

The same sort of complex attitudinal variations are found,
especially among women, on the question of whether women
should work after marriage (see Figure 23.11). Among women,
the peaks and troughs of the opinion that they 'should stay in
the home after marriage' precisely match those of the opinion
that 'men shouldn't help with housework' – the three peaks being

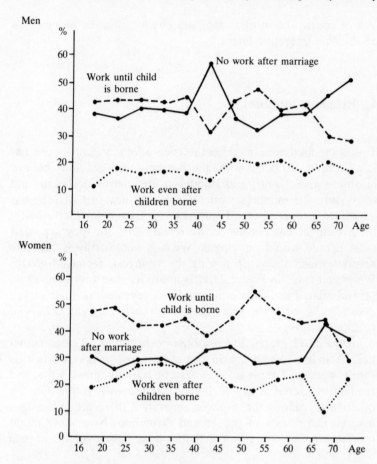

Figure 23.11 *Attitudes toward employment of women after marriage and childbearing*

in the groups over sixty-five, in their forties, and in their late teens.

If a generation is taken to span twenty-five years, then sure enough, the mothers of these late-teenaged women are in their forties, and *their* mothers are over sixty-five. Alternating with them are the women in their fifties (the Taisho-born generation, known for their 'worldliness'), and their daughters, the progressive postwar generation in their twenties. It is the women in particular among whom this chain phenomenon is conspicuous.

473

Yet of course the mother-daughter chain cannot be assumed to be the sole operative factor.

4   Religious attitudes

This is the final area in which the generational variations are not at all simple. To begin with, the numbers who generally believe in Shinto gods (*kami*) and Buddhism are sharply declining, and conversely the numbers who do not hold any sort of religious belief are increasing (see Figure 23.12). Except for the rapidity, these changes are not especially remarkable, for they are what most people would anticipate. What is noteworthy is the tiny reversal which shows up among the youngest, teenaged group. While that trend in Figure 23.12 is not in itself so very significant, several related and surprising trends are revealed by other survey questions which probe more deeply into activities and beliefs of religious nature.

Figure 23.13 graphs the responses concerning religious activities. Activities which are in the strict sense religious, such as shrine worship, temple services, ascetic training, grave visits, and reading of sacred texts, do indeed decline with youth. On the other hand, among the younger generation there are increases – marked increases – in prayer and divination. Now these might be dismissed as leisure-time activities done half in fun or, in such

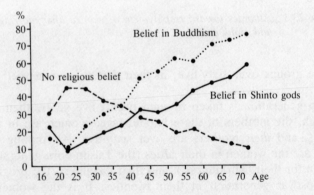

Figure 23.12 *Generational variation in religious attitudes – I*

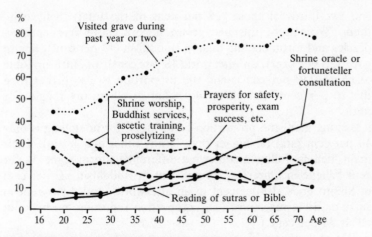

Figure 23.13 *Generational variation in religious activities*

cases as prayers for entrance-exam success, as mere formalities. No doubt such an interpretation is partially correct. However, Figure 23.14 shows that the numbers who 'believe in' miracles or divination (*mikuji*) or fortunetelling are in fact on the rise. On questions concerning religious *activities*, among the 37 per cent of the younger generation who responded that they had 'consulted a shrine oracle or a fortuneteller at least once in the past year or two,' more than half also said they 'believed in' them.

Among women in particular, nearly half the respondents in their late teens (44 per cent) consulted oracles or fortunetellers,

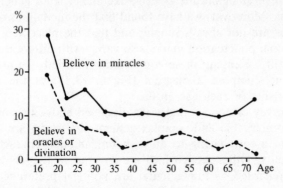

Figure 23.14 *Generational variation in religious attitudes – II: belief in miracles, oracles, divination*

475

and two-thirds of those (28 per cent of the total) 'believe in' them. Women of this age group believe more frequently in oracles and fortunetelling than in Buddhism (17 per cent), Shinto gods (26 per cent), an afterworld (8 per cent), or sutra or Bible teachings (10 per cent); and the proportion is also higher than the 26 per cent who claim 'no belief at all in any religion or faith.'

Among men, the proportion believing in fortunetelling is only 10 per cent (still far higher than in any other age group). Their main 'beliefs' follow a somewhat different pattern: some 34 per cent believe in 'miracles,' 16 per cent in Buddhism, 23 per cent in Shinto gods, 10 per cent in an afterworld, and 8 per cent in sutra or Bible teachings. (The proportion reporting 'no belief at all' is 34 per cent.)

Out of the heart of the contemporary rationalized system, like demon-children of its rationalism, comes this maturing generation of men believing in miracles and women believing in divination, a resurgent faith in the supernatural, taking the form of a diffused, secularized esotericism.

Conclusion: the dual framework of generational composition

We have seen that the mentality of the Japanese population, at least in several significant aspects, exhibits striking generational variations. Moreover, we have found that the modalities of those variations are not always simple; and that the placement of the generational punctuation marks also varies with different aspects of mentality. Keeping these complexities in mind, we may now venture to compose a diagram (Figure 23.15) of the leading characteristics of each age group.

The survey categories that were discussed above because they display remarkable and complex generational shifts are all also important areas, having to do with fundamental characteristics of mentality. Other areas which are covered by the surveys and can be regarded as fundamental are political preferences, and views on 'work and leisure.' But since views on work and leisure showed little variation by age group (the major differentiations

476

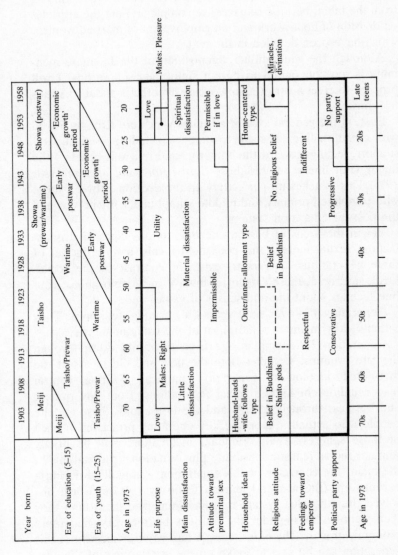

Figure 23.15 *Generational composition of Japanese mentality in the 1970s*

accorded with education and gender), only the political areas of party support and feelings toward the emperor are added into the table of generational composition (Figure 23.15). Missing from the table, because of excessive complexity, are the attitudes on division of housework and on employment of married women, which have been detailed in the text.

Although the generational composition of the Japanese mentality is too convoluted to permit simple generalizations, I will proceed to erect a very rough working hypothesis about its stratifications.

First, in the general area of attitudes which are strongly linked with directionalities of social *ideology* – including political-party support, feelings toward the emperor, and religious beliefs – the major fault line separates those *born before and after the year 1933*. This matches up perfectly with the division between those who completed primary and middle school under the prewar and the postwar education systems.

Yet in the areas of basic value orientation, types of dissatisfaction, sexual mores, and household ideals, a different set of three generations appears to exist. In contrast to the social-ideological field, these categories involve more amorphous, routine feelings about life and senses of value.

Generation 1 is over sixty years old, mainly Meiji-born. They rather rigidly maintain a moralism of the traditional type.

Generation 2, ranging in age from the fifties down through the late twenties, straddles both the new and old layers of the first-noted ideological generation pattern. Bearing central responsibilities in today's social instituitions, from government and business through schools and the household, these are the people who actually shape the key operating principles in each of those spheres. Their dominant inclinations may be briefly summarized as realistic sensibility plus situational rationalism. In the main, the character of this generation was molded during a perilous era (the war and immediate postwar years) which dissolved the old value system that had immersed them, and they then went on to shoulder the burdens of 'recovery' and rapid economic growth. The *older segment* and *younger segment* of this generation can be said to make up the core groups of the *conservative* and *progressive* movements within Japan's corporations and labor unions.

Generation 3 (or 4, if weight is given to the older and younger segments of the previous generation) is the group rising to the surface in the society of the 1970s. At the outset they hold conceptions of a different nature and within a *different dimension* than the polarized field of generation 2. Having been reared and molded in an era of relative economic security, this generation has never known harsh material poverty, but on the other hand they carry a special sensitivity to various strains arising from that 'affluent society.' Their dominant inclinations may well involve some sorts of spiritual craving, as expressed in their preoccupation with human relations, and in the spiritual quality of their sense of dissatisfaction. Meanwhile, on the ideologically informed field of consciousness (political and religious inclinations), where we first noted a bifurcation, they are with some frequency going about forming their own third force. That would be no mere next stage to the pre- and post-1933 factions, but rather something foreign, in a different dimension. In politics, for example, it is not a question of their conservatism or progressism, for they make up a generation with 'no preference,' on a plane perpendicular, as it were, to the conventional spectrum. This is beyond the ken of either the conservatives or progressives of today, who cannot cope with the phenomenon even when they are capable of grasping it.

Will they proceed with age to be absorbed into the value systems of their predecessors, or will they forge their own independent values? Or, without taking any clear direction, will they gradually permeate the whole social field with their anchorless yearnings? In short, is the consciousness of the youngest group nothing more than a manifestation of the immaturity and privilege of youth, or is a truly new generation coming on stage? In theory this is a problem to be entrusted to surveys in the next decade, and in reality it is a serious question for us all.

(1984)

A note on changes in the 1980s

Data from the repetition in 1988 of the same survey confirms that most of the above-described trends of the 1970s either continued or intensified during the 1980s. Some of the key points are outlined below.

I am most grateful to the NHK Opinion Survey Section for permission to use here the 1988 data which, with minor exceptions, has not yet been published. (In 1988, 3,853 usable responses were obtained from a sample of 5,400 persons.)

Dissatisfaction with life

A comparison of Figure 23.16 with Figure 23.1 shows that overall, the stratum of the dissatisfied has remarkably declined (this point is analyzed in the next chapter).

Looking at the generations, we find that the only clear peak is among those in their early twenties; the lesser peak which was visible in 1973, among those in their early thirties, has vanished. The reason (based on other data), is that the material dissatisfactions of those now in middle age were completely wiped away by economic prosperity.

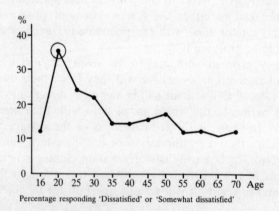

Percentage responding 'Dissatisfied' or 'Somewhat dissatisfied'

Figure 23.16 *Rates of overall dissatisfaction with life (men and women, 1988)*

'Work' value orientation

A comparison of Figure 23.17 and Figure 23.6 shows that between 1973 and 1988, the peak age among 'work-minded' males has shifted from the thirties to the fifties. Thus virtually the same generation of men (born in the 1930s) continues to be

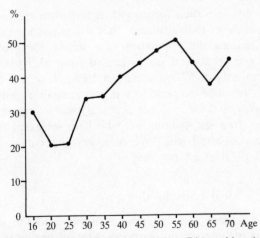

Those taking one of the following positions on work and leisure: 'Take some leisure time, save most energy for work' or 'Work is life's purpose, all energy is devoted to it.'

Figure 23.17 *Variation by age of work orientation among men, 1988*

the core group of Japanese whose strongest value orientation is toward work. The fixed retirement age of fifty-five remains common in Japan, which means that in the 1990s the generation that most likes to work will lose the chance to work! During the latter 1980s, this was one factor stimulating discussion about postponing the fixed retirement age (lengthened life expectancy, naturally, was another factor).

Sexual mores

The drastic age-group difference seen in 1973, with young people inclined to condone premarital sex (Figure 23.7), was hypothesized above as being not dependent upon age in itself, or stage of life, but rather characteristic of a generation (in the narrow sense). My supposition was that as those young people grew older, they would maintain the same opinion, and accordingly there would be a major shift among Japanese as a whole. The data from fifteen years later proves that forecast correct.

The crossover group, i.e. the borderline generation where opposite attitudes on premarital sex coexist in fairly equal proportion, shifted from around age thirty in 1973, to around age fifty in 1988 (male and female combined). As the younger generation who accepted premarital sex in 1973 progressed through their thirties and into their forties (when they themselves are not the 'beneficiaries' of that attitude), they maintained their belief. As a result, among the population as a whole, the group who do not rule out premarital sex increased from 37.5 per cent in 1973, to a majority of 57.1 per cent in 1988. However, for 30.9 per cent of the 1988 respondents it is permissible only when 'deeply in love,' and for 22.6 per cent only when 'engaged to be married'; the 'free sex' contingent, who believe sexual relations need not be connected with love or marriage, remained about as rare as in 1973, at 3.6 per cent.

Image of the ideal household

In 1973, the majority of Japanese subscribed to the ideal of 'Father pours his energy into working, Mother dedicates herself to household duties' (the outer/inner-allotment type). But among the youngest age bracket (high teens) only, the most popular ideal was 'Father also pays attention to the family, and Mother is devoted to making a happy home' (the home-centered type). (See Figure 23.9).

An interesting question at that time was whether the disposition of the high-teen group was the posture of emotionally dependent 'children,' or whether it revealed a generational shift of values. The late-1980s survey shows that the latter is the case. In 1988, the outer/inner-allotment type of ideal, which had been held by the majority of Japanese until the early 1970s, ranked first only among the generations over age forty-five. In each age bracket up to forty-four, the home-centered type was the top choice. The 'children's ideal' that was limited to the high-teen bracket in 1973 is becoming the most popular ideal for the 1990s among the entire population.

Religious attitudes

In 1973, only the younger generation exhibited a high rate of belief in 'oracles and fortunetellers' and in 'miracles.' In the later 1970s and the 1980s this became a large trend. (This point is analyzed in detail in the next chapter.)

Conclusion

The data from fifteen years on confirm that the main variations by generation in the 1973 data were on the whole not influenced by absolute age or stage of life, but were *generational* (in the narrow sense) characteristics, strong enough to persist *over time*.

Especially in the areas of ideal family image and 'religious' postures, the attitudes which in the early 1970s were only beginning to emerge among the young as a 'new mentality' have, in many cases, not only persisted with that age group but also engulfed the succeeding generation. Hence they have molded a large element of the Japanese mental climate of the 1990s. This pattern can also be seen in aspects which were not touched on here, such as political attitudes: the choice of 'no support for any political party' which was dominant only in the youngest generation of 1973, led for all ages up to the thirties in 1988. It seems that in modern Japan, a grasp of the mentality of the younger generation is a powerful tool for predicting the mind of the coming era.

(1991)

24 The Changing Mentality of the Young

The shifts in a society's mentality over time can be described in strict numerical terms only by comparing the results of surveys taken at different times, in which both the questions and the response options are identically worded. This seems obvious, and yet such identical sets of data from different times are quite scarce, as researchers well know. One of the main merits of the survey discussed here is precisely such consistency. Entitled 'Mentality of the Japanese,' it was conducted in 1973 and again in 1978 by NHK, the national broadcasting organization. By comparing the data from the two administrations of the survey, it is possible to grasp in objective, quantitative terms the tremendous shifts which occurred during the 1970s in the mentality of the younger generation of Japanese (or at the least, in its outward expression).

To make full use of the special advantage of these surveys to illuminate the issue at hand, the results were retabulated for this study and analyzed according to the following design:

I   For the 16-to-29 age group (within limits where the parameter did not become too small), more detailed double- and triple-cross analysis was performed.

II In each retabulation category, items for which there was statistically significant variation between the 1973 and 1978 surveys were noted, and internal correlations were considered.

Multi-cross aggregation in step I was done as follows:

A   The young people were first broken into six base groups by sex and age: (Male / Female) × (16–19 / 20–24 / 25–29). Those base groups were each broken down into these retabulation categories:

1   Locality: Cities of 100,000 or more / Villages and townships of less than 100,000

2 Occupation: Men: Blue collar / White collar / Other
  Women: Blue collar / White collar / Other
3 Political preference: Conservative parties / Progressive parties / No preference / Other
4 Value orientation: Pleasure / Utility / Love / Right

B Respondents were separated into two categories by sex, and then into subcategories which were further subdivided and retabulated by:

1 Locality: Tokyo and Osaka / Tokyo and Osaka suburbs / Other cities of 500,000 or more / Cities of 100,000 or more / Cities of less than 100,000 / Villages and townships
2 Education: Middle school graduate / High school graduate / Junior college or vocational school graduate / University graduate / High school student / University student
3 Occupation: Men: Self-employed / Sales and service / Blue collar / White collar / Other
  Women: Self-employed / Sales and service / Blue collar / White collar / Housewife / Other
4 Political Preference: Liberal Democratic Party / Socialist Party / Komeito / Democratic Socialist Party / Communist Party / New Liberal Club / No preference
5 Value orientation: Pleasure / Profit / Love / Right
  (Note on political preference: Totals for each party include supporters of the party plus those who indicated the party when asked, 'Which party could you support if you were to choose?' Those listed as 'No preference' indicated no party and also said 'None' when asked the same question.)

I Deus ex machina

Having restrained the impulse to rush ahead to particular topics of interest, the first step was an impartial scan of all the data from 1973 and 1978, to identify where the most dramatic change could be seen. Interestingly enough, it was in the area of religious attitudes. Some of the data indicated states of mind which might well be considered non-religious under certain traditional conceptions; hence the term 'religious' is here used advisedly. At any rate, the fluctuation in 'religious' mentality is so remarkably apparent that it deserves to be the initial clue in our analysis.

Ten of the fourteen response categories for religion-related questions (excluding 'None,' 'Other' and 'No response') yielded statistically significant differences from 1973 to 1978 when tabulated for young people as a whole, and each of those ten *increased* in the later survey. They are:

- *Four types of religious activity*: 'Make grave visits once or twice per year'; 'Went to pray at least once in the past year or two for health, prosperity in business, success in university entrance exams, etc.'; 'Keep traditional charms or amulets about the person'; and 'Consulted a shrine oracle or a fortuneteller at least once in the past year or two.' And,
- *Six items of religious faith*, for which 'belief' was indicated: God, Buddha, Afterworld, Miracles, Power of Charms or Amulets, and Fortunetelling or Divination.

Like Columbus's egg, these increases may not seem so remarkable in retrospect. We must remember that the conventional expectation would be for those 'religious' activities and beliefs to decline as more and more progress is made toward 'modernization'. How many social scientists and social thinkers have regarded modernization as equivalent in meaning to rationalization and secularization, or as superordinate to those concepts, or at least as a parallel phenomenon. Let us try, then, to retain some of the initial sense of shock as we review the data in some detail.

Table 24.1 provides an overview of those ten factors, arrayed in the six base categories of sex and age. It allows us to see at a glance *which strata* show particularly remarkable change.

Looking first at the base categories in Table 24.1, it is clear that the increase in 'religious' consciousness among the youth of the 1970s is borne more by *young women* than by men. Among men in their later twenties, not a single item showed significant

The Changing Mentality of the Young

Table 24.1 Change in religious mentality and activity

	Total	Male			Female		
	16–29	16–19	20–4	25–9	16–19	20–4	25–9
Religious activity							
Grave visit	46<51%	41 49	37 39	44 52%	47 53	50 48	52 57%
Prayer	22<33	32 40	17<29	22 25	23<51	21<34	19 26
Charms	30<37	23<35	31 26	27 33	34 44	37 38	26<41
Fortunetelling	32<38	30 36	24 30	25 21	44 52	42<52	28<38
Religious belief							
God (*kami*)	20<26	23 28	8<21	15 21	26 32	22 26	25 27
Buddha (*hotoke*)	8<21	16 16	9 10	18 20	17 24	14 17	27 30
Afterworld	6<13	10<20	4<10	4 9	8<17	5<17	6 9
Miracles	18<24	34 33	18<28	14 19	22<32	10<25	18 14
Charms	10<17	12 18	6 10	6 10	14<29	14 18	9<16
Fortunetelling	11<16	10 10	4 6	4 5	28 34	14<21	9<15

In each column, 1973 at left, 1978 at right; < = significant difference.

upward variation. Among the women, belief in prayer, the after-world and miracles increased markedly in the younger, typically pre-marriage age bracket, while the simpler sorts of religious activity and belief – fortunetelling and charms – stayed proportionally rather high beyond the typical age for marriage. For men, an increase in religious consciousness in the early-twenties age group stands out. However, this is centered around the 'miracles' category, and comprises the early-1970s generation of high-teens who showed strong disposition for the occult. A comparison of the various figures confirms that such 'beliefs' seem to have persisted into adulthood.

Let us turn to the content of religious consciousness. Among the ten items with significant variation which make up Table 24.1, 'Grave visits' and 'Buddhist belief' are highly traditional religious elements in Japan. For those two the table shows that, while there is indeed significant movement for the younger generation as a whole, none of the base categories had significant variation on its own, and furthermore the change for the entire group is not as pronounced as for some of the other items. These patterns tell us that the two traditional items are not central to the change of religious mentality among the younger generation in the 1970s.

As for 'god,' or *kami*, the Japanese word has many meanings, but as a minimum the following three meanings are included: (1) traditional Shinto gods; (2) the Christian God; and (3) occult-style or so-called contemporary gods. In which of these senses has awareness of god been on the increase recently?

Men in their early twenties comprise the base category in which there was a marked increase in the belief in god. Yet on the question of belief in 'the teachings of the Bible, Buddhist sutras, etc.,' men in their early twenties were the *smallest* group in 1978, and that figure had declined from 1973 (from 7.8 per cent to 4.8 per cent). A check for which particular types of young people are gravitating toward belief in 'god,' shows that it is not farm villagers but rather urbanities (from 7 to 24 per cent), and those with value orientations of Pleasure (from 5 to 18 per cent) and Utility (from 7 to 31 per cent).

Taken together, these trends suggest that for men in their early twenties, and perhaps for the younger generation in general, the increasing belief in 'god' is not aimed at the traditional Shinto gods, nor at a Christian-style god, but rather at some type of contemporarily styled god. Incidentally, there was a notable increase of male university students believing in 'god(s)' (from 6 per cent to 21 per cent, while female university students went from 9 per cent to 25 per cent).

The remaining seven items appear to be the pivotal elements in the augmentation of 'religious' consciousness among young people.

To determine *which types* of young people are the primary bearers of these seven mentalities and behaviors, the (retabulated) data is rearranged for easy overview in Table 24.2. For the same seven items, to facilitate comparison with the earlier survey, data for the groups with significant increase is presented in similar form in Table 24.3. Viewing these two tables conjointly, we can grasp the composition and transition of the increase in 'religious' mentality among the younger generation during the 1970s. (Greater reliance on symbols would have made these tables more compact, but I believe that retaining the specificity allows images to well up more easily.)

First, the group which is the major carrier of these attitudes

Table 24.2 *Main young carriers of religious mentality and behavior*

Fortunetelling (activity)	Females 16–24, F high school students, F university students, F office clerks, F saleswomen, F urbanites, Democratic Socialist Party, Love females
Fortunetelling (belief)	Females 16–19, F high school students, F university students, Love females
Charms (activity)	Females 16–19, F high school students, F farm villagers, Love females
Charms (belief)	Females 16–19, F high school students, F farm villagers
Prayer (activity)	Males/females 16–19, M/F high school students, self employed males, females in regional cities, Love females
Miracles (belief)	Males/females 16–19, F high school students, M university students, salesmen, M farm villagers, New Liberal Club, Pleasure males
Afterworld (belief)	Female university students, salesmen, Right females

Table 24.3   *Religious mentality and behavior among young people:*
groups exhibiting significant increase during the 1970s

Fortunetelling (activity)	Females 20–9, M/F university students, urbanites, Love females
Fortunetelling (belief)	Females 20–9, F university students, housewives
Charms (activity)	Males 16–19, females 25–9, housewives, Love females
Charms (belief)	Females 16–19 and 25–9, F high school students, salesmen, Love females
Prayer (activity)	Females 16–19, M/F 20–4, F high school students, F office clerks, F factory workers, farm villagers, Love females, Utility males
Miracles (belief)	Females 16–19, M/F 20–4, F university students, F office clerks, salesmen, farm villagers, Love females, Pleasure males
Afterworld (belief)	Males/females 16–25, M/F high school students, F factory workers, salesmen, farm villagers, Love females, Pleasure and Utility males

is youths in their high teens, centered around *female high school students*. Yet at the same time there is a rapid increase on the whole among those in their twenties. This tells us that, as we have already seen with respect to the belief in miracles, it is not simply a stage which was passed through at a certain age and died out with adulthood, but rather it is in some sense the consciousness of a generation. The tendency for the ages of these groups of carriers to grow along with the maturing of this generation is clear, up to this point at least.

Marx is well known for his theory that the mentality of the ruling class pervades the entire society, while Kracauer claimed that it is the middle class whose mentality saturates society. In contemporary Japan another force is at work: it seems that *children's culture* and *youth culture* are, through the agency of the mass media, flowing throughout society. I believe that the new 'religious' consciousness is, among other things, an aspect of that phenomenon.

Second, along with generational factors, there is generally high correlation between this new 'religious' mentality and primary values (life goals). Women with *value orientations toward Love* are the main carriers, and at the same time a steady increase is occurring within the group. The Love-orientation statement of one's life's desire as 'Living in harmony with close ones' indicates the *dependency* type, according to the value factor analysis of C. W. Morris. This suggests a possible connection of this religious consciousness of the young generation with the so-called *amae* mentality, and with societal character.

Third, while the typical elements of the first and second tendencies are fortunetelling/divination and charms/amulets (and assocated practices and beliefs), there is a rather different demographic pattern for afterworld belief. Also, although the prayer-activity and miracle-belief groups are basically similar to the fortunetelling/divination and charms/amulets groups, several dissimilarities are also present.

Fourth, detailed breakdown of the afterworld-belief data shows that the core is female university students, not high school students. Also, among the main carriers of this item the primary value is not Love, but rather Right. This is notable in that it seems to suggest a connection with Christian beliefs; belief in an afterworld reward generally serves as a support for moral action, hence the data might be interpreted on the basis of motivation. The *trend*, meanwhile, is toward marked increase among those indicating Love orientation, as well as Pleasure and Utility. In 1973 it was the Right orientation in both genders which coincided most frequently with afterworld belief, but in 1978 that orientation was much less outstanding among women and dropped to the bottom among men (see Table 24.4). The parameters for Pleasure, Utility, and Love orientations are far higher among both sexes than that for Right, making the latter a rather trivial factor among all young persons who believe in an afterworld (the distribution ratio is 4.8 per cent for men, 9.3 per cent for women). Thus even afterworld belief, the only one of the seven items with something of a particular group of carriers, had its Christian-style kernel swallowed up by the wave of mass-societal new carriers. The spread of afterworld belief among a new stratum, including high school students and other high-teenagers (see Table 24.3), evidently represents a similar state of affairs.

Fifth, by combining prayer activity and miracle belief, which express similar tendencies, into a common base group with for-

Table 24.4   *Change in afterworld belief, by primary value orientation*

	Orientation	1973		1978	Parameter
Young men:	Pleasure	4.7%	<	14.7%	143
	Utility	4.4	<	12.0	133
	Love	6.5		12.3	187
	Right	*12.5*		*9.4*	32
Young women:	Pleasure	6.3		12.0	158
	Utility	6.7		10.6	188
	Love	3.8	<	15.3	255
	Right	*16.7*		*20.5*	39

< = significant difference.

tunetelling and charms, the strata of positive respondents are broadened to include: (1) not only teenage women, but also teenage men; (2) not only high school and university students, but also sales personnel and the self-employed; and (3) not only Love-oriented women, but also Pleasure- and Utility-oriented men. Thus the belief formation is not limited to 'romantic girls'; it is also grounded in young groups whose lives embrace more worldly apprehensions.

Finally, looking back to Table 24.1, we find that for both charms and fortunetelling the practitioners outnumber the believers. It is not a case of practicing what you preach, but of 'practice without preaching.' From this we might infer that many of their 'religious' activities are presently without any substantial belief, and are performed as an element of *leisure activity*. On the other hand, it should not be overlooked that the proportion of 'believers' is increasing, and increasing more rapidly than that of 'practitioners.'

On the whole, the young people of today hold many beliefs in suprarational phenomena, ranging from the 'occult boom' to UFOs, computer fortunetelling, and science-fiction-style miracles. And it seems that within such beliefs, however modern and mechanistic they may seem, the emotional desire for 'something religious' persists in its primordial form.

My hypothesis is that there are two key factors which constitute the backdrop to this 'religious' mentality of today's young people, and which further provide a context of meaning and explanatory linkage for nearly all of the significant variations between the first and second surveys, including those outside the 'religious' sphere. Those keys are:

1 Dependence on 'Mother Reality'
2 Satiation with modern rationality

II Dependence on a mother-like system

Growing satisfaction with the status quo

The sense of satisfaction with one's present life increased significantly among young Japanese in all respects – on the material plane and the spiritual plane, in personal as well as societal terms, and as an overall assessment – between the 1973 and 1978 surveys (see Table 24.5). Even where dissatisfaction was highest, concerning the physical environment of society, more than half of the respondents were satisfied in 1973, and the proportion had grown to two-thirds by 1978. In assessing their overall situations, the proportion of young persons who were dissatisfied with present conditions declined sharply from 24 per cent to 14 per cent; some 85 per cent were satisfied with the status quo.

Broken down by age group, the data show various patterns of similarity in the areas of both material and spiritual well-being (see Table 24.6). Higher degrees of material satisfaction, on

Table 24.5 *Changing levels of satisfaction with life (men and women, age 16–29)*

	Satisfied			Dissatisfied		
	1973		1978	1973		1978
Personal material situation	64.0	<	72.4%	30.1	>	21.1%
Personal spiritual situation	60.7	<	66.2	31.4	>	24.2
Society's material situation	55.4	<	66.7	40.0	>	28.9
Society's spiritual situation	64.7	<	72.4	29.6	>	21.2
Overall assesment	75.6	<	85.2	23.7	<	14.4

> or < = significant difference.

Table 24.6 *Declining levels of dissatisfaction with life*

	Personal material situation		Societal material situation		Personal spiritual situation		Societal spiritual situation	
	1973	1978	1973	1978	1973	1978	1973	1978
Male								
16–19:	21	17%	31	28%	36 >	23%	24 >	15%
20–4:	42 >	22	44 >	27	42	37	32 >	20
25–9:	40	31	48 >	30	33	27	32	25
Female								
16–19:	13	12	32	27	24	25	17	11
20–4:	25	19	38	30	31 >	22	32	24
25–9:	34 >	23	43 >	31	26 >	17	34	29
High school students								
Male	18	13	31	24	37 >	22	23 >	13
Female	10	13	34	24	19	24	11	8
White collar								
Male	50 >	30	52 >	32	30	32	37	26
Female	29	22	36	31	23	20	26	21
Housewives								
16–29:	36	26	46 >	34	27	18	37	35

> = significant difference.

personal and societal planes, were found among both men and women over twenty years of age. The main factor here is a dissipation by 1978 of the serious dissatisfaction with material conditions displayed by this generation in 1973. Meanwhile, among teenage men there were notably higher levels of spiritual satisfaction, both personal and societal; or to put it the other way around, there was notably less dissatisfaction. For women over twenty, too, dissastisfaction with spiritual conditions declined.

In order to furnish more concrete images of the transition, the data on age-group shifts is retabulated in the lower part of Table 24.6.

Most conspicuous are the falling levels of dissatisfaction among male high school students, male white-collar workers, and young housewives. Specifically, among *male high school students* dissatisfaction with spiritual conditions showed a remarkable decline; this was the main component of a decline in the corresponding age group of teenage men. For female high school students, the earlier level of dissatisfaction was not so high, and hence this tendency is not apparent. Among *white-collar males*, who in 1973 had shown extreme dissatisfaction with material conditions both personally and societally, amounting to some 50 per cent, there was a distinct diminishment to the 30 per cent level. This group exerted strong influence on the age bracket of men in their twenties (upper part of Table 24.6). The trend for female white-collar workers was similar, but the difference was not statistically significant. The decline in dissatisfaction among women over twenty had more to do with *housewives*. As the table shows, there were sizeable drops in their dissatisfaction with material conditions and with personal spiritual conditions.

The particular category of young people in which the trend toward overall *satisfaction* is most remarkable is *Socialist Party supporters* (see Table 24.7). They accounted for many of the dissatisfied in 1973, but in 1978 the proportion expressing satisfaction with overall conditions was nearly 90 per cent, even higher than that for young people as a whole.

Contraction and softening of radicalism

As the previous paragraph suggests, the general growth in young people's feelings of satisfaction with the status quo is closely

Table 24.7 *Satisfaction with overall life condition (age 16–29)*

		Aggregate		Socialist Party supporters	
	1973		1978	1973	1978
1 Satisfied	14.1	<	17.9%	12.6	15.7%
2 Somewhat satisfied	61.5	<	67.3	58.5	< 72.7
3 Somewhat dissatisfied	20.7	>	13.3	26.9	> 11.1
4 Dissatisfied	3.0	>	1.1	2.0	0.5
1 + 2 (Satisfied)	75.6	<	85.2	71.1	< 88.4
3 + 4 (Dissatisfied)	23.7	>	14.4	28.9	> 11.6

> or < = significant difference.

linked to a transformation in political consciousness. To begin by stating the conclusion: The trend in radical thinking was a *decline* in extension and at the same time a *softening* in intension.

The diminished extent is evident from the direct data on political preference. Table 24.8 shows that among young people as a whole there was a significant decrease in support for the Socialist Party and the Communist Party, and a significant increase in the 'No preference' column. The declines were quite serious, with the Socialist tally in 1978 at less than two-thirds its 1973 level, and the Communist tally at less than half.

Table 24.8 *Changing political preferences of young people*

	1973		1978
Liberal Democratic Party	23.1		22.2%
Socialist Party	15.0	>	9.6
Komeito	2.9		3.5
Democratic Socialist Party	2.5		1.4
Communist Party	5.3	>	2.4
New Liberal Club	–		2.3
Social Democratic Union	–		0.1
Other	0.3		0.1
No preference	46.3	>	54.0
No response	4.6		4.5

> or < = significant difference.

The Socialist decline was sharpest among urban males, centering on blue-collar workers (Table 24.9). The Communist support rate fell most drastically among teenage men, especially university students, as well as young housewives, and generally in the

Table 24.9 *Decline of Socialist Party support among employed males (16–29)*

	1973		1978
Blue collar	24.1	>	13.4%
White collar	20.5		13.2
Sale/service	20.4		8.6

> = significant difference.

suburbs of the two major cities (Table 24.10). Support among male university students dropped to one-sixth the former level, from 12.2 percent in 1973 to 1.9 per cent in 1978; female support was unchanged, 3.2 per cent to 3.1 per cent. Young housewives' support rate dropped to 0.6 per cent, one ninth of the 1973 level of 5.4 per cent. Meanwhile, the most conspicous increase in the 'No preference' category was with late-twenties blue-collar workers, while a boomlet of New Liberal Club support was sustained by such groups as young women in the big-city suburbs and university students.

Table 24.10 *Decline of Communist Party support among young urbanites*

		1973		1978
Men:	Tokyo and Osaka	7.1%		2.4%
	Tokyo and Osaka suburbs	9.8	>	2.9
	Cities over 500,000	8.5		1.9
Women:	Tokyo and Osaka	11.1		3.2
	Tokyo and Osaka suburbs	5.5	>	0.0
	Cities over 500,000	9.3		3.4
Male university students		12.2	>	1.9
Young housewives (16–29)		5.4	>	0.6

> = significant difference.

Synthesizing this data, we can identify two concurrent streams of the 1970s: (1) Male workers – traditionally solid supporters of progressive parties – deserted the Socialist Party to state 'No preference'; and (2) A 'floating' block, largely students and young housewives in big cities and suburbs, shifted away from the Communist Party and toward the new type of conservatives.

To gauge how 'submissive' the supporters of progressive parties have become, in thought and in action, we could observe various quantifications, including the higher levels of satisfaction noted at the end of the previous section. Let us take as a model the survey questions on 'organization and militancy' around the issue of pollution. Table 24.11 shows how 'organization and militancy' declined among young people in general, while among supporters of progressivism the rate of decline was, generally, even greater for the youngest respondents. This tendency was especially prominent among teenage male progressives.

Table 24.11   *Decline of organization and militancy among supporters of progressive parties (age 16–29)*

'In the event of a pollution problem threatening life and residents in this area, I would . . .

	. . . wait and see'			. . . rely on those with influence.'			. . . start a movement.'		
	1973	1978	+/−	1973	1978	+/−	1973	1978	+/−
All respondents	17 <	24	+7	29 <	36	+7	50 >	37	−13
Socialist Party supporters	14 <	22	+8	26 <	36	+10	59 >	42	−17
Male progressive party supporters									
16–19	2 <	28	+26	24	38	+14	70 >	31	−39
20–4	21	26	+5	18 <	42	+14	59 >	32	−27

> or < = significant difference.

The delegationists

Along with the growth of the 'wait-and-see' faction in Table 11, there was also growth of the delegating faction ('rely on those with influence'). The same trends are evident in the data from a general question on 'desirable forms of political activity' (Table 24.12).

While significantly fewer chose the most passive response of simply electing representatives, the corresponding increase shows up not in the personal conduct of political activity, but rather in the method of appealing to politicians and depending upon them. The largest such increases among young men were in the categories of farm villages, blue-collar, and conservative party support; but among young women they were in just the opposite categories of big-city suburbs, white-collar, and progressive politics. For both men and women, it was realists with the Utility value

Table 24.12   *Change in 'desirable forms of political activity'*

		1973		1978
1	Elect politicians who will take action on our behalf as our representatives	58.5	>	52.7%
2	When an issue arises, make appeals to our political respresentative so that our views will be reflected in the political process	13.4	<	21.4
3	Regularly carry out activities in support of our preferred party or group, in order to realize our aims	21.1		20.6

> or < = significant difference.

orientation who correlated most strongly with the increased preference for the dependent formula of politics.

Passive reliance on the system

A fascinating topic cries out for consideration in connection with these points: nationalism and its changing forms. Table 24.13 presents the changing attitudes in various aspects of nationalism. We find that for young people as a whole, despite significant growth of positive feelings about Japan as a home and as a nation, there was a significant decline of the mentality of wanting to serve the nation.

Table 24.13   *Changing style of nationalism among young people*

	1973		1978
I am glad I was born in Japan	84.9	<	88.0%
Japan is a first-rate country	28.1	<	34.9
In my own way I want to be of service to Japan	62.4	>	58.1

> or < = significant difference.

Consistent cynicism toward all types of concrete political action was elicited by a set of questions on 'the sense of political effectiveness' of voting, demonstrations, petitions, etc. Nonetheless, a more positive overall attitude toward the political system came out in 1978 than in 1973, in response to the abstract, general question, 'To what degree are the opinions and desires of we the general citizenry reflected in the nation's politics?'

The feeling that it is good to be born Japanese increased solidly, and the idea that Japan is a first-rate nation also gathered strength, but *at the same time* the active intent to be of service to Japan had weakened. Furthermore, there was skepticism about the efficacy of specific political action, and *at the same time* a general sense of confidence that one's opinions and ideas were substantially reflected in the political process.

Conclusion: the system as mother

The fundamental worldview of the younger generation of the late 1970s has shifted largely toward a certain definite image. They tend to believe that even if they don't carry out any particular activity themselves, the real world will probably prepare an environment in which they can obtain satisfaction, and that at present this has already been done for them. It is an image of a mother or a father. In particular, it is the image of the mother or father of the early 1960s, when *Konnichi-wa*, *aka-chan*, 'Hello, Darling Baby' was the biggest hit song: the era when the nation as a whole celebrated the ideal of dotingly raising a child or two, to the extent that it became part of the basic personal experience of a generation. It is a world in which there most assuredly exists some entity that will provide the answers to your questions, point out a direction for your life, and grant your unfulfilled wishes.

III Fermentative dissolution of the modern world

Changing value orientation

We may look to the fundamental value orientations of young people to indicate their preferred modes of living. As shown in Table 24.14, the rational, self-centric Utility value orientation declined significantly from 1973 to 1978, while the emotional, sociocentric Love value orientation grew significantly.

In another, similar trend, we find that the status of economic power, stressing 'the things required to make life complete,' went down, while that of 'harmonious relationships' went up.

Interestingly, on the topic of relations with neighbors, the proportion of people who want to 'get together and confer about things, and interact on the basis of mutual assistance,' i.e. those desiring deep human relations, declined significantly among

Table 24.14 *Change in primary value orientation of young people*

	1973		1978
Live for today, enjoying freely: *pleasure* (self-centric emotional)	26.3		26.1%
Lay solid plans, build an affluent life: *utility* (self-centric rational)	32.6	>	27.8
Live in harmony with close ones: *love* (sociocentric emotional)	33.6	<	38.3
Pool our strengths, do right in the world: *right* (sociocentric rational)	5.5		6.2

> or < = significant difference.

Japanese as a whole, with only young people showing an opposing trend of increase (for all Japanese, from 34.5 per cent in 1973 to 31.9 per cent in 1978; for young people, from 19.5 per cent to 21.1 per cent). In particular, there was a marked increase among urban females in the high teens, centering around high school students (from 17.3 per cent to 28.3 per cent) and university students (from 3.2 per cent to 18.8 per cent).

Changing attitudes toward work

Changing attitudes toward work and leisure go hand-in-glove with the above value shifts. Table 24.15 demonstrates a change toward moderation which seems appropriate to the youth of this time: the attitude placing fairly strong emphasis on work declined significantly, while the concept of parity between work and leisure became significantly more widespread. In fact, the most numerous faction among young people shifted from those giving priority to work in 1973, to those giving equal priority to the two in 1978. But the telling point here is that the most rapidly defecting element of the earlier work-emphasis faction was not students or housewives, but young male workers, precisely those who are most directly connected to the issue. The breakdown by occupational category of work emphasis among young men is:

White collar	1973: 47.3%	>	1978: 29.7%
Blue collar	42.5	>	29.1
Sales/service	53.7	>	31.4

Table 24.15   *Changing attitudes toward work and leisure*

	1973		1978
A life worth living is found in leisure, not work	5.0%		3.9%
Finish work quickly to enjoy maximum leisure	21.1		19.2
Put similar amounts of energy into work, leisure	32.0	<	39.3
Take some leisure time, save most energy for work	35.9	>	32.1
Work is life's purpose, all energy is devoted to it	3.8		4.5

> or < = significant difference.

Paradoxically, the sales/service employees also registered a notable increase in 'all energy to work' responses (from 1.9 per cent to 11.4 per cent); they stand out as a disjointed category. (By way of comparison, the white-collar proportion indicating 'all energy to work' went from 3.6 per cent to 3.3 per cent, and blue collar 5.2 per cent to 5.5 per cent. Meanwhile, female sales/service employees responding 'all energy to work' multiplied from 2.4 per cent to 12.2 per cent.) This situation merits some reflection, especially in light of the current situation of sales employees. But be that as it may, the main trend among young people in general is clearly a declining emphasis on work.

We saw above that larger numbers of young people wished to have warm relations with their neighbors. When it came to human relations in the workplace, the trend was the opposite, in the form of a significant decline (52.0 per cent to 47.0 per cent). It was quite dramatic in the later-twenties age bracket (men from 49.4 per cent to 28.6 per cent, women from 51.1 per cent to 31.2 per cent).

On questions concerning the conditions of the 'ideal job,' in 1978 significantly more young people said they wanted 'no fear of losing the job.' Of course business retrenchment can be a serious problem, but this may reflect another factor as well, namely a mentality in which the job is seen as the major guarantor in a passive life. (The total of respondents ranking job security as the first or second most important factor nearly doubled, from 12.7 per cent to 23.3 per cent.) Among Japanese as a whole, besides this response, there were increases for two others, 'Making full use of specialized knowledge or skills' and 'A job involving responsibility and leadership.' Among young people only, however, the specialization factor drew a lowered response (from 23.4 per cent to 22.2 per cent) while the leadership factor was unchanged (2.3 per cent). Here again, it seems that work is not associated with the idea of expending positive personal effort, but is perceived instead as patronage and as a framework for a stable life. This calls up the image of their abstracted 'father' figure, who simply brought home a salary from some unknown workplace.

Changing attitudes toward sex

A marked change in the sexual morals of young people was already apparent in 1973; along with a decline in reverence toward the emperor, it stood out as one of the sharpest signs of a generation gap. In the 1978 survey the same trend – the disappearance of the taboo on premarital sex – made continued progress. As Table 24.16 shows, the attitude that 'Sexual intercourse is permissible if a man and a woman are deeply in love' has become the maincurrent among young Japanese.

Table 24.16　*Disappearance of the taboo against premarital sex*

Premarital sex:		Impermissible		Permissible if engaged		Permissible if in love		Marriage, love irrelevant	
		1973	1978	1973	1978	1973	1978	1973	1978
All young people		35 >	26%	19	21%	35 <	43%	6	7%
Males:	16–19	21	19	16	16	42	49	8	8
	20–24	12	10	21	18	52⟍	59	10	10
	25–29	25	19	27	23	37 <	51	8	7
Females:	16–19	51 >	39	11	17	28	36	6	7
	20–24	43 >	25	19 <	27	33⟍	38	5	9
	25–29	49 >	36	19	24	25 >	36	3	3

> or < = significant difference; arrows discussed in text.

The change is most noticeable in the *late-twenties* age bracket for both men and women. These results indicate that this trend in the mentality of the young, which first appeared in the 1973 survey, survived the maturing of that generation (note the arrows in Table 24.16). More than just a temporary romanticism or recklessness during youth, it is a fixed element of the spirit of a generation. Moreover, for most Japanese, the passage from early to late twenties involves crossing the threshold of one's own marriage. In other words, we know that this was no mere selfish insistence on one's own rights, for there is also a willingness on the part of the generation of already-marrieds to allow such behavior among their juniors. When a moral standard is supported by such a range of public opinion, it begins to become something socially fixed. Thus while the 1978 trend can be seen at a glance to represent a quantitative extension of the former survey, it seems also to hold qualitative significance.

Broken down by locality, the increase of the permissive attitude was especially pronounced in middle-sized cities of 100,000 to 500,000 people (from 38 per cent to 55 per cent for men, 26 per cent to 38 per cent for women), and among women in the larger regional cities (from 23 per cent to 44 per cent), adding something of a spatial dimension to the growth of the trend.

In what Max Weber called a 'lifting of spells' (*Entzauberung*), modernity has dismantled many taboos. The sex taboo, too, insofar as no concrete trouble is involved, loses its ground for continued existence as rationality presses relentlessly onward. 'Youth without frustration to sublimate.' Yet at the same time the modern world may by its exertions be demolishing one of the foundations of its own driving force.

Changing images of the family

The image of the family is also changing. To begin with, the model of the ideal household is moving to a significant degree away from the inner-outer concept of 'father works, mother keeps house,' and toward the mutual-independence concept of 'father and mother have their respective jobs and interests' (see Table 24.17).

Orientation toward the mutual-independence pattern increased notably among men and women in their later twenties – already known, appropriately enough, as the 'new families' (from 12.9 per cent to 20.2 per cent for men, 17.6 per cent to 25.5 per cent for women). An especially remarkable expansion of this trend among unemployed young housewives (9.4 per cent to 14.5 per cent) articulates the spread of a 'self-reliance' orientation among that group. Also standing out among this later-twenties group were the 'realists' with Utility-oriented values (3.3 per cent to 20.3 per cent for men, 14.5 per cent to 26.3 per cent for women); the exponential increase among these husbands likely reflects not

Table 24.17   *Changing image of the ideal family among young people*

	1973		1978
Father reigns as master of the house, mother backs him up and wholeheartedly serves	19.6%		18.6%
Father and mother are each enthusiastically absorbed in their own jobs and interests	16.3	<	21.3
Father pours his energy into working, mother diligently maintains the household	36.8	>	31.4
Father also pays attention to the family, and mother is devoted to making a happy home	24.6		27.3

> or < = significant difference.

so much the ideal of sexual equality, as the realistic motive of dual earning power.

Participation by the husband in kitchen chores and other housework received significantly larger support in 1978 (from 55.6 per cent to 62.1 per cent), with especially strong change among women in their twenties (58.4 per cent to 69.1 per cent for ages 20–4; 55.0 per cent to 68.2 per cent for ages 25–9). Here again, the Utility-oriented realists among the women displayed conspicuous rates of change (63.2 per cent to 82.7 per cent for ages 20–4; 51.3 per cent to 71.7 per cent for ages 25–9). Yet the Utility-oriented men who agreed that wives should get jobs were not so enthusiastic about the idea of helping out themselves with the housework (58.6 per cent to 59.0 per cent for ages 20–4); 53.3 per cent to 65.2 per cent for ages 25–9).

On the topic of employment for married women, among young people as a whole the view that they should stay home after marriage declined, while support for employment after bearing children showed a definite increase (see Table 24.18).

There seems to be some contradiction here of the change in young people's attitudes toward work, which was discussed around Table 24.15. Could there be a connection between young people in general having dropped their illusions about professional work, and the expansion of the view that women should be allowed to work after marriage and childbearing?

A qualitative change is under way in the basic image of an 'occupation': it is no longer seen as the arena in which people's energies are to be solely and completely concentrated, but rather

Table 24.18 *Attitudes of young people toward wife, work and home*

	1973		1978
After marriage she should devote herself entirely to running the household	33.0	>	26.1%
After marriage she should hold a job until a child is born	44.4		44.9
After marriage and even after childbirth she should keep working as much as possible	19.5	<	27.0

< or > = significant difference.

as one field of engagement, allowing for appropriate amounts of attention to other areas of one's life. In this light, the view that women should have careers, and the clamor raised over the issue by a minority of the preceding generation, seem a bit pathetic. The diffusion of the attitude that women who are married and have children 'should keep working *as much as possible*' seems not to be backed up by a fervent work ethic. On the contrary, it is clearly associated with a perception of professional work as somewhat more lightweight than was previously thought.

The modern world has been built on the pattern of an image of man (primarily an image of the male) as pouring every bit of vitality into work which is taken as a 'calling.' The reality, however, is that the work in this image was guaranteed the necessary attention by means of a devotion in the background to the household; in short, the image was propped up by the 'shadow work' of women. Japanese society, which has developed so rapidly through the concept that an occupation requires all or at least the major portion of one's energies, is in fact supported by an image of the household that comes from an 'inner-outer' work allotment model.

That model conflicts with one of the basic ideals of the modern era itself, the concept of equality. Moreover, the technological revolution brought forth by the modern era itself, along with the corresponding changes in the forms of business, have led to the replacement of that pattern in many areas of work with types of labor that, although still required by society, do not necessarily require such concentration of one's energy, and indeed are hardly worth it.

The modern world is thus undergoing deconstruction, for as a result of its own logic it is in the process of unraveling the types of social relations and life models from which it has formed itself.

Conclusion: the postmodern mentality

Taken comprehensively, the above factors point to some observable changes in the pattern by which the values of human interaction are arranged. I have developed a model for expressing the pattern in terms of two scales, the authoritarian-egalitarian scale and the utilitarian-emotional scale.

First, on the authority-equality scale, as one would expect, young people shifted significantly toward the egalitarian type (from 53.6 per cent in 1973, to 58.3 per cent in 1978), while on the utility-emotion scale they shifted significantly toward the emotional end (52.6 per cent to 57.5 per cent). Second, among the four types of value consciousness resulting from a perpendicular combination of the scales, young Japanese showed significant increase in the area of the *egalitarian-emotional* type (from 29.1 per cent to 33.5 per cent), while the largest decrease was in the area of the opposite type. (See Figure 24.1.)

This remarkably increasing type differs from the representative Modern Type (egalitarian-utilitarian), as well as from the representative Premodern Type (authoritarian-emotional). It also differs from the authoritarian-utilitarian pattern which is visible in so many developing societes where rapid modernization is under way. Since, as we saw above, a shift along the utilitarian-emotional scale from utility toward emotion was clearly visible, we can accurately locate it as occurring *after* the modern era, rather than during a transition period to modernization.

It is possible to place the four value patterns found in human relations in historical context, as recorded in Figure 24.1: the Premodern Type (I), the Protomodern (or Modern-tending) Type (II), the Modern Type (III) and the Postmodern Type (IV). In Japan's case, they correspond to the patterns of arrangement of values in human relations in (I) traditional communities; (II) the historical stage of rapid development under the authoritarian style of the half-modern Emperor system, from the Restoration of 1868 to the defeat of 1945; (III) the situation during the period from the postwar democratizing reforms through the high-economic-growth era of the 1960s; and (IV) the situation since the closing moments of the high-growth era.

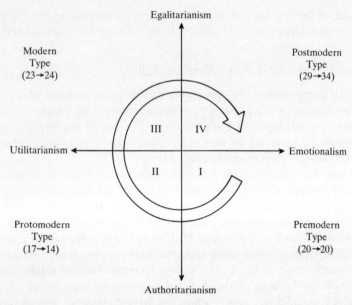

Numbers in brackets are for 1973 (left) and 1978 (right)

Figure 24.1 *Intensification of the egalitarian–emotional pattern*

All of the principal changes in the mentality of young Japanese
which are reported in this chapter can be viewed as corresponding to the *shift from type III to type IV*, that is, as indications
of various aspects of the shift from the mentality of the Modern
Type to that of the Postmodern Type: From disavowal of 'the
religious' to trial-and-error groping for its contemporary forms.
From self as subject, confronting the surrounding world and
reforming the near-at-hand, to an existence which flirts with
dissolving the subject into the distance of surroundings joyfully
accepted. From a spirit of rational self-control within a future-
oriented temporal outlook, of egoistic rule over various domains
of life within sharply distinguished spaces and times (work and
leisure, workplace and home, married life and single life, adulthood and childhood, etc.) – to an existence which accepts the
'nowness' of life in which those various domains cross over and
commingle. And from a consciousness which welcomes everything 'rational,' to a meta-rationality which exists on its own in
association with 'things rational' and 'things suprarational.'

At the opening of the 1970s, the rebellion against modern

rationality by Japanese youth was suppressed and dissolved. But now the modern ferments itself within its very sufficiency, and dismembers its fermenting self.

Where is this fermentative dissolution taking us? That is not the topic here. Yet it can be seen that this dissolutional ferment is in fact us ourselves. Without our own clarification of what sort of world we aspire to, without a lucid grasp of the entirety of the contemporary world, of the *self-contradictions of our own existence* and their self-betraying distortions of any truly desirable vision, neither talk of despair nor talk of hope is anything more than delusion.

(1984)

IV A note on changes in the 1980s

Data from the 1988 version of the same NHK survey has been made available, as explained in the concluding Note of the last chapter. I am able to report here that the variations in mentality during the 1980s tend to reinforce the main hypotheses of this chapter. (Some of the results of the 1983 survey are also included. For 1983 and 1988 I draw on the basic data for younger men and women, without double- and triple-cross aggregation.)

Religious orientation

Table 24.19 extracts and updates seven key elements of religious activity and belief from Table 24.1. Despite one or two exceptions, the data show that among men and women in their early twenties, the overall increase in religious orientation which was apparent in the 1970s has not only continued but intensified during the 1980s.

Satisfaction with the status quo

The younger generation's overall sense of satisfaction with their present circumstances has very slightly declined in the 1980s, but remains at an extremely high level (see Table 24.20). The main reason for the slight decline was increased dissatisfaction on the

Table 24.19   *Change in religious mentality and activity (to 1988)*

	Males, 20–4			Females, 20–4		
	1973	1978	1988	1973	1978	1988
Consulted fortuneteller	24 <	30 <	36%	42 <	52	48%
Believe in fortunetelling	4	6 <	10	14 <	21	21
Possess charm(s)	31	26	28	37	38	37
Believe in charms	6 <	10 <	16	14	18 <	25
Prayed	17 <	29	29	21 <	34	37
Believe in miracles	18 <	28	23	10 <	25 <	33
Believe in afterworld	4 <	10 <	21	5 <	17	22

> = significant difference.

Table 24.20   *Percentage of young men and women expressing satisfaction with life*

	1973	1978	1988
Age 16–19	77	88	88%
20–4	74	81	76
25–9	76	86	82

Percentage responding 'satisfied' or 'relatively satisfied'.

personal mental level among men in their early twenties. (Refer to Table 24.5.)

Political party support

The 1980s data on party preference shows that in the early-twenties age group, support for 'progressive' parties continued to decline, while the no-preference attitude increased even more markedly. (Table 24.21; refer to Table 24.8.)

Table 24.21   *Changing political party preferences (ages 20–4)*

	1973	1978		1983	1988
Liberal Democratic Party	21	21		22	16%
Socialist Party	16	11	>	5	5
Komeito	2	2		5	3
Democratic Socialist Party	2	1		3	2
Communist Party	4	3		2	1
Social Democratic Union	0	0		1	1
No party preference	52	58		61 <	70

> or < = significant difference.

Nationalism

The trend noted above as 'passive reliance on the system,' including the increase of passive nationalism and the decline of active nationalism, is still more apparent among people in their early twenties during the 1980s. (Table 24.22; refer to Table 24.13.)

Table 24.22   *Changing sense of nationalism (ages 20–4)*

	1973		1978		1983	1988
I am glad I was born in Japan	82		86	<	93	91%
Japan is a first-rate country	27	<	35	<	46	44
In my own way I want to be of service to Japan	53		54		49	47

< = significant difference.

Value orientation

In the 1980s there was an increase in emotional orientation, and especially a continued increase in the 'love' value orientation. (Table 24.23; refer to Table 24.14.)

Table 24.23   *Change in basic value orientation (ages 20–4)*

	1973		1978	1983	1988
Self-centric emoptional (*pleasure*)	31		26	26	29%
Self-centric rational (*utility*)	30		28	29	26
Sociocentric emotional (*love*)	31	<	38	41	43
Sociocentric rational(*right*)	6		6	3	1

< = significant difference.

Attitudes toward work and leisure

Again in the 1980s, young people giving top priority to work grow relatively fewer, while those emphasizing leisure in life grow relatively more numerous. (Table 24.24; refer to Table 24.15.)

Sexual mores

Regarding the permissibility of premarital sex, both the disappearance of the 'requirement' of marriage, and the increase of

Table 24.24   *Changing attitudes toward work and leisure (ages 20–4)*

	1973		1978		1983		1988
A life worth living is found in leisure, not work	9		6		6	<	13
Finish work quickly to enjoy maximum leisure	25		19		21		21
Put similar amounts of energy into work, leisure	32	<	41		48		49
Take some leisure time, save most energy for work	30		30	>	22		16
Work is life's purpose, all energy is devoted to it	3		5		3		2

< or > = significant difference.

the 'requirement' of love have intensified in the 1980s. The variations are particularly notable among women. As mentioned in the concluding Note of the previous chapter, these attitudes are prevalent among older adults as well. (Table 24.25; refer to Table 24.16.)

Table 24.25   *Attitudes toward premarital sex*

	Age	Men				Women			
		1973	78	83	88	1973	78	83	88
Impermissible	20–4	12	10	5	6%	43 >	25	17	20%
	25–9	25	19	13	7	49 >	36	27 >	11
Permissible if engaged	20–4	21	18	19 >	10	19 <	27	22	22
	25–9	27	23	18	18	19	24	23	28
Permissible if in love	20–4	52	59	58	67	33	38 <	54	49
	25–9	37 <	51	55	57	25 <	36	43 <	57
Marriage and love irrelevant	20–4	10	10	15	14	5	9	7	5
	25–9	8	7	12	16	3	3 <	7 >	1

> or < = significant difference.

Image of the ideal family

The husband-wife ideal subscribed to by most Japanese until 1970 – 'Father pours his energy into work, mother diligently maintains the household' (which recent observers have termed 'traditional' but is actually 'classical modern') – began to lose support among the younger generation in the late 1970s, as noted above. Table 24.26 shows that the shift became very clear in the

Table 24.26 *Change in images of the ideal family (ages 20–4)*

	Men				Women			
	1973	78	83	88	1973	78	83	88
Husband leads, wife follows	15	21	19	18%	19	20	20	14%
Husband and wife independent	19	20	16	16	18	24	22	25
Husband works, wife tends home	34	30	23	23	33	31	21 >	12
Husband joins in home tending	26	27 <	42	19	29	25 <	36 <	48

> or < significant difference.

1980s, especially among women (refer to Table 24.17). In its place, while there was a temporary growth of the independent-partners ideal in the late 1970s, in the 1980s the weight moved suddenly to the 'home-centered' pattern, or the ideal that 'Father also pays attention to the family, and mother is devoted to making a happy home.' In the 1970s that image was the most popular only among those in their high teens (see Chapter 7, Figure 7.9).

Wives, work and housekeeping

The norm that 'after marriage a woman should devote herself entirely to the family' began to fade among women in the 1970s, and in the 1980s it began to decrease among men as well. Yet there may be a gap between young spouses, for the women increasingly believe in working after a child is born, while the men are unswervingly inclined to keep them at home. (Table 24.27; compare Table 24.18.)

Conclusion

Although there are various differences on small points, nearly all of the main elements of the new shifts in mentality of the 1970s continued, or intensified, through the 1980s.

From the 1990s we can look back on the 1970s as, if nothing else, the time when the seed of the mentality of the Japanese up to this point (the 'postmodern mentality' or, strictly speaking,

Table 24.27 *Attitudes toward wife, work and housekeeping (ages 20–4)*

	Men				Women			
	1973	78	83	88	1973		78	83	88
She should devote herself to running the household	36	36	32	24%	26	>	16	19	20%
She should hold a job until a child is born	43	47	47	55	49		49	48	38
Even after childbirth she should work if possible	18	16	19	16	22	<	33	30	38

> of < = significant difference.

the post-'high-growth' atmosphere) began to develop among the youngest generation of adults into a cloud that would eventually fill the sky.

That cloud is *akarui* – light and bright, a 'brilliant' cloud. I close with a sketch on the *akarui* norm that was virtually compulsory for the young generation in the 1980s 'consumption society' of Japan. It comes from a report that a student recently submitted, and though it is fictional, it roused the actual sympathies of many other students.

Once there was a lonesome girl. She was always wishing she could become a 'brilliant girl.' She went to ask her teacher for advice on how she could turn into a 'brilliant personality.' The teacher, too, found the question perplexing. 'I don't really know. . . . But wait, here's something you can do. You know the McDonald's in front of the school. There's a girl working there in a clown costume, and she is wildly brilliant. Everyone there starts feeling brilliant just because she's around. You should hang around there sometimes, and see what she has to say.' The girl who had come for advice replied, 'But Teacher, that clown is me, that's my part-time job.'

(1991)

25 Reality, Dream and Fiction: Japan, 1945–90

'Reality' has three antonyms: Ideal vs reality. Dream vs reality. Fiction vs reality.

Looking back from 1990, the mentality of Japan during the 45 years since the defeat of 1945 divides into three basic tonal values. They span periods of about 15 years each, periods which can be characterized by those three anti-realities.

From 1945 to 1960 was the time when the Japanese tried to live out Ideals. From 1960 through the first years of the 1970s they tried to live out Dreams. From the mid–1970s to 1990 they have been trying to live out Fictions. In terms of the economic growth that brought forth a fundamental transformation of society, they may be defined as the 'pre-high-growth', the 'high-growth' and the 'post-high-growth' periods.

The mentalities of living out Ideals and living out Fictions are opposite ways of confronting reality. The Ideal seeks realization, and the urge to confront ideals is an urge to confront reality. Realism movements, in photography and other expressive forms, have often been mounted on idealistic engines. But in the spirit that seeks Fiction there is no longer any love of reality. It was Fiction as a statement, as an expression, indeed as a way of life, Fiction drifting toward the deodorization of reality, that gave Japan, especially urban Japan, its distinctive coloration in the 1980s.

The 'ideal' period (1945–60)

After the smashing of the mythical age of the Fifteen-Year War (starting with the Manchuria Incident of 1931), the first thing that was exposed among the smoldering ruins was: Reality. On the ground of the cities, where everything manmade was

515

destroyed by the urban scorched-earth policy of the American air force, shards of glass and steel lay formless, transmuted to simple matter, scattered and heaped up by the animal urges of human beings. And what the urges of that animal, filtered through the surplus swellings of its cerebral cortex and frontal lobe, began the next day to raise up anew was: Ideals.

There were two dominant ideals in Japan just after the war: the ideal of American democracy and the ideal of Soviet communism. Though opposed to each other, these two idealistic camps stood together as the progressives of the time, squaring off against the 'realistic' conservative authorities.

Again, those who pursue the ideal also pursue Reality. A leading polemicist of the postwar progressives, Masao Maruyama, laid out the following logic in an essay on 'The Pitfalls of "Realism." ' Reality has two sides: one is the reality by which we are limited and determined, and the other is the reality which is determined and formed by our efforts; the so-called realists see only the first side, ignoring the path of reforming reality; and the only ones who see the true reality are those who also see the side that we can carve with our own hands. This clearly exposes the real inclination of the idealists (as opposed to fictionalists). Meanwhile, American democracy and Soviet communism themselves, each grounded in its own progressive view of history, had no doubt that their ideals were the inevitable future of mankind, and in due course were bound to become 'reality.'

What about the realism of the common people? When I was growing up after the war, I heard adults talking like this: A young woman is taking her time in getting married, and her parents remark, 'Our daughter has high ideals.' The ideals in question would be the high socioeconomic status and earning potential of a suitor. That was the essential meaning of 'ideal' as it was used in actual conversation. Ideal marriage, ideal job, ideal home, ideal electric rice cooker. Even the 'realists' pursued the same things, the ideals of higher living standards, of material enrichment, which were to become the driving force for economic recovery.

The realism of the Japanese of this period grew out of the deep impression that, in the final analysis, they had lost the war to the 'sheer material strength' of America. Under the American occupation which spanned the first half of this period, that materialistic conviction grew stronger by the day in every corner of the country. People's desires shifted somewhat, following an instinctive order of urgency and corresponding to the phases of economic revival; one sociologist divides this period of economic resuscitation into three five-year phases: the 'food years,' 'clothing years' and 'shelter years.' But at all levels, the principal energy behind the ambitions was that longing for the American Way of Life. It made idealists out of the realists of the time, for they were pursuing the things they had never had.

Looking back from the Fiction Period of today at the Japanese of that era, when idealism was realism and realism was idealism, we may be sure that they had no doubts about Reality.

The Japanese of the nineteenth century were content to translate 'photograph' as 'copy of reality' (*shashin*). This says much about their attachment to reality, their dependence upon it. When Technicolor was introduced in the 1950s, the Japanese of the Ideal Period translated it as 'natural color' (*tennenshoku*). They could just as well have used characters for 'technical color' or 'artificial color,' but they chose a name which flips over the value emphasis. It was the golden age of the movies, before the diffusion of television, and the theaters erected huge signs on the streets proclaiming, 'Totally Natural Color.' Evidently there still stirred a desire akin to that which had interpreted the photograph as a 'copy of reality.' Yet when color television penetrated Japan in the 1960s, there was no talk of 'natural-color television.'

At the close of the Ideal Period in the late 1950s, the novel *Season of the Sun* ignited a youth culture that was dubbed 'the sun tribe.' The hero of this book displayed a highly substantive manner of courtship, thrusting his erect penis through the paper of a *shōji* door. At the time it was something 'new' which was seen to mark the passing of the 'postwar condition,' although it appears through the lens of 1980s literary awareness as just a typical physical technique of the 'reality' period.

The 1960 Ampo uprising against the extension of the American mutual security pact was the final showdown between the idealists and realists of the period. When the Cabinet forced the extension through the Diet, the two idealist factions – those for American democracy and those for Soviet communism – joined forces and struck out together against the realists. They lost, and the Ideal Period in postwar Japan came to its end.

The dream period (1960 to the early 1970s)

The 1960s brought a basic transformation of Japanese society. The two main policies of the Ikeda government (1960–4) were 'the organic law of agriculture' (1961), and 'the general plan of nationwide development' (1962). The former was aimed at the drastic reorganization of the traditional rural communities that had formed the very basis of the society, mainly through 'structural improvement of agriculture.' The latter promoted the establishment of new industrial cities', and other projects which facilitated nationwide industrialization and urbanization. The social effects of these interrelated policies were: (1) concentration of public investment in industrial development by cutting off protection for the small farmers who formed a major part of the society at that time; (2) formation of a large pool of actual and latent manpower by 'discarding the poor peasants', which caused a massive urban inmigration; and (3) putting the agricultural sector under the control of the modern capitalistic system ('chemicalization' of agriculture, reorganization of the distribution and processing systems for foodstuffs, etc.). In short, these policies provided (1) capital, (2) labor and (3) markets, which were necessary for 'rapid economic growth'.

The result was the total reorganization of the archipelago with many 'new industrial cities', coastal industrial zones, and other forms of areal industrial development. The portion of the population engaged in primary industries (agriculture, forestry and fishing) showed a drastic reduction from more than 30 per cent in 1960 to 18 per cent in 1970 (12.7 per cent in 1975). The number of households of farmers without any side job (*sengyō-nōka*) fell by 60 per cent during the 1960s. At the same time there was an obvious increment of white-collar workers in the growing cities. (See Table 25.1).

These changes in social structure caused a transformation of the family structure as well. The extended family system, which had formed the basis of the society together with the rural agricultural communities, had been maintained for quite a long period, through the first century of modernization (1860s–1950s). Unlike the European and North American countries, the average size of a Japanese family did not diminish as modernization progressed (4.89 persons in 1920, the year of the first national census, and 4.90 in 1955). But, from the late 1950s, it dropped sharply, to 3.55 in 1970, (see table), and 3.48 in 1971. Even in the USA, which experienced a high pitch of modernization, it took 60 years for the average family size to diminish from 4.9 to 3.5 (1890–1950). Japanese society ran through that change in just 16 years around the 1960s. The numerical change of family size from 4.9 to 3.5 meant a qualitative and structural change from the traditional family system to the nuclear family. That meant the transformation of family relationships, male-female relationships, the life courses of women, the lifestyles of men, modes of growing up for children, the forms of 'problems' in people's lives, and other factors affecting the character of generations.

Table 25.1 *Structural change of Japanese society during the period of 'High Economic Growth'*

I Class structure (%)				
	1950	1965	1970	1975
Entrepreneurs	1.9	2.7	3.8	5.9
Self-employed	58.9	45.7	34.9	29.4
Farming, forestry and fishing	44.6	30.6	18.1	12.1
Employees	38.2	50.5	60.1	63.3
Professional, technical and clerical	11.9	14.2	18.7	21.3
Sales and service	4.3	7.8	10.5	11.5

II Farming households (ten thousands)					
	1926 . . . 1955	1960	1965	1970	1975
Total Number	556 . . . 604	606	567	540	495
Pure farming households*	409 . . . 211	208	122	84	62

* Without any side job (*sengyo noka*)

III Family size (persons)					
	1920 . . . 1950	1955	1960	1965	1970
	4.89 . . . 4.97	4.90	4.53	4.01	3.55

As part of a nationwide social-psychology survey in 1963, respondents were asked to choose colors to symbolize the several eras of Japan's modern century. The results offer a spectrum of historical images in the public eye:

Meiji Period	Purple
Taisho Period	Yellow
Early Showa Period	Blue/Green

War Years	Black
Postwar Years	Gray
Present (1963)	Pink

The purple, yellow, and blue/green images of prewar eras are not on our schedule here (see Chapter 16). In sharp contrast to wartime 'black' and postwar 'gray,' the popular social psychology of the early 1960s had a self-awareness of its own time as 'pink.' Indeed, in the current vernacular it was a time of 'tranquility.'

Through a memory mechanism which psychologists call backward inhibition, recollections of a calm period just before some violent experience are easily lost. Due to the brief but dramatic disturbances of the late 1960s, the preceding interval of tranquility is today largely overlooked. But from inside the period itself, there was a sense of the virtual 'end of history,' as if after the upheavals of war and defeat and recovery, there was nothing more of consequence that could happen to the country. It was a dreamy feeling of having arrived at a happy ending. Of course there were some who were impatient, complaining that the poor were being left behind by the 'sense of prosperity,' and some who criticized the 'tranquil mood' itself as vulgar or tedious. But the commonly shared sense was that it was a time of 'happiness.' And so it was – a happiness that was implicitly naive, cynical, ironic.

Popular songs, as discussed in Chapter 1, are the data which most sensitively reflect the periodic fluctuations of the social psychology of the people, and a major turning point in the history of the modern Japanese popular song occurred during this period. The *enka* and *kayokyoku* ballad forms which had been established during the 1920s – half-modern, half-traditional melodies keyed to a minor-sounding pentatonic scale – were pushed aside by purely Western/modern melodies which, for the first time and with spectacular force, became the dominant trend. The two big hits of 1961, Ueki Hitoshi's '*Suudara bushi*' and Sakamoto Kyu's '*Ue o muite arukō*,' led the way in smashing open the conventional world of *enka* sensibilities. As was discussed in Chapter 8, Ueki's singing was the exact opposite of *enka* vocalization. The *enka* technique, in the tradition of *naniwa-bushi* recitation, calls for maximum constriction of the throat and nose during exhalation, so that the voice is repeatedly distorted and squeezed. Ueki's words shoot cleanly out without the slightest resistance. Absence of the sense of resistance was precisely the sensibility of this period.

In the broadcast media of the early 1960s, the theme song of the leading 'home drama,' *Ukkari fujin to chakkari fujin*, was heard every day: 'It's a small town / It's a small family / It's a small garden / But we have plenty of dreams / Dreams, dreams, at number 10 Dreamhills Street.' That theme, like the super hit song of 1963, 'Hello, Darling Baby' was a typical expression of the dream of 'my-home-ism' – a Japanese–English term that characterizes the era. The bestselling books of the period exhibited two prominent, apparently contradictory, tendencies – the 'dry' titles of how-to manuals (*How to Double Your Fund, Money Building Manuals*, etc.) and the 'wet' titles of romantic love (*Gazing at Love and Death* etc.) In reality, those tendencies correspond in complementary ways to the dreams of the masses of urban immigrants of that final uprooting phase of modernization, who had lost their country homes as well as their traditional family ties, who thirsted for and were striving to build their *new homes*, the new bases of their lives, both materially and mentally.

If the Dream Period began as a time of 'warm dreams,' it closed from the late 1960s as a time of 'hot dreams.' The wave of youthful rebellion that washed over the advanced capitalist countries, notably America, France and Germany, also reached a corresponding crest in Japan, which had just then come abreast of those countries with the high-growth spurt.

The radical youth of the late 1960s were not pursuing the ideals of democracy and communism which the Ampo movement had sought a few years earlier. On the contrary, they wanted liberation from the new forms of oppression and discrimination which had been brought forth by the idealist political movements and organizations of the previous period, and by the realization of the economic ideals of the realists who opposed them. The targets of their attacks were the reality born of democratic idealism (postwar democratism); the reality born of communist idealism (Stalinism and the old left); and the fruits of the realization of the realists' ideals (modern rationalism and its managerial system). In short, it was an all-out rebellion against the various ideals of the Ideal Period.

The majority of young people seemed to feel no connection to the struggle; no doubt they were repulsed by the directly political – or rather, physical – form of the movement, symbolized by the *geba* staves of the militants. Meanwhile, the hot dreamers, those who believed they were incubating the forms and lifestyles of the new age, soared among the diverse cultural experiments of the time, such as the hippie movement and the flower children, which were ongoing before and after the uprising. Even after the politically prominent element of the movement was physically suppressed and exhausted by the authorities, the dreams which were glimpsed amid the fervor of the time remained on the field, in an assortment of communal situations and in various modes of exploratory expression, as experiments in creating newly liberated spaces and times and sensibilities.

The fiction period (mid-1970s to 1990)

The oil shock of 1973 signaled the end of rapid economic growth, which Japan enjoyed intermittently through the 1960s. A negative rate of real economic growth was recorded in 1974 for the first time since the war. The Economic White Paper that year was called 'Beyond Economic Growth'; in 1975 it was 'New Approaches to Stability,' in 1976, 'Stengthening the Foundations for Renewed Development,' in 1977, 'The Japanese Economy Adapts for Stable Growth.' The mid–1970s thus witnessed the switch from the 'high-growth' track to the 'path to stability,' the turning point between 1963, when the White Paper charted 'The Road to Becoming an Economically Advanced Nation,' and 1980 when it arrived at 'Japan's Trials and Problems as an Economically Advanced Nation.'

Two of the trendy words of 1974, 'eschatology' (*shūmatsuron*) and 'gentleness' (*yasashisa*), reflected society's consciousness of that shift in the social structure. Those two ideas persisted as keynotes in the sensibility of the next dozen years. Literature – from Murakami Ryū's *Almost Transparent Blue* (1976), to Tanaka Yasuo's *Indefinably Crystal* (1981), Murakami Haruki's *End of the World and Hard-Boiled Wonderland* (1985), and the works of Banana Yoshimoto in the late 1980s – expressed the sense of terminality and the many variations of 'gentleness' (though eschewing those particular terms). It had been purified by the embers of fury and heat of earlier eras which, in keeping with the passing of time, it then shed completely. Where the color value of the 1960s was pink, that of the 1980s would be an almost transparent white. It is exemplified in the basic tonal value of the film 'Kitchen' (1989), directed by Morita Yoshimitsu and based on a work by Banana Yoshimoto.

Another Morita film, 'Family Game' (1983), depicts the customary atmosphere of the family – that ultimate stronghold of the 'real,' the 'live,' the 'substantive' in society – as uprooted from the depths of its daily life, and fabricated by what may be called the fictionalizing power of the time. The novel seating arrangement of the family at table attracted a great deal of attention. Rather than facing each other as they would for a classic family meal, they sit in a row along a counter, like customers at a bar. This is no happy family circle. There is no eye contact, the lines of sight are parallel. Critics, caught up in classical realism, protested that such a family was 'unnatural' or 'unrealistic.' But the fact was that in the many Japanese families of the 1980s who ordinarily ate while watching television, the seating positions were functionally parallel, reckoned by spiritual disposition if not line of sight. With its use of this parallel gaze, 'Family Game' staked out a certain reality of its own. Turning the tables, it expertly nailed down the non-reality, the unnaturalness, indeed the *fictionality* of reality itself in our time.

The stages designed by Yamazaki Tetsu, a playwright popular with the younger generation of this period, realize the fundamental fictionality of the contemporary 'family.' After a classically perfunctory exchange between a husband, who is reading the newspaper, and his wife, who is sewing, she confirms that, 'Once again, we have had our daily conversation between husband and wife.' 'Family happiness' is being staged. Which is to say that the reality of the time is being articulated. Offstage, too, we are exhorted by local governments to 'set aside fifteen minutes a day to talk with your children' so as to prevent juvenile delinquency. 'Well, let us begin the talking between father and son' – a sense of fictionality about even the most basic part of the relationship.

The perpetrator of a series of kidnappings and murders of little girls in 1989, one Miyazaki Tsutomu, lived in a single room surrounded by thousands of videotapes stacked up even over the windows. There he inhabited a world of images. Back in the

Ideal Period, the typical sex offender was Kodaira Yoshio, who lured housewives with a promise to show them 'a place that sells rice cheap' and violated them. In the Fiction Period the young video fan enticed little girls with a promise to 'take your picture,' photographed them, eliminated them, and savored the images. From the realism of life and flesh to the realism of undressed phantoms.

Calling a photograph a 'copy of reality,' the nineteenth-century Japanese, as we have noted, hungered for the real. To that contemporary young man, photography means 'the copy is what is real.' It has evolved into a living medium in which epistemology equals ontology. The 'copy' and the 'real' have exchanged places.

A friend who teaches at a vocational school for journalists asked his students, who were about 20 years old, to write essays on the topic, 'Does reality exist in contemporary society?' Most of them concluded by stating that reality exists with the unreality of the world.

The urbanologist Yoshimi Shunya undertook a detailed analysis of Tokyo Disneyland when it opened in 1983. Examining the strategy of creating a manmade space which is complete in itself by fully excluding the outside world, he found that it is just a condensed model of the hyperreal existence of present-day Tokyo (consistent with Baudrillard's study of the Los Angeles Disneyland).

Historically, the city of Tokyo has had various symbolic centers which embody the city's several eras, the progression being from Asakusa to Ginza to Shinjuku to Shibuya (as described in another of Yoshimi's studies). Within our postwar purview, Shinjuku was the center embodying the Dream Period, and Shibuya the center embodying the Fiction Period.

Shibuya was previously one of the disorderly series of neighborhoods which served as adjunct city centers. Since the 1970s, in an urban production on a grand scale orchestrated by capital from the Seibu organization, it has been transformed into a giant amusement park-like space that embodies the hyperreal sensibility in ultramodern fashion. Things exist in this space on condition that they be 'cute,' 'happening,' 'smart' or 'beautiful.' Yoshimi points out that, 'It sets up frames of exclusion against the "unattractive," the "passe," the "unclean." ' One of the hot dreamers of Period II, Yamao Sansei, a poet and a charismatic hippie leader, moved to the southern island of Yakushima and became a farmer. He visited Tokyo every year or so, but never changed his style of ragged jeans and boots. By the late 1970s that style was heresy, yet one could still be proud of the acknowledged heresy. But in the Tokyo of the late 1980s, at least in the eyes of the Shibuya scene, he could only feel 'out of it.' The amusement-park space senses something in those ragged jeans and boots with which it will not coexist. That is the smell of earth, the smell of sweat.

Here is exclusion as a pressurized sensitivity, aiming to 'deodorize' the real, the raw, the 'natural.' (Next: A gigantic new marketplace named Insenseland, kept up via compulsory washing?)

Any society is inevitably based on some kinds of work which are 'unclean' or 'passe,' with the smells of sweat and earth, at the starting points of production as well as the endpoints of consumption. In place of the 'smart' and 'beautiful' residents of fabricated spaces who refuse to soil their hands, those jobs are being filled by workers from other countries (whose numbers increased sharply during this period for the first time) or by Japanese-Brazilian 'reverse immigrants.' Or else, through foreign trade and the export of capital, those tasks fall to the farmers and fishermen and laborers of unseen worlds. In the visual frame of the city as a sterilized amusement park, seeing them is self-forbidden, mutually forbidden. The gross is not spoken of. It is not thought of. It is a 'cute' world of Marie Antoinettes with their naive ruthlessness.

Tokyo in the 1980s talked of the shift of its commercial hubs 'from the three wards to the three A's' – from the established centers of Chiyoda, Chuo and Minato Wards, to the 'international city' neighborhoods of Akasaka, Azabu, and Aoyama. There lies the '24-hour information city,' abreast of the New York and London markets, attuned to the situations at Suez and Panama. Inside their artificially lighted, artificially heated space-times, the business elites and non-elites have completely dismantled, abstracted and reorganized the bodily rhythms of the human animal. As they manage their information, they stock their drawers and attache cases with sets of tablets and capsules – vitamins and digestives, caffeine and sleeping pills, energizers and tranquilizers – to suppress symptoms of mind and body. The catchphrase of one of the best-known television commercials of

1990, for an energizer named Regain, asks 'Can you fight for twenty-four hours?' with the picture showing 'Japanese businessmen' flying all over the world, fighting with the time differentials.

The ultimate problems facing the contemporary world – environment, pollution, resources, energy – occur at the interfaces with external nature, around the limits of its exploitation and disorganization. And the medications and mind/body troubles are other forms of battle, which are developing at the interfaces between contemporary human beings in contemporary society and their own *inner* nature, around the limits of its exploitation and reorganization.

Fictional spaces, fictional times. How much farther will they go?

Once, toward the end of the 1960s, I interviewed a group of copywriters, which was the vanguard profession at that time. Among other inquiries I asked which seemed to them more worthwhile, (1) to advertise a *really* worthy item by informing the masses of advantages, or to advertise an ordinary item by making it *appear* to have some special value? All of the several participants chose the latter case; one added, 'making common things special.' Their words were tinted with a prominent shadow of cynicism. Later, in the 1980s, I had the chance to talk with the leading copywriters of the time. When I recounted the above exchange, one professional of the younger generation responded: 'Textbook answer.' Such a way of thinking seems already to have become scripture, part of the theory of ordinary economic conduct, as the creating of 'added value' through 'information.' There is no longer a shadow of cynicism. Rather, they seem to be simply enjoying a kind of game. The cynicism has been made *structural*, rendered unconscious. This demonstrates the connection between the cultural phenomenon of 'fictionalization' and the transformations of the social structure which led to the 'mass consumption' and 'information' societies.

My intent is not to simply denounce such social phenomena as mass consumption or 'hyper-informationalization.' These are the ways by which Japanese capitalism, like other advanced forms of capitalism, has overcome its structural dilemma. The classical capitalist system was, as criticized by classical socialist ideology, threatened by periodic crises of overproduction or limited final demand. To avert crisis, capitalist societies tended to pursue policies of military or imperial expansion. The contemporary, postmodern system of capitalism seems to have succeeded to solve the classic dilemma of 'crisis or war,' in a manner totally unexpected by the classical socialists (or even by the capitalists themselves): *self-reproduction of the consumer market, the creation of artificial demand through information.*

Obviously it has been far better that Japanese economy achieved enduring prosperity in that way, rather than making up the ultimate demand through military expansion. But the better is not necessarily the best. There seem to be many other ways to keep activating the economy without military expansion. Completion and perfection of social overhead capital, including improvement of the meager housing situation; investment in education; appropriate responses to the problems of the aging society; more substantive aid to needy countries; international cooperation to solve global problems of environment and resources, and to enrich the soil for cultivation of the arts and sciences. There must be various concepts and images of society which provide outlets for the energy of a population in ways that do not ruin our external and our internal natures, and do not breed structural nihilism. Searching and living them out may be the primary task of our society for the coming century.

Index